Modern Essays in English

Modern Essays in English

Edited by JOSEPH FRANK

The University of Rochester

LITTLE, BROWN AND COMPANY   *Boston · Toronto*

Acknowledgments

An appropriate acknowledgment to various publishers for permission to reprint these pieces will be found at the start of each essay. I do, however, wish to thank my colleague Russell Peck. The Appendix was largely his idea, and his practical advice and literary sensitivity have been helpful in editing this anthology.

Contents

vii

Creative Possibilities

Appendix

Introduction

The Atomic Age was born in the summer of 1945. Its adolescence —like most adolescences—was characterized by tantrums, feelings of guilt, a sense of living dangerously, and a rapid growth in strength. Though now having passed the age of twenty-one and technically arrived at manhood, the Atomic Age is still frighteningly and exhilaratingly young. And we are part of it.

Yet history is a continuum: at any given moment a new generation is being born, an old one dying—and the world is always in a state of transition. But now, for the first time in its long evolution, the human race is faced with the clear possibility of extinguishing itself by its own powers of destruction or of distinguishing itself by its own powers of construction. It is the pressing reality of this fear and this hope that gives the Atomic Age its unique schizoid quality. We are aware that we are balancing on a teeter-totter poised between the abyss and the stars.

All art, no matter how nostalgic or prophetic, necessarily reflects the era in which it is produced. In an age which is self-conscious about its newness, its difference from the past—such as Periclean Athens or Medician Florence or Elizabethan England—art is especially responsive to its own time and place. In the Atomic Age both the level of historical self-consciousness and the rate of overt change are so high that our art is even more responsive to its time and place, is indeed often pointedly contemporary. Modern painting mirrors a fragmentation of values, a concern for the subconscious, and a universe in which Einsteinean probabilities have replaced Newtonian certainties. Modern music echoes an electronic age in which improvisation, cacophony, new tonalities are all part of our jazzed-up physical and intellectual environment. Modern literature, with its sensitivities to the cumulative influence of Marx and Darwin and Freud, its awareness of megalopolis, its sense of an empyrean devoid of God, its implicit schizophrenia, also reflects our world.

Each essay in this book is modern, not only because it was written after 1945, but because it reveals the impact of the Atomic Age on a sensitive and articulate spokesman. The essay is an ancient form, going back at least to Hellenistic Greece and reaching an early peak in the *Essais* of Montaigne. But from the "Characters" of Theophrastus to next week's issue of *The New Yorker* the essay has always had two distinguishing features: it is addressed to an audience not restricted to specialists, and it shows, either directly or indirectly, a mind in the process of thinking—hence the word "essay" with its connotations of attempting, of tentativeness. An essay can deal with any subject; it can range from the stiffly formal to the casually informal; it can be short or long, gay or sad, colorful or drab, scientific or mystical; in fact, it can be—and has been—any and all of these in a variety of effective combinations. Even so, the modern essay has qualities which set it apart from its predecessors.

Almost every contemporary essay with any literary pretensions is argumentative: the author has a case to make or an axe to grind. He may be extremely informative, but he is almost never dispassionate. As a result, his emphasis is more on persuading than instructing. Probably this has always been true; it is now conspicuous. Second, it is difficult to put contemporary essays into such categories as impersonal/personal, neutral/slanted, analytic/descriptive. The large majority are eclectic and fit badly, if at all, into conventional subdivisions. Finally, the essay of today has certain stylistic tendencies that separate it from the past.

Most modern essays show relatively little concern with traditional rhetorical devices and arrangements. This is not to say that the contemporary essayist ignores rhetoric, but rather that he is more interested in its subliminal effects than in its surface patterns. If one attempts to apply Renaissance or Neoclassic or any

other conventional "rules," he will usually find that these rules—
these rhetorical habits—are not pertinent. The contemporary essayist is also less concerned than his literary ancestors with patterned sound effects. Many of the authors represented here are
masters of rhythm and alliteration and assonance, but none of
them systematically tries to achieve the balanced regularity of
a Dr. Johnson or the studied irregularity of a Thomas Browne or
Bernard Shaw. And in matters of diction the bulk of today's
writers make an extra effort to be colloquial, to talk with rather
than to their audience. These current stylistic tendencies are, in
relation to the past, matters of degree not of divorce, but they
do suggest that the modern essay speaks with its own distinctive
voice.

That voice, sometimes shrill, sometimes cajoling, sometimes a
whisper, sometimes a shout, can be clearly heard in the pages
that follow. I have tried to assemble a collection which would
both transmit that voice and range widely in subject and tone.
From a massive array of possibilities I chose those essays that
seemed noteworthy for their literary excellence, though such
excellence could be of many and mingled types: scholarly, humorous, prophetic, contentious, nostalgic, dramatic, etc. In short,
Modern Essays in English is a deliberately rich mixture, with
ingredients that are, I think, of the highest quality.

The arrangement of this collection is intellectual rather than
rhetorical. The first ten pieces can generally be described as
providing *background* for today. Thus the opening article sets
up broad problems of historiography and takes a comprehensive
glance at the past five centuries. Or Agee's piece recalls the
world of childhood and the apparently stable world that existed
on the eve of World War I. The next fourteen essays are more
concerned with *foreground,* with our current problems. For instance, Langer, Barzun, Faulkner, Trilling, and Kronenberger—
each from a different vantage point—comment on the dilemmas
of mass society and mass culture. Or Baldwin, standing on the
Alps, sees the Negro problem in extremely broad perspective,
while Salisbury, from close up, peers into a big-city slum. The
concluding ten essays then deal with the *creative possibilities* in
our tense world. Bronowski, for example, shows that the creative
impulse of both artist and scientist is essentially the same; Stein-

berg argues for the underlying traditionalism of modern painting, Cage for the anti-traditionalism of modern music; and Katherine Anne Porter concludes that life and culture will go on, in spite of the Atomic Age.

Following each essay is a short biographical statement about the author, a résumé of the important rhetorical devices and stylistic features that characterize the selection, and a few deliberately provocative questions about its style and content. At the end of the book the Appendix provides a brief sampling of the traditional essay in English.

Background

GEOFFREY BARRACLOUGH

Metropolis and Macrocosm. Europe and the Wider World, 1492–1939

Ever since the end of the war a change has come over our conceptions of modern history. We no longer feel that we stand four square in a continuous tradition, and the view of history we have inherited, the history which has western Europe at its centre, seems to have little relevance to our current problems and our current needs. In the Second World War "the collapse of the traditional European system became an irrevocable fact," and "what is called the 'historic Europe' is dead and beyond resurrection."[1] "The old Europe of the years between 1789, the year of the French Revolution, and 1939, the year of Hitler's War, has gone for ever."[2]

This fundamental change is bound to have repercussions upon the writing of modern history, in particular upon the inescapable assumptions of historians. There is still, for those who lived through the period beginning with the great depression of 1929, a morbid interest in the *post mortem* type of history, of which Sir Lewis Namier had made himself the master; but such history avails little as orientation among the dilemmas which face us in the post-war constellation of world-affairs, and it is natural and

From *History in a Changing World,* by Geoffrey Barraclough. By permission of the University of Oklahoma Press.

[1] H. Holborn, *The Political Collapse of Europe* (1951), x.
[2] A. Bullock, *Hitler. A Study in Tyranny* (1952), 738.

inevitable that a younger generation of historians should turn away from the older preoccupations, which no longer correspond to a living need, and attempt to hammer out a new vision of the course of modern history, to replace the world-picture which the war has torn to shreds.

In some cases this reaction has taken the form of a critique of the assumptions which had become the unquestioned foundations of western historiography—in particular, the assumption, which nineteenth-century economic developments seemed to prove, that Europe, the "microcosm" at the heart of an expanding world-economy, was destined to transform all other civilisations and carry over into the hemispheres the system of a balance and concert of powers, by which it was loosely integrated.[3] The illusory nature of these assumptions is already common knowledge;[4] it is not merely that imperialism has produced a reaction in the political field, the strength of which we are only beginning to feel, but that throughout Asia and Africa it has been accompanied by rejection of what are somewhat misleadingly called "western values," i.e. moral and religious assumptions which, in practice at least, the bulk of the population in the west has already discarded. European predominance in Asia is seen to-day as a temporary phase—almost as a breach in historical continuity—that has now passed.[5] In European history itself the old tendency to exaggerate the role of the "historic core," springing from the empire of Charlemagne, has given way to a better appreciation of the significance for us all of the enduring factors in Russian history—not merely its impact on the western world from the days of Peter the Great, but the importance of the period from the end of the eleventh to the middle of the sixteenth centuries in which the essential features of Russian culture, distinguishing it from Western Europe, took shape.[6] We realize better that historic Europe includes not only the Germanic peoples looking to Rome, but the Slavonic peoples looking to Byzantium and later to Mos-

[3] Cf. L. Dehio, "Ranke und der deutsche Imperialismus," *Hist. Zeitschrift* CLXX (1950), 307–328; also ibid. CLXXIII (1952), 77–94, and CLXXIV (1952), 479–502.

[4] Cf. A. J. Toynbee, *The World and the West* (1953).

[5] K. M. Pannikar, *Asia and Western Dominance* (1953).

[6] Cf. W. Philipp, *Hist. Zeitschrift* CLXXVI (1953), 590.

cow, the "Third Rome."[7] And instead of emphasizing the impact
of Europe on the New World, historians to-day are giving greater
attention to the impact of the New World on Europe, or are at
least seeking to treat their history not as that of separate continents but as directly related elements in the history of a world
which, since the Industrial Revolution, has become ever more
closely integrated.[8]

Underlying this change of orientation is not so much new
knowledge as a new vision playing on old facts, and a realization
of the inadequacy of old formulations in a new situation. The
older historiography, with its myopic concentration on Europe
and on the European powers and—where it looked further afield
—its independent treatment of the history of America and the
overseas territories as distinct units or spheres moving in a separate
axis, had discredited history and denuded it of sense and significance; it seemed to be lost in a world of nationalities which
has disintegrated visibly before our eyes. The effort of the newer
writers is therefore directed to blasting a way through the blank
wall, against which our previous historiography had come to a
halt; to opening a path for the historian into the future; and to
restoring the connexion between past and present, between history and life, which had perished.

Two main postulates underlie the new view. The first is the
realization that what has been called "the European age," which
may be dated roughly from 1492 to 1914, was not a steady culmination, but a phase with its beginning and its end, lying between the preceding "Mediterranean" and the succeeding "Atlantic" ages.[9] The second is that the history of this age cannot
profitably be studied in isolation, particularly for us who stand
outside its limits, and are interested as practical persons above all

[7] H. F. Schmid, "Eastern Europe in the light of world history," *Eastern
Review*, I (1948), 7–23; S. H. Gross, *Slavic Civilisation through the Ages*
(1948); H. Ludat, "Die Slaven und das Mittelalter," *Die Welt als Geschichte*
XII (1952), 69–84; O. Halecki, *Borderlands of Western Civilisation. A
History of East Central Europe* (1952).

[8] Cf. M. Silberschmidt, "Wirtschaftshistorische Aspekte der neueren
Geschichte," *Hist. Zeitschrift* CLXXI (1951), 245–261.

[9] O. Halecki, *The Limits and Divisions of European History* (1950),
29, 61.

else in the establishment, during the "European age," of the foundations of the period which, after the wars of 1914–18 and 1939–
45, was to succeed it; that, in particular, the distinction between
European and American history, as though they were two trams
running simultaneously down parallel tramlines, is as unreal and
deceptive as would be the attempt to-day to draw a dividing-line
between the economic and political problems of the European
and the American continents.

There have, of course, from Tocqueville and Burckhardt on-
wards, always been historians who have perceived the temporal
limitations of the "European age," and were acutely conscious that
it was running to its close; but they remained eccentric and exceptional, and exerted no clear influence over the tradition of
historical writing. To-day it is different. The failure of the old
historiography to provide reliable guidance—for example, in regard to the rise of Russia to the rank of a world-power—its
extraordinary capacity, which has bred widespread scepticism as
to the "use" of history, to get the portents wrong, because it failed
(if, indeed, it did not often deliberately refuse) to take a wider
view, have cleared the decks. Much of the writing to-day, naturally enough, is still tentative, a groping after new formulations,
and he who attempts a new synthesis does so at his peril. But
already we have from a German historian a challenging re-
examination of the whole course of international relations for the
five centuries following the fall of Constantinople[10]—a reappraisal
which has placed the political history of modern Europe in an
entirely new light by setting it in an extra-European context—
and there is evidence that this work will not stop short at the
political level. The impact of the outer world on European politics, and the transforming effects of that impact are now evident.
Equally important is the economic impact—considered as a
whole, and not merely in relation to isolated incidents, such as
the periodic effects of American slumps—and its transforming
effects upon the whole superstructure of ideas and institutions in
the modern world. And precisely this is the field which the
American historian, Walter Prescott Webb, has chosen to investigate anew. For Webb, the opening of the frontier lands of the

[10] L. Dehio, *Gleichgewicht oder Hegemonie. Betrachtungen ueber ein
Grundproblem der Leueren Staatengeschichte* (1948).

western hemisphere to a static European society in 1492, is the beginning of a new epoch in the story of mankind. Thereafter "in the history of western civilisation the two are inseparable," and "the interaction between the two," a "gigantic process extending over more than four centuries," is for him the essential "drama of modern history."[11]

Whatever reservations we may have to formulate as to its positive results, Webb's work deserves recognition as a bold attempt to re-examine along new lines the fundamental postulates of modern history; even where, we may think, it fails to convince, it helps us to clarify the issues, and above all else to see the present not as a continuation of, but as a break with past development. For Webb, as for Halecki—though the terms he uses are different—the "European age" is a thing of the past; and if, viewing it as a past age, he seeks to re-appraise its character and the elemental forces which determined its beginning and its end, it is not to discover guiding lines leading out of it into the future, but on the contrary to make clear the fundamental differences in environment which place us to-day before new circumstances, in which the experience of the past offers no sure guide.

The conventional starting-points of modern history, for historians in western Europe, are the Renaissance and the Reformation. Walter Prescott Webb takes another view. There had been other renaissances, a long series reaching back to the time of Charlemagne; there had been reformers without number before Luther. But the earlier reforms had withered, the earlier renaissances had failed to produce a decisive turning in the human mind. Why was it that the sixteenth century registered a permanent advance, where other centuries had experienced only a transient stimulus? Was it simply the gathering impetus, which now suddenly burst the banks and carried all before it, or was it that a new factor, a new "propelling force," so changed the external environment and "enlarged the field in which the human mind could operate," that the decisive leap into the future which had baffled earlier generations became suddenly feasible? Webb's answer is clear and categorical. The supreme architect of the

[11] W. P. Webb, *The Great Frontier* (1952), viii, 8, 11.

modern world, for him, was Christopher Columbus; the decisive event, differentiating the modern era from all previous recorded history, was the discovery of the New World in 1492, and the series of voyages, explorations and discoveries which followed in its wake. Decisive, because the vast accretion of new territory, "of gold and silver, of new foods for every empty belly and new clothing stuffs for every half-naked back," opened up possibilities no previous society had known. Down to 1492, for all its political upheavals, society had been static in essential things. The rise of empires, Persian or Roman or Carolingian, did not add to wealth, but simply transferred it to other hands. Apart from insignificant increments, due to the slow recovery of forest and marsh, "the land area available to Europeans" remained substantially unchanging; and the consequence was that population, pressing hard on the means of subsistance, was stable too. The idea of progress had not been born; "heaven alone, which could be reached only through the portals of death, offered hope to the masses."[12]

The discovery of the New World completely altered this situation. It added to the old inhabited areas—the "closed world" of the Metropolis—the whole "frontier" zone, the unexploited habitable regions revealed by the explorations of the fifteenth, sixteenth and seventeenth centuries—"three new continents, a large part of a fourth, and thousands of islands in oceans hitherto hardly known." What this signified figures best make clear. The population of the "Metropolis" in 1500, about 100 million, was crowded into an area of three and three-quarter million square miles, giving an average density of 26.7 persons per square mile. But now "to the 100 million people of the Metropolis was suddenly made available"—in addition to the exportable wealth, gold and silver, timber, furs—"nearly 20 million square miles of fabulously rich land practically devoid of population, an area more than five times as great as all Europe." The result was that "the population density was reduced to less than five persons per square mile, and each individual could have an average of 148 acres instead of 24." In addition, however—and far more immediately effective—there was the impact on the Metropolis of the wealth of the New World. It was American treasure, and American treasure alone, "that reversed the long descent of prices and sent them slanting up-

---

[12] Webb, *The Great Frontier*, 9, 143.

wards to such heights as to constitute a revolution." It was the "windfalls" of the frontier—those commodities which fell into the hands of explorers and adventurers almost for the taking—that brought about the capital accumulation which made the Industrial Revolution possible. As Webb says, "it is inconceivable," that the people of Europe in 1500, confined to their original area, "could by any stretch of their genius or by any invention they might make produce the wealth and create the boom which they enjoyed during the following four centuries." The frontier was "the matrix of the modern world." "Without its frontier modern Europe would be so different from what it is that it could hardly be considered modern at all."[13]

Modern history is therefore the drama of the impact of the Metropolis on the frontier and of the frontier on the Metropolis. If Western Europe—the Metropolis—is considered alone, its history does not make sense; for "the story of the Great Frontier and the Metropolis rises high above the fragments of both"; it is the unity of which each singly is the imperfect part. It was through contact with the frontier in the New World that the institutions handed down from the Middle Ages disintegrated; and "the character of the modern age is due in large measure to the fact that it had a frontier setting, that it grew up in an economic boom induced by the appropriation and use of frontier resources, and that its institutions were designed and modified to meet the needs of a booming society."[14]

In 1500 "wherever man turned, some guardian was telling him what to do, what to believe, what to think. All round he was walled in by authority, which saw to it that he moved in a prescribed groove." The frontier was "the fifth column of liberty." It put a premium on the individual, made possible "his temporary supremacy over institutions." "Democracy," says Webb, "is a frontier institution, so far as the modern world is concerned." On the frontier the old-world "baggage" of "ideas about rank, status and

[13] Ibid., 7, 10, 16, 17, 144, 174. As instances of the "windfalls" of the frontier Webb cites the examples of the gold and silver brought back by Drake in the *Golden Hind*—which provided the capital behind the Levant and East India Companies—and the dividend paid in 1687 by Sir William Phipps—"what is probably the biggest dividend in business history, 10,000 per cent as against a paltry 4,700 per cent paid by Drake about a century earlier" (ibid., 197, 201).

[14] Ibid., 11, 140.

relative position" was jettisoned, because it was useless; and instead there arose a new creed of equality. The institutions of the
old corporate class-conditioned European society of the *ancien
régime* "wore themselves out against the abrasive frontier grind-
stone." And in their place—spreading back to the Metropolis—
arose the characteristic institutions and outlook of a frontier
society: individualism, equality, democracy, the "religion of
work," "unbridled optimism," "rude manners," the profit-motive—
a mixed bag, indeed, for the frontier "ruthlessly crushed out many
fine qualities which human beings derive from leisure," but a
mixture without which modern civilisation, in the Metropolis as
well as in the New World, would be unrecognizable.[15]

It is easy to take these changes for granted "as merely another
logical step in the orderly progress of an endowed people." To do
so is to miss the essential point. We are apt to assume that man
"achieved freedom by his own efforts"; in reality, the whole sub-
structure and the whole superstructure of modern civilisation rest
upon a "windfall." "The modern age," in other words, "was an
abnormal age and not a progressive orderly development which
mankind was destined to make anyway." "The institutions developed in this exceptional period were exceptional institutions . . .
quite different from what might be expected in the course of
human affairs." Like the ideas that went with them—ideas, for
example, about the relations of the individual and government—
they were "highly specialized to meet boom conditions," and as
such bound to undergo violent change as soon as "boom conditions" passed "away and history returned to normal." And precisely that is what has happened. The "Age of the Frontiers" is an
age which has passed. Between 1890 and 1910 the frontier closed.
As we have seen, the ratio of population to land in 1500 was about
27 to the square mile; by 1900 it was again approaching that mark;
by 1930 it had passed it; a decade later it was touching 35. There
was a "pause" lasting about a generation, from 1900 to 1930; but
"by 1940 the big house was much fuller than the little house was
in 1500."[16]

Just as the opening of the "frontier" marked the beginning of
a new era, so the closing of the "frontier" marks its passing. The

---

[15] Ibid., 5, 30, 31, 34, 35, 49 sqq., 55, 265, 303.
[16] Ibid., 14, 15, 18, 107, 141, 160, 413.

repercussions are already being felt all along the line. "Frontier individualism is now old, a thing of history," something to look back on, representing the "goal of an extinct period"; and the modern individual, "caught between the closing frontier and the expanding production of the machine," feels himself "useless, baffled and defeated." He sees the economic system he knew in process of falling about his ears; "and the case is not much different in our attitude toward democracy." Even if scientific discovery and technology can maintain the abundance which "made the profit-motive tenable" and carried society "along the road to capitalism," it will still "bring with it a new set of needs" and "it will be necessary to specialize in another direction determined largely by . . . whatever force dominates society."[17]

Hence "we should not be so obtuse as to believe that the means of management are the same as those of conquest, or that frontier institutions will necessarily serve a metropolitan society." Obsessed by the idea of guarding against the restrictions they had escaped, in the form of absolutism and mercantilism, people failed to see that out of their new condition, out of "abundance and freedom," "new institutions as menacing as the old ones," were arising. Of these none was more important than the business corporation, "the pattern-maker of institutionalized modern life." "Corporateness is now the primary fact and the dominant force." "Curbed on all sides by corporations or government agencies or labour unions, or associations," the individual is "approaching anonymity in the modern corporate culture"; "the chief choice left to him is a choice of curbers." "Like the reluctant ox, he comes slowly to the yoke, but he comes nevertheless." "It is not that people are no longer willing to take risks, but rather that they are overborne by a sense of futility in striving for what seems unattainable." Nevertheless the result is a situation "which makes it possible for the corporate organizations . . . to gather their recruits," and "gives the few bold leaders their opportunity . . . to command an army more noted for its docility than for its courage." Above all else, it is a situation "favourable to the dictator," who rises from "the cemeteries of dead hopes and aspirations."[18]

This is the new age upon which we are entering; and of neces-

[17] Ibid., 109, 128, 414.
[18] Ibid., 71, 78, 101, 103, 107–109, 113, 118, 119, 131, 418.

sity our entry into it "will be accompanied by basic changes in the
nature of the institutions which grew up in the earlier one"—
particularly in "those institutions which best fulfilled the needs of
a frontier society." "Society as it thickens will become more closely
integrated and its members more interdependent. Governments
will tend to become stronger, using more compulsion in order to
meet their obligations. . . . The individual will become relatively
less important and will lose his identity in a growing corporate
life." "Capitalism of the nineteenth-century type will decline with
the passing of the boom on which it was based." Society itself will
"go through a process of devolution and retrogression rather than
evolution and progress," losing "much of its dynamic character,"
and "rural life" will "tend to become more important" as "city
life" becomes "less alluring," until in the end men looking back
will see "the Age of the Frontier" and all its ideas and institutions
as "an aberration, a temporary departure from the normal, a
strange historical detour."[19]

Such are Webb's arguments. Their force is due to the fact that
they are based not on chance observation of contemporary trends
but upon a rigorous historical analysis which, if true, is inexorable.
Few of his arguments are new in themselves. His debt to Turner's
famous "frontier concept" is obvious;[20] and scarcely less marked,
in his analysis of boom conditions, is his debt to Keynes and to
Earl Hamilton, the historian of the sixteenth-century price revolution.[21] His own contribution is to bring familiar concepts and arguments within the fold of an encompassing vision which illuminates
them afresh. Nor is it a serious criticism that his narrative—in
common with many other great simplifying visions—is sometimes
crudely expressed and marred by error in detail. It should nevertheless be noted that he does not hold "that the frontier originated
ideas or institutions, but only that it altered them, often in a
spectacular manner"; he does not claim that it was the only
factor, but simply that it was the formative factor, which provided

[19] Ibid., 414–415.
[20] F. J. Turner, *The Frontier in American History* (1920).
[21] Cf. J. M. Keynes, *A Treatise on Money* II (1930), 148 sqq.; Earl J.
Hamilton, "American Treasure and the Rise of Capitalism," *Economica*
(1929).

the impetus otherwise lacking.[22] It might be argued that he exaggerates the role of the "frontier" and pays too little attention to economic developments within Europe since the Industrial Revolution, to the coal of South Wales and the Ruhr and the development of the iron and steel industries, as factors in the creation of modern industrial civilisation. To this criticism his answer would be that the capital accumulation and the economic milieu favourable to technical progress, which were pre-conditions of the Industrial Revolution, owed their existence to "frontier exploitation"; that, however formidable in themselves, they were secondary consequences, and the "frontier," which "increased manifold the room over which European people could move; and the body of wealth which they could acquire," was primary.[23] It is, no doubt, true that the "fertilization of industry by commercial capital" derived ultimately from the frontier, was a less straightforward process than Webb appears to suggest;[24] but whatever nuances might be introduced, it would be difficult to write off his generalization as unfounded. Undoubtedly the historical situation at every stage was more complicated than he indicates; but this fact does not in itself impair the force of his argument, and we are still entitled to ask, what is its validity, not at this or that particular point, but as a comprehensive view of the course of world-history since the age of Columbus.

To this fundamental question—all criticism in detail apart—the answer must be that Webb illuminates part of the scene, but does not illuminate the whole scene because his vision—though wider than that of the average western European historian—is still not world-wide. His study, he says, "is confined to the empty lands of North and South America, Australia, and that portion of the Dark Continent comprised in the Union of South Africa"; Asia "has no part" in his "exposition."[25] The limitation is arbitrary; for it rules out a phase in the relations of Frontier and Metropolis comparable in scale to, and no less heavy in consequences than those

[22] *The Great Frontier*, 239; cf. pp. 15, 101, 143, 173, 174, 258.
[23] "The early stages of the Industrial Revolution were the middle stages of the frontier revolution"; *The Great Frontier*, 129. Cf. ibid., 75, 101, 238, 410. Cf. M. Dobb, *Studies in the Development of Capitalism* (1946), 207 sqq.
[24] Cf. for example Dobb, op. cit., 195.
[25] *The Great Frontier*, 9.

with which he deals: the history of the Russian frontier. It may
be true that, relatively, the extent of European colonization, beginning in the Middle Ages—in Prussia, for example, and other
trans-Elbean lands—is too small to set beside that of the New
World, though the repopulation of the Hungarian plain in the
eighteenth century, after the expulsion of the Turks, was so vast
a movement that Hungary at that time has been compared with
America.[26] But all historians are agreed that in Russian history
the "frontier," moving across Asia to the Pacific, has been as important a factor as it was in that of the United States; and in
excluding Russia and Russian expansion from his scheme, Webb
not only violates the unity of history, but also vitiates his own
conclusions.

The elementary geo-political facts are sufficient to demonstrate
this limitation. The Soviet Union is as large both in extent and
numbers as the whole of the North American continent; it is four
times the size of Europe, and yet has less than half its population.[27] This itself implies a ratio of land and population radically
different from that upon which Webb's whole argument rests. In
fact, where Webb establishes for 1940 a figure of approximately 35
inhabitants per square mile, the figure for the Soviet empire is no
more than 22—a figure, significantly, still below the European
ratio of 1500.[28] In addition we may take into account—by contrast with the "ruinously rapid rate of soil exploitation" in North
America—the slow tempo of Russian colonisation in Asia, which
only got going on a major scale after 1891.[29] If we accept Webb's
postulates, only one conclusion is possible: namely, that the turn
of the wheel which he claims to have been completed by about
1910 in the western hemisphere, has not yet occurred in the Soviet
Union, that the Soviet frontier is not yet "closed," and therefore

[26] Nevertheless we should remember that two-fifths of modern Germany
—estimated by its pre-war frontiers—was added by colonization in little over
two centuries, between 1125 and 1346; cf. G. Barraclough, *The Origins of
Modern Germany* (1946), 251.

[27] B. H. Sumner, *Survey of Russian History* (1944), 9; "throughout Russian history," he adds, "one dominating theme has been the frontier."

[28] Assuming a population of 192 millions; cf. A. Mousset, *Le monde slave*
(1946), 8. The figure of the 1939 Soviet census is 170 millions, but this
covers an area smaller than the Russian empire; cf. Sumner, op. cit., 391.

[29] Cf. Sumner, op. cit., 17, 55.

that the decline, the "devolution and retrogression," that set in in the west with the closing of the frontier, does not apply in the Russian orbit.

It is, however, another question whether we can accept Webb's postulates, and in particular the statistical basis upon which he works. To throw together the land area and population of Europe and the New World, as he does, may illuminate certain facts in their relations, but it obscures others. Even if "the influence of the frontier on the Metropolis was indivisible," if "it exerted its influence on non-owners as well as on the proprietors"—if, for example, "Spanish gold prospered England and Holland and France," and we should not allow "the concept of colonies and empires" to "obscure its common characteristics and the unity of the force it exerted"[30]—the fact remains that its impact was uneven. It is certainly worth emphasizing that the wealth of the New World was not canalized by political frontiers; but that does not mean that political frontiers counted for nothing. When, for example, Webb states that the discoveries "made available nearly 20 million square miles" for the inhabitants of the Metropolis,[31] it is fair to point out that this availability was largely theoretical, and that in many directions it became illusory when political action in the form of immigration laws checked and even halted the flow of population. When Hitler in 1939 drew President Roosevelt's attention to the fact that the United States, with a population scarcely one-third greater than that of Germany, possessed more than fifteen times as much living space,[32] he unerringly put his finger on the inherent weakness of any argument comprising the European metropolis and the New World in one formula. To treat either the New World or the Metropolis as a "unity," as Webb postulates, is itself of dubious validity; but it will suffice for present purposes to emphasize the broad distinction between the two "colonial" regions, the Asian and the American, and Europe. Europe, with its relatively small land-area and its high population,

[30] *The Great Frontier,* 11, 21, 410.
[31] Ibid., 17.
[32] *Documents on International Affairs,* 1939–1946, I (1951), 255. "In this state," he had already remarked, "there are roughly 140 people to each square kilometer—not 15, as in America" (p. 254).

stands apart from the one as it does from the other; and the only safe course, for the purpose of analysis, is to treat each area separately.

This fact becomes even clearer if we turn to the political and institutional developments, which Webb associates with the influence of the frontier. It is a plausible (though by no means new) argument that the values of individualism were born on the frontier and "that democracy is a frontier institution so far as the modern world is concerned"; but a finer analysis—particularly if, unlike Webb's, it is extended to include Russia—will not stop at this point. Democracy, as a descriptive term, has been used from the time of Aristotle to denote a variety of ills, a number of different political systems; and it is important—not in order to make moral judgments, to castigate the one or the other as merely "a semblance of democratic forms,"[33] but simply in order to secure a sound basis for historical analysis—to distinguish between the democracy of the frontier lands, of Russia and the United States, and that of Europe. There are adequate reasons, if we so wish, for describing all three forms of government as democratic, provided that we realize that such a description does not imply identity between them, or even identity between any two. Neither Russian nor American democracy—despite obvious inter-connexions and cross-influences—is the type of democracy we know as a historical fact in western Europe, if only for the reason that they are products of a totally different environment. For Webb the class structure of modern Europe, the privileges of groups and local communities, the corporations which existed to bolster and defend these privileges, constitute both restraints on liberty and the antithesis of democracy. For the European historian who is in a position to compare both the United States and Russia, they are likely, on the contrary, to appear as the very core and kernel of European democratic institutions. Whether we like it or not, Cromwell's famous dictum: "Where is there any bound or limitt sett, if . . . men that have noe interest butt the interest of breathing shall have a voice in elections?"[34] is an essential ingredient of European democratic practice; and "liberty" and "privilege" in

---

[33] *The Great Frontier*, 165, 166.

[34] Cf. C. H. Firth, *The Clarke Papers* I (1891), 309. I have cut out the double negative of Cromwell's statement in the defective copy of the short-

European political tradition are historically not antitheses but co-ordinates, at some periods even synonyms.[35] In western European experience democratic practice has resulted from the action of estates and—on the continent, if not in England—of provincial groupings, fighting for their "rights";[36] it is for that reason and in that sense that it has so often been described as "empirical" or "pragmatic," the product of historical circumstances rather than of systematic theory.[37] We do not need to nourish any illusions about the limitations of democracy of this type, still less—as is now so common in Germany—to entertain nostalgic longings on its behalf; but it would be blindness to ignore the historical force of the traditions upon which it rests.[38]

From this point of view the historian in western Europe is more likely to contrast Europe with America and Russia, the two societies of the great open spaces, than to range Europe and the United States together as one type, in contrast to Russia.[39] In America, the dismantling of the corporative structure introduced by the early settlers—the collapse of guild-organisation and apprenticeship, the destruction of the village-community, the disestablishment of the church, and the introduction of a free system of land-tenure in place of entail and primogeniture—had occurred before the end of the eighteenth century.[40] In Russia, except per-

---

hand notes. The text is reprinted in A. S. P. Woodhouse, *Puritanism and Liberty* (1938), 59.

[35] Cf. G. Tellenbach, *Church, State and Christian Society at the time of the Investiture Contest* (1940), 16 sqq.—an important statement of the relations of *privilegium* and *libertas* which, no doubt because of the special context in which it is found, has not received the general attention that it deserves.

[36] It is sufficient to refer to Mill's classic statement in the historical introduction to his essay *On Liberty* (Everyman's Library edition, 66).

[37] Cf. G. H. Sabine, *A History of Political Theory* (1938), 665; M. Oakeshott, *The Social and Political Doctrines of Contemporary Europe* (1939), xviii; C. E. M. Joad, *Guide to the Philosophy of Morals and Politics* (1938), 770, 788.

[38] Cf. for the whole of the above paragraph and for what follows, D. Gerhard's impressive study, "Regionalismus und ständisches Wesen als ein Grundthema europäischer Geschichte," *Hist. Zeitschrift* CLXXIV (1952), 307–337.

[39] Cf. M. Beloff, "Is there an Anglo-American political tradition?" *History* XXXVI (1951), 77, and passim.

[40] Cf. Gerhard, op. cit., 327–328; for primogeniture and entail, cf. Webb, op. cit., 259–268.

haps on the western frontiers, such a social structure had never existed.[41] As in America, the open spaces, the moving frontier, the flow of population, stood in the way of the formation of stable social and regional groups comparable to those of the west; even the provincial and district assemblies of the nobility were weak.[42] And, as in America, the open frontier and the existence of free land created possibilities for the sudden rise of the individual, which find their parallels in America rather than in western Europe.[43] Indeed, in Russia, as in America, the open frontier has been the source of liberties—the history of the Cossacks is the best evidence of that[44]—but these liberties were never incorporated in fixed institutions in such a way as to withstand the extension of state power and the transformation of the structure of frontier society.[45] Here, in fact, we touch the essential difference between the "democracy of the frontier," and the historically conditioned democracies of western Europe; and it may be argued that "the democracy of the frontier," for Webb the only true democracy, is a fragile growth precisely because it lacks the support of ingrained institutions, because it is related to a theoretical structure of individual rights and based on the atomized individual standing alone in society, whereas western democracy has its roots in groups and associations which effectively bind individuals together as a counterpoise to the power of Leviathan. "Take away corporations and communities," wrote Bodin, "and you ruin the state and transform it into a barbaric tyranny."[46] Not the least significant feature in the situation in Germany leading to the rise of Hitler was the undermining, by economic and other factors, of the old-standing corporate associations, from the *Länder* to the trade unions and the Christian churches. We may well think that Russian history is evidence of the fragile nature of "frontier democracy," that the weakness of local institutions and the mobility of the population go far to explain the triumph of

[41] Cf. Gerhard, op. cit., 312.

[42] Sumner, op. cit., 76.

[43] Cf. Gerhard, op. cit., 329–333.

[44] Cf. Sumner, op. cit., 49 sqq.

[45] Cf. A. von Schelting, *Russland und Europa im russischen Geschichtsdenken* (1948), 274–278.

[46] J. Bodin, *Les six livres de la république* (Geneva, 1629), 502 (bk. iii, cap. 7); cf. *Six Books of the Commonwealth* (transl. M. J. Tooley, 1955), 107.

autocracy. And if that is so, we may attach particular importance to Webb's chance remark, that "if totalitarianism comes, it will come hardest among the people who made the most of individualism, the Americans of the United States."[47] In spite of contemporary political and ideological divergencies, there may well, in short, be fundamentally more affinity beween the two extremes than between either extreme and the mean.

The foregoing reflections, summary as they are, may serve to throw into relief some of the main limitations of Webb's arguments, as a comprehensive picture of the development of modern society. They indicate three main reasons why his thesis fails to convince, although it helps to illuminate certain aspects of modern history. The first is that he exaggerates the influence of frontier institutions, and seriously underestimates—indeed, virtually ignores—the effects of industrialization and of the shift of population from the land to the great urban centres, which is so outstanding a feature of more recent American history. Even in the United States, in short, there are good reasons to think that the frontier was not the sole or even the main factor in the evolution of political and social democracy,[48] while it still has to be satisfactorily explained why, if decisive, it failed to produce parallel results in South or Latin America.[49] Secondly, he fails to perceive that, in the Metropolis, what we may call "frontier values" have never been accepted as the norm of human existence, and that their influence has been limited historically by counter-currents coming from the heart of western society. European historians are accustomed to see this reaction—with its ideal of an organically articulated society, built up of groups and associations, in contrast to the ideal of a uniform egalitarian society—as finding its outlet in the Romantic movement after 1815; indeed, many would regard it as the essence of the Romantic movement, and it is of the deepest historical significance that, whereas European rationalism of the eighteenth century had powerful repercussions

[47] *The Great Frontier,* 122.

[48] This has rightly been emphasized by P. Marshall, "The Great Frontier," *Past and Present* VII (1955), who effectively assembles American criticism of Turner's "frontier" thesis.

[49] Webb's summary treatment of this problem (pp. 87–89), in which he emphasizes exclusively the "rigidity and stability of the Catholic church" as a differentiating factor, is inadequate and unsatisfactory.

in America and in the Russia of Catherine the Great, the Romantic movement remained, in its political aspects, a western European phenomenon affecting Russia only in so far as it was diverted into Slavophile channels, and thereby sharply differentiating the temper of European thought from that of Russia and of America alike.[50] We may, if we like, call this temper conservative, provided we realize it is not the conservatism of political parties; and it is again of the deepest historical significance—wherever our personal sympathies may lie—that the force of this conservatism in Europe, as events since 1945 have demonstrated, is not spent, and that it still exists as a powerful check to the levelling and atomizing influence of "frontier civilisation," though in what direction its influence will be exerted no one can foretell.

But Webb does not merely exaggerate the influence of the frontier and underestimate the strength of contrary forces. His third major error is to misinterpret the role of frontier institutions, which historically have weakened the safeguards of individual rights and so have marked a dilution rather than an advance of the democratic tradition which Europe inherits from its Middle Ages. It is another question whether the new "democracy" is, except in the most indirect way, a product, as Webb supposes, of the frontier; whether it is not more simply the result (as indicated above) of the growth both in the United States and in Europe of an amorphous urban proletariat which, inadequately represented by the older political associations, gave rise to a new political machinery to cope with its requirements and implement its aspirations. Nevertheless, no one would deny the force of the institutions and ideas which Webb, rightly or wrongly, has identified with the frontier. But to admit their force does not imply that we must welcome their advance as progress. On the one side, we can see all too plainly—for all the obstacles have been torn down—the wide road leading from "frontier democracy" to totalitarianism. On the other side, we can assert with a good deal of conviction that diversity, regional differentiation, and stability—the very things that the levelling force of the frontier attacked—are part and parcel of the indispensable foundations of civilisation.[51]

[50] Cf. for example G. Ritter, "Ursprung und Wesen der Menschenrechte," *Hist. Zeitschrift* CLXIX (1949), 233–263.

[51] Cf. Gerhard, op. cit., 337, and Oakeshott, op. cit., xix.

Nevertheless, it remains true that Webb is right in emphasizing the importance of the closing of the frontier, the cessation of the boundless opportunities for the individual which it betokened, and the problems of a frontierless society. Even in Russia the time cannot be far distant when the frontier will have closed. But whereas Soviet Russia claims to have its own answer to the problems of a frontierless society, western society, in Europe and in America, is still entangled in the "philosophy of a free and un-fettered world," still "trying to harness the dreams of yesterday . . . to the machines of to-day and to-morrow," and searching among the debris of the old for new or "substitute" frontiers.[52] On these "unreal images of new frontiers" Webb is caustic and astringent; in particular, he is sceptical of the common assumption that the problems of a frontierless society can be circumvented by science which, in place of the open frontier that has gone, can give us the infinite possibilities of a "scientific frontier" stretching in-definitely ahead, and a new abundance produced by scientific means.[53] Science, he insists, cannot create abundance; it may "speed up the rate at which resources already in existence" can be "utilized," but its end-effect is destructive. Indeed, by fostering "a population that is expanding with explosive force all over the world," it is more likely to add to our problems than to solve them. The solution to these problems, if they are to be solved, can only come on the political level.

But this solution is complicated by the fact—to which Webb scarcely refers—that the conquest of the frontier, for good or for evil, has made the whole world one. There is no "overspill" area left, no outlet for surplus population, not even room for man-oeuvre. Precisely because the unification of the world—in every sense save the political sense—is something unique in history, it has created a situation without parallel in the past.[54] The question to-day is whether we can devise new means of coping with this new world-situation. One of the virtues of Webb's analysis is that —parting company from most of his compatriots—he realizes that the newness of our situation leaves no room for the classical indi-

---

[52] *The Great Frontier*, 121, 133.

[53] Ibid., 280–302.

[54] Cf. A. J. Toynbee, "The Unification of the World and the Change in Historical Perspective," *Civilisation on Trial* (1948), 62–96.

vidualistic remedies, and makes no attempt to fob us off with the
empty clichés—"the middle way," "constitutional co-operation,"
"spiritual rebirth," and the like[55]—of threadbare liberalism. It is a
cardinal weakness, on the other hand, that he ignores the achievement of Communism and the fact that Communism—whether we
like it or not—provides the only alternative to date which has not
lost constructive force and imaginative grip; it offers at least a plausible solution for the countless millions of "under-privileged" in
Asia and Africa as well as in Europe, to the problems of a frontierless society. But there is another way out, of which Hitler has
given us a foretaste,—the conquest of "living-space" at the expense of others. It is the classical solution and probably the line
of least resistance in a world of contending powers, with a resur-
gent Asia looming ever larger in the background; but it is a
solution which entails famine, bloodshed, want, destruction, and
its result can only be the survival—of which past history gives us
so many examples—of the least fit, and the crudest, the earthiest
and the least civilized.

[55] Toynbee, op. cit., 27, 39, 40, 142, and passim.

✦

GEOFFREY BARRACLOUGH   Born in England in 1908, Professor Barraclough is a prominent, prolific, and provocative historian.

*"Metropolis and Macrocosm. Europe and the Wider World, 1492–
1939"* (1954) An example of scholarly writing at its best, this article
presents a carefully organized argument. The author uses such rhetorical devices as classification, definition, and comparison to refute some
widely held historical assumptions and to set up new areas for exploration. He has a good ear and bolsters his analysis with interesting sentence variety. The reader can enjoy watching a logical and well-in-
formed mind proceeding inductively through a mass of complex
materials.

✦

*1. In what ways, if any, does the new frontier of space affect the
argument? 2. What should be the basic assumptions of a historian writing about the modern world?*

H. R. TREVOR-ROPER

Niccolò Machiavelli

In 1530 two Italianate Englishmen discussed politics together. Reginald Pole, who tells us about the conversation, was a somewhat priggish character: his ideal, he said, was Plato's *Republic*. Thomas Cromwell was sceptical. Such views, he said, were now out of date: the duty of a stateman was to see through such verbiage to the reality of politics; and since Pole's studies in Padua had evidently been inadequately supervised, he obligingly offered to lend him, in manuscript (for it had not yet been printed) a more up-to-date manual of politics. He afterwards forgot to send the book (he was rather busy in the next decade), but Pole read it and remembered it with a good deal of virtuous pain. It was, he said, "written by the finger of Satan." It was *The Prince* of Machiavelli.

No man, perhaps, until Marx, has had so various, so revolutionary an effect on political thought as Machiavelli. A scholarly official and observant ambassador of the Florentine Republic, a friend (in spite of his views) of Popes and Cardinals, he seemed, in his lifetime, a distinguished academic figure. After his death, his most famous work, *The Prince*, was at last published, with papal blessing, and in twenty years ran into twenty-five editions. Then, at mid-century, opinion began to harden. The Council of

From *Men and Events* (English title: *Historical Essays*) by H. R. Trevor-Roper. Copyright © 1957 by W. A. Evill and A. D. Peters. Reprinted by permission of Harper & Row, Publishers; the author; Macmillan & Co. Ltd. (London); and The Macmillan Company of Canada Limited.

Trent ordered the destruction of his works. At Rome he was denounced as a detestable atheist. In Germany the Jesuits burnt him in effigy. In France the hatred felt for Catherine des Medicis and her Italian court was concentrated on his head. He penetrated to Scotland as "Mitchell Wylie," the spirit embodied in that sceptical politician Maitland of Lethington. In England the dramatists made him a universal bogey-man, "the murderous Machiavel," the type and patron of poisoners and assassins. His works were banned in England as in Rome. Poets, peoples, governments, Protestants, Pope—all seemed united in detestation of that name.

And yet, behind that solidarity of ignorance and prejudice which so often unites governments and people, the greatness of Machiavelli was never forgotten. Long before his works had been printed, the Italian booksellers had employed professional copyists to reproduce them. Long after they had been banned, manuscript translations passed from hand to hand in England, and the Italian text was piratically printed in London for learned readers. Already by 1540 Pole declared that Machiavelli "had poisoned England and would poison all Christendom." Thomas Cromwell's disciple, Richard Morison, read him privately in Germany with his secretary Roger Ascham, the tutor of Queen Elizabeth; Sir John Cheke read him, the tutor of King Edward VI; Cheke's brother-in-law William Cecil, Lord Burghley, read him, and Queen Elizabeth's other servants, Sir Christopher Hatton and Sir Thomas Smith; Sir Walter Raleigh read him, and Sir Francis Bacon, and Raleigh's friend "the Wizard Earl" of Northumberland.[1] And as they read, little by little the cloak of respectability wore gradually thinner, the pretence of secrecy was dropped, the name of their master was discreetly avowed and quietly praised. Even so, it was not till the eve of the Puritan Revolution that his greatest works, *The Discourse on the First Ten Books of Titus Livy* and *The Prince* were at last published in English. Even then the editor took care to apologise for so bold a gesture. *The Prince,*

[1] That Hatton read Machiavelli is shown by Thomas Bedingfield's dedication to him of his translation of the *Florentine History* (1595), "which . . . your Lordship hath heretofore read in the Italian tongue." The 9th Earl of Northumberland's copy is still at Alnwick Castle: it is the Italian text secretly published in London (with the imprint of "Palermo") in 1584.

he allowed, was a poisonous work; and yet, he added, even poisons, if carefully used, can be medicinal: "the Lamprey, they say, hath a venomous sting runs along the back of it; take that out, and it is served in a choice dish for dainty palates." Within a few months the twenty years' crisis had begun. In that revolution the last shreds of humbug were torn away, and the greatest of its political thinkers, examining their revolution with a new technique, were no longer afraid to glorify their teacher. John Lilburne, and the twin authors of *Oceana*, James Harrington and Henry Neville, all praised "the divine Machiavel"—"the best and most honest of all the modern politicians," "one of the wisest, most judicious and true lovers of his country, of Italy's liberties and freedom, and generally of the good of all mankind, that ever I read of in my days"; and when at last, in 1675, the first English translation of Machiavelli's whole works was published, its editor was the surviving republican philosopher, Henry Neville.[2]

What was the new science which Machiavelli had invented; which had so outraged the world that only revolutionaries, a hundred and fifty years later, could dare to praise him openly? To us it seems innocent enough. Machiavelli humanised the study of politics. Rejecting old ideas that human institutions depended on divine prescription or *a priori* reasoning, he declared the simple proposition that the material of history does not change, that valid general laws of political behaviour can therefore be deduced from the past, and that modern politics should be regulated by these scientific laws. These laws are of course as many and various as human experience: there is one set of laws for tyrants wishing to seize and retain absolute power, another for democrats wishing to prevent such tyranny. Machiavelli is not directly concerned with such differences of purpose: he is a pure

[2] It is frequently stated that Neville himself was not only the editor but also the translator of Machiavelli's works. This statement derives ultimately from the Life of Neville prefaced to Thomas Hollis's edition of Neville's *Plato Redivivus* (1763). But in fact this preface is an unacknowledged plagiarism—with additions and omissions by Hollis—from Antony Wood's *Athenae Oxonienses*, and the statement that Neville "translated Machiavelli's works" is one of Hollis's additions. I can find no evidence for it; and in fact one at least of the translations in Neville's edition was taken from an earlier publication which seems quite unconnected with Neville (*The Marriage of Belphegor*, printed in *The Novels of Dom Francisco de Quevedo*, London 1671).

intellectual concerned to work out the general laws of political cause and effect, regardless of the practical use to which they may be put. To work them out, all that is needed is a deductive faculty and a stretch of history. Since history is recurrent, one stretch is theoretically as good as another; in fact, as an Italian humanist, Machiavelli chose to comment on contemporary Europe by reference to the history of Republican Rome. So a book with the dry title of *Discourses on the First Ten Books of Titus Livy* became the medium of the new theory which shocked the world.

Thus in theory the science of Machiavelli, like all science, is entirely neutral as to political aims. Political forms and political methods are to be valued not in themselves but according as they achieve the purpose for which they are intended. Whatever the political form, the real rulers are seldom more than forty or fifty men, and certain institutions, certain rules of method are essential to any form of government. A republic can no more dispense with ultimate dictatorial authority (like the Venetian Council of Ten) than a prince; religion and certain other forms of fraud are essential instruments of all governors; no revolutionary power can tolerate its avowed enemies: "he who establishes a tyranny and does not kill Brutus, and he who establishes a republic and does not kill the sons of Brutus, will not last long."

And yet, however he try, can a political philosopher really be entirely neutral? It may be that the rules for establishing or overthrowing tyranny are, for their different purposes, equally valid; but what if the question is asked whether tyranny or freedom is more conducive to the peace, the prosperity, or the happiness of a people? This is an entirely neutral question soluble, in Machiavelli's theory, by entirely neutral methods; nevertheless, its answer implies a preference which can hardly be distinguished from a moral preference. So, obliquely, but by his very method, Machiavelli in his *Discourses* allows his own political preference to emerge. Fundamentally he is a citizen, and a republican. He does not believe in single rulers or unitary states. Political life is to him an essential of civilisation, and feudal gentry, who render such life impossible, he abominates. If vigorous city life leads to class-conflict, these are a sign of health, not corruption: "to me those who condemn the quarrels between the nobles and the plebs seem to be cavilling at the very cause of Rome's continued freedom." Further, as between aristocracy and democracy he is a democrat. Aristocracies, like Sparta and Venice, may preserve themselves longest, but only democracies, which refresh their ruling class, can expand. The methods of expansion for all governments are the same: war and conquest; and war and conquest also have their scientific rules.

Nevertheless, if Machiavelli is a republican, his very theory requires that such a preference can never be absolute. Times and necessities change and different circumstances have different rules. "No state, be it republic or kingdom, is either first established or radically changed except by a single person." Machiavelli lived in a time of European crisis: he saw French and Spaniards and Swiss invading Italy and a corrupted Papacy strong enough to foment the evil, too weak to cure it. For such a crisis he judged that a single person was necessary; and so in the end this Florentine republican, with absolute intellectual consistency, called for a tyrant to save Italy. Tyranny has its own rules, and Machiavelli never pretended to like them. But if there was one thing which he liked less it was intellectual muddle, half-measures, "that middle course which is the most prejudicial that men can take," the technical failure to relate means to ends. If the situation called for a tyrant, then it called for the methods appropriate to a tyrant. . . . So the writer of the *Discourses* became also, without any change of philosophy, the writer of the *Prince*.

So also he acquired that bad name which has never really forsaken him. It is an *idée fixe* among men that neutrality is impossible, and no protestations have really persuaded them that Machiavelli did not secretly approve his own propositions. Certainly he protested. He did not, like those modern ideologues who miscall themselves his disciples, pretend that cruelty and treachery were positive virtues. The methods of Philip of Macedon, he declared, "are exceedingly cruel and repugnant to any human, let alone any Christian community. It were far better to avoid them and live in obscurity than to reign as king by such methods. Nevertheless, if a man wants to reign . . . ." He protested in vain. The doctrine that the end justifies the means has been firmly ascribed to him. Even the Jesuits, who hated him, could not altogether rob him of the discredit of that doctrine; and when John

Donne staged his infernal competition for Satan's favour, he chose as his finalists Ignatius Loyola and Machiavelli.

The controversy continues. Machiavelli's latest editor[3] (himself a Jesuit) almost overheats himself in his eagerness to clear his order of the dreadful imputation. "Let me begin by stating plainly," he writes, "that I reject this doctrine root and branch, and regard it, together with its corollaries, as most pernicious." But why all this moral indignation? Machiavelli's clarity is more instructive than Fr. Walker's heat, and if we examine the question cooly, we soon find the answer. Machiavelli and the Jesuits both in fact taught that the end justifies the means, but their meaning was different. The word "end" is misleading: it can mean "intention" or it can mean "result." Machiavelli's word was *effetto*— "result:" he had no patience with good intentions and expressed his contempt of the Gracchi "whose intention was more creditable than their prudence." A neutral political analyst, observing cause and effect, he only justified one in relation to the other. The doctrine of the Jesuits was different. They were not neutral observers. Indeed, they set themselves up as the official leaders of anti-machiavellianism, and it was against Machiavelli that their prize pupil, Giovanni Botero, advanced his theory that it is not the result but the intention which justifies the means, and thereby launched his new phrase *Ragion di Stato*, Reason of State.

It is interesting to look back at the last four centuries of history and observe the consequences of these two different doctrines that the end justifies the means: the doctrine of Machiavelli and the doctrine of the Jesuits. Machiavelli was a layman, and empirical philosopher who, believing no form of government to be absolute, sought only to recommend, for whatever purpose seemed desirable, the most practical, the most scientific, the least costly means. His great disciple is Bismarck, to whom politics were "the cult of the possible." The Jesuits, having ideals, believed that all means were justified which were intended (even if they failed and whatever the cost) to serve those ideals. From Plato's priest-king to Lenin and Hitler that tradition is clear. On the whole, like Thomas Cromwell, I prefer Machiavelli.

[3] *The Discourses of Machiavelli*, translated and edited by Leslie J. Walker, S. J. (London 1950).

H. R. Trevor-Roper   Born in England in 1914, he is now Regius Professor of Modern History at Oxford. The author of many books and articles, he has consistently been versatile, controversial, and uninhibited.

"Niccolò Machiavelli" (1951) An objective weighing of evidence which leads to a personal and disputable conclusion, this essay is a model of tight organization and of a clear, fast-paced, assertive style.

1. *What arguments and rhetorical devices does the author use to support his preference for Machiavelli? 2. Can you see any flaws in his reasoning? 3. How would Machiavelli feel about the world today?*

GARRETT MATTINGLY

Curtain Raiser

Fotheringhay, February 18, 1587

Mr. Beale had not brought the warrant until Sunday evening but by Wednesday morning, before dawn outlined its high windows, the great hall at Fotheringhay was ready. Though the earl of Shrewsbury had returned only the day before, nobody wanted any more delay. Nobody knew what messenger might be riding on the London road. Nobody knew which of the others might not weaken if they waited another day.

The hall had been cleared of all its ordinary furniture. Halfway along its length a huge fire of logs blazing in the chimney battled against the creeping chill. Towards the upper end of the hall they had set up a small platform, like a miniature stage for traveling actors, jutting twelve feet into the hall, eight or nine feet wide, and less than three feet high. At one side a pair of stairs led up to it, and the fresh wood of the scaffolding had been everywhere decently covered in black velvet. On the platform, in line with the stairs, stood a single high-backed chair, also draped in black, and three or four feet in front of it a black cushion. Next to the cushion and rising above it something like a little low bench showed where the velvet imperfectly concealed an ordinary wooden chopping block. By seven in the morning the stage managers were satisfied, the sheriff's men trying to look soldierly in morion and breastplate and to hold their halberds stiffly had taken their places, and the chosen audience, two hundred or more knights and gentlemen of the neighborhood peremptorily summoned for that early hour, had filed into the lower end of the hall.

The star kept them waiting more than three hours. In the almost thirty years since she had wedded a future king of France in the glittering, devious court beside the Loire she had failed repeatedly to learn some of the more important lessons of politics, but she had learned how to dominate a scene. She entered through a little door at the side, and before they saw her was already in the great hall, walking towards the dais, six of her own people, two by two, behind her, oblivious of the stir and rustle as her audience craned forward, oblivious, apparently, of the officer on whose sleeve her hand rested, walking as quietly, thought one pious soul, as if she were going to her prayers. Only for a moment, as she mounted the steps and before she sank back into the black-draped chair, did she seem to need the supporting arm, and if her hands trembled before she locked them in her lap, no one saw. Then, as if acknowledging the plaudits of a multitude (though the hall was very still), she turned for the first time to face her audience and, some thought, she smiled.

Against the black velvet of the chair and dais her figure, clad in black velvet, was almost lost. The gray winter daylight dulled the gleam of white hands, the glint of yellow gold in her kerchief and of red gold in the piled masses of auburn hair beneath. But the audience could see clearly enough the delicate frill of white lace at her throat and above it, a white, heart-shaped petal against the blackness, the face with its great dark eyes and tiny, wistful mouth. This was she for whom Rizzio had died, and Darnley, the young fool, and Huntly, and Norfolk, and Babington and a thousand nameless men on the moors and gallows of the north. This was she whose legend had hung over England like a sword ever since she had galloped across its borders with her subjects in pursuit. This was the last captive princess of romance, the dowager queen of France, the exiled queen of Scotland, the heir to the English throne and (there must have been some among the silent witnesses who thought so), at this very moment, if she had her rights, England's lawful queen. This was Mary Stuart, Queen of Scots. For a moment she held all their eyes, then she sank back into the darkness of her chair and turned her grave inattention to her judges. She was satisfied that her audience would look at no one else.

The earls of Kent and Shrewsbury who had entered with her, almost unobserved, had seated themselves opposite, and Mr. Beale was standing, clearing his throat and crackling the parchment of the warrant he had to read. He need not have been nervous. One doubts whether anyone was listening. "Stubborn disobedience . . . incitement to insurrection . . . against the life and person of her sacred Majesty . . . high treason . . . death." Nothing in the phrases could have mattered to Mary Stuart or to any person in the hall. Everyone knew that this was not the sentence for a crime. This was another stroke in a political duel which had been going on as long as most of them could remember, which had begun, indeed, before either of the enemy queens was born. Sixty years ago the parties had begun to form, the party of the old religion, the party of the new, and always, by some trick of fate, one party or the other, and usually both, had been rallied and led by a woman. Catherine of Aragon against Anne Boleyn, Mary Tudor against Elizabeth Tudor, Elizabeth Tudor against Mary of Lorraine, and now, for nearly thirty years, Elizabeth Tudor against Mary Stuart, the prisoner on the scaffold. The shrewdest politicians might wonder how for almost two decades England had managed to contain both these predestinate enemies and keep them both alive.

Whatever Elizabeth had done, Mary Stuart had, of course, sought by every means in her power to destroy her cousin and bring her low. In a duel to the death like theirs there were no foul strokes. When the arms of strength had fallen from her hands she had used whatever weapons weakness could grasp: lies, tears, evasions, threats and pleadings, and the hands and lives of whatever men her crowns, her beauty or her faith could win to her cause. They had proved two-edged weapons at last; but if they cut her now, she had dealt wounds with them, and kept her cousin's realm in greater turmoil from her English prison than ever she had been able to do from her Scottish throne. And she meant to strike one blow more. She turned a bored chin on Mr. Beale's concluding phrases.

The dean of Peterborough was even more nervous than Mr. Beale. She let him repeat his stumbling exordium three times before she cut him contemptuously short. "Mr. Dean," she told him, "I shall die as I have lived, in the true and holy Catholic faith. All you can say to me on that score is but vain, and all your prayers, I think, can avail me but little."

This, she was sure, was the one weapon which would not turn in her hand. She had been closely watched at Fotheringhay, but not so closely that she could have no word from the daring, subtle men who slipped in and out of the Channel ports in disguise. The north was Catholic, they said, and the west, and even here in the heretic's own strongholds, even in the midlands, even in London, more and more turned daily to the ancient faith. While the heir to the throne was a Catholic, likely to succeed without a struggle on her heretic cousin's death, those thousands had been quiet, but now, should the heretic slay her orthodox successor, surely they would rise in their wrath to sweep away all this iniquity. And there were Catholic kings beyond the seas who would be more eager to avenge the Queen of Scots dead than ever they had been to keep her alive.

That Mary herself was a devout Catholic is one of the few things about her not open to dispute, but it was not enough for her simply to die in her faith. The duel would go on. All men must know that she had died not only in her faith, but for it. Perhaps she had not always been its steadiest pillar. Perhaps her dubious intrigues had sometimes harmed her cause more than her devotion had helped it. Now the glittering sweep of the axe would cut off forever the burden of old mistakes, silence the whispered slanders, and her blood would cry out for vengeance on her enemies more unmistakably than her living voice could ever have done again. For years she had favored an ambiguous motto, "My end is my beginning." Martyrdom might make good both the promise and the threat. She had only to play this last scene well.

So she held the crucifix high, visible all down the long hall as she flung defiance at her judges, and her voice rose with a kind of triumph above the voice of the dean of Peterborough, always higher and clearer than his rising tones, arching over the vehement English prayers the mysterious, dominating invocations of the ancient faith. The queen's voice held on for a minute after the clergyman had finished. Her words were in English now; she was praying for the people of England and for the soul of her royal cousin Elizabeth; she was forgiving all her enemies. Then for a moment her ladies were busy about her. The black velvet gown fell below her knees revealing underbodice and petticoat of crimson silk and she stepped forward, suddenly, shockingly, in the color of martyrdom, blood red from top to toe against the somber background. Quietly she knelt and bowed herself low over the little chopping block. "In manus tuas, domine . . ." and they heard twice the dull chunk of the axe.

There was one more ceremony to accomplish. The executioner must exhibit the head and speak the customary words. The masked black figure stooped and rose, crying in a loud voice, "Long live the queen!" But all he held in his hand that had belonged to the rival queen of hearts was a kerchief, and pinned to it an elaborate auburn wig. Rolled nearer the edge of the platform, shrunken and withered and gray, with a sparse silver stubble on the small, shiny skull was the head of the martyr. Mary Stuart had always known how to embarrass her enemies.

*

GARRETT MATTINGLY Born in 1900 in Washington, D.C.; died in 1962. A professor of history who specialized in the Renaissance, his three books on that subject are outstanding. The following essay is the prologue to his *The Armada*.

"*Curtain Raiser*" (1959) To get at the essence of a significant moment in history the author employs theatrical devices—an emblematic setting, quick vignettes, the flashback of the movies—as well as narrative and descriptive techniques. Further, in keeping with the pace, condensation, and drama of his account, he is generous in his use of imagery, metaphor, and simile. The result is excitement without cheap sensationalism.

*

1. *What purpose is accomplished by describing this event as if it were a play?* 2. *What might be a modern equivalent to the execution of Mary?* 3. *Discuss the selection and ordering of detail in terms of their dramatic effectiveness.*

C. V. WEDGWOOD

The Last Masque

The dress designed for King Charles I to wear in the masque which concluded the Christmas festivities of the year 1639–40 was of pale blue embroidered with silver thread. Inigo Jones, who had designed the sets for every masque for the last thirty years, had once again revived the fashions of his youth with their tight-fitting doublets and padded breeches. For the sleeves he had adapted one of his favourite flower motifs: calyx-shaped over-sleeves enveloped the King's shoulders and upper arms, like the inverted cups of gigantic bluebells. The doublet, closely moulded to his slight figure, was so thickly stitched over in silver whorls and posies that the blue background hardly showed. His padded breeches were of slashed blue and silver, the blue edged with filigree thread. Long white silk stockings encased his small but well-made legs, exposed up to the thigh. His dancing pumps were all but concealed under huge silver shoe-roses. A quilled ruff of fine muslin framed his face, and his greying hair, carefully curled, was surmounted by a three-cornered hat of cloth of silver above which nodded two tiers of well-matched ostrich plumes.

King Charles was mature for masquerading. He was in his fortieth year and, but for his Master of the Ordnance, Lord Newport, the oldest performer in that year's festivities. Although the King had been rehearsing with his usual assiduity since the previous October, his more serious and distinguished courtiers had

Reprinted from *Truth and Opinion* by C. V. Wedgwood, by permission of Joyce Weiner Associates.

been too deeply engaged in the affairs of the nation to have much time to spare. Apart from the eight lords he had chosen to attend him, the performers were mostly drawn from the pages and musicians, the small fry of Whitehall.

The King's part was suited to his age and dignity. He had only to appear on a throne of honour raised high above the stage and later to partner the Queen in a stately dance. It was the responsibility of Inigo Jones to see that no embarrassing accidents occurred. "The peece of tymber of ye engyne of ye Kings seate to be strongly nayled and fastened" he scribbled on his sketch of the backstage mechanics.

The King's seat on the English throne in January 1640 was less comfortable than the stout wooden contraption designed for him by Inigo Jones. The atmosphere of gaiety which normally surrounded the Christmas celebrations of the Court was notably absent, and although both the King and Queen appeared as enthusiastic about their masque as usual, there was in their conduct a hint of pretence. The iron-handed minister, Wentworth, recently recalled from Ireland and created Earl of Strafford, had been in frequent audience with the King. He was not among the masquers. Both his austere presence and that of the buff-coated officers who now haunted the palace disturbed the jocund mood proper to the season.

The words of the masque had been written by William Davenant, the music composed by the Queen's master musician, Louis Richard, a Frenchman long resident at the English Court. In the opinion of everyone, not least of Inigo Jones himself, words and music were secondary to the scenic inventions for which they provided the vehicle. But a plot and a subject of some kind there had to be. King Charles, therefore, would impersonate the character of Philogenes, the lover of his people, a beneficent ruler conferring the blessings of peace upon a chorus representing the grateful nation. The king rehearsed the part in the intervals of the harassing Council meetings at which he decided to equip an army of thirty thousand foot and three thousand horse to keep his rebellious subjects in order.

The trouble had begun a year before in Scotland, but showed signs of spreading southward. In the previous summer, confronted by a superior force of rebel Scots at Berwick, the King had had to make temporary concessions to the rebels and withdraw without striking a blow. It had been a harsh forewarning of difficulties to come. His English troops, raised with difficulty, had been meagre and mutinous. An odd kind of volunteers, a wit had said, for not a man of them had come willingly. Murmurs against the King's church policy, against prelacy and popery, were growing loud in every English county. On the march north against the Scots, Lord Say and Lord Brook had refused to take the special oath of allegiance tendered by the King to all his followers, promising "most constantly and cheerfully even to the uttermost hazard of life and fortune to assist him against any rebels whatsoever." He had had to place them under arrest: only for a few days, of course, but it had been an unseemly and perplexing incident. When Lord Say was released he went home and took his contingent of troops with him, announcing that they had come solely as his attendants.

Yet with an obscure tenacity the King rejected the evidence of his subjects' discontent. This must be something superficial, temporary. It could not be that he, King Charles, the good, the just, who referred his every action to God and his conscience, should be wantonly defied merely because he wanted to impose a beautiful uniformity of worship throughout his dominions.

After he had made his temporary concessions to the rebel Scots at Berwick, agreeing to suspend his religious reforms in their country for the time being, he had reviewed the army which had marched against him. The troops, in innocent enthusiasm, threw up their blue bonnets and cried "God save King Charles and down with the Bishops." He was not pleased: he would compel them to respect his bishops yet. To the Scots lords who waited on him he had been cold. When they made to kiss his hand, he withheld it and only slightly raised his hat in a general salutation before taking his seat. His puzzled eyes travelled over their faces, seeking the private reasons for their public opposition. To his certain knowledge there were only five or six of them to whom, in his own phrase, "he had not done courtesies." In his opinion past courtesies should have secured present loyalty; he could conceive of none but personal motives for rebellion. That these men should seriously, for reasons of conscience or patriotism, object to the liturgy that he had had specially composed for Scotland was beyond his imagination.

When he left Berwick after the pacification he had learned his lesson after his own fashion. In future, he announced, "I shall not command but where I am sure to be obeyed." He would be patient and wily; opponents could be removed, bribed, persuaded. He would call into being again the old animosity between English and Scots; he would raise a larger army. He would compel obedience. He would do everything except abandon the policy which he knew to be pleasing to God.

As he moved southwards to London the warm reception of his English subjects, profoundly relieved that there was to be no war, applied a deceptive balm to his injured spirit.

> *Others by war their conquests gain,*
> *You, like a God, your ends obtain,*
> *Who, when rude chaos for his help did call,*
> *Spoke but the word and sweetly ordered all . . .*

The Cambridge poet Cowley told him what he wanted to hear. The pacification at Berwick had been of his choosing; he had not been defeated; he, the merciful King, had decided not to fight.

The theme was taken up and elaborated in the masque for which on the afternoon of Tuesday, January 21st, 1640, the whole Court, with a number of ambassadors and distinguished guests, had assembled in the building behind the banqueting house of Whitehall. For the occasion the cares of state had to be excluded, like the bleak January weather, beyond the world of expensive make-believe which was to be conjured up on the stage of the Queen's Dancing Barn. The name had been rudely given to the new building by the Puritans, but in reality it was the King's Dancing Barn, for it had been his idea. Once they had used the banqueting hall itself for masques, but since the painted canvases of Rubens had been hoisted into place on the ceiling, the King feared the damaging effect of candles and torches on their colours. He had given order for the temporary wooden building alongside and it had been constructed to the designs of Inigo Jones, with a permanent stage measuring fifty-two feet in height and forty-two feet from side to side of the proscenium arch. The stage itself was raised from seven to eight feet above the floor of the room, allowing for the construction and working of substantial mechanism underneath.

The seats and boxes in the auditorium were designed to accommodate spectators according to their rank. The central place this afternoon was filled by the royal children and their grandmother. The children, of whom the eldest was not yet ten, were a handsome, high-spirited group, taking strongly after their mother's family—large features, high colouring, bouncing vitality. Their maternal grandmother, Marie de Medici, the only adult royalty among the audience, since the King and Queen had disappeared into their robing-rooms, commanded the scene. She was a substantial woman in her later sixties, her fat-enveloped face eloquent of character rather than intelligence.

After quarrelling for the last time with her son, the King of France, she had thrown herself embarrassingly on the hospitality of her daughter, the Queen of England. In the delicate state of English public opinion the presence of the extravagant Italian visitor with a large train of priests and servants, made an unfortunate impression. Her manner of living at St. James's Palace, which her son-in-law had assigned to her, emphasized inopportunely his Queen's foreign and Roman Catholic connections.

The masque had been devised with the Queen's mother and the royal children in mind. In deference to Marie de Medici's ignorance of English there was little speaking, and the usual interludes of spoken comedy had been replaced by a series of farcical dances. For the delight of the children the scene changes were to be many and all the incidents short.

While the usual preliminary hitches occurred and were dealt with behind the scenes, the audience had plenty to occupy it in deciphering the meaning of the allegorical figures and symbols painted on the cornice, the proscenium arch and the drop-curtain which concealed the stage. In the centre of this curtain appeared the classical name of the performance they were about to see— *Salmacida Spolia*—and those who understood the allusion could explain to those who did not how certain savage tribes had been subdued by the Greeks of Halicarnassus, not by force of arms, but by visiting the fountain of Salmacis, where they saw and learnt to appreciate the superior civilization of the Greeks. So, it was to be understood, the rebellious Scots would learn to appreciate the superior qualities of episcopal government. On one side of the stage two female figures, representing Reason and Intellectual Appetite, were clasping hands. Opposite them "a grave old man representing Counsel" kept company with an armed woman for Resolution. On the deep cornice which surmounted the stage, figures of women and children with symbolic attributes jostled one another. Here were Fame and Safety, Riches, Forgetfulness of Injuries, Commerce, Felicity, "Affection to the country, holding a grasshopper," Prosperity and Innocence.

Presently an anticipatory hush foretold the rising of the curtain. Fans of matched and curled ostrich feathers ceased their movement and lay still in velvet laps; white explanatory hands dropped into repose; all faces turned the same way and, rustling over its roller at tremendous speed, up went the curtain.

Before them, in the cavern of the stage, was a scene of gloom and tempest. Trees with tormented branches bowed before the gale. In the distance angry waves broke over a rock and a storm-driven ship shuddered under a lightning-riven sky. The rattling of metal sheets in the wings added to the awful effect. In the middle of the stage stood a huge round object, recognizable from the outlines painted upon it as the great globe itself.

The audience had possessed themselves of the horror of the scene when with a clap of thunder the globe split in half and a hideous Fury "looking askance with hollow envious eyes" came snarling to the front of the stage, torch in hand. In a harsh male voice, belying her female draperies, the creature began to speak:

> How am I grieved the world should everywhere
> Be vexed into a storm, save only here?
> Thou over happy, too much lucky isle . . .

In rhymed couplets the monster declared her intention of destroying the peace of England. Lest the meaning should be still in doubt, the speaking Fury was joined by three others who emphasized the point in a menacing dance.

This was the opening anti-masque. The first of the scene-changes followed. The shutters forming the wings slid back along grooves out of sight, revealing another series of shutters behind them. The dark clouds which hung down from the top of the scene were wound up creakingly while others of a different hue began to appear. The stormy sea at the back of the stage divided down the middle and slid apart to reveal another painted scene. Since it was not the fashion for the curtain to drop during these operations, there had long been arguments among the producers of masques as to the best way of diverting the attention of spectators. An Italian producer—and the Italians were the acknowledged masters of the masque—advised the placing of stooges far back among the audience to cause a disturbance at the critical moment. The simulated cracking of wood as though a tier of the gallery were collapsing, or a cry of "Fire! Murder! Help!" could be guaranteed to draw all attention away from the stage. But the stooges sometimes acted too well; there had been panics and whole theatres had been emptied in a stampede for safety. Inigo Jones preferred his own invention—a gyrating coronal of three concentric circles of candles set off by reflectors which, being set in motion when a scene change was to take place, delighted and dazzled the audience so that they had eyes for nothing else.

But there is no sign of the use of this invention, or of anything else, among the numerous sketches which were made for the masque of 1640. The scene-changes in this, the most mechanically ambitious of all his masques, were apparently effected with so much rapidity that they needed no concealment. The scenery was wound off at each side and up and down from below and above. Behind the numerous canvas clouds which were suspended from braces in the roof and lowered or raised at will, all manner of rapid modifications could be made in the scenery and furnishings of the top part of the stage. They were wonderful clouds, carefully painted and cut after the numerous loving and lyrical sketches which have survived in his papers, small and large, round and elongated, billowing cumulus clouds carefully copied from nature to serve the higher ingenuities of his art.

Before the eyes of the spectators, therefore, the stormy sea and lowering sky gave place to a landscape of smiling summer. Across the painted sky jerked a painted Zephyr on a cloud breathing a flowery breeze from his fat cheeks. Below stretched a saffron-yellow cornfield, improbably framed in arching elm trees round whose knotted trunks grape-bearing vines were garlanded.

Meanwhile, below the stage strong hands turned the windlass which governed the silver chariot now slowly descending from the clouds. Two persons were unsteadily seated within it—a woman in blue ornamented with bulrushes, and a young man "in a carnation garment embroidered all with flowers." In mid-air the two broke into a duet. The lady, who represented Concord, expressed her reluctance to remain longer among the ungrateful people of Great Britain. Her companion, who was the Good Genius of Great Britain, remonstrated with her. The people might be unappreciative, he admitted, but they had a King whom she must surely find it a pleasure to serve:

> Yet stay, oh stay, if but to please
> The great and wise Philogenes.

It was true, the couple pursued their argument, that the people were sullen and ungrateful and would not accept their monarch's benevolent control; but to reward so good a King, Concord might yet give his people another chance. The harmonious lecture on politics at an end, the chariot reached stage-level and the two heavenly beings climbed out of it and departed in different directions to see whether their persuasions would soften the hearts of the ungrateful subjects of Philogenes.

Their endeavours would take time, as some of the better-informed members of the audience may well, a little grimly, have been thinking. The passage of time had, however, been allowed for by Davenant in composing his libretto: after their departure the remaining anti-masques, a series of twenty separate comic dances, were to be presented, mostly by the young members of the Court, pages and young gentlemen, with their fortunes to make, who had grasped the opportunity of displaying their amiable talents before the great. Of this half-hour's frolic nothing has remained but Davenant's brief descriptive note on each entry and a few unidentifiable sketches of grotesques by Inigo Jones. Most of the dances were funny and most of the jokes were topical: ballets about doctors and prescriptions, about Rosicrucians and Roaring Boys, Jealous Dutchmen and Mad Lovers. Occasionally the mind's eye can supply a guess from the stage direction: "Four Grotesques or drollities in the most fantastical shapes imaginable"; or, the sentimental interlude, a shepherd dancing a pastoral *pas seul;* or pure farce, "a nurse and three children in long coats, with bibs, biggins, and muckenders." Then there was the dance specially put in for the Queen's dwarf, Jeffrey Hudson; "three Swiss, one a little Swiss, who played the wag with them as they slept." Three feet high and twenty-one years old, Jeffrey Hudson concealed an alert intelligence in his mouse-coloured head and a valiant spirit in his breast. His portraits reveal the full-size personality in the midget figure. A year or two later he would be a captain of horse and would be knighted, not undeservedly, for courage in the field.

When he had first been brought to the King, Charles had already been in possession of two other notable curiosities—his giant porter, and "Old Parr," the English Methuselah, said to be a hundred and fifty years of age, and brought to Court by the Earl of Arundel. "You have lived much longer than other men," said the King, when the venerable father was presented to him; "what have you done that was more remarkable?" The rustic replied with what had long been his best crack: "Please your Majesty, I did penance for a bastard when I was above a hundred years old." King Charles uttered a freezing reproof; but if he regretted old Parr's morals he valued his years and used to boast that his kingdom contained the tallest man, the smallest man, and the oldest man in the world.

But Old Parr's vitality had not survived the pace of life at Court; both he and the giant porter were long since dead, and Jeffrey Hudson, capering waggishly upon the prostrate bodies of his fellow-dancers, was now the sole survivor of the astounding trio.

The interludes had now lasted for long enough. Concord and the Genius of Great Britain had assembled the full chorus of the "Beloved People" of England in the wings. The last ballet, a rollicking affair of a Spanish riding-master and his pupils, galloped off the stage. The side shutters rattled once more along their grooves, the clouds were lowered and raised, and the cornfields at the back changed to a mountain landscape, in the midst of which, on a high, hollow mountain, above defiles of rock and pine, the clouds hung mysteriously low. While the scene was changing the chorus had crowded on to the stage and facing the very centre of the audience began to sing a compliment to the

Queen Mother. There she sat, the stupid, stout, unloved widow of Henry of Navarre. "Your beauty kept his valour's flame alive," they shamelessly chanted, "Your Tuscan wisdom taught him how to thrive."

Now, at last, the great moment had come. The chorus of the Beloved People ranged themselves politely on each side of the stage so as not to impede the view. The low clouds above the mountain rose, the last of the obstructing shutters slid out of the way, "and the King's Majesty and the rest of the masquers were discovered sitting in the throne of Honour, his Majesty highest in a seat of gold, and the rest of the Lords about him."

There they stood, in their bluebell doublets, like the King's, their white stockings, their silver hats and ostrich feathers: in the midst Charles himself, looking for once a great deal larger than life, for the sharply narrowing perspective of Inigo Jones's sets made no allowance for the actual size of the performers who were to appear backstage. Larger than life, therefore, and very regal, he sat, with his cousin Lennox on his right, and the Earl of Carlisle on the left, tall young men with fair, horsy, well-bred faces; six other lords were ranged at suitable distances round about. Instantly the Beloved People broke into laudatory song.

> *Since strength of virtues gained you Honour's throne*
> *Accept our wonder and enjoy our praise!*
> *He's fit to govern there, and rule alone,*
> *Whom inward helps, not outward force, doth raise.*

Certainly King Charles's throne rested on no effective outward force in spite of his present efforts to remedy the deficiency. But at the moment the spectators were not paying much attention to the words even if they could distinguish them. The King's throne, lords and all, had been slowly lowered to ground-level; he rose and at the same time there appeared, high up under the cornice, the largest and most solid of the many clouds which had yet descended from the pulleys in the heavens. "A huge cloud of various colours," Inigo Jones described it. It was indeed vast, since it concealed—or, to maintain the illusion, it carried—no less than eleven people. As it reached mid-air and mid-stage, it was seen slowly to open, revealing "a transparent brightness of thin exhalations." "Tinsel" is the word scribbled on Inigo Jones's sketch, but it is possible that the rays which broke from the cloud were not all tinsel. There may have been light effects managed by reflectors, for Inigo Jones fancied himself at tricks of the kind. Whatever the nature of the "transparent brightness," in the heart of it among her "martial ladies" sat the Queen herself.

When the ladies were rehearsing for the masque, the Earl of Northumberland wrote to his sister that they were the worst set of faces he had ever seen on such an occasion. But he was prejudiced; neither of his own sisters—one the celebrated beauty Lady Carlisle—had been chosen. If their portraits are to be trusted against his word, they were a pretty enough collection. There was the sweet-faced Duchess of Lennox, exchanging eye-signals with her husband on the King's right: they were deeply in love. There was the lymphatic blonde, Lady Carnarvon, a convinced Puritan who had stipulated that she would only appear in the Queen's masque if it was not performed on a Sunday. There was the handsome, headstrong Lady Newport, carrying her sorrows with a high head; no eye-signals here although Lord Newport stood opposite her close by the King. He was the Puritan of this marriage and her adoption of the Roman Catholic religion a year or two back had done more than the bearing of three imbecile children to alienate him from her for ever. There was the glowing bride, Lady Kinalmeaky, whom the King himself had given away three weeks before.

But the Queen herself drew all eyes. In looks she hardly competed with the younger women who surrounded her. She was thirty years old and pregnant for the ninth time. She had lost her looks in her first childbed and was in the habit of saying—judging all other cases from her own—that no woman was beautiful after eighteen. She was a scrawny little woman with an ivory skin, a figure slightly twisted, features too large for the meagre face, and teeth which, as a niece once unkindly said, protruded from her mouth like guns from a fortress. But the King worshipped her and he was not the only one. Plain, old before her time, in wretched health, she dominated her younger and handsomer ladies by the electric animation of her personality. Her prominent eyes sparkled; when her thin, long mouth parted into a smile it was a chord of music. So she sat, mistress of stage and Court, from her throne in the multi-coloured cloud, a diminutive figure in carnation silk with plumed helmet and scarlet baldric and an antique sword at her side, the undoubted Queen of the Amazons.

As her cloudy car touched the ground the King advanced, took her by the hand and led her in procession from the stage to the place where her mother sat among the audience. The lords and ladies sought their wives or the partners allotted to them and followed in stately dance.

The King and Queen were now seated in the midst of the Court, but it remained for the Beloved People to sing a final salutation. For the last time all the handles were being turned off-stage; for the last time the clouds laboured up and down. For the last time the pictured cloths opened to reveal the last back-drop. It was the noblest and most elaborate of all Inigo Jones's effects and his sketch-books show that he had drawn it time and time again before he was satisfied. The scene was one of "magnificent buildings composed of several pieces of architecture. In the farthest part was a bridge over a river, where many people, coaches, horses and such like were seen to pass to and fro: beyond this, on the shore were buildings in perspective, which shooting far from the eye showed as suburbs of a great city." The whole represented, by implication, the King's extensive building programme in London to which Inigo Jones himself had so largely contributed. He did not, of course, go so far as to include drawings of the Piazza at Covent Garden or the new west front of St. Paul's Cathedral—the bridge was frankly modelled on a recent new bridge in Rome—but only the slowest courtier could fail to take his meaning. Here, almost as large as life, was the final representation of the blessings which King Philogenes had poured upon his Beloved, and strangely ungrateful, People.

For the moment the menacing discontent of England and Scotland, the cabals and intrigues of the King's enemies, the rude things that his people wrote on walls and sometimes even in pamphlets, were forgotten. On the final chords of Louis Richard's long-lost music three more cloudy chariots jerked across the sky above the city and opened to reveal all the musicians playing on their instruments to present the music of the spheres. Last of all, in the centre of the stage "the heavens opened full of deities which celestial prospect, with the Chorus below, filled the whole scene with apparitions and harmony." In the general exclamation of the audience, the merry accompaniment of the fiddlers, the creaking of the mechanism, Davenant's words may not have been altogether distinguishable. The Beloved People vociferously saluted the wisdom of their reigning King.

> *All that are harsh, all that are rude,*
> *Are by your harmony subdued,*
> *Yet so into obedience wrought*
> *As if not forced to it, but taught.*
> *Live still, the pleasure of our sight*
> *Both our example and delight . . .*

Inigo Jones was delighted with his effects. By his own account they were "generally approved of, especially by all strangers that were present, to be the noblest and the most ingenious that hath been done here in that kind." The one other opinion that has come down to us is markedly different. Young Robert Read, nephew of one of His Majesty's principal Secretaries of State, wrote some days later to his cousin Tom Windebanke in Ireland. "The mask was performed last Tuesday night, myself being so wise as not to see it. They say it was very good, but I believe the disorder was never so great at any."

There was room for disorder among all those pulleys and cog-wheels, those ascending and descending chariots and clouds, those quadruple scene changes. Which windlass jammed while the stage-hands strained at the handle, what backdrop stuck as it went up, leaving the scene half-cornfield and half-stormy sea? Did the Beloved People like sheep go astray all over the stage? For a moment the imagination pictures the frantic, furtive signals, the forgotten cue whispered in agitation, the audience sometimes restive, sometimes laughing, and the vacant eyes of Marie de Medici, vaguely aware of compliment, but blind to meaning.

The allegory of tempest giving place to joyous calm, of Philogenes bestowing peace on his applauding people, was de-fiantly inept. Among the eight blue-and-silver lords about the King there were three at least who vehemently opposed his policy in public, and among the rest not one who did not conceal a dark anxiety under the radiant *mine de circonstance* demanded by the part. Young Lennox, who nine years later was to offer vainly to die in his master's place, knew well and feared the temper of his countrymen in the north. The bewildered Earl of Lanark, a lip-biting, over-burdened, conscientious young man, had in the last few days been presented with the impossible appointment of Secretary of State for rebellious Scotland. Among the English lords there were Russell and Fielding who were well aware from their Puritan kinsmen and friends that the King's reputation in England had never stood so low—an indignant city, a restive gentry, a depressed and uneasy people. The accidental disorders on the stage added their unintentional, tacit note of satire to the last masque ever to be danced by King Charles.

The last chorus ended, the clustered wax candles were lighted in all the sconces, the musicians from their cloudy gallery began to play again, the masquers mingled with the audience and the King and Queen danced among their courtiers. The rhythmic patter and swish of the dancing feet, the hum of voices, the susurration of silks, filled for the last time the Queen's great Dancing Barn.

Beyond the precincts of Whitehall, skewering rashers of bacon from the glowing coals of their winter fires, or warming knotted hands at the blaze of wood and the glow of turf, the people of England in town and country talked of their own affairs, made love or made baskets, darned the day's tears in worn clothes, smoked a pipe of tobacco or took a pot of ale after the day's work, before huddling by families on to their flock mattresses to sleep. A few were talking politics, more than a few were praying. The revolving world carried the island and all on it through the darkness to the late winter dawn and brought nearer by one day that January morning nine years in the future, when King Charles, haggard and dignified, would enact outside Whitehall the last scene in the story of Philogenes.

ˆ

C. V. WEDGWOOD Born in England in 1910, Miss Wedgwood is a historian but not attached to any university. She has written many books on European history, especially on seventeenth-century England, and she is noted for her depth of scholarship and brilliance of style.

"The Last Masque" (1950) This essay offers excellent possibilities for analyses of tone, the subtle use of persona, and the maintenance of an objective historical perspective. The style is rich, rapid, colorful, and the irony of the event is given full play. By skillfully piling up details and by abundant metaphors, similes, and allusions the author recreates a sense of splendor and of impending disaster.

ˆ

1. *What is the function of the concluding paragraph?* 2. *Are there any details in this essay that you would omit? that you would add?* 3. *What would be a modern parallel to Charles's last masque?*

ERIK H. ERIKSON

The First Psychoanalyst

*The 100th birthday of Sigmund Freud presented an
occasion to introduce a new generation of German
students to an event in the history of European
thought which had been all but obliterated by National Socialist teaching: the discovery of psychoanalysis. The following address was delivered at a
ceremony held jointly by the universities of Frankfurt
and Heidelberg, at the University of Frankfurt, on
May 6, 1956.*

I

It is a solemn and yet always a deeply incongruous occasion when
we select an anniversary to honor a man who in lonely years
struggled through a unique experience and won a new kind of
knowledge for mankind. To some of us, the field created by
Sigmund Freud has become an absorbing profession, to some an
inescapable intellectual challenge, to all the promise (or threat)
of an altered image of man. But any sense of proprietary pride in
the man to be honored this year should be sobered by the thought
that we have no right to assume that we would have met his
challenge with more courage than his contemporaries did in the
days when his insights were new. It seems fitting to use his cen-
tenary to review some of the dimensions of lonely discovery.

Reprinted from *Insight and Responsibility* by Erik H. Erikson, by permission of W. W. Norton & Company, Inc. Copyright © 1964 by Erik H.
Erikson.

50

It is not easy (unless it be all too easy) for a "Freudian" to speak of the man who *was* Freud, of a man who grew to be a myth before our eyes. I knew Freud when he was very old, and I was young. Employed as a tutor in a family friendly to him I had the opportunity of seeing him on quiet occasions, with children and with dogs, and at outings in the mountains. I do not know whether I would have noticed Freud in a crowd. His notable features were not spectacular: the finely domed forehead, the dark, unfathomable eyes, and certain small indomitable gestures—they all had become part of that inner containment which crowns the old age of good fighters.

I was an artist then, which can be a European euphemism for a young man with some talent, but nowhere to go. What probably impressed me most was the fact that this doctor of the mind, this expert of warped biography, had surrounded himself in his study with a small host of little statues: those distilled variations of the human form which were created by the anonymous artists of the archaic Mediterranean. Certainly, of Freud's field, of conflict and complaint and confession, there was no trace in their art. This respect for form, so surprising in a man who had unearthed mankind's daimonic inner world, was also obvious in his love for proud dogs and for gaily bright children. I vaguely felt that I had met a man of rare dimensions, rare contradictions.

When I became a psychoanalyst myself, this same old man— now remote from the scene of training and gathering—became for me what he is for the world: the writer of superb prose, the author of what seems like more than one lifetime's collected works: a master, so varied in his grandiose one-sidedness that the student can manage to understand only one period of his work at a time. Strangely enough, we students knew little of his beginnings, nothing of that mysterious self-analysis which he alluded to in his writings. We knew people whom Freud had introduced into psychoanalysis, but psychoanalysis itself had, to all appearances, sprung from his head like Athena from the head of Zeus.

The early Freud became better known to us only a very few years ago, through the accidental discovery of intimate letters written before the turn of the century. They permitted us to envisage Freud the beginner, the first, and for a decade, the only, psychoanalyst. To pay homage to him means, in the passage of time, to acknowledge a lasting bond and yet also to take leave of what is now history.

II

For orientation and comparison, let us consider the circumstances of another discovery of the nineteenth century, the discovery of a man who was also lonely and calumniated, and who was also eventually recognized as a changer of man's image: Charles Darwin. Darwin came upon his evolutionary laboratory, the Galapagos Islands, on a voyage which was not part of an intended professional design. In fact, he had failed in medicine, not for lack of talent, it would seem, but partially because of an intellectual selectivity which forbade him to learn passively—a self-protective selectivity of the kind for which old Bernard Shaw, in retrospect, patted himself on the back when he said, "My memory rejects and selects; and its selections are not academic. . . . I congratulate myself on this."

Once embarked on the *Beagle*, however, and on his way to his "laboratory," Darwin showed that dogged, that prejudiced persistence which is one condition for an original mind's becoming a creative one. He now fully developed his superior gift, namely, "noticing things which easily escape attention, and observing them carefully." His physical stamina was inexhaustible. His mind proved ready for the laboratory and the laboratory seemed to have waited for him. He could fully employ sweeping configurations of thought which had ripened in him: cutting across existing classifications which assumed a parallel, linear origin of all species from a common pool of creation, he saw everywhere transitions, transmutations, variations, signs of a dynamic struggle for adaptation. The law of natural selection began to "haunt him." And he perceived that man must come under the same law: "I see no possible means of drawing the line and saying, here you must stop."

Darwin, at the age of twenty-seven, went home with his facts and theory, and traveled no more. He gave the scientific world a few papers primarily on geological subjects; then he withdrew to the country, to work for twenty years on the *Origin of Species:* he *made* it a long and lonely discovery. He now became physically incapacitated by insomnia, nausea, and chills. His doctor-father could not diagnose his disease, but declared his son too delicate for a career out in the world. The son became a life-long invalid. If his hypersensitivity was a sign of hereditary degeneracy, as some doctors believe, then there never was a degenerate guided more wisely in the utilization of his degeneracy by an inner genius of economy. For, "I could . . . collect facts bearing on the origin of species . . . when I could do nothing else from illness." Not that Darwin did not realize what this restriction of his life-space did to him: when, at the end, even Shakespeare seemed so "intolerably dull" as to nauseate him, he deplored the "curious and lamentable loss of the higher aesthetic tastes" and spoke of an "enfeeblement of the emotional part of our nature."

I do not wish to speculate here on the dynamics of a psycho-neurosis in a man like Darwin. But I do know that a peculiar malaise can befall those who have seen too much, who, in as-certaining new facts in a spirit seemingly as innocent as that of a child building with blocks, begin to perceive the place of these facts in the moral climate of their day. "We physicists have known sin," Oppenheimer has said; but it does not take the use of scientific data for mankind's material destruction to make a scientist feel or behave as if he had sinned. It is enough to have persisted, with the naïveté of genius, in the dissolution of one of the prejudices on which the security and the familiarity of the contemporary image of man is built. But a creative man has no choice. He may come across his supreme task almost accidentally. But once the issue is joined, his task proves to be at the same time intimately related to his most personal conflicts, to his superior selective perception, and to the stubbornness of his one-way will: he must court sickness, failure, or insanity, in order to test the alternative whether the established world will crush him, or whether he will disestablish a sector of this world's outworn fundaments and make place for a new one.

Darwin only dealt with man's biological origins. His achieve-ment, and his "sin," was a theory that made man part of evolved nature. In comparing Darwin's approach to nature with his approach to man, a recent biographer remarks half-jokingly, "In any case, no man afflicted with a weak stomach and insomnia has any business investigating his own kind."

As we now turn to Freud, the psychological explorer, I hope to make the reader wonder whether anybody *but* one at least temporarily afflicted with psychosomatic symptoms, one temporarily sick of his own kind, could or would investigate his own species—provided that he had the inclination, the courage, and the mental means of facing his own neurosis with creative persistence. A man, I will submit, could begin to study man's inner world only by appointing his own neurosis that angel with whom he must wrestle and whom he must not let go until his blessing, too, has been given.

III

What was Freud's Galapagos, what species fluttered what kinds of wings before his searching eyes? As has often been pointed out derisively, his creative laboratory was the neurologist's office, the dominant species hysterical ladies—"Fräulein Anna O.," "Frau Emmy v. N.," "Katarina" (not a Fräulein, because she was a peasant).

Freud was thirty when, in 1886, he became the private doctor of such patients. He had not expected to be a practitioner; he had, in fact, received his medical degree belatedly. His mind, too, had been "selective." At the age of seventeen he had chosen medicine, in preference to law and politics, when he heard Goethe's "Ode to Nature": the unveiling of nature's mysteries, not the healing of the sick, provided the first self-image of a doctor. Then came *his* professional moratorium. As in an ascetic reaction to romantic indulgence he committed himself to the physiological laboratory and to the monastic service of physicalistic physiology. What geology was to Darwin, physiology was to Freud: a schooling in method. The ideology of the physicalistic physiologic method of the time was formulated in an oath by two of its outstanding teachers, DuBois Reymond and Brücke: "to put in power this truth: No other forces than the common physical chemical ones are active within the organism. . . . One has either to find the specific way or form of their action by means of the physical mathematical method, or to assume new forces equal in dignity to the chemical physical forces inherent in matter."[1] *New forces equal in dignity*—we shall return to this phrase.

[1] Ernest Jones, *The Life and Work of Sigmund Freud*, New York: Basic Books, 1953.

When Freud exchanged the academic monastery for the medical parsonage, he had fully developed a style of work which would have sufficed for an impressively productive lifetime. He had published many papers on physiological and neurological subjects, and had two major works in preparation. Thus, when he became a practicing neurologist, he left a future behind him. But he had married the girl who had waited for him, and he wanted a family, in fact, a large one; he had earned the right to have confidence in himself.

Yet, a future anticipated in a man's configurations of thought means more than time not yet spent. To give up the laboratory meant to relinquish a work-discipline and a work-ideology to which Freud had been deeply committed. The work of a specialist catering to the epidemiological market was lacking in what Freud nostalgically called an inner tyrant, i.e., a great principle. Luckily, he had met an older practitioner, Dr. Joseph Breuer, who had shown him that there was a laboratory hidden in the very practice of neurology.

Freud's new laboratory, then, were patients, mostly women, who brought him symptoms which only an overly-serious and searching observer could accept as constituting a field activated by dignified forces. These ladies suffered from neuralgic pains and anesthesias, from partial paralyses and contractions, from tics and convulsions, from nausea and finickiness, from the inability to see and from visual hallucinations, from the inability to remember and from painful floods of memory. Popular opinion judged the ladies to be spoiled, just putting on airs—"attention-getting" some of us would call it today. The dominant neuropathology of the day, however, assumed some of their disturbances to be a consequence of hereditary degenerative processes in the brain. Freud, too, had learned to treat these patients like partially decerebrated bundles, or like children without a will: he had learned to apply massage and electricity to the affected body part and to dominate the patient's will by hypnosis and suggestion. He might, for example, order the hypnotized patient to laugh out loud when encountering in the future a certain thought or a person or place, the sight of which had previously caused a fit or a paralysis. The awakened patient did laugh out loud, but more often than not, she would become afflicted again, and in connection with something else.

But Freud, like Darwin, could not believe in linear descent—in this instance, of isolated symptoms from defects of the brain. In an array of symptoms he, too, looked for a common principle, a struggle for equilibrium, a clash of forces. And he was convinced that challenging phenomena must have a hidden history. As Freud listened to his hypnotized patients, he realized that they were urgently, desperately offering him series of memories which, seemingly fragmentary, were like variations in search of a theme— a theme which was often found in a historical model event.

Here no detail could be too trivial for investigation. A patient suffers from a persistent illusion of smelling burned pancakes. All right, the smell of burned pancakes shall be the subject of exhaustive analysis. As this smell is traced to a certain scene and the scene vividly remembered, the sensation disappears, to be replaced by the smell of cigars. The smell of cigars is traced to other scenes, in which a man in an authoritative position was present, and in which disturbing subjects had been mentioned in a connection which demanded that the patient control her feelings.

It fits our image of those Victorian days—a time when children in all, and women in most circumstances were to be seen but not heard—that the majority of symptoms would prove to lead back to events when violently aroused affects (love, sex, rage, fear) had come into conflict with narrow standards of propriety and breeding. The symptoms, then, were delayed involuntary communications: using the whole body as spokesman, they were saying what common language permits common people to say directly: "He makes me sick," "She pierced me with her eyes," "I could not swallow that insult," or, as the song has it, "I'm gonna wash that man right out of my hair." Freud the neurologist now became "haunted" by the basic conviction that any neurotic symptom, traced along a path of associated experiences (not of neurological pathways), would lead to the revival in memory of earlier and earlier conflicts, and in doing so would yield a complete history of its origin.

As Freud proceeded with his reconstruction of the pasts of his patients, a dangerous insight dawned on him; such conflicts as his patients revealed were, in principle, shared by all men. It would be hard, indeed, "to draw the line and say here you must stop." He became aware of the fact that man, in principle, does not remember or understand much of what is most significant in his childhood, and more, that he does not want to. Here, a mysterious *individual prehistory* seemed to loom up, as important for psychology as Darwin's biological prehistory was for biology.

But Darwin had at his disposal the whole tradition of an ancient science. For Freud's psychologic findings, there were, at first, only physiologic methods, his own speculations, and the sayings of writers and philosophers, who, in their way, it seemed, had known it all. Yet, it appears to be part of a creative man's beginnings that he may change his field and yet maintain the manner of work which became part of his first identity as a worker. Freud had investigated the nature of brain lesions by slicing the brains of young animals and foeti. He now investigated memories as representative cross sections of a patient's emotional condition. In successive memories, he traced trends which led, like pathways, to the traumatic past; there experiences of a disruptive nature loomed like lesions interfering with growth. Thus, the search for traumatic events in the individual's forgotten prehistory, his early childhood, replaced the search for lesions in early development.

Psychology, of course, is the preferred field for a transfer of configurations of thought from other fields. The nature of things, or better, man's logical approach to things, is such that analogies —up to a point—reveal true correspondences. But the history of psychology also reveals how consistently neglectful and belated man is in applying to his own nature methods of observation which he has tried out on the rest of nature. That man, the observer, is in some essential way set off from the observed world, is clear. But this difference calls for a constant redefinition in the light of new modes of thought. Only thus can man keep wisely different rather than vainly so. Before Copernicus, vanity as well as knowledge insisted that the earth must be in the exact nodal center of God's universe. Well, we know now where we are. Before Darwin, man could claim a different origin from the rest of the animal world with whom he shares a slim margin of the earth's crust and atmosphere. Before Freud, man (that is, man of the male sex and of the better classes) was convinced that he was fully conscious of all there was to him, and sure of his divine values. Childhood was a mere training ground, in charge of that intermediary race, women.

In such a world female hysteria was implicitly acknowledged by men and men doctors as a symptom of the natural inferiority, the easy degeneracy, of women. When Freud presented to the Vienna Medical Society a case of *male* hysteria, the reaction of his colleagues convinced him that years of isolation lay ahead of him. He accepted it then and there: he never visited that society again. Yet, their reaction proved to be only one small aspect of a memorable crisis in which a new science was almost stillborn, by no means only because of professional isolation, but also because of disturbances in the instrument of observation, the observer's mind. Freud's early writings and letters permit us to see a three-fold crisis: a crisis in therapeutic technique; a crisis in the conceptualization of clinical experience; and a personal crisis. I shall try to indicate in what way all three crises were, in essence, one, and that they were the necessary dimensions of discovery in psychology.

IV

First, then, Freud's change in technique. The textbooks describe it as the replacement of the cathartic and the suggestive methods by the psychoanalytic one. In Freud's *Studies in Hysteria*,[2] however, a pervasive change in the doctor-patient relationship is clearly traced. Freud judged some of his patients to be outstanding in character and talents, rather than degenerate. He began to let himself be led by the sequence and the nature of their communications. With amused surprise he would admit that a hypnotized patient, in suggesting to him that he should stop interrupting her with his authoritative suggestions, had a point. She fortified her point by unearthing memories which he would not have suspected. He realized that in hypnosis the patients had at their disposal a depth of understanding and a freedom of affect which they did not marshal in normal life. This he had not imposed by suggestion: it was their judgment and their affect, and if they had it in hypnosis, it was part of them. Perhaps, if he treated them like whole people, they would learn to realize the

[2] Sigmund Freud, "Fragment of an Analysis of a Case of Hysteria" [1905], *Standard Edition*, 7:3–122, London: Hogarth Press, 1953.

wholeness which was theirs. He now offered them a conscious and direct partnership: he made the patient's healthy, if submerged, part his partner in understanding the unhealthy part. Thus was established one basic principle of psychoanalysis, namely, that *one can study the human mind only by engaging the fully motivated partnership of the observed individual, and by entering into a sincere contract with him.*

But a contract has two partners, at least. The changed image of the patient changed the self-image of the doctor. He realized that habit and convention had made him and his fellow physicians indulge in an autocratic pattern, with not much more circumspection or justification than the very paternal authorities who he now felt had made the patients sick in the first place. He began to divine the second principle of psychoanalysis, namely, that *you will not see in another what you have not learned to recognize in yourself.* The mental healer must divide himself as well as the patient into an observer and an observed.

The intellectual task faced here, namely psychoanalytic insight and communication, was a massive one. Today, it is difficult to appreciate the psychosocial task involved. Freud had to relinquish a most important ingredient of the doctor role of the times: the all-knowing father role, which was safely anchored in the whole contemporary cult of the paternal male as the master of every human endeavor except the nursery and the kitchen. This should not be misunderstood: Freud did not, overnight, become a different man. Indeed, there are many who will see nothing in the nature of renunciation of paternalism in him. But we are not speaking here of opinions and roles in the modern sense, of personalities subject to change like the body styles of automobiles which retain little logical relation to the inner motor of the thing, nor to the laws of the road. True roles are a matter of a certain ideologic-esthetic unity, not of opinions and appearances. True change is a matter of worthwhile conflict, for it leads through the painful consciousness of one's position to a new conscience in that position. As Justice Holmes once said, the first step toward a truer faith is the recognition that *I*, at any rate, am *not* God. Furthermore, roles anchored in work-techniques are prepared in the intricacies of a man's life history. Whoever has suffered under and identified with a stern father must become a stern father

himself, or else find an entirely different quality of moral strength,
an equal measure of strength. Young Martin Luther's religious
crisis is a transcendent example of the heights and the depths of
this problem.

Freud, as we have seen, had sought a new inner tyrant in a
work-ideology shared with esteemed minds. He had relinquished
it. Now, he discarded the practicing neurologist's prevailing role
of dominance and of license. This, then, is the first aspect of
Freud's crisis: he had to create a new therapeutic role for which
there was no ideological niche in the tradition of his profession.
He had to create it—or fail.

v

The second problem which isolated Freud in those years was
the course taken by his search for the "energy of equal dignity"
which might be the quantity and the power in mental life; for
the mental mechanisms which normally maintain such power in a
state of constancy; and for those inner conditions which unleash
its destructiveness. The power, as we saw, was first perceived as
"affect," the disturbance in the machine, as a "damming up." A
long treatise recently found with some of Freud's letters reveals
the whole extent of Freud's conflict between the creative urge to
say in psychological terms what only literature had known before
him, and on the other hand, his desperate obedience to physiology. The treatise is called "A Psychology for Neurologists."[3] It
was written in 1895, sent to his friend Fliess, and forgotten.
Freud introduces it thus: "The intention of this project is to
furnish us with a psychology which shall be a natural science:
its aim, that is, is to represent psychical processes as quantitatively
determined states of specifiable material particles and so to make
them plain and void of contradictions." Freud proceeds to develop
a model for the organization of these "particles," a sensitive
machine for the management of qualities and quantities of exci-
tation, such as are aroused by external and internal stimuli.
Physical concepts are combined with histological concepts to
create a kind of neuronic Golem, a robot, in which even con-

[3] Sigmund Freud, *The Origins of Psychoanalysis: Letters to Wilhelm
Fliess, Drafts and Notes: 1887–1902*, edited by Marie Bonaparte, Anna
Freud and Ernst Kris, New York: Basic Books, 1954.

sciousness and thought are mechanistically explainable on the basis of an over-all principle of inner constancy. Here Freud, at the very beginning of his career as a psychologist, tried to create a mind-robot, a thinking-machine, in many ways related to the mechanical and economic as well as the physiological configurations of his day. As Freud wrote triumphantly to his friend: "Everything fell into place, the cogs meshed, the thing really seemed to be a machine which in a moment would run of itself." But one month after Freud had sent this conception to his friend, he recanted it. "All I was trying to do," he writes, "was to explain defense (against affect), but I found myself explaining something from the very heart of nature. I found myself wrestling with the whole of psychology. Now I want to hear no more of it." He now calls the psychology a "kind of aberration." This manuscript, found only accidentally, documents in a dramatic way the pains to which a discoverer will go *not* to haphazardly ignore the paths of his tradition, but to follow them instead to their absurd limit, and to abandon them only when the crossroad of lone search is reached.

In the meantime, clinical work had brought Freud within sight of his crossroad. His patients, he had become convinced, were suffering primarily from "the damming up" of one irrepressible "affect," namely, sexual sensuality, the existence of which had been consistently denied by their overclothed parents, while engaged in only with furtive shame and degradation by many of their mothers. In the epidemiological fact of widespread female hysteria, Freud faced the specific symptoms of the Victorian age, the price paid, especially by women, for the hypocritical double standard of the sexes in the dominant classes, the masters of commerce and the would-be masters of industrial power. However, the most glaring epidemiological fact (compare poliomyelitis, or juvenile delinquency) does not receive clarification until a seasoned set of theoretical configurations happens to suggest a specific approach. In introducing the energy concept of a sexual libido, which from birth onward is the fuel in all desiring and loving, and which our mind-machine must learn to transform according to our goals and ideals—in this concept Freud found at once the most fitting answer to the questions posed by his patients' memories, and the theory most consistent with his search for a "dignified force." But alas, it was also the most irrationally repugnant solution thinkable in his prudish times, and a solution of emotional danger to the observer. For, indeed, where "to draw the line?"

Here Freud's genetic fervor led to a faulty reconstruction. Certain of being on the right track, and yet shaken by inner and outer resistances, he overshot the mark. In search for a pathogenic Ur-event, he was led to regard as historically real the patients' accounts of passive sexual experiences in the first years of childhood, and to consider the fathers of the patients the perpetrators in such events. He later confessed: "The analysis had led by the correct path to such infantile sexual traumas, and yet, these were not true. Thus, the basis of reality had been lost. At that time, I would gladly have dropped the whole thing." But finally, "I reflected that if hysterics trace back their symptoms to imaginary traumas, then this new fact signified that they create such scenes in fantasy, and hence psychic reality deserves to be given a place next to actual reality." Freud would soon be able to describe psychic reality systematically as the domain of fantasy, dream, and mythology, and as the imagery and language of a universal unconscious, thus transforming into a scientific dimension what had been age-old intuitive knowledge.

In the meantime, had his error detracted from the "dignity" of sexuality? It does not seem so. Knowing what we know today, it is obvious that somebody had to come sometime who would decide that it would be better for the sake of the study of human motivation to call too many rather than too few things sexual, and then to modify the hypothesis by careful inquiry. For it was only too easy to do what had become civilization's "second nature," that is, in the face of the man's sexual and aggressive drives forever to beat a hasty retreat into romanticism and religionism, into secrecy, ridicule and lechery. The patients' fantasies were sexual, and something sexual must have existed in their early years. Freud later called that something *psychosexuality*, for it encompasses the fantasies as well as the impulses, the psychology as well as the biology in the earliest stages of human sexuality.

Today one can add that Freud's error was not even as great as it seemed. First of all, sexual (if not always genital) seductions of children do occur, and are dangerous to them. But more important, the general provocation and exploitation of the child's immature emotions by parent and grandparent for the sake of their own petty emotional relief, of suppressed vengefulness, of sensual self-indulgence, and of sly righteousness must be recognized not only as evident in case histories, but as a universal potentiality often practiced and hypocritically rationalized by very "moral" individuals, indeed. Samuel Butler's *The Way of All Flesh* is probably the most forceful statement on record. What today is decried as "momism" in the United States existed in analogous form in the father's role in the Victorian world: it is only necessary to think of Hitler's official account of his father-hate, and the appeal of this account for millions of young Germans, to know that this is a smoldering theme of general explosiveness. In finding access to the altogether fateful domain of man's prolonged childhood, Freud discovered that infantile man, in addition to and often under the guise of being trained, is being ruefully exploited, only to become in adulthood nature's most systematic and sadistic exploiter. Freud's search thus added another perspective of as yet unforeseeable importance to the image of man.

Yet, this discovery, too, had to pass through its lonely stage. Freud had made a significant mistake, and he was not one to shirk the responsibility for it either publicly or privately. He made it part of his self-analysis.

VI

We know about this first self-analysis in history from the letters, already mentioned, which Freud wrote to Dr. Wilhelm Fliess of Berlin. The extent and the importance of Freud's friendship with Fliess was not even suspected until the letters revealed it.

The two doctors met for what they called their "congresses," long weekends in some mountainous city or town. Their common heritage of education permitted them to roam in varied conversation, as they walked vigorously through the countryside. Freud seems to have shared Nietzsche's impression that a thought not born in locomotion could not be much good. But among the theories discussed by the two doctors, there were many which never saw the light of publication. Thus, Fliess, for many years, was the first and only one to share Freud's thinking.

Psychoanalysts do not seem to like this friendship much; Fliess, after all, was not even a psychoanalyst. Some of us now read of Freud's affection for this man wishing we could emulate that biographer of Goethe who, in the face of Goethe's claim that at a certain time he had dearly loved a certain lady, remarks in a footnote: "Here Goethe is mistaken." Freud, we now say, must have overestimated this friendship in an irrational, almost pathological way. But what, after all, do thinkers need friends for? So that they can share speculations, each alternately playing benevolent authority to the other, each being the other's co-conspirator, each serving as applauding audience, and as cautioning chorus. Freud calls Fliess his "*Other* one," to whom he can entrust what is not ready for "the *others*." Fliess, at any rate, seems to have had the stature and the wide education which permitted Freud to entrust him with "imaginings, transpositions, and guesses." That Freud's imaginings turned out to be elements of a true vision and a blueprint for a science, while Fliess's ended in a kind of mathematical mysticism, provides no grounds to belittle the friendship. The value of a friend may sometimes be measured by the magnitude of the problem which we leave behind with him.

The friendship seems to have been unmarred by irrational disturbances, until, in 1894, Freud consulted Fliess in regard to his own symptoms and moods, which he condenses in the word *Herzelend*—something like "misery of the heart." Fliess had cauterized swellings in Freud's nose and had urged him to give up his beloved cigars. Suddenly, the intellectual communication appears jammed: "I have not looked at your excellent case histories," Freud writes, and indicates that his latest communication to Fliess "was abandoned in the middle of a sentence." He continues: "I am suspicious of you this time, because this heart business [*Herzangelegenheit*] of mine is the first occasion on which I have heard you contradict yourself." At this time, Freud speaks of his discoveries with the anguish of one who has seen a promised land which he must not set his foot on: "I have the distinct feeling," he writes, "that I have touched on one of the great secrets of nature." This tedium of thought seems to have joined the "heart misery" and was now joined by a mistrust of his friend. He wrote, "Something from the deepest depths of my own neurosis has ranged itself against my taking a further step in understanding of the neuroses, and you have somehow been involved."

Freud, at this point, had developed toward Fliess what later, when he understood it, he called a transference, i.e., that peculiar mixture of overestimation and mistrust, which man is so especially ready to bestow on people in significant positions—doctors and priests, leaders and kings, and other superiors, competitors, and adversaries. It is called transference, because, where it is neurotic, it is characterized by the blurring of an adult relationship through the transfer to it of infantile loves and hates, dependencies and impotent rages. Transference thus also implies a partial regression to childish attitudes. It was this very area which, at that time, Freud was trying to understand in his patients. Yet, in Freud, it was quite obviously related to the processes of creativity. We have seen how young Freud, in his student days, had subdued an almost incestuous eagerness to "unveil nature" by the compensatory concentration on laboratory work. He had thus postponed a conflict by realizing only one part of his identity. But when, in his words, he "touched on one of the secrets of nature," he was forced to realize that other, that more creative identity. For any refuge in the established disciplines of scientific inquiry was, as the project proved, forever closed. It is in those moments when our divided selves threaten to drag each other down, that a friend, as Nietzsche said, becomes the life-saver which keeps us afloat and together.

Freud thus discovered another principle in his new work, namely, that *psychological discovery is accompanied by some irrational involvement of the observer, and that it cannot be communicated to another without a certain irrational involvement of both*. Such is the stuff of psychology; here it is not enough to put on an armor of superiority or aloofness in the hope that, like the physicist's apron, it will protect vital organs against the radiation emanating from the observed. Here, only the observer's improved insight into himself can right the instrument, protect the observer, and permit the communication of the observed.

In his transference to Fliess, Freud recognized one of the most important transferences of all: the transfer of an early father-image on later individuals and events. And here we can recognize the pervasiveness in these crises of the great father theme. We saw this theme in Freud's determination not to play autocratic father to patients already crushed by autocracy; we recognized this theme as the core of his tendentious error in the genetic reconstruction of his patients' childhood; and we observe it in his filial reactions to Fliess. A dream, he now reported to Fliess, had clearly revealed to him the fact, and the explanation for the fact, that an irrational wish to blame all fathers for their children's neuroses had dominated him. Yet, one senses at the same time the need of the creative man to have his creativity sired, as it were, by an over-valued friend—a need which often leads, and in Freud's life periodically led, to almost tragicomic involvements.

Having established, then, both the actual and the fantastic aspects of a universal father-image, Freud now could break through to the first prehistoric *Other* of them all: the loving mother. He was free to discover the whole Oedipus complex, and to recognize it as a dominant theme in literature and in mythologies around the world. Only then could he understand the full extent to which he, when sick and bewildered, had made a parent-figure out of Fliess, so that that mystic *Other* might help him analyze himself "as if he were a stranger." He concluded that "self-analysis is really impossible, otherwise there would be no illness . . . I can only analyze myself with objectively acquired knowledge." This insight is the basis for what later became the training analysis, that is, the preventive and didactic psychoanalytic treatment of every prospective psychoanalyst.

The friendship, for other reasons too, had outlived itself. It ended when Freud, in a way, could least afford to lose it, namely, around the turn of the century, after the appearance of *The Interpretation of Dreams*.[4] Freud then, as later, considered this book his most fundamental contribution; he then also believed it to be his last. And, as he wrote, "not a leaf has stirred." For months, for years, there were no book reviews, no sales to speak of. Where there was interest, it was mostly disbelief and calumniation. At this time, Freud seems temporarily to have despaired of his medical way of life. Fliess offered a meeting at Easter. But this time Freud refused. "It is more probable that I shall avoid you," he writes. "I have conquered my depression, and now . . . it is slowly

[4] Sigmund Freud, *The Interpretation of Dreams* [1900], *Standard Edition*, 4, London: Hogarth Press, 1953.

healing. . . . In your company . . . your fine and positive biological discoveries would rouse my innermost (impersonal) envy.
. . . I should unburden my woes to you and come back dis-
satisfied . . . no one can help me in what depresses me, it is my
cross, which I must bear." A few letters later, he refers to his
patients' tendency to prolong the treatment beyond the acquisition of the necessary insight: "Such prolongation is a compromise
between illness and health which patients themselves desire, and
. . . the physician must therefore not lend himself to it." It is clear
that he has now recognized such "prolongation" and "compromise"
in his friendship as well, and that he will refuse to permit himself
a further indulgence in the dependence on Fliess. But he will
sorely miss him—"my one audience," as he calls him.

In the course of this friendship a balance was righted: feminine
intuition, childlike curiosity, and artistic freedom of style were
recognized and restored as partners of the masculine "inner
tyrant" in the process of psychological discovery. And Fliess? According to him the friendship was ship-wrecked on the age-old
rock of disputed priorities: Freud, he said, envied him. And, indeed, Freud had expressed envy that Fliess worked "with light,
not darkness, with the sun and not the unconscious." But it does
not seem probable that Freud would have changed places with
him.

VII

These, then, were the dimensions of the crisis during which and
through which psychoanalysis was born. During these years Freud
at times expressed some despair and confessed to some neurotic
symptoms which reveal phenomenological aspects of a creative
crisis. He suffered from a "railroad phobia" and from acute fears
of an early death—both symptoms of an over-concern with the
all too rapid passage of time. "Railroad phobia" is an awkwardly
clinical way of translating what in German is *Reisefieber*—a fever-
ish combination of pleasant excitement and anxiety. But it all
meant, it seems, on more than one level that he was "coming too
late," that he was "missing the train," that he would perish before
reaching some "promised land." He could not see how he could
complete what he had visualized if every single step took so much
"work, time and error." As is often the case, such preoccupation

with time leads to apprehension centered in the heart, that metro-
nome and measure of endurance.

In the letters the theme of time overlaps with a geographic
restlessness. He thinks of emigrating, maybe to Berlin, to England,
or to America. Most striking is a theme of European dimensions,
namely, an intense, a "deeply neurotic" urge to see Rome. At first,
he wants to arrange to meet his friend, his "one audience," there.
But he writes, "We are not in Rome yet," or, "I am further away
from Rome than at any time since we met, and the freshness of
youth is notably declining." Only when his fundamental work,
The Interpretation of Dreams is published, does Freud decide to
spend Easter in Rome: "Not that there is any justification for it, I
have achieved nothing yet [*es is nichts erreicht*] and in any case,
circumstances will probably make it impossible."

What did Rome mean to Freud? It was a highly "overdeter-
mined" and thus a highly condensed theme. We recognize in it
the fate of Hannibal, who had kindled the imagination of the
Jewish boy: the Semitic warlord had never conquered Rome.
Beyond this, the Eternal City is the goal of many roads, all of
which are superbly condensed in the final wish which Freud sent
to Fliess: "Next Easter in Rome." Here we recognize the educated
German's eternal *Sehnsucht* for Italy (*"dahin, dahin"*); the Israel-
ite's longing for the ancestral home as expressed in the prayer
at Passover, "Next year in Jerusalem"; and within it all a remnant
of that infantile wonder once experienced by the little Jewish boy
on the holiday of resurrection, under the eager guidance of the
Kinderfrau, his Catholic nanny. I know that this kind of "over-
determination," embracing various periods of a man's life and, at
the same time, reconciling ambivalent divisions in his affects and
in his imagery, seems to lack the parsimony of other sciences: but
such is the material of psychoanalysis.

Only in the very last of the letters to Fliess does Freud seem to
have found his position in time and space: "I have readers . . .
the time is not yet ripe for followers." The last letter, written in
the last year of the 19th century, admits, "We are terribly far
ahead of our time." Freud is now forty-four years of age.

But lest anyone form the faulty image of a lamentably torn and
tormented man and physician, it must be reported that the Freud
of those years was what to all appearances we would call a well-

adjusted individual, and what then was a decent and able one: a man who took conscientious care of all the patients who found their way to his door, who with devotion and joy raised a family of six children, who was widely-read and well-groomed, traveled with curiosity, walked (or, as we would say, exercised) with abandon, loved good food and wine wisely, and his cigars unwisely. His "railroad phobia" did not keep him from traveling. And, when he wrote about his being "arbeitsunfaehig" (unable to work), he meant that his writing was not keeping up with his aspirations. But he was not too "well-adjusted" to entertain the dreams, the passions, and the fears adhering to extraordinary vision; nor too "decent" to approach a few things in life with decisive, with ruthless integrity. All of which in a way he could ill afford, for the times were bad for a medical specialist; it was the time of one of the first economic depressions of the modern industrial era, it was a time of poverty in plenty. Nor did the self-analysis "reform" or chasten Freud. Some of the vital conflicts which pervaded the friendship with Fliess remained lifelong, as did some of the early methodological habits: in *Totem and Taboo*, Freud again reconstructed—this time on the stage of history—an "event" which, though an unlikely happening in past actuality, yet proved most significant as a timeless theme. But that early period of Freud's work gave to the new method of inquiry its unique direction, and with it gave its originator that peculiar unity of peculiarities which makes up a man's identity, thus forming the cornerstone of his kind of integrity, and posing his challenge to contemporaries and generations to come.

Freud's self-revelations in the *Interpretation of Dreams* as well as in his letters have provided ample leeway to both his friends and his adversaries for placing emphasis on one or the other of the inner contradictions which characterize genius. Any exclusive emphasis, however, on the infantile or the great, the neurotic or the creative, the emotional or the intellectual, the medical or the psychological aspects of a creative crisis sacrifices essential components. Here, I like to quote a sentence which Professor Cornford puts into the mouth of Pythagoras: "What is your warrant for valuing one part of my experience and rejecting the rest? If I had done so, you would never have heard my name."

VIII

The unique direction given by Freud to the new method of inquiry consisted of the introduction into psychology of a system of co-ordinates which I can only summarize most briefly. His early energy concept provided the *dynamic-economic* co-ordinate, dealing with drives and forces and their transformations. A *topographic-structural* co-ordinate emerged from his study of the partitions within that early mind-robot; while the *genetic* co-ordinate takes account of the origin and the development in stages of both drive and structure.[5] Generations of psychoanalysts have endeavored to find proper places for each new observation and each new theory in these co-ordinates, which thus have provided a method of cross-checking not easily appreciated by the untrained. On the other hand, Freud's case-studies have given to the study of lives a daimonic depth to be found before him only in drama, in fiction, and in the confessions of men endowed with passionate introspection.

Since those early days of discovery, psychoanalysis has established deep and wide interrelationships with other methods of investigation, with methods of naturalist observation, of somatic examination, of psychological experiment, of anthropological field work, and of historical research. If, instead of enlarging on all these, I have focused on the early days, and on the uniqueness of the original Freudian experience, I have done so because I believe that an innovator's achievement can be seen most dramatically in that moment when he, alone against historical adversity and inner doubts, and armed only with the means of persuasion, gives a new direction to human awareness—new in its focus, new in its method, and new in its inescapable responsibility.

The dimensions of Freud's discovery are contained in a triad which, in a variety of ways, remains basic to the practice of psychoanalysis, but also to its application. It is the triad of a *therapeutic contract*, a *conceptual design*, and *systematic self-analysis*.

In psychoanalytic practice, this triad can never become routine. As new categories of suffering people prove amenable to psycho-

[5] David Rapaport, "The Structure of Psychoanalytic Theory: A Systemizing Attempt," in *Psychology: A Study of a Science*, Vol. III, edited by Sigmund Koch, New York: McGraw-Hill, 1959.

analytic therapy, new techniques come to life, new aspects of the mind find clarification, and new therapeutic roles are created. Today, the student of psychoanalysis receives a training psychoanalysis which prepares him for the emotional hazards of his work. But he must live with the rest of mankind in this era of what we may call anxiety-in-plenty, and neither his personal life nor the very progress of his work will spare him renewed conflicts, be his profession ever so recognized, ever so organized. Wide recognition and vast organization, in fact, will not assure—they may even endanger—the basic triad, for which the psychoanalyst makes himself responsible, to wit: that as a clinician he accept his contract with the patient as the essence of his field of study and relinquish the security of seemingly more "objective" methods; that as a theorist he maintain a sense of obligation toward continuous conceptual redefinition and resist the lure of seemingly more profound or of more pleasing philosophic short cuts; and finally, that as a humanist he put self-observant vigilance above the satisfaction of seeming professional omnipotence. The responsibility is great. For, in a sense, the psychoanalytic method must remain forever a "controversial" tool, a tool for the detection of that aspect of the total image of man which in a given historical period is being neglected or exploited, repressed or suppressed by the prevailing technology and ideology—including hasty "psychoanalytic" ideologies.

Freud's triad remains equally relevant in the applications of psychoanalysis to the behavioral sciences, and to the humanities. An adult studying a child, an anthropologist studying a tribe, or a sociologist studying a riot sooner or later will be confronted with data of decisive importance for the welfare of those whom he is studying, while the strings of his own motivation will be touched, sometimes above and sometimes well below the threshold of awareness. He will not be able, for long, to escape the necessary conflict between his emotional participation in the observed events and the methodological rigor required to advance his field and human welfare. Thus, his studies will demand, in the long run, that he develop the ability to include in his observational field his human obligations, his methodological responsibilities, and his own motivations. In doing so, he will, in his own way, repeat that step in scientific conscience which Freud dared to make.

IX

That shift in self-awareness, however, cannot remain confined to professional partnerships such as the observer's with the observed, or the doctor's with his patient. It implies a fundamentally new *ethical orientation of adult man's relationship to childhood:* to his own childhood, now behind and within him; to his own child before him; and to every man's children around him.

But the fields dealing with man's historical dimension are far apart in their appraisal of childhood. Academic minds, whose long-range perspectives can ignore the everyday urgencies of the curative and educative arts, blithely go on writing whole world histories without a trace of women and children, whole anthropological accounts without any reference to the varying styles of childhood. As they record what causal chain can be discerned in political and economic realities, they seem to shrug off as historical accidents due to "human nature" such fears and rages in leaders and masses as are clearly the residue of childish emotions. True, scholars may have been justly repelled by the first enthusiastic intrusion of doctors of the mind into their ancient disciplines. But their refusal to consider the historical relevance of human childhood can be due only to that deeper and more universal emotional aversion and repression which Freud himself foresaw. On the other hand, it must be admitted that in clinical literature (and in literature turned altogether clinical) aversion has given place to a faddish preoccupation with the more sordid aspects of childhood as though they were the final determinants of human destiny.

Neither of these trends can hinder the emergence of a new truth, namely that the collective life of mankind, in all its historical lawfulness, is fed by the energies and images of successive generations; and that each generation brings to human fate an inescapable conflict between its ethical and rational aims and its infantile fixations. This conflict helps drive man toward the astonishing things he does—and it can be his undoing. It is a condition of man's humanity—and the prime cause of his bottomless inhumanity. For whenever and wherever man abandons his ethical position, he does so only at the cost of massive regressions endangering the very safeguards of his nature.

Freud revealed this regressive trend by dissecting its pathological manifestations in individuals. But he also pointed to what is so largely and so regularly lost in the ambivalent gains of civilization: he spoke of "the child's radiant intelligence"—the naive zest, the natural courage, the unconditional faith of childhood which become submerged by excessive ambitions, by fearful teaching and by limited and limiting information.

Now and again, we are moved to say that a genius preserved in himself the clear eye of the child. But do we not all too easily justify man's mass regressions by pointing to the occasional appearance of leaders of genius? Yet, we know (and are morbidly eager to know) how tortured a genius can be by the very history of his ascendance, and how often a genius is driven to destroy with one hand as he creates with the other.

In Freud, a genius turned a new instrument of observation back on his childhood, back on all childhood. He invented a specific method for the detection of that which universally spoils the genius of the child in every human being. In teaching us to recognize the daimonic evil in children, he urged us not to smother the creatively good. Since then, the nature of growth in childhood has been studied by ingenious observers all over the world: never before has mankind known more about its own past—phylogenetic and ontogenetic. Thus, we may see Freud as a pioneer in a self-healing, balancing trend in human awareness. For now that technical invention readies itself to conquer the moon, generations to come may well be in need of being more enlightened in their drivenness, and more conscious of the laws of individuality; they may well need to appreciate and to preserve more genuine childlikeness in order to avoid utter cosmic childishness.

x

Freud, before he went into medicine, wanted to become a lawyer and politician, a lawmaker, a *Gesetzgeber*. When, in 1938, he was exiled from his country, he carried under his arm a manuscript on Moses, the supreme law-giver of the Jewish people whose unique fate and whose unique gifts Freud had accepted as his own. With grim pride he had chosen the role of one who opens perspectives on fertile fields to be cultivated by others. As we look back to the beginnings of his work, and forward to its implications, we may well venture to say: Freud the physician in finding a method of healing himself in the very practice of emotional cure has given a new, a psychological rationale for man's laws. He has made the decisive step toward a true interpenetration of the psychological with the technological and the political in the human order.

If, in the meantime, others see in him primarily the destroyer of precious illusions, if not of essential values, I would remind you of an event that took place in this city, Frankfurt am Main. It was from here that, in 1930, the Secretary of the Goethe Prize Committee informed Freud of his award, which was later received for her ailing father by Anna Freud, in a ceremony in the old (and now rebuilt) *Roemer*. In his dedication the Secretary suggested that "the Mephistophelic bend toward ruthless disillusion was the inseparable counterpart of the Faustian veneration of man's creative potentials." In his letter of acceptance Freud affirmed that nobody had recognized more clearly his "innermost personal motives."

✦

ERIK H. ERIKSON   Born in Germany in 1902, trained in both psychology and psychoanalysis, he is now a professor of psychology at Harvard and the author of three books and many significant articles.

"The First Psychoanalyst" (1956) By comparing Darwin and Freud, the author arrives at psychological hypotheses which apply generally to human nature and human greatness. As he probes Freud's life he plays the personal against the impersonal, the result being an analysis of several subjects simultaneously—objective, comprehensive, and challenging—yet one which never disguises Erikson's enthusiasm for Freud.

✦

1. *What qualities in his own life and character contributed to Freud's psychoanalytic discoveries? 2. In what ways does the author reveal his discipleship to Freud?*

JAMES AGEE

Knoxville: Summer 1915

We are talking now of summer evenings in Knoxville, Tennessee in the time that I lived there so successfully disguised to my-self as a child. It was a little bit mixed sort of block, fairly solidly lower middle class, with one or two juts apiece on either side of that. The houses corresponded: middle-sized gracefully fretted wood houses built in the late nineties and early nineteen hundreds, with small front and side and more spacious back yards, and trees in the yards, and porches. These were softwooded trees, poplars, tulip trees, cottonwoods. There were fences around one or two of the houses, but mainly the yards ran into each other with only now and then a low hedge that wasn't doing very well. There were few good friends among the grown people, and they were not poor enough for the other sort of intimate ac-quaintance, but everyone nodded and spoke, and even might talk short times, trivially, and at the two extremes of the general or the particular, and ordinarily nextdoor neighbors talked quite a bit when they happened to run into each other, and never paid calls. The men were mostly small businessmen, one or two very modestly executives, one or two worked with their hands, most of them clerical, and most of them between thirty and forty-five.

But it is of these evenings, I speak.

Supper was at six and was over by half past. There was still daylight, shining softly and with a tarnish, like the lining of a shell; and the carbon lamps lifted at the corners were on in the light, and the locusts were started, and the fire flies were out, and a few frogs were flopping in the dewy grass, by the time the fathers and the children came out. The children ran out first hell bent and yelling those names by which they were known; then the fathers sank out leisurely in crossed suspenders, their collars removed and their necks looking tall and shy. The mothers stayed back in the kitchen washing and drying, putting things away, recrossing their traceless footsteps like the lifetime journeys of bees, measuring out the dry cocoa for breakfast. When they came out they had taken off their aprons and their skirts were dampened and they sat in rockers on their porches quietly.

It is not of the games children play in the evening that I want to speak now, it is of a contemporaneous atmosphere that has little to do with them: that of the fathers of families, each in his space of lawn, his shirt fishlike pale in the unnatural light and his face nearly anonymous, hosing their lawns. The hoses were attached at spiggots that stood out of the brick foundations of the houses. The nozzles were variously set but usually so there was a long sweet stream of spray, the nozzle wet in the hand, the water trickling the right forearm and the peeled-back cuff, and the water whishing out a long loose and low-curved cone, and so gentle a sound. First an insane noise of violence in the nozzle, then the still irregular sound of adjustment, then the smoothing into steadiness and a pitch as accurately tuned to the size and style of stream as any violin. So many qualities of sound out of one hose: so many choral differences out of those several hoses that were in earshot. Out of any one hose, the almost dead silence of the release, and the short still arch of the separate big drops, silent as a held breath, and the only noise the flattering noise on leaves and the slapped grass at the fall of each big drop. That, and the intense hiss with the intense stream; that, and that same intensity not growing less but growing more quiet and delicate with the turn of the nozzle, up to that extreme tender whisper when the water was just a wide bell of film. Chiefly, though, the hoses were set much alike, in a compromise between distance and tenderness of spray, (and quite surely a sense of art behind this compromise, and a quiet deep joy, too real to recognize itself), and the sounds therefore were pitched much alike; pointed by the snorting start of a new hose; decorated by some man playful with the nozzle; left empty, like God by the sparrow's fall, when any single one of them desists: and all, though near alike, of various pitch; and in this unison. These sweet pale streamings in the light lift out their pallors and their voices all together, mothers hushing their children, the hushing unnaturally prolonged, the men gentle and silent and each snail-like withdrawn into the quietude of what he singly is doing, the urination of huge children stood loosely military against an invisible wall, and gentle happy and peaceful, tasting the mean goodness of their living like the last of their suppers in their mouths; while the locusts carry on this noise of hoses on their much higher and sharper key. The noise of the locust is dry, and it seems not to be rasped or vibrated but urged from him as if through a small orifice by a breath that can never give out. Also there is never one locust but an illusion of at least a thousand. The noise of each locust is pitched in some classic locust range out of which none of them varies more than two full tones: and yet you seem to hear each locust discrete from all the rest, and there is a long, slow, pulse in their noise, like the scarcely defined arch of a long and high set bridge. They are all around in every tree, so that the noise seems to come from nowhere and everywhere at once, from the whole shell heaven, shivering in your flesh and teasing your eardrums, the boldest of all the sounds of night. And yet it is habitual to summer nights, and is of the great order of noises, like the noises of the sea and of the blood her precocious grandchild, which you realize you are hearing only when you catch yourself listening. Meantime from low in the dark, just outside the swaying horizons of the hoses, conveying always grass in the damp of dew and its strong green-black smear of smell, the regular yet spaced noises of the crickets, each a sweet cold silver noise threenoted, like the slipping each time of three matched links of a small chain.

But the men by now, one by one, have silenced their hoses and drained and coiled them. Now only two, and now only one, is left, and you see only ghostlike shirt with the sleeve garters, and sober mystery of his mild face like the lifted face of large cattle enquiring of your presence in a pitchdark pool of meadow; and now he too is gone; and it has become that time of evening when people sit on their porches, rocking gently and talking gently and watching the street and the standing up into their sphere of

possession of the trees, of birds hung havens, hangars. People go
by; things go by. A horse, drawing a buggy, breaking his hollow
iron music on the asphalt; a loud auto; a quiet auto; people in
pairs, not in a hurry, scuffling, switching their weight of aestival
body, talking casually, the taste hovering over them of vanilla,
strawberry, pasteboard and starched milk, the image upon them
of lovers and horsemen, squared with clowns in hueless amber. A
street car raising its iron moan; stopping, belling and starting;
stertorous; rousing and raising again its iron increasing moan and
swimming its gold windows and straw seats on past and past and
past, the bleak spark crackling and cursing above it like a small
malignant spirit set to dog its tracks; the iron whine rises on rising
speed; still risen, faints; halts; the faint stinging bell; rises again,
still fainter; fainting, lifting, lifts, faints forgone: forgotten. Now is
the night one blue dew.

Now is the night one blue dew, my father has drained, he has
    coiled the hose.
Low on the length of lawns, a frailing of fire who breathes.
Content, silver, like peeps of light, each cricket makes his com-
    ment over and over in the drowned grass.
A cold toad thumpily flounders.
Within the edges of damp shadows of side yards are hovering
    children nearly sick with joy of fear, who watch the un-
    guarding of a telephone pole.
Around white carbon corner lamps bugs of all sizes are lifted
    elliptic, solar systems. Big hardshells bruise themselves,
    assailant: he is fallen on his back, legs squiggling.
Parents on porches: rock and rock: From damp strings morning
    glories: hang their ancient faces.
The dry and exalted noise of the locusts from all the air at once
    enchants my eardrums.

On the rough wet grass of the back yard my father and mother
have spread quilts. We all lie there, my mother, my father, my
uncle, my aunt, and I too am lying there. First we were sitting
up, then one of us lay down, and then we all lay down, on our
stomachs, or on our sides, or on our backs, and they have kept
on talking. They are not talking much, and the talk is quiet,

of nothing in particular, of nothing at all in particular, of nothing at all. The stars are wide and alive, they seem each like a smile of great sweetness, and they seem very near. All my people are larger bodies than mine, quiet, with voices gentle and meaningless like the voices of sleeping birds. One is an artist, he is living at home. One is a musician, she is living at home. One is my mother who is good to me. One is my father who is good to me. By some chance, here they are, all on this earth; and who shall ever tell the sorrow of being on this earth, lying, on quilts, on the grass, in a summer evening, among the sounds of the night. May God bless my people, my uncle, my aunt, my mother, my good father, oh, remember them kindly in their time of trouble; and in the hour of their taking away.

After a little I am taken in and put to bed. Sleep, soft smiling, draws me unto her: and those receive me, who quietly treat me, as one familiar and well-beloved in that home: but will not, oh, will not, not now, not ever; but will not ever tell me who I am.

✦

JAMES AGEE   Born in 1909 in Knoxville, Tennessee; died in 1955. A Harvard graduate, he became a movie critic, poet, novelist, and writer for the movies and television. His *Let Us Now Praise Famous Men* shows how intimately he knew and loved the land and the people it barely supported. "Knoxville: Summer 1915" serves as a prologue to his posthumously published novel *A Death in the Family;* the essay was found among his papers and added to the novel by its editors.

"*Knoxville: Summer 1915*" (1957) The tone is complex: a blend of sweet and sour, of childish nostalgia and adult disillusionment, of the centripetal and the centrifugal. The diction involves an intricate interplay between details of hard fact and elusive—sometimes illusive—experience. The syntax displays delicate subordination and runaway sentences, and this, combined with the many overtly lyrical passages, produces a carefully controlled impressionism. The essay's ostensibly digressive logic helps to carry the implied argument.

✦

1. Why and how does the author use sound effects? 2. What evidence might you find that Agee was familiar with the techniques of moviemaking? 3. Is the overall mood happy or sad?

The President

At thirty years of age he was teaching history and political science to the girls at Bryn Mawr College. He did not enjoy his work, for the students could not be expected ever to vote or play a part in the governing of the nation, and their girlish ways did not stimulate him to do his best lecturing. They admired him and faithfully wrote down his jokes in their notebooks, but their response to constitutional law was limited.

He threw himself into the writing of a college textbook, *The State*, and supplemented his $1,500 a year salary by delivering lectures at Johns Hopkins. But when Wesleyan College asked him to join its faculty, he was happy to leave Bryn Mawr; he was "hungry for a class of *men*," he wrote a friend. In his new post he taught political economy, the histories of France, England and the United States. In 1890, getting on to thirty-five, he returned to his alma mater, Princeton.

He stayed there twenty years. As a professor, he was one of the most popular in the university's history, and the highest-paid of his day. He was a wonderful classroom orator, precise, artful, knowledgeable. He related his lectures to the doings of the times as he illustrated the developments of political institutions, and his jokes and dramatizations were marvelously apt. Often the students applauded and stamped their feet at the end of the class. He worked with the boys on extracurricular activities, coaching the debating societies and helping out with the football team. At home during his free hours he wrote extensively— essays, political treatises. Also short stories. (Everything else sold well, but his attempts at fiction brought only rejection slips.) He wrote books about the political history of the country, a life of George Washington, a five-volume history of the American people. He rode a bicycle from his home to his classes. At home were the three little daughters growing up, and in the classrooms were hundreds of young men who would leave Princeton thinking him the finest teacher they had ever seen. When in 1902 the head of Princeton resigned, the university trustees unanimously picked as replacement the head of the Department of Jurisprudence and Political Economy.

Head of the university, he gave up his writing and teaching and turned to administrative duties, but still he remained extremely popular with the students. He told them he was not to be addressed as Professor or Doctor[1] but simply as Mister. He performed well at one of the most important tasks—getting money from the alumni—and he revised and strengthened the curriculum, modernizing it and making it far more demanding. The old Princeton way of gracious living vanished; one disgruntled student wrote home the place was "getting to be nothing but a damned educational institution." That was what the plan had been.

The tutorial system was instituted at the university. Fifty young men, preceptors, were hired to work with students in an intimate and personalized manner. The standards of the university rose even higher, and many inadequate students fell by the way. One such boy was expelled for cheating, and his mother came to plead for his reinstatement with the man who had passed upon the expulsion. She said she was undergoing serious medical treatments and that the shock of having her boy expelled might well bring those treatments to naught. The answer was, "Madam, you force me to say a hard thing, but if I had to choose between your life or my life or anybody's life and the good of this college, I should choose the good of the college." But he could eat nothing at luncheon that day.

[1] His Ph.D. was from Johns Hopkins.

Hazing bothered him; he came upon some sophomore forcing a freshman to pick up twigs with his teeth and acidly said, "Isn't that a fine occupation for a gentleman?" The rather snobbish fraternity-like eating clubs of the university also bothered him. He proposed to abolish the clubs and their anti-intellectual approach in favor of a plan which would have the students of all backgrounds eat, study and live together in dormitories. Princeton graduates loyal to their old eating clubs fought the proposed move, but to the public at large which became aware of the controversy, it seemed as if the head of the university were fighting the battle of democracy in his attempt to shatter the citadels of Princeton's socially elect. He failed in the battle, but popular opinion in New Jersey and elsewhere translated him into the champion of the poorer boys struggling with the richer.

Another argument began. It concerned the graduate school. The university's head wanted the graduate students to work and study on the campus itself and not, as some others desired, in separate buildings some distance from the heart of the campus. The first idea became associated with the conception of a democratic mingling of the graduates and undergraduates, the second idea with that of a standoffish aristocracy.

The question was fought with violence. The head of the university lost. He resigned his post. But he left with the aura of a man who fought for the democratic way. It was 1910, and faced with a gubernatorial election, the New Jersey political bosses chose him to run on the Democratic ticket. He seemed to be very much the college professor; to the politicos he looked to be malleable. They saw him as a dupe, but he saw himself as the agent of Reform. After the bosses of Jersey City and Newark pushed through his nomination, he went campaigning, saying to the people who heard him, "If you give me your votes I will be under bonds to you—not to the gentlemen who were generous enough to nominate me." He was elected and to the disillusionment of the politicians proved that he meant what he had said. They termed him an "ingrate," but it did not matter. As Governor he pushed through reform measures to destroy the boss system and end corruption in state elections. He set up a public utilities commission to establish fair rates for transportation and communications, and laws were passed regulating the work of children and women, the handling of food, the schools. New Jersey had been the very symbol of the complacently corrupt turn-of-the-century business corporation's fief; now the bosses were driven away and the corporations tamed.

In 1912 he was nominated for the Presidency. His election was a certainty, for the Republicans were split, with the incumbent President, Taft, running on the regular party ticket, and the former holder of the office, Roosevelt, campaigning as a Progressive on the "Bull Moose" ticket. The returns in, the President-elect went vacationing to Bermuda. He went bicycle riding with his daughters and turned his head sideways to look at the ocean because someone told him the view was best from that angle. The cable system to the United States was out of order for five days, and he said that made him happy, for he needed peace to think. But he was a public figure now, and reporters dogged his footsteps. He came back from a ride with Jessie [his daughter] and asked the photographers not to take her picture while she was wind-blown from the exertion; when a camera popped he rushed at the man who ignored him and raised his fists as he threatened to chastise him physically.

Back at Trenton, he received a steady stream of visitors seeking appointment to high posts, but he kept his own counsel and refused to be hastened into making known his selections for the Cabinet. (Those who came, however, were generally ignored when the time came for him to announce his choices. He did not think it seemly that men should so nakedly seek power.) In the end his Cabinet was generally marked down as a weak one.

As President he did not consult with the Senators and Representatives. When he wanted to tell them something, he sent for them. There was little give-and-take when they appeared. He explained what was desired, and dismissed callers. When men offered information he already possessed, he cut them off by saying, "I know that." He could not abide callers who meandered about without coming to the point; they wearied him with their palaver and proffered good-fellowship. With his Cabinet he was pleasant and even affable, but he did not care for long extended discussions, preferring written memorandums. At the Cabinet meetings he offered cigars—although he did not smoke himself—and told jokes, but did not get involved in the minor problems of the various departments. When something important came up, he digested the memorandums on the subject with remarkable speed, sent for the Secretary in question, analyzed the problem in a few sentences, and recommended a solution. No one ever had trouble understanding him, and no one had to wait long for a written reply to a written question. (It rarely took more than a day for a Secretary to get an answer to a query.) No one ever dictated to a stenographer faster and more surely than the President. Few of these dictated replies ever needed doing over, for everything he said was right the first time. He was like that in his verbal habits also. Each sentence was gotten out correctly; there was never any stumbling or beginning again. He could not conceal his impatience with men who began to say something, stopped, and took off in a new direction.

At table there was never any business discussed, and never any guests who would talk of public matters. All the conversation was erudite and cheerful. In the Congress they criticized him for this and said that what he wanted was a few tough-minded sons instead of the gay and easygoing daughters. The sons would throw things back in his teeth, Senators told each other, and make the President less inclined to ignore the advice of other people. On the golf course, also, there was no business talk. No Senators or Representatives went along on the auto rides, for the rides were for relaxation. The President said he had a certain amount of energy and was not going to squander it by taking up business matters when he was not in his office during working hours.

In his first year he did more than most of his predecessors had done in complete terms. Tariffs were lowered, the Federal Reserve System was born, and the Federal Trade Commission and a strong anti-trust law. Personal income taxes were levied to make up for the losses in tariff revenue. The rights of laboring men were strengthened, and vocational schools were given federal assistance. At his inauguration he had motioned to an empty space in front of the Capitol and, indicating the men and women held back by police, said, "Let the people come forward." That was the theme of his administration; that was the meaning of the New Freedom.

In 1916 he was renominated. In order to receive his formal notification on a spot not the property of the government, he rented a New Jersey estate and was there through Election Day, when it seemed that Charles Evans Hughes was the winner. The apparent loss did not ruffle the President; he went to bed early after remarking that it seemed his programs had not been completely understood by the voters. The morning after (legend has it) a reporter calling at the Hughes home was told that President Hughes could not be disturbed. The tally was that close. It came down in the end to how California would go, and when the last returns from the mountain polling places were in, the state was in the Democratic column.

By then, by 1916, the domestic program was in the background, for the talk was all of whether the United States would go to the war. A Democratic slogan, "He Kept Us out of War," was credited with the President's victory, but he knew best of all that a German lieutenant looking through a submarine periscope could make nonsense of the slogan.

The Americans did not want to fight, not in the main. Nor did their President, who remembered from his youth what Sherman had done to the South. From the White House went unending notes to the contesting British and Germans as the President twisted one way and then another in his attempts to avoid the war. During the first half of his term there had been a skirmish between American marines and some Mexicans at Vera Cruz, and when the handful of American deaths was reported to the President he whitened and staggered. To go to France in force would mean dead men in their tens of thousands. In the President's eyes the soldiers he would have to send to face machine guns and artillery shells were akin to his boys back at Princeton. That is what he usually called them—"boys," not "soldiers" or "men."

But the war, it seemed, could not be avoided. He sat before dawn one day in April on the South Portico, and the First Lady awakened and came to him with an overcoat, some biscuits, a glass of milk. In the rain of an April evening he went with the words he had written to the House Chamber of the Capitol. His fingers trembled as he turned the pages, and in the silences between his sentences the sound of drops could be heard hitting upon the roof. He said, "It is a fearful thing to lead this great peaceful people into war, into the most terrible and disastrous of all wars, civilization itself seeming to be in the balance. But the right is more precious than peace . . ."

On the plaza outside, cavalry Regulars from Fort Myer sat their horses to keep the crowds back and guard against disturbances of the kind which earlier in the day saw an anti-war pacifist strike

Senator Henry Cabot Lodge of Massachusetts in the face. (Lodge
hit back before the pacifist was dragged away.) Soon the Regulars would be indistinguishable from the farmers and clerks, the
college boys and mechanics, and in the Oval Room of the White
House the President would give off singing the nonsense songs of
Princeton in favor of "Over There" and "There's a Long, Long
Trail A-Winding."

". . . and we shall fight for the things which we have always
carried nearest our hearts—for democracy, for the right of those
who submit to authority to have a voice in their own governments,
for the rights and liberties of small nations, for a universal
dominion of right by such a concert of free peoples as shall bring
peace and safety to all nations and make the world itself at
last free."

(Something would have to come of it. America would bring the
justice and peace of a just and peaceful nation to the world.)

"To such a task we can dedicate our lives and our fortunes,
everything that we are and everything that we have, with the
pride of those who know that the day has come when America
is privileged . . ."

(Else what would it all be for, the dying boys and the sunken
ships?)

". . . to spend her blood and her might for the principles that
gave her birth and happiness and the peace which she has
treasured.

"God helping her, she can do no other."

There was a moment of silence. Then a great roar of applause
rolled up to him. Mixed in it were the high rebel yells of South-
erners. The troops of cavalry formed up, and with Cary Grayson,
Joe Tumulty and the First Lady he drove in silence back to the
White House past the crowds of cheering people. "My message
today was a message of death for our young men," he said. "How
strange it seems to applaud that."

The Americans went to France and Pershing and his staff to a
grave where an officer said, "Lafayette, we are here!" The way
it got back was that the handsome and soldier-like head of the
American Expeditionary Force said it himself, and that was right,
because it was what he *should* have said. There was something

different about the soldiers the Americans sent abroad under him in that AEF. Such soldiers, perhaps, were never seen before. They sang. They laughed a great deal. They believed in themselves, their country, their way. They were young, confident and open; to the Europeans it seemed that they were indeed godlike, untouched, sure of the sacredness of their mission, which was to give the world a new order and make the world clean and right.

And the war was fought and won. The New World had come to redeem the Old, and when it came time to ask for peace the enemy applied to the leader of that New World. And the guns stopped. That the night ended meant there must be a dawn, and that the dawn must compensate for the dead in their millions, for the girls who would get old and older and who would die as old maids whose lovers-that-should-have-been lay, forever young, in Flanders or Mesopotamia or Gallipoli. In parts of France the poison gas would cling to the roofs of caves for twenty years; the trench-system outlines under the fields could be seen from airplanes forty years later. The Sacred Way up to Verdun, the Lost Battalion, the Chemin des Dames, the Australians coming off their transports past the sunken *River Clyde*, the British boys in their 174 cemeteries crammed into the Ypres Salient, the Italian artillerists dueling with the Austrians in the snow; the English staff general going up forward for the first time and crying, "Good God, did we really send men to fight in that?" the Yank non-com with "Come on, you sons of bitches! Do you want to live forever?" the mules drowning in the shell holes, "Madelon" —it all had to be paid for, something must come out of it, it could not have all been done for nothing. The world was crying out for the price to be paid.

Three weeks after the Armistice was signed, on December 4, 1918, the President of the United States, the man who with his soldiers had brought the dawn, sailed for Europe to work on a final peace treaty and to form a League of Nations which would give the world justice and security and prevent war forever.

"You carry overseas with you," Ellen's brother [the brother of Wilson's first wife; she had died in 1914] wrote him, "the hearts and hopes and dreams and desires of millions of your fellow Americans. Your vision of the new world that should spring from the ashes of the old is all that has made the war tolerable to many of us. That vision has removed the sting, has filled our imaginations, and has made the war not a tragedy but a sacrament. Nothing but a new world is worth the purchase price of the war, and the comfort of millions of us is that you have the vision to glimpse it and the power to realize it in action."

Off Brest before dawn of December 13, at four-twenty in the morning, lights were sighted on the horizon and a welcoming fleet of American warships steamed up. By seven twenty-five, nine battleships were standing alongside the warship and five destroyers that had escorted the *George Washington* across the ocean. Each fired a 21-gun salute as it came by. Twelve destroyers followed the battleships. A little after ten Brest could be seen by the President and the First Lady standing on the bridge with Cary Grayson and the First Lady's secretary, Edith Benham. As they headed in, two French cruisers and nine French destroyers came up from the south firing salutes, the black puffs of smoke visible in the air moments before the roll of the guns could be heard. By eleven-thirty they were fifteen miles off shore, with the *George Washington* leading and the *Wyoming*, the *Pennsylvania*, the *Arkansas*, the *Florida*, the *Utah*, the *Nevada*, the *Oklahoma*, the *New York*, the *Texas* and the *Arizona* ranging behind in double column. The French squadron and the American destroyers followed through a calm sea and under a sky brightening after a dark morning. At one o'clock they entered the narrow strait into the harbor, and the shore batteries in the ten forts on both sides of the cliffs began firing salutes one after the other. The fleet below returned the honor gun for gun, and the booming from the heights and from the water mingled with the clouds of black smoke pouring forth. As the *George Washington* went in, military bands on top of the cliffs crashed into *The Star-Spangled Banner* and *The Marseillaise*. The pounding of the guns was deafening, but when they reached the harbor the noise grew even greater as the sound of the continual firing mixed with the whistles and sirens of the shore craft, ships dressed and yards manned.

A little after one-thirty the *George Washington* dropped anchor a mile off shore, and the escorting and welcoming fleets took up stations around it. As far as the eye could see across the mile-long harbor, ships were standing to, and weaving through them came boats carrying welcomers. Margaret [another daughter], who had been abroad singing for the troops, came on board with Pershing and a contingent of French officers and dignitaries who bore bouquets and clicked their heels as they bent to kiss the First Lady's hand. Admiral Sims walked up to Pershing, whom he had not seen in some months, and made them all laugh: "Hello, Jack, how the hell did you do it? I didn't know you had it in you." Two hours later, after lunch, they went ashore in a tender, the President standing by the French Ambassador to the United States, Jules Jusserand, who pointed out the sights. All along the terraced shore they could see fishermen in wooden shoes, velvet coats and flat hats, and women in colorful Breton headdresses and peasant bodices. They reached the quay, where a specially constructed platform was waiting. It was covered with masses of greens and flowers, and as the tender came to it a French marine band burst into the National Anthems of first America and then France. The tender was made fast and the party went ashore, the First Lady escorted by Pershing and the President coming last, walking up the gangplank alone with his silk hat held in his hand in response to the cheers rolling toward him. The French troops and the Americans presented arms, hands slapping smartly on the rifles, and the Mayor of Brest stepped forward to present the President with a large parchment roll made fast with a ribbon of red, white and blue and containing the greetings of the Brest City Council. The Mayor's seven-year-old daughter handed a bouquet to the First Lady and received a kiss in return.

The visitors got into open automobiles and began to ascend the steep road up the cliff to the railroad station, where the private train of President Poincaré of France waited to carry them to Paris. All along the route American soldiers stood at attention, and Ike Hoover, the White House usher, thought he could see their chests swell with pride to be so near their President. Above the road, over the troops and the shouting Bretons and cheering children waving American flags, hung printed signs: HAIL THE CHAMPION OF THE RIGHTS OF MAN. HONOR TO THE APOSTLE OF INTERNATIONAL JUSTICE. HONOR AND WELCOME TO THE FOUNDER OF THE SOCIETY OF NATIONS. The President held his hat in his hand and smiled even though he took note that the sign about the founder of the society of nations was a little premature. At the railroad station there was a pavilion decorated in red silk and the Mayor made a speech, saying destiny brought the American leader to release the people of Europe from their tortures. The train had huge armchairs and picture windows, and at four o'clock they pulled out of the station. Just before they left, the Mayor's little girl came in again with a bouquet which she shyly pushed forward. The President made as if to take the flowers and hand them to the First Lady, but the child hung on and finally got out, "Pour Mademoiselle Veelson," and Margaret bent laughing to kiss her.

All along the line to Paris people stood waiting to shout greetings. And in the capital itself the next day there waited the largest throng in the history of France. The weather ever since Armistice Day had been rainy and muddy, but on the day they arrived there was a soft and clear autumn-like sky and a brisk west wind. It seemed the whole of France stood in the streets. From the Madeleine to the Bois de Boulogne not a square foot of space was clear. Stools and tables were put out by the concierges of houses along the parade route, with places on them selling for ten, twenty or fifty francs, depending upon the affluence of the customer. Carpenter horses and boards were arranged into improvised grandstands, and men and boys clung to the very tops of the chestnut trees. The housetops were covered with people. Captured German cannons were ranged along the line of march and the cannons were covered. Lines formed of thirty-six thousand French soldiers, the cream of the Army, stood fast to hold back the crowds; they parted only to allow wounded comrades in wheel chairs to gain places inside the lines so as to see the visitor. The people had gathered hours before the train was due in Paris and stood waiting and looking down toward the station, a tiny bandbox on the edge of the Bois reserved for official arrivals of visiting royalty.

Past them went the chasseurs in blue berets and the spahis in scarlet and white robes, the President Poincaré and Premier Clemenceau. The military bands along the route formed in compact groups and stood silent, and in fact a great silence fell all over Paris and the hundreds of thousands of people, a silence that grew ever more deep, so that when the time came for the train's arrival only the chomping of the cavalry horses could be heard in the completely jammed streets. Then at ten o'clock the first booming of the batteries on Mont Valérien was heard off in the distance: the train was in Paris. Moments later the sound of *The Star-Spangled Banner* came floating up the boulevards from the station and a stir went through the waiting multitudes. After the guns and the music came a new sound, like the distant rumblings of thunder, and it grew louder in turn to the ears of those who stood waiting at the Porte Dauphine and on the Champs Elyseés and Pont Alexander III, in front of the Chamber of Deputies and in the Place de la Concorde: "*Wil-son. Wil-son.*" And then he was in the streets of Paris in a two-horse victoria, sitting by the President of France, with the Garde Républicaine, swords on shoulders and plumes dancing, going on ahead, the cheers coming like waves as he moved. "Vive Wil-son! Vive Wil-son! Vive Wil-son!"

Never, even on Armistice Day, had such cheers been heard. From the windows poured roses, violets, forget-me-nots, holly, greens. The people screamed in holy fervor to the man standing in the victoria and holding outstretched his tall hat. He went under draped flags, and bunting, and an immense electric sign: WEL-COME TO WILSON. The military bands beat on their drums and the bugles sounded; the noise was lost in the roaring cheers for the man who would save France from another 1870 and another 1914. The air was filled with coats and jackets thrown aloft after the hats. A huge banner stretched across the Champs Elysées: HONOR TO WIL-SON THE JUST. Flowers rained down onto the First Lady, so that people could barely see her as she rode in the carriage behind her husband. The President of France looked dazed and pale; he seemed terrified almost by the emotion before him. The American Secret Service men were in a frenzy of fear for their charge, but it was impossible to do anything; the crowds were too enormous, the noise too loud, the press of bodies too great. People grew giddy; women wept as they screamed his name.

"No one ever had such cheers," wrote the journalist William Bolitho. "I, who heard them in the streets of Paris, can never forget them in my life. I saw Foch pass, Clemenceau pass, Lloyd George, generals, returning troops, banners, but Wilson heard from his carriage something different, inhuman—or superhuman. Oh, the immovably shining, smiling man!"

It seemed the Arc de Triomphe would fall before this cascade of sound. His carriage went under it—the first time within the memory of living man this had happened. The Premier of France said, "I do not think there has been anything like it in the history of the world."

Later in the day the President spoke at a luncheon, exchanging toasts with the French President: "All that I have said or tried to do has been said and done only in the attempt to faithfully express the thoughts of the American people. From the very beginning of this war the thoughts of the people of America turned toward something higher than the mere spoils of war. Their thought was directed toward the establishment of the eternal principles of right and justice."

That day French soldiers joined hands to drag German cannons down the street at a run; French girls screaming with laughter went along as passengers. That day the overloaded branches of a tree near the Madeleine broke and half a dozen doughboys tumbled all over the sidewalk—but it was a day when nothing could go wrong and they all jumped up unhurt and trooped away, laughing. That day *Le Petit Parisien* headlined: VIVE WILSON! VIVE WILSON! and *La Liberté* said Paris had given to him all its fire and all its heart. That night Paris was ablaze with illuminations and the boulevards were thronged with singing, dancing, confetti-tossing crowds.

He went to England. French ships escorted him to mid-Channel; British craft took up the duty there. At Dover the Lord Mayor in wig and robe greeted him, and little English school-girls draped in American flags threw flowers in his path. In London a wintry haze hung in the air, but the flags and bunting and triumphal arches made of choice flowers, richly berried holly, and gilt golden eagles in front of Charing Cross seemed to glimmer as the guns in Hyde Park and the Tower pumped off blanks to announce his coming. A detachment of the Scots Guards was at the station, and the band of the Grenadiers, and of course the King in field marshal's uniform. They went out over red carpets to the great high red-and-gold royal carriages drawn by beauti-fully groomed bays with red harness and silk on their manes and surrounded by a Sovereign's Escort and postilions and footmen in royal livery. The people filling the Strand broke out into a roar for the man who would save England from another Continental war with its horrors of gas and mud, and they got under way, the carriages, the Royal Standard Bearer, the clattering horse escort going by Venetian masts, by the National Gallery almost hidden by flags and bunting, by the rigid ranks of the Coldstream Guards. For blocks in all directions the streets were completely jammed; the newspapers said two million people stood to see him. From Hyde Park Corner down Constitution Hill the lampposts were draped in scarlet with flags and emblems bearing Imperial and civic emblems. The Royal Horse Guards band was at Hyde Park Corner to crash into *The Star-Spangled Banner* when the carriages came to it, and bells and chimes rang out over all London. He stood not simply to raise his hat but to wave it boyishly. They went to Buckingham Palace, where the Welsh Guards band waited, and from the balcony looked over at the crowd reaching all down the Mall to the Admiralty half a mile away, overflowing St. James's Park on one side and the Green Park on the other. The crowd screamed for him to speak and waved tiny American flags hawked all through the city that day—"a penny each and all silk"—and he laughed and waved his hand to say no, there would be no speech, and went inside but in a few moments had to go out in answer to the immense rolling sound of hundreds of thousands of voices chanting in unison, "WE WANT WILSON." The First Lady waved a Union Jack as she stood with her husband and the King and Queen. Never had London heard the cheers that reached up toward them.

A royal state dinner, the first held since Great Britain went to war, was given in the palace. Everything on the table was of gold —the candelabra, dishes, forks, spoons, knives. On three different sides of the room were hung gold dishes not used during the dinner; many were the size of tea trays. Beefeaters from the Tower stood in their red uniforms holding in their motionless hands unmoving halberds. Liveried servants were everywhere. The King's hands trembled as he read off a toast; the President replied extemporaneously, addressing his hosts as "Sir" but not "Your Majesty."

They left London and went up to Carlisle near the Scottish border and to the little church in which the Reverend Thomas Woodrow, his grandfather, had preached. He stood in front of the communion rail, declining to stand in the pulpit, and spoke to the congregation of the little girl who had worshiped in this

church before she went to America and womanhood and ultimately motherhood, and of her sense of duty and of what she had
taught her son. He spoke of what that son believed: "We shall
now be drawn together in a combination of moral force that will
be irresistible . . . it is from quiet places like this all over the
world that the forces accumulate which presently will overbear
any attempt to establish evil." He went along into the vestry to
sign the book and the First Lady was glad for his moment of
seclusion, for she saw what it meant to him to be in this church.

They went back to Paris and from there to Italy on the royal
train of that country. At ten-thirty on the morning of January 2,
1919, they crossed the Franco-Italian frontier at Mentone to the
accompaniment of cheers from the Italian troops lined up by the
barriers. They headed south, their way at night lighted by blazing
bonfires of welcome. In Rome an Alpine infantry guard of honor
waited along with the Mayor's Guard in crimson and gold and
silver helmets with plumes. In the royal carriage they rode with
the King and Queen to the Quirinal Palace. Airplanes roared and
a dirigible drifted over the streets covered with golden sand
brought from the Mediterranean in compliance with an ancient
way of honoring heroes. From the windows of the old houses
hung rare old brocades and velvet with coats of arms embroidered
upon them, and flowers rained down as swords, handkerchiefs,
flags, hats, epaulets flew up into the air. The great cheers re-
bounded off the Baths of Diocletian and seemed to stir the banners crying HAIL THE CRUSADER FOR HUMANITY and WELCOME TO
THE GOD OF PEACE. Triumphal arches were emblazoned with texts
from his writings and in the shopwindows all over Rome his
picture stood with burning candles before it. The officials kissed
the hand of the man who would return Italy to its former glory;
his signature they pressed to their hearts. When he stood on the
balcony of the Quirinal he threw kisses to the throngs and they
in return hailed him as no one in Rome had ever been hailed, not
Caesar and his legions returned from the conquest of Gaul, not
anyone. *Epoca* said: "He launched his country into the great
conflict with the sole aim of making justice triumph. He comes to
Rome and will walk up the Capitoline Hill, whence were dictated
to the world the laws of right and justice." The *Corriere d'Italia:*
"We thought justice and right had disappeared from the world,

when his figure arose." He went to call on Pope Benedict XV and en route to St. Peter's a child was knocked out of its mother's arms by the wild crowds. Margaret saw the accident and had the child, whose nose was scratched, brought to her. She fondled it and kissed the bruised nose and the people went mad, falling on their knees to kiss her hand and screaming, "Long live Miss Wilson! Long live America!"

They left Rome for Milan and again he blew kisses to the wildly cheering people gathered in what the newspapermen said was perhaps the greatest mass of people ever in one spot at any single time in the history of the world. He was gay and easy with the crowds; he waved his arms in time with a band. In Turin the students at the university begged him to speak and he put on one of their blue caps and wore it while saying a few words. The First Lady thought as she looked at him, How young and virile!

He returned to Paris as the man of whom it was said that he could bring to the earth that peace and good will of which the angelic choir sang upon the occasion of the birth of the Messiah at Bethlehem; of whom it was said that no such moral and political power and no such evangel of peace had appeared since Christ preached the Sermon on the Mount; of whom it was said that only Augustus nineteen centuries before had had such an opportunity to create a new world. In the children's ward of a Vienna hospital a Red Cross worker gently told the young patients that in that year of defeat for Austria there could be no Christmas gifts; they cried back, "Wilson is coming. Then everything will be all right." A French teacher asked her class to "describe President Wilson and give your own ideas about him," and one little girl wrote that he wore no beard so there would be more room on his face for the children to kiss. Another wrote, "I wish that President Wilson may never die." In the area of the Allied intervention in northern Russia his picture was almost as common in the peasant huts as the ever-present icon, and from Egypt an American wrote that the natives held him to be the Mahdi, the Mohammedan Messiah calling for revolt that would drive out the English so that he might send Americans to help govern the country. His name was recited as an incantation by the effendis, the harem women, the imams and mullahs; with tomtoms beating and pipes shrilling, crowds in the East cried for hour after hour, "Yahia Dr. Wilson." ("Long

Live Dr. Wilson.") In the mountains of the Balkans the villagers settled petty disputes by saying, "President Wilson would have it so." Shakespeare, Caesar, Alexander—two thirds of the earth's inhabitants never heard these names, wrote William T. Ellis, but his name and creed "have found lodgment in a greater number of human minds than any platform or name save Jesus or Mohammed."

On the *George Washington* coming over, the President once grew pensive. "What I seem to see—with all my heart I hope I am wrong—is a tragedy of disappointment," he had said.

1

GENE SMITH Born in 1929, he is a newspaperman and free-lance writer with a lifelong interest in American history. *When the Cheering Stopped—the Last Years of Woodrow Wilson,* from which the preceding is a chapter, is his first book.

"The President" (1964) The style is extremely simple, deceptively so, for the shadow of subsequent events gives almost every sentence a double meaning. These terse, declarative sentences, with their rapid, easy-flowing rhythms, italicize the neat and naive attitudes so soon to be shattered. The author uses the device of sampling to accumulate a mass of details within a carefully patterned, apparently repetitive and yet subtly varied syntax.

1

1. *What is the author's underlying view of Wilson's personality and character? 2. In what ways might he be considered unfair in his selection of evidence and in his emphases?*

A Search for the Poet's Tomb

Granada, I found, had not changed much in outward appearance during the past fifteen years. A new modernistic building put up here, a shop gone there, and the usual decrease in the number of cafés and increase in the number of banks. (The palatial bank is as much a symbol of modern Spain as the cathedral was of Spain in the Middle Ages.) Yet the change in atmosphere was striking. Granada had always been a sober town, as austere and conventional as a provincial capital in Castile, though tempered by a certain Andalusian refinement, but now it seemed to me that it was more than austere—it was sad. There were fewer signs of extreme poverty and hunger than I had seen elsewhere in Spain, for the irrigated *vega*, or plain, to the west eases the life of the city, but the faces of the passersby were gloomy and sullen, the principal squares had lost their animation, and there were police everywhere.

The morning was gray and windy as I set off to explore the old Moorish part of the city known as the Albaicín, with its steep, cobbled lanes, its white houses rising one above another, and its terraced gardens. A stream of women and children moved up and down the street, but few men. There was a feeling of tension. After I had climbed a certain distance, I caught, on my right, the sounds of dogs barking and the harsh jangling of a guitar; they came from the whitewashed caves of the gypsy quarter. Then I reached a little square, with trees and a crenellated gate, and in a few minutes was out on the open hillside, above the houses.

How touching, in some way I cannot describe, are those *terrains vagues* of old cities, where the last houses meet and mingle with the countryside! Here was a wall of dried mud, there an agave plant, and a fig tree that, clumsy and babyish, groped in the air with its blunt fingers. An old woman carried a pitcher, a man leaned against the wall and gazed at his shoes, and far below, beyond the city, lay the flat, green plain, stretching away to the rim of mountains. From it, there rose the crowing of cocks —faint, shrill, and charged with distance and memory—into the gray sky that spread over everything. This was the Albaicín as it used to be—yet why did it seem so changed, so different? As I stopped and listened to the cock crows, the answer came to me. This was a city that had killed its poet. And all at once the idea entered my mind to visit, if I could find it, Federico Garcia Lorca's grave.

I decided first to drive to Fuente-Vaqueros, the village where Lorca was born and brought up, though I knew I would not learn much there; Federico moved away in 1912. The village lies some dozen miles from Granada, on the *vega* and at the edge of an estate that was once Godoy's and is now the seventh Duke of Wellington's. It was a beautiful drive, past clear, swift-running irrigation channels islanded with watercress, like streams near my home in England; plantations of thin, mast-like poplars; barns for drying tobacco. The village was low, white and dusty; through the middle of it ran a broad thoroughfare planted with pollarded trees, and at one end of the plaza stood the usual group of unemployed laborers, staring in front of them with wooden expressions. Mules, ox-carts, pigs, goats, children—the whole place was one great farm, smelling of the soil and of the farmers' round of labors.

The house where Federico had lived was one of the largest in the village, a white, two-storied building with balconies, a roof of brown tiles, and a concealed garden behind. Its unpretentious simplicity gave it an exceptional charm. Next to it stood the church, long, low, color-washed, with a miniature tower—the image of a toy church in a child's picture book. Unfortunately, like so many other Spanish churches, it was defaced by Falangist

symbols and claptrap set up over the porch. I paid my respects to
the poet's aunt and cousin, who lived close by, but as I had sur-
mised, they knew very little of Federico's career. After that, there
was nothing more to be seen, so I started out on the return
journey, over roads deeply rutted by oxcarts, between flat fields
and the green poles of poplar trees.

Next morning, I set out on foot to climb the hill to the cemetery
of Granada. The sun was shining and a dry wind raised the dust
in eddies. Passing through the elm woods that surround and
smother the Alhambra, the great acropolis and Moorish bastion
east of the city, I took the road up which, morning after morning
during the Civil War, the lorries packed with Loyalist prisoners
had struggled. The foreign residents of the Washington Irving
Hotel, half a mile from the cemetery, had listened to them changing gears, I knew, and had pulled the blankets over their heads
when, so little time later, the shots rang out. Afterward, the night-
ingales, noisy as frogs, had resumed their chug-chugging. Soon I
could discern, crowning the hill in front of me, the high white
walls of the cemetery where for generations all the *hijos de
Granada* have been buried. As I came up to it, I could see that a
new enclosure, several acres in extent, had been added. I entered
this newest part, where the sun glared down and the loose earth
was blown about by the wind, and began to wander among the
graves. Then I came upon a man driving a small donkey loaded
with a pannier of dirt.

"I am looking for a grave," I began, and explained the circumstances.

"Well," he said, "you will have to inquire at the office. The
names of all those who were shot at the cemetery are recorded
there."

"Really?" I exclaimed, for I was surprised that the Civil Guards
had taken the trouble to do this.

"Oh, yes," he said. "Those who were shot here were shot by
order of the military authorities, and so all the formalities were
observed. On every grave, a marker was put up with the name of
the unhappy soul upon it, and when three or four were buried
together in the same grave—well, three or four names were
inscribed."

"Were you here then?"

"Not me. I spent the war fighting on the Red side. When it finished and I'd done my term in the labor camps, I got this job digging graves."

Leaving his donkey, the gravedigger accompanied me to the office. There a little old man, shabby and frail, came scraping up to us. On his nose, which was very thin, he wore a pair of steel-rimmed spectacles, and on his head an official peaked cap that was too large for him. He listened to my inquiries with an air of reserve and obsequiousness, but the whole cast of his face expressed fear and sadness, as well as a certain wariness. Whom did I say I was looking for? Federico García Lorca? Ah, yes, he remembered the name, for I was not the first person who had asked about him. Only last year, some foreigners—Argentines, he thought—had driven up to the gate with a wreath of flowers. But he had been unable to satisfy them. Señor García Lorca's remains had been put in the bone pit after the five years in the earth required by Church law, because no one had paid the fee for their removal to a permanent resting place.

"Could I see the pit?"

"Certainly. There is no objection." And he handed the gravedigger a large key. Then, with the same sad, deferential manner with which he had addressed me, he turned to bow to a funeral party that had just arrived.

Jangling the key and talking breezily of the secrets of his trade—how long, for example, it took corpses to decay in the local earth—the gravedigger led the way across the dusty, sun-drenched hillside, pitted with humble graves. Then he stopped before a gate in a high wall. "Here we are," he said, unlocking it. "This is the ossuary."

A curious, sweetish smell and a disagreeable, uneasy feeling of isolation and silence met us as we entered. Pulling myself together, I saw that we were in a sort of open court littered with torn and blackened fragments of clothing. It was as though a rag fair had been held there a dozen years before, or a collection of gypsy caravans had made the place their camping ground. But quickly my eyes were drawn from these sordid things to a pit in the center of the enclosure. It was some thirty feet square, to all appearances deep, and filled to within six feet of the top with skulls and bones. Among these lay a few parched and shrunken bodies, wrapped in moldering cerements, in distraught postures, as though they had come flying down through the air.

"Here you have what was once the flower of Granada," said the man. "Look well and you'll see the bullet holes." And, in fact, nearly every skull was pierced through.

"But what is that?" I asked. Stretched across the rubble of bones, in an attitude of rigid attention, was a complete and well-preserved corpse, dressed in a braided green uniform. Its face, a little greenish, too, with dark markings, had the severe, concentrated look of a man who is engaged in some important task.

"Ah, that one!" exclaimed the gravedigger. "He's a fine bird. A colonel, if you please, in the Civil Guard. He's been lying for fifty years or so in one of the upper niches in the wall, and that's why he's so well mummified. Even his complexion is as fresh as if he had just been laid out. We took him up the other day because his family have stopped paying the rent, and here he is." A colonel of the police guarding the bones of the men his successors had shot! Goya could not have thought of a better subject.

"And how many would you say are buried in this pit?" I asked.

"Well, the list of those officially shot has eight thousand names. All but a few of them are here. Then, there are a thousand or so more who had the originality to die natural deaths. *Vamos,* say nine or ten thousand altogether. And all good friends, good companions."

"Why do you say that?"

"Well, why not? They're all there together." He laughed as we turned to go. After locking the gate, we walked to the cemetery entrance, passing on the way the donkey, still patiently waiting with its load of soil.

"Can you point out to me where the executions took place?" I asked.

"I'll take you there," he said. "Then you won't lose yourself."

"But will that get you into trouble?"

"No, why should it? They were officially shot, weren't they? By order of the military authorities. A great act of justice!" He led me out through the iron gates to the wall that bounded the lower side of the cemetery. The bullet marks were still there, and a few red stains. The prisoners had been bundled out of the lorries at dawn and machine-gunned in groups, their rope manacles still on them. Only the city councillors of Granada, Socialists all, had been granted the privilege of lighting cigarettes and so showing the traditional contempt and defiance. There they had stood, looking at a red plowed field planted with olive trees and sloping up to the gradually brightening sky. After that, nothing.

The more I thought over the results of this expedition, the less I was satisfied with them. The old man at the office had been elusive, it seemed to me. The gravedigger's emphasis on official executions suggested that there had been other executions, which could not be so classified. I decided to return to the cemetery that afternoon and to demand to see the list of those executed. If Lorca was really buried there, surely his name would be on it.

At four o'clock, therefore, I was back again. This time, I made my way into that part of the cemetery where the middle classes are buried, either in niches cut in the patio walls or in more expensive marble tombs under the cypress trees. Here I started a conversation with two gravediggers, one of whom, the older and more talkative, had been in Granada when the military rising began. I asked them to show me where those executed in 1936 and not eventually consigned to the bone pit had been reburied.

"You've come straight to the spot," replied the elder gravedigger. "The most celebrated ones are all here." And he led me to the grave of Montesinos, the Socialist mayor of Granada, who was Lorca's brother-in-law, and then to those of the city councillors and other officials. Next came the graves of various doctors, including that of a famous specialist in children's diseases. The gravediggers, who were taking a professional interest in showing me the sights, now took me to a different part of the cemetery, where, among other things, I saw the corner in which the postmen were interred; they had been shot, it appeared, because their jobs were wanted by other people. After this came what the gravediggers evidently regarded as the highlight. In the civil section, where non-Catholics and prisoners who had refused confession were buried, stood the tomb of the Protestant pastor whose crime was that he had kept a free school for poor children in the Cuesta Gomerez. Unhappy man, he had been well liked by the foreign residents, including those who were Catholics, but even a British consul's friendship could not save him. I observed that the tombstones here all had the same formula for the epitaph, saying "ceased to exist" instead of "died," and, at the end, "Your mother [sister, daughter] will not forget you." It would no doubt have been unwise to mention the unforgetfulness of brothers, sons, or fathers.

"All this is very interesting," I said, at length, "but the person I am looking for is not here. Perhaps you can tell me where he is buried. He is called Federico García Lorca."

"That is a famous name," said the elder of the gravediggers. "There is much talk about him."

"He is famous all over the world," I replied. "His poems are read from Buenos Aires to New York and London. Some of them have been translated into English."

"There you are!" exclaimed the gravedigger to his companion. "These foreigners know more about us than we know about ourselves. I tell you, there's as much knowledge in one of their little fingers as there is in the whole of our bodies. Compared to them, we're nothing."

"That's it," agreed his friend solemnly. "Just savages."

"You don't understand me," I said. "This man whose grave I am looking for was a friend of mine. When, many years ago, I lived in Granada, I used to know him."

"Ah, that makes a difference," the old man said. "Still, I must tell you that you've come to the wrong place. He is not here."

"I have been told that he is. Anyhow, I want to see the lists."

"They are at the office. But I warn you that his name is not on them. I have been through them all many times."

"What are they like?"

"Well, there is just a list of names with a number after each. When the name was not known, as often happened, there was written 'man' or 'woman.' "

"Perhaps he was one of those unknowns."

"No, he was not. I tell you he is buried somewhere else—at Viznar."

"Viznar?"

"Yes, in the trenches in the ravine. They shot him there."

"How do you know?"

"How is anything known? These things come out." And he refused to say any more about it.

In the office, I found the old caretaker alone, entering something in a ledger with a scratchy pen. I told him I was not satisfied that García Lorca's remains were in the bone pit and asked to see the books in which the names of those shot had been recorded.

"I cannot show them without permission," he said, glancing up at me sharply. "You must go to the military authorities."

"At least tell me if my friend's name is on the lists."

He looked at me through his glasses in his half-frightened, half-appealing way.

"No, señor, it is not. The person you are asking about was not buried here."

"Then he was buried somewhere else?"

"Evidently."

"At Viznar?"

His eyes met mine for a moment in an uncertain glance. Then, without a word, he made a slight inclination with that perpetually deferential body of his and turned away. I could see his thin, bent back, and the scruff of gray hair that ran down his neck under his dirty collar, as he scratched with his pen on the pages of the ledger. I went out.

The next two days were spent in making further inquiries. I had once known many people in Granada, and though some of them were dead or absent, there were others who were ready to tell me what they could. And whenever I asked about García Lorca, I heard the name Viznar, if any place was mentioned at all. Viznar is a small village a few miles away in the hills, and a *barranco,* or ravine, adjacent to it was one of the Falangist burial grounds. Such places are all over the country. But no one I met had visited the site, and the story of Lorca's being buried there remained hearsay. Further acquaintance with the two grave-diggers at the cemetery, however, showed me that they belonged to a sort of fraternity concerned with the things of the dead, and that they had access to information that was not available to other people. Also, they were without prejudices; their interest in these matters was professional. This inclined me to believe that when they said García Lorca was buried at Viznar, they had good reasons for thinking so.

A number of facts were clear. Lorca had arrived in Granada a day or two before the military rising, and, at the first news of this, had taken refuge in the house of a friend and fellow-poet, Luis Rosales, close to the cathedral. The circumstance that Rosales' brother, who also lived there, was a leading Falangist appeared to assure complete protection, yet a couple of days later, during a temporary absence of his hosts, a car full of armed men drew up at the door and carried him away. None of his friends ever saw him again.

For twelve years, Spanish censorship did not allow Lorca's name to be mentioned or his works to be published. Then, in December, 1948, José María Pemán, the leading publicist and author laureate of the regime, wrote an article in *ABC*, one of Madrid's foremost newspapers, decrying his murder as a crime against the nation by unknown persons. The reason for this change in the official attitude seems to have been that Lorca's many admirers in the Argentine had created a bias against the Franco regime that was affecting the commercial negotiations going on at the time between the two countries. The blame had therefore to be shifted from the leaders of the military rising and the Falange to certain irresponsible and criminal persons. But to what persons? Only one other segment of opinion was then allowed to exist in Spain—that of the clericals. The Falangist story, as it is usually told, is as follows: A day or two after the beginning of the rising, a rumor reached Granada that the playwright Benavente had been shot in Madrid by the Reds. A Catholic Conservative deputy to the Cortes, Ruiz Alonso, was sitting in a café with several friends. "Well, if they have killed Benavente," he exclaimed, "we have García Lorca. Why doesn't someone go out and fix him?" And so, like Fitzurse obeying Henry II's hint that Becket would be better dead, a couple of men got up and went out.

Now, there is nothing inherently improbable in such a story. García Lorca had scandalized the narrow-minded and provincial citizens of his town in the same way that Picasso scandalizes many people today. But there is more to be said about the motives for assassinating him than that. Lorca was not only a poet; he was also the brother-in-law of the Socialist mayor, Montesinos, and the intimate friend and collaborator of Fernando de los Ríos, the leading Socialist intellectual of Granada. Thousands were shot for less reason than this, and though Lorca had influential friends on the Right, he must have had even more enemies there, not only among the Catholic Conservatives but in the ranks of the Falange. So far as I was able to discover, all the *Escuadras Negras,* the Black Squads who carried out the shootings, wore Falangist insignia. And who, one may ask finally, would have dared to take him from the house of such a Falangist as Rosales unless he had the connivance and protection of other Falangists? Thus, there seemed no reason that García Lorca's death should not have taken place at a Falangist center like Viznar. The only point to be settled was—had it?

As it happened, I was able to obtain a strong corroboration of the gravediggers' assertion that it had. A friend gave me the name of a person well known in the city who, I was assured, could tell me the whole story. I contrived to meet him. My reasoning was quite sound, this person said. García Lorca had been shot in the *barranco* at Viznar, after being made to dig his own grave. He had been driven there straight from Rosales' house. There could be no possible doubt about it, my informant said, for he himself had spoken to a man who had been present and who had recognized Lorca. And he added other details. His serious manner convinced me that he was speaking the truth, and as he was not a clerical, there could be no question of his being actuated by political bias. "Among ourselves we don't talk of these things," he said, "but we haven't forgotten them. They lie at the bottom of our minds, and many people who have done things they should never have done are racked by fear and contrition. Those most deeply implicated find themselves cold-shouldered or tormented by hints and pointed allusions, and some have fallen ill or gone mad from brooding. And now it seems that Heaven is punishing Spain for the evil her sons have committed. On both sides, of course—on both sides."

The next step, clearly, was to go out to Viznar and see whatever was to be seen there. Since my expedition required speed and secrecy—for a visit to one of these burial places was, I fully realized by now, a delicate affair, possibly a dangerous one had I been a Spaniard—it was important that I should hire a driver who would not show too much curiosity about my movements. But to my dismay, the man I had chosen was at the last minute replaced by another driver, who was not only alert and intelligent but a strong supporter of the regime; though not a Falangist, he had been a chauffeur for some important general during the war. I should have to find some way of eluding his vigilance.

Outside Granada, the car left the main road and began to climb in sharp twists and curves between terraces of grain and olive trees. Soon we reached the village—a hamlet, really, of tall white houses crowding around the church.

"Where shall I stop?" asked the chauffeur.

"Here in the square," I answered. "I want to visit the cemetery, where a friend of mine is buried, and I will go on foot."

Silent with astonishment, the chauffeur looked around at me and then stopped the car.

"The cemetery is probably locked," he said.

"Then send someone to fetch the key."

He continued to stare at me for a moment, and then got out of the car, collared a small boy, and sent him off for the caretaker. At length, an old woman appeared, with the key in her hand.

"I'll come with you," the chauffeur said. But when he heard that the cemetery lay some distance from the road, he turned back reluctantly to guard his car.

The old woman and I followed a narrow path along the edge of one of the *bancales,* or stone-walled terraces, through drooping feminine olive trees and sun-struck grain and beans; below us on the left was the green, flat plain, with Fuente-Vaqueros in the distance. The old woman prattled away. Her mother, she told me, had always had a great devotion to the dead. Night and day, she had kept a lamp burning for them in the cemetery, and even when it rained, and even when snow fell, she would go there to tend it. "Ay, *Dios mio,*" she used to say, "if it is wet and cold for us, isn't it colder and wetter still for them? There they lie, *los pobrecillos,* out in that place with nothing to comfort them." Then, when she was dying, when she was about to set out on her last journey and join them, she had said to her daughter, "Ay, *hija mía,* how can I bear to die? For when I am gone, who will tend the lamp in the cemetery; who will look after the poor dead?" And so she, her daughter, had answered, "I will tend the lamp and look after the dead, please God, as long as I live." And her mother, hearing that, had died in peace. The guardian of the key went on to say that though she worked at a factory, at a wage of one peseta a day, she never failed to find time every evening to visit the cemetery and pray there. To her it meant more than the Church, more than the saints. She felt such pity for those poor dead, lying there so far from the village and its animation. Even when oil to keep the lamp burning was hard to get, she managed to find some. Eventually, she fell silent, but as she walked, she kept sighing and turning her beads and murmuring snatches of prayer, among which one caught a great many "*Ay, Ay*"s and "*Madre mía*"s and "*Pobrecillos*"s.

Soon we came to the cemetery, a little, high-walled enclosure. Inside was a commotion of mounds and hollows, with, here and there, a few cheap wooden crosses and artificial wreaths, mostly broken and dilapidated—the rubbish heap of a country where the only things ever thrown away as useless are dead bodies. The woman apologized: This was a poor village—the rich were taken for burial to Granada. And at once she began to pray again, interspersing her monotone with exclamations of how cold it was to come here on winter evenings, and yet what a small sacrifice this was to make to the Lord.

The time had come for me to say what I wanted.

"Listen," I said. "I have come here in search of the grave of a man who was shot as a Red during the first days of the war. Can you help me?"

She did not answer, so I repeated my request.

"There are three or four buried here," she finally muttered, and led the way to the place. Then, as I stood reading the names on the crosses, the impulse to talk became too great for her, and she told me their story. One day some Civil Guards had brought these men here in manacles and had shot them against the wall. But as soon as the Guards had left, one of the men, who had only been wounded, had begun to creep away. Along the hill he had gone, under the olive trees, dragging himself on his hands and knees and leaving a trail of blood on the ground. Someone had seen him and given word to the Guards, though, and they had brought him back and shot him again, this time dead. *Ay*, such a pity! The whole village had wept as though he were their own. Later, they heard that a pardon had come for him. But of what use, *Dios mío*, were pardons to him then? After many years, two women had come to visit his grave. Tall women, beautifully dressed in black from head to foot, and they had wept a great deal. And after they had finished weeping, they had prayed and had asked her to pray, too.

I now felt that I must put my cards on the table.

"My friend is not buried here but in the trenches in the *barranco*," I said. "Do you know where they are?"

"In the pits, you mean. *Ay, ay*, who doesn't know? But since those days no one has dared to go there."

"Will you tell me how I can find them?"

"They're quite close. I'll take you."

We were leaving the cemetery when a man wearing a brass-studded bandoleer slung diagonally across his chest appeared. He introduced himself as the *regidor* of the village municipality and asked, very politely, what my business was. I replied that I was looking for the grave of a friend who had been shot during the war. I wished, before returning to my country, to say a few prayers over it.

"Have you found it?" he asked.

"Not yet. It seems that he is buried in the pits."

The man did not speak for some moments. Then he said, "If you wish to go there, that is your affair. But you must excuse me if I do not accompany you. The *consejo* has no jurisdiction in such matters."

"I shall be there only a few minutes," I said, to reassure him.

"The fewer the better. *Vaya usted con Dios.*"

The old woman and I set off. After following the path for some time, I found that we were back on the main road, beyond the village. "Where does this road lead?" I asked.

"To the spring that is just beyond the *barranco*," replied the woman. "There it stops. That is why it is called the Camino de la Fuente [Spring]. In the days before the war, people walked along it on Sunday evenings and took the air. They drank water from the spring, for this water is famous all around these parts, and very fattening, and the children played there. But now no one goes along it, no one."

The last patch of cultivation was coming to an end, and the road began to plunge into the mountains. On our left, just below it, stood a large red house, ugly and new, and built, apparently, as a summer villa. It was known, the woman told me, as La Colonia. Before the military rising, it had been a sort of Brown House for the Falangists of Granada, where they had met and received training. They had also brought their girls there and danced. Then, when the war broke out, it had been put to a different use. Every night, three or four lorries had roared up the road with their loads of prisoners and had left them there. A Falangist priest was waiting to confess them, and the parish priest was fetched as well; poor man, he had had to be present—that was the regulation. Then they were taken down to the ravine to be—*Dios mío,* you understand—some by the light of the lorries' headlamps and some at dawn. Women, too. The *Escuadra Negra* (here the woman lowered her voice) stuck at nothing.

"And who dug the graves?"

"In the basement of the house they kept prisoners for work of that sort, and later on, so it was said, they shot them, too. *Ay, Dios mío,* what terrible things were done! To think that Christian men should do such terrible things!"

Ahead of us, the road twisted like a snake. It dipped into a ravine—the *barranco*—crossed over the now dry stream bed by a bridge, came out again, ran on a little way, and ended. All around us were bare, shaly slopes and occasional dry bushes. Below lay the green *vega* and its villages, among them the one where Federico had been born, and above us a mountain of harsh gray rock rose sheer, its summit crowned with stunted pines and pointed rock pinnacles. On one of these had been placed an iron cross.

A few minutes more and we had reached the bridge. As we drew near it, the woman ceased her chatter and began to mumble prayers and to tell her beads with increasing energy. A little side path led up the dry watercourse, and there, fifty yards on, was the place. It was a gentle slope of blue clay, scattered with rushes and thin sedge grasses growing in the deposit left by the freshets that ran when the stream was in spate. The entire area was pitted with hollows and dotted with low mounds, at the head of each of which had been placed a rough, unlettered stone. I began to count them, but gave up when I realized that the number ran into the hundreds.

"They buried them here in shallow trenches and then pushed earth over them," said the woman. "What a thing to do! Weren't they all sons of God, and Christians who crossed themselves as we do?" And she began to pray in a low tone: "Holy and Immaculate Virgin, be with us now and in the hour of our death. . . ."

As I stood there on the pitted clay, I heard a sound, and saw that my car had followed us and was drawn up near the bridge. The chauffeur had got out and, to the evident alarm of the woman, was making his way along the path toward us. However, when he saw me standing motionless with bared head, he stopped and removed his hat, too.

I waited, trying to fix the scene in my mind. In front was the red, shaly side of the *barranco*—just one little sample of the interminable barren mountain slopes of this country; on the right, visible through the open end of the ravine, lay the green *vega*, with the Sierra de Elvira rising, like a volcanic island, out of it. Above, the mountain. Such had been the poet's last view, as the dawn rose in brightening circles in the sky and the cock crows floated up from the plain, sounding like their own echoes. I picked a blue grape hyacinth, the only flower growing there among the rushes, and came away.

✦

GERALD BRENAN   Born in England in 1894, historian, journalist, writer of travel books, he is intimately acquainted with Spain and its people.

"A Search for the Poet's Tomb" (1950) The style, though simple, captures the color, excitement, and poignance of the search for Lorca's grave; yet the narrative is profound as well as immediate. The author has a responsive eye and delicate ear, and he skillfully uses dialogue to pace and punctuate his account.

✦

1. *How and why does the author recurrently contrast life and death?* 2. *Is it significant that Lorca was a poet rather than, say, a banker?* 3. *In what ways is this essay both more and less than a guidebook to a section of Spain?*

JOHN F. KENNEDY

Inaugural Address

January 20, 1961

We observe today not a victory of party but a celebration of freedom, symbolizing an end as well as a beginning, signifying renewal as well as change. For I have sworn before you and Almighty God the same solemn oath our forebears prescribed nearly a century and three-quarters ago.

The world is very different now. For man holds in his mortal hands the power to abolish all forms of human poverty and all forms of human life. And yet the same revolutionary belief for which our forebears fought is still at issue around the globe, the belief that the rights of man come not from the generosity of the state but from the hand of God.

We dare not forget today that we are the heirs of that first revolution. Let the word go forth from this time and place, to friend and foe alike, that the torch has been passed to a new generation of Americans, born in this century, tempered by war, disciplined by a hard and bitter peace, proud of our ancient heritage, and unwilling to witness or permit the slow undoing of those human rights to which this nation has always been committed, and to which we are committed today at home and around the world.

Let every nation know, whether it wishes us well or ill, that we shall pay any price, bear any burden, meet any hardship, support any friend, oppose any foe to assure the survival and the success of liberty.

This much we pledge—and more.

To those old allies whose cultural and spiritual origins we share, we pledge the loyalty of faithful friends. United, there is little we cannot do in a host of co-operative ventures. Divided, there is little we can do, for we dare not meet a powerful challenge at odds and split asunder.

To those new states whom we welcome to the ranks of the free, we pledge our word that one form of colonial control shall not have passed away merely to be replaced by a far more iron tyranny. We shall not always expect to find them supporting our view. But we shall always hope to find them strongly supporting their own freedom, and to remember that, in the past, those who foolishly sought power by riding the back of the tiger ended up inside.

To those peoples in the huts and villages of half the globe struggling to break the bonds of mass misery, we pledge our best efforts to help them help themselves, for whatever period is required, not because the Communists may be doing it, not because we seek their votes, but because it is right. If a free society cannot help the many who are poor, it cannot save the few who are rich.

To our sister republics south of our border, we offer a special pledge: to convert our good words into good deeds, in a new alliance for progress, to assist free men and free governments in casting off the chains of poverty. But this peaceful revolution of hope cannot become the prey of hostile powers. Let all our neighbors know that we shall join with them to oppose aggression or subversion anywhere in the Americas. And let every other power know that this hemisphere intends to remain the master of its own house.

To that world assembly of sovereign states, the United Nations, our last best hope in an age where the instruments of war have far outpaced the instruments of peace, we renew our pledge of support: to prevent it from becoming merely a forum for invective, to strengthen its shield of the new and the weak, and to enlarge the area in which its writ may run.

Finally, to those nations who would make themselves our adversary, we offer not a pledge but a request: that both sides begin anew the quest for peace, before the dark powers of destruction unleashed by science engulf all humanity in planned or accidental self-destruction.

We dare not tempt them with weakness. For only when our arms are sufficient beyond doubt can we be certain beyond doubt that they will never be employed.

But neither can two great and powerful groups of nations take comfort from our present course—both sides overburdened by the cost of modern weapons, both rightly alarmed by the steady spread of the deadly atom, yet both racing to alter that uncertain balance of terror that stays the hand of mankind's final war.

So let us begin anew, remembering on both sides that civility is not a sign of weakness, and sincerity is always subject to proof. Let us never negotiate out of fear, but let us never fear to negotiate.

Let both sides explore what problems unite us instead of belaboring those problems which divide us.

Let both sides, for the first time, formulate serious and precise proposals for the inspection and control of arms, and bring the absolute power to destroy other nations under the absolute control of all nations.

Let both sides seek to invoke the wonders of science instead of its terrors. Together let us explore the stars, conquer the deserts, eradicate disease, tap the ocean depths and encourage the arts and commerce.

Let both sides unite to heed in all corners of the earth the command of Isaiah to "undo the heavy burdens . . . [and] let the oppressed go free."

And if a beachhead of co-operation may push back the jungle of suspicion, let both sides join in creating a new endeavor, not a new balance of power, but a new world of law, where the strong are just and the weak secure and the peace preserved.

All this will not be finished in the first one hundred days. Nor will it be finished in the first one thousand days, nor in the life of this Administration, nor even perhaps in our lifetime on this planet. But let us begin.

In your hands, my fellow citizens, more than mine, will rest the final success or failure of our course. Since this country was founded, each generation of Americans has been summoned to give testimony to its national loyalty. The graves of young Americans who answered the call to service surround the globe.

Now the trumpet summons us again—not as a call to bear arms, though arms we need; not as a call to battle, though embattled we are; but a call to bear the burden of a long twilight struggle, year in and year out, "rejoicing in hope, patient in tribulation," a struggle against the common enemies of man: tyranny, poverty, disease and war itself.

Can we forge against these enemies a grand and global alliance, North and South, East and West, that can assure a more fruitful life for all mankind? Will you join in that historic effort?

In the long history of the world, only a few generations have been granted the role of defending freedom in its hour of maximum danger. I do not shrink from this responsibility; I welcome it. I do not believe that any of us would exchange places with any other people or any other generation. The energy, the faith, the devotion which we bring to this endeavor will light our country and all who serve it, and the glow from that fire can truly light the world.

And so, my fellow Americans, ask not what your country can do for you; ask what you can do for your country.

My fellow citizens of the world, ask not what America will do for you, but what together we can do for the freedom of man.

Finally, whether you are citizens of America or citizens of the world, ask of us here the same high standards of strength and sacrifice which we ask of you. With a good conscience our only sure reward, with history the final judge of our deeds, let us go forth to lead the land we love, asking His blessing and His help, but knowing that here on earth God's work must truly be our own.

JOHN F. KENNEDY   Born in Brookline, Massachusetts in 1917; assassinated in Dallas, Texas in 1963; author and thirty-fifth President of the United States.

Inaugural Address (1961) President Kennedy's Address illustrates the fact that speeches of important leaders have to be as carefully written as the most formal essay. Part of his rhetorical effectiveness is the result of a strongly accentuated rhythm, a rhythm which is stately and impressive. One could almost do a syllable count, matching phrase for phrase, clause for clause, construction for construction. To create a sense of inevitable logic, the President uses frequent and emphatic guideposts: e.g., not . . . but . . . for; then . . . for . . . and yet; We . . . Let us . . . let us . . . let us.

1. What qualities made this speech exciting to many Americans? 2. Is it still relevant? 3. What are the traits which show that it was meant to be heard rather than read?

The Big Bite—April, 1963

The rite of spring is in the odor of the air. The nerve of winter which enters one's nose comes a long far way like a scythe from the peak of mountains. To the aged it can feel like a miasma up from the midnight corridors of a summer hotel, empty and out of season. Winter breath has the light of snow when the sun is on it, or the bone chill of a vault. But spring air comes up from the earth—at worst it can be the smell of new roots in bad slimy ground, at best the wine of late autumn frost is released from the old ice. Intoxication to the nostril, as if a filbert of fine sherbet had melted a sweet way into the tongue back of the throat down from the teeth. Spring is the season which marks the end of dread—so it is the season of profound dread for those who do not lose their fear.

Looking back on the winter and fall, one thinks of a long season of dread. There was that week toward the end of October when the world stood like a playing card on edge, and those of us who lived in New York wondered if the threat of war was like an exceptional dream which would end in a happy denouement (as indeed it did) or whether the events of each day would move, ante raised on ante, from boats on a collision course to invasions of Cuba, from threats of nuclear reprisal to the act itself, the Götterdämmerung of New York. Or would the end come in-

Reprinted by permission of G. P. Putnam's Sons from *The Presidential Papers* by Norman Mailer. Copyright 1960, 1961, 1962, 1963 by Norman Mailer.

stantly without prevision or warning, we would wonder as well, were we now heroes in a movie by Chaplin, was our house at the edge of the cliff, would we open the door and step into an abyss? There was dread that week. One looked at the buildings one passed and wondered if one was to see them again. For a week everyone in New York was like a patient with an incurable disease—would they be dead tomorrow or was it life for yet another year?

We sat that week in New York thinking of little. When movies are made of the last week on earth, the streets thrive with jazz, the juveniles are unrestrained, the adults pillage stores, there is rape, dancing, caterwauling laughter, sound of sirens and breaking glass, the roller coaster of a brave trumpet going out on its last ride. But we sat around. All too many watched television. Very few of us went out at night. The bars were half empty. The talk was quiet. One did not have the feeling great lovers were meeting that week, not for the first time nor for the last. An apathy came over our city. A muted and rather empty hour which lasted for a week. If it all blew up, if it all came to so little, if our efforts, our loves, our crimes added up to no more than a sudden extinction in a minute, in a moment, if we had not even time before the bomb (as civilians did once) to throw one quick look at some face, some trinket, some child for which one had love, well, one could not complain. That was our fate. That was what we deserved. We did not march in the street or shake our fists at the sky. We waited in our burrow like drunks in the bullpen pacing the floor of our existence, waiting for court in the morning while the floor was littered with the bile that came up in our spit and the dead butts of our dying lung's breath. Facing eternity we were convicts hanging on the dawn. There was no lust in the streets nor any defiance with which to roar at eternity. We were guilty.

We gave our freedom away a long time ago. We gave it away in all the revolutions we did not make, all the acts of courage we found a way to avoid, all the roots we destroyed in fury at that past which still would haunt our deeds. We divorced ourselves from the materials of the earth, the rock, the wood, the iron ore; we looked to new materials which were cooked in vats, long complex derivatives of urine which we called plastic. They had no odor of the living or of what once had lived, their touch was alien to nature. They spoke of the compromise of incompatibles. The plastic which had invaded our bathrooms, our kitchens, our clothing, our toys for children, our tools, our containers, our floor coverings, our cars, our sports, the world of our surfaces was the simple embodiment of social cowardice. We had tried to create a world in which all could live even if none could breathe. There had been a vast collective social effort in the twentieth century— each of us had tried to take back a critical bit more from existence than we had given to it.

There was a terror to contemplate in the logic of our apathy. Because if there was a God and we had come from Him, was it not the first possibility that each of us had a mission, one of us to create, another to be brave, a third to love, a fourth to work, a fifth to be bold, a sixth to be all of these. Was it not possible that we were sent out of eternity to become more than we had been?

What then if we had become less? There was a terror in the logic. Because if there was a God, there was also in first likelihood a Devil. If the God who sent us out demanded our courage, what would be most of interest to the other but our cowardice?

Which of us could say that nowhere in the secret debates of our dreams or the nightmare of open action, in those stricken instants when the legs are not as brave as the mind or the guts turn to water, which of us could say that never nor nowhere had we struck a pact with the Devil and whispered, Yes, let us deaden God, let Him die within me, it is too frightening to keep Him alive, I cannot bear the dread.

That is why we did not roar into the street and shout that it was unnatural for mankind to base its final hope on the concealed character of two men, that it was unnatural to pray that Kennedy and Khrushchev taken together were more good than evil. What an ignoble suppliant hope for civilization to rest its security on two men, no more, two men. What had happened to the dream of the world's wealth guarded by the world's talent, the world's resource?

We sat in apathy because most of us, in the private treacherous dialogues of our sleep, had turned our faith away from what was most vital in our mind, and had awakened in depression. We had drawn back in fright from ourselves, as if in our brilliance lay madness, and beyond the horizon dictated by others was death. We had been afraid of death. We had been afraid of death as no generation in the history of mankind has been afraid. None of us would need to scream as eternity recaptured our breath—we would be too deep in hospital drugs. We would die with deadened minds and twilight sleep. We had turned our back on the essential terror of life. We believed in the Devil, we hated nature.

So we watched the end approach with apathy. Because if it was God we had betrayed and the vision with which He had sent us forth, if our true terror now was not of life but of what might be waiting for us in death, then how much easier we might find it to be blasted into eternity deep in the ruin of ten million others, how much better indeed if the world went with us, and death was destroyed as completely as life. Yes, how many of the millions in New York had a secret prayer: that whomever we thought of as God be exploded with us, and Judgment cease.

✦

NORMAN MAILER   Born in Long Branch, New Jersey in 1923, author of three novels and three collections of essays, his *The Naked and the Dead* may well be the best American novel written about World War II.

"The Big Bite—April, 1963" (1963) In this angry analysis Mailer employs the rhetorical devices of oratory (e.g., series of questions, the editorial we), and his voice, equipped with a fine sense of rhythm and modulation, seems to be speaking to and for a large group. The style is unusually varied in its syntax and diction, and consistently hard hitting.

✦

1. *What constitutes Mailer's Devil?* 2. *How do the essay's shifts in tone contribute to the argument?*

Foreground

D. W. BROGAN

A World They Never Made

"A world they never made." I am fully aware of the dangers inherent in applying to a people of one hundred seventy millions
a poet's insight into personal psychology. And in beginning my
discussion of the world in which the American people to their
great discomfort find themselves, I am not professing to expound
an exact or even an approximately verifiable science. I am attempting something both more humble and more bold, the calling
of the attention of Americans to what I, a sympathetic foreigner
but nevertheless a foreigner, think is the first cause of their discomfort, the first cause of the degree of suspicion, apprehension,
bewilderment with which many, many Americans regard the
world of 1959 and the world that they see lying beyond 1959.

To begin with, it is a world they never made. In making that
judgment on the contemporary world the average American is
not indulging in more than the usual human allowance of per-
missible shorthand. In one sense the United States is most decidedly one of the makers of the modern world; in some respects
the United States is the chief maker of the modern world. But
in the sense in which I am using the metaphor, the poet's insight,
the world that the American today is forced to regard and fear
is one that he feels little responsibility for making and little con-
sequent capacity for understanding. Not only is it a world defying

his sense of both what is reasonable and what is right. It is a world that somehow or other has replaced the other, better, happier, more harmless world that lay alongside the United States, in few relations with it but those relations friendly, hopeful, innocent.

The American does not like the world in which he finds himself (who does?), but he dislikes it the more because it has replaced a world that may indeed never have existed. It certainly did not exist in the simple innocent form in which the American tradition remembers it, but it was not totally mythical and had some if not all of the attractiveness that the tradition lends it. The American today, it seems to me, has slowly accepted the fact that this is a case of Paradise Lost, not just Paradise Mislaid, and naturally he laments his exile from Eden. Naturally he fears the flaming sword that sweeps between him and the innocent garden of his youth.

It is time, I am sure, to leave metaphor, to leave poetry, and to try to present in more prosaic terms the nature of the present dilemma that perplexes the American, the nature of some of the varying characteristics of the world in which the American has to live. What is the first that has to be stressed, the first American disillusionment?

It is, I think, the discovery that progress is an ambiguous term. All of us, or most of us, know that progress—the view that the world more or less inevitably and easily got better and better—is a novel idea in the history of the human mind. It seemed more natural until quite recently in our human story to look to the past, to a golden age in which mankind lived happily under the benevolent protection of the "laws of nature and of nature's God" for the epoch of human felicity. I do not know that at any time in past history mankind thought it was living in the golden age or even in the silver age. At best it was the age of iron that each generation saw itself embedded in. But in the past things were better till we paid for "the crude apple that corrupted Eve."

It was against this traditional pessimism of the human race, reflected in legend all over the earth, that the idea of progress—the idea that the present was better than the past, the future better than the present—was a protest and one that since, say, the late fifteenth century began to captivate the Western mind.

To find the line of progress, to move along that line, to cooperate with the winning forces of destiny, to welcome with open hands the gifts of nature, given the more lavishly when those hands were capable of using and developing the gifts—these were the first duties of modern man. And if man did his duty he would be rewarded from a horn of plenty of an unprecedented size and generosity.

> The world's great age begins anew,
> The golden years return.

They return; but far more golden than in the past, for Shelley saw the future of the free man in the free society as much more attractive than the golden age of the Greeks. We stand on the shoulders of the ancients, said Bacon, and naturally we see farther and reach higher. I could multiply the citations but I need hardly do so. The theme is the commonplace of our Western tradition, finding some of its most eloquent expression in America in the Declaration of Independence, some of its most adroit and plausible exemplification in the writings and achievements of Franklin. "He snatched the lightning from heaven, and the sceptre from tyrants." So wrote Turgot of the American who, as politician and technological innovator, best justified American hopes at the birth of the American Republic. Franklin, Jefferson, the names say a lot.

But more important than the great names of great men is a fact about American life that I want to emphasize now and shall have occasion to emphasize again. It was not only the great Americans who believed in progress, it was all Americans. This country was born in the age of progress, baptized in the religion of progress, created and peopled by men and women who believed in progress, in some amelioration for themselves, in more for their children; it was in hope as well as in resentment and rebellion that they had crossed the Atlantic to a new world that, often unconsciously, they knew they had to make and resolved, again often unconsciously, to make better. Many attempts have been made, some of them profound and just, to characterize the American people. Surely one of their marks, until very recent times, has been that they have been a people of hope, of believers in amelioration. They have been a people for whom the bonds of tradition have not been allowed to justify inertia, the acceptance of visibly inferior conditions simply because that was the way of the fathers.

This hopefulness of the American view of life can be illustrated in many ways. Professor Perry Miller has shown us how the early American Calvinists, grim, fatalistic, pessimistic as they may seem, as they must seem to preachers of "togetherness," were in fact by the standards of seventeenth-century Europe optimistic, ill-disciplined, cheerfully inconsistent. With them, as with Dr. Johnson's would-be philosopher friend, "cheerfulness would keep breaking in." The new world offered new possibilities and "no man who had been born in Boston needed to be born again."

It would be possible to cast shadows on this picture. The greatest of Americans, that is, the man I consider the greatest of Americans, had a strong streak of pessimism in his nature. As much as Dr. Reinhold Niebuhr, Lincoln had a sense of man's essentially tragic situation. So it is expressed in that great but not 100 per cent American document, the Second Inaugural; so it is revealed in Lincoln's quotation from *Macbeth* at the moment of his triumphant return from captured Richmond:

> Duncan is in his grave;
> After life's fitful fever he sleeps well.

But the greatest men of a nation are too great to be fully or merely representative and the representative American has, until recently, seen the story of the human race as on the whole a success story and one part of it as undoubtedly a success story, the history of the United States, the creation here, on this continent, of the last, best hope of earth. And if melodramatic pessimism is a luxury Americans could allow themselves because they did not really doubt that theirs was a success story, the pessimism that I seem to note today is not merely melodramatic; it is real, alarmed, and shows for the first time a realization that the human story may go wrong, that the old pessimistic cyclical theory of human destiny may be the true one—and that the American people are inextricably involved in the common, dangerous, and only intermittently hopeful destiny of the human race. For the American is beginning to realize that he can neither remake the world according to the American plan (for many Americans, necessarily God's plan) nor contract out. If the human race would obey or imitate, all would be well soon, if not now. But the hope of obedience or imitation is weak if not dead.

This, it seems to me, is the first ground for American discontent and alarm. The world is not visibly going the American way and is still less visibly content to let the Americans go their way, "the world forgetting, by the world forgot."

What were the American hopes that have been shattered? The first is that the United States having made herself by her exertions would save the world by her example. How deep that faith was, how justified, a cursory glance at history abundantly illustrates. In an international as well as in a national sense, America had erected a standard to which all good men could and, it was confidently believed, *would* repair. It was not for nothing that the founders of the Republic adopted a proud Latin motto: "Novus ordo seclorum," a new order of the ages. (You will find this device on one of the three sacred documents of the Republic: not on the Declaration, not on the Constitution, but on the dollar bill).

In a world still sunk in tyranny, empty tradition, political and religious servility, the new Republic shone, free from the sins of the past, bright with the greatest hopes known in the upward history of man-upward, for no one, in America at least, doubted that, as an American poet was to put it with great effect if bad Latin, the banner with the strange device bore the inspiring motto "excelsior." It is easy to make fun of the poem, of the poet, of the sentiment, but to do so is to sin against the spirit of America— and to fail to understand both the greatness of the hopes and the present chill of the fears.

It was not a matter of mere national pride or conceit. The virtuous republic of Washington was a model, not a mere pattern laid up in heaven but taking form in the remote American forest. The very hostility of conservative thinkers like de Maistre was proof of the fascination of the new state and the new society. Hopes dashed by the course of the French Revolution came to life again as the mild rule of Washington and then of Jefferson was contrasted with the Reign of Terror and the baleful, comet-like career of Napoleon. The great news was out; a free and orderly society could be created and mankind had far more hope of happiness open to him than had, until this happy day, been

dreamed of. Again I could multiply the instances, from the re-
pentance of his early hostility by William Cobbett to Goethe's
famous praise of the new society:

Amerika du hast es besser.

But chronology supplies the most adequate example. It is a
hundred years since the most profound and permanently valuable foreign commentator on the American scene and the
American system died. And one of the lessons that Alexis de
Tocqueville wanted to teach Europe—and especially France—
was that the possibilities of human happiness, if not of exceptional human achievement, were greater than Europeans, especially conservative Europeans regretting the old order that
America condemned by her success, had ever admitted to be
possible. That way the Western world was going and that way,
drab or dull as it might be, the greatest happiness of the greatest
number lay.

On the shining picture a most ominous shadow lay—slavery.
So the Civil War was both the punishment of American sin and
the justification of faith in America. The victory of the North was
a triumph for the cause of human freedom and dignity and John
Bright, addressing a great meeting in favor of extending the
franchise, interrupted his oration to give out the simple but meaningful message, "Richmond has fallen." So Walt Whitman was
hailed by Swinburne; so all liberal Europe (including that semi-
representative figure, Karl Marx) welcomed the triumph of the
Union. And the victors felt—and rightly felt—that this triumph
not only was theirs but was the most manifest proof that faith in
human progress and in a kindly destiny for mankind was justified.

That faith was naïve, so naïve that a quite different triumph,
that of Bismarck's Prussia, was welcomed as a victory for the same
good cause and the unification of Italy was welcomed both
because national unity was a good thing and because it meant a
decline, perhaps a fatal decline, in the power of Giant Pope. And
the homage of imitation and admiration was not confined to
statesmen and poets. It was made more manifest in the floods of
immigrants who poured in, the greatest folk movement of which
we have any adequate record. The Statue of Liberty was no more
eloquent of America's role in the upward spiral of mankind than

was Castle Garden and then Ellis Island. Every immigrant was a vote for America and the American way of life. It is my belief that the memory of this golden day still colors the American attitude toward the outside world and that some of the average American's discontent with that outside world springs from a deep regret that those days of automatic leadership for all the advancing peoples of the world seem to be over. They have of course been over for a long time. It was pointless to stress the sentiments of the poem of Emma Lazarus when the United States no longer welcomed the poor and the oppressed in the old, generous and, if you like, reckless way. Moreover, as Socialist criticism of the capitalist order grew in strength in Europe, the determinedly un-Socialist economy and political system of the United States became a stumbling block, a stone of offense to the makers and shakers of Europe. The United States became less the country that had freed the slaves than the country that had hanged the Chicago anarchists, less the country of Lincoln than of the Standard Oil Company. And it was not only on the Left that the American image lost some of its dazzling brilliance.

The success story of Bismarck's Germany to some degree offset the success story of the United States. If it was Commodore Perry who forced the Japanese to go to school, they went to school at least as much to Prussia as to the United States or to Britain. Nor was this the only disillusionment. The formal imitation of American constitutional methods in Latin America gave only ambiguously gratifying results. The innocence with which Louis Kossuth had been hailed after the failure of the Hungarian rising of 1849 was hard to recapture when the finally triumphant Magyars turned out to be oppressors themselves.

The innocent, egalitarian farmer's republic had become the greatest industrial power in the world with all the problems of social order and justice that this dangerous promotion involved. America was virtuous; America was right; America was promises; but America was not quite so innocent, not quite so conscious of deserved and spontaneous admiration.

The year 1914 was, it is now easy to see, the watershed. Then began our dangerous, disorderly, unpredictable world. Then the faith in automatic progress received its first, perhaps its greatest, blow. Yet to the innocent American, on the farm, in the corner store, in the White House, the lesson of 1914 seemed plain. America had it better; the murderous quarrels of Europe had not been and should not be exported. America should stay above the battle and with malice toward none should only step in to bind up the nations' wounds. Such was the high ambition of the most famous New Jersey statesman, and who can think that Woodrow Wilson was wrong in his first ambition, which was to be a mediator and not a victor? It is not my place to discuss or decide why that ambition failed and Wilson had to combine the two so different roles of being the head of a victorious coalition and the creator of a just and lasting peace. My purpose is to remind you that the Wilson of the last months of 1918, the first months of 1919, was the last American to revive in Europe (and outside Europe) the old faith in the good faith, the healing power, the moral superiority of the United States. With him there crashed a faith that has never been fully restored.

And that crash was all the more important because a new and baleful star had arisen, for surely the most important result of the First World War was not the Russian Revolution, that might have come anyway, but the Bolshevik Revolution, which I believe was made possible only by the war—and by the Allied victory, for that saved the Bolsheviks from destruction by the Germans.

The Russian Revolution is so much one of the turning points in world history that I need do no more than remind you of the fact, but the point I want to stress is that it had, among other results, one highly relevant for our purpose, the setting up of a rival and deeply hostile center of attraction to that still exercised by the United States.

In 1919 the American people made a desperate and totally hopeless effort to return to the peace that they had known yesterday. How quickly the crusading fervor wore off! How soon it was implausibly asserted that all American policy need do was to reverse the sins and errors of 1914–1919! Let America mind her own business; let her remember in a phrase of President Coolidge's (that may have been misunderstood) that "the business of the United States is business." Much could be said about this policy, if that it can be called. But it had one fatal fault. It ignored the fact that the world of 1919 was a world that owed its shape very largely to the power and policy of the United States. That policy may have been an error, that power may have been wrongly asserted, but the fact was there. The new and disillusioning world that the American people turned their back on was a world in whose making the American people had had a great share. For the sin of 1914 the innocent Republic had had no share of guilt. For the world of 1919–1939 the Republic, still in its own estimation innocent, had if not guilt at least a share in its creation.

Nothing could be further from my intentions than to indict American policy or the American people. It is easy to see how tempting it was to withdraw from the sinful outer world and to give only such leadership as was compatible with formal irresponsibility. But America had a share in the responsibility for the destruction of the hopes of 1919. Just before the outbreak of the second war an intelligent Frenchman, said that *all* the great powers involved—Britain, France, Germany, Russia, America— had committed enough sins, positively and negatively, to account for the disastrous state of the world. Perhaps the sins of the United States were mainly negative, but sins there were. But the American people did not see it in that light. They saw a series of undeserved slurs, a mass of undeserved hate, a degree of unprecedented ingratitude descend on the innocent Republic. They saw, with bitterness, what had happened to democracy in the world that they had hoped to make safe for it. They forgot, as Chesterton said at the time, that the world could not simply be made safe for democracy, for it is a dangerous trade.

Yet the contrast between impoverished Europe and booming America, if it fed hatred, envy and malice, also bred reluctant admiration. Europe, even the Soviet Union, was ready to go to school to the masters of them that knew. André Siegfried declared that the world would have to choose between Gandhi and Henry Ford, and in a more material, less ideologically impressive fashion the United States was for a brief moment, again, the last best hope of earth. Then came the catastrophe from which, in my opinion, American prestige has not fully recovered and whose reverberations still weaken her world position.

It is again far from my intention to assess responsibility for the smash of 1929 or for the long and slow haul of the American economy out of the slough of despond into which the American people were plunged and in which they, in a sense, remained until the coming of the Second World War. What I am concerned with is the impact on the outer world and the rebounding of that impact on the American view of the outer world.

It seems to me to matter little whether Europe made the smash or whether the United States pursued its own destruction. Seen from the outside, what mattered was that the great exemplar of a liberal economy had failed, that the policy of abundance had failed, that the secret of high wages (as it had been optimistically described) had been lost.

The decline in European faith in the American political way of life that had occurred so precipitately in 1919–1920 was followed by an equally precipitate decline in faith in the American economic way of life. All the radical, Socialist fear and suspicion of American capitalism was revived; it was reinforced, made more formidable by the rise of communism, now the doctrine, the political weapon of a great state. Everywhere democratic values plummeted down like so many overpriced stocks. In the crash the feeble new democratic institutions and habits of Germany and Japan were smashed as the feeble democratic institutions of Italy had been smashed in the previous decade. Whether on the Left or on the Right, the day seemed to be to the authoritarian way of life. The answer lay not in free cooperation but in some form or other of dictatorship. True, in the first years of the New Deal the spectacle of a democratic leader taking the initiative was a refreshing novelty. But the successes of the New Deal were limited and not easily imitable in countries with less abundant resources. Franklin D. Roosevelt remained a symbolic leader in a world of dictators or of drab and timid parliamentary chiefs like Chamberlain and Daladier, but the American people were too committed to isolation for him to do more than exemplify principles and moral passions. He could advise; he could not lead, even if he had been determined to lead—which it is not quite certain that he was.

The world that drifted to war or was rapidly pushed to war (I think the latter is the truer view) was a world for which the United States, by her immediate past and by her power, had a great responsibility but in which her role was played ineffectually and evasively. As far as the second war was "the unnecessary war," as Sir Winston Churchill was later to call it, the main fault for not avoiding it must fall on the rulers—and peoples—of Britain and France. But there is some American share to be noted and I am convinced that much of the faith that the American people later put into the United Nations came from a sense of inadequacy and guilt in the recent past.

In the Second World War the role of the United States was curiously reversed. In the first war the American material contribution, although decisive, was limited in time and extent. In the second it was immense in time, in extent, in impact. It can be justly said that only for the United States was the Second World War truly a world war, that the United States alone threw her massive power into all theaters of war and that power was an indispensable condition of victory in all parts of the globe. It is true that the United States did not suffer as much as Russia or Britain—not to speak of Germany. But the world had an unforgettable lesson in the realities of American power. That lesson has not been forgotten.

On the ideological side the picture is not quite so impressive. True, President Roosevelt had difficulties to face that did not face President Wilson. He had an ally in the Soviet Union as embarrassing, at times, as the czardom would have been to Wilson had it survived. The very violence of the defiance of the democratic dogma by Nazi Germany was a kind of handicap. Imperial Germany and Republican America had more in common than had the Third Reich and the United States, and whether the policy of "unconditional surrender" was a mistake or not it was a natural mistake. But for these and other reasons, some personal and some political, the United States in the Second World War was not the admitted and solitary center of an ideological crusade. It was not in F.D.R.'s power, adroit orator as he was, to stir the masses of the world as Wilson had done and perhaps Wilson's successor was too conscious of Wilson's mistakes and Wilson's fate to wish to imitate him. Then death came before Roosevelt's policy was tested, before he could use the fund of good will and trust that he had accumulated.

Whatever the reasons, the United States in 1945 stood rather on a pinnacle of material power than on a peak of political leadership. Nothing in a sense was further from the minds of the American people than a desire to mount the peak of leadership. Innocently, the American people knew that they had won and deserved victory and believed that they had won, as they had deserved, peace. The new United Nations, the amicable continuance of wartime relations with the Allies (of whom the cunning British were as much to be feared as the rude Russians), would deal with the urgent questions. Meantime the American people could busily beat swords into plowshares or their equivalent and resume the slow upward climb to the old prosperity that had been temporarily lost. That climb proved easier and quicker than had been feared. What proved harder was the seeking of peace and the ensuring of it.

There was no question in 1945 of the United States not being a maker of the world of 1945. If the American public underestimated the difficulty and the duration of the task that fell on it, it did not for a moment deny that it had a share and a responsibility for the state of the world and for its salvation. Indeed, one of the most remarkable and comforting and creditable signs of the maturity of the American people has been found in the fact that no challenge put to them since 1945 has found them wanting in either generosity or courage. Even wisdom has been in more abundant supply than veterans of 1919 might have feared.

But it was soon found that virtue and good will were not enough. For one thing, they were supposed to call out equivalent virtues in other people and they did not conspicuously do so. The liberated and saved countries of Western Europe were barely capable of mere survival. The great power of Eastern Europe, in its most desperate need, yet preferred power to plenty and showed neither will to true accommodation of interests nor capacity to understand the real roots of American policy.

There were faults on both sides, faults committed during the war and after the war. But in 1947, contemplating the world around it, the American people, whatever their grievances against the foresight or lack of it of their rulers, could truthfully acquit themselves of any desire to exploit victory or to impose their will. If they preached and in a sense practiced and imposed democracy in Germany and Japan, they did so in good faith and in no spirit of revenge. If they were disappointed in their efforts, the disappointments were often taken philosophically or humorously.

The Teahouse of the August Moon was a fable applicable in more places than Okinawa. On the whole, the results of American leadership and munificence in both Germany and Japan gratified the American people, who took possibly too complacent a view of their success as re-educators.

It was elsewhere that the American public suffered its great disillusionment and had fostered in it that attitude of resentful wonder at the outside world that is part of the American problem today. First of all, America was faced with the paradox not merely of ingratitude but of wrongly directed gratitude. It was not only that so many millions in France, in Italy, in Britain even, did not sufficiently appreciate what they owed to American power and generosity. It was that they felt or professed to feel more gratitude to the remote Soviet Union that had no doubt been a main force in bringing down the Nazi power but had not freed Paris or Rome from the Nazi forces or London from the daily menace of V-1 and V-2.

I shall certainly make no attempt to justify this error of morals and of judgment. Nor can I do more than allude to some reasons for it. All of Europe was exhausted, morally as well as physically debilitated, and full of more or less conscious resentment of the apparent prosperity and immunity of the United States. The contrast between New York and London in 1947 was dramatic enough for anyone who went to America frequently. To those who only knew of the earthly paradise by report it was humiliating, maddening or inexplicable. Or it was explicable simply. The Americans had taken the chance of the war vastly to enrich themselves. And they could only have done that at the expense of their allies. The old sullen Socialist suspicion of American capitalism revived. The contrast between the austerity of England, the gross inequalities of well-being in France and Italy, and what was rumored of the paradise over the ocean was more than human nature could bear. What the Americans had they owed to others. It was their duty, their interest to share it. Instead of being grateful for such acts of generosity as the Marshall Plan, Europeans should rather praise themselves for their magnanimity in letting the Americans do their duty! In this period I more than once recalled Napoleon's explanation of why the brothers and sisters whom he had made kings and princes were so ungrateful. "They think I have cheated them of their due share in the inheritance of our father the late King." So much of Europe felt regarding the plenty and the bounty of the United States.

It would be wrong to attach too much importance to this European attitude (which was far from universal) or to the natural American resentment of it. The Marshall Plan succeeded; Western Europe was saved from ruin and from communism and if the rescued were not adequately grateful or adequately conscious of the abyss from which they had been saved, the Americans were and are a pragmatic people. They had done what they set out to do and, although it would have been nice to be thanked for it, success is better than gratitude. And if the European nations by 1950 were in a position to answer back and be sassy, that was proof of the success of American policy. Like the parent of a troublesome teen-ager, the American as taxpayer and voter felt a mixture of pride and annoyance. But pride predominated.

But it was not in Europe that the average American was most disappointed. It was in Asia; it may soon be in Africa. It would be absurd to attempt to allocate praise or blame for the events in China, sometimes summed up in a misleading shorthand phrase as "the loss of China." But nothing is more natural or more defensible than the spontaneous American reaction to the discovery that China had been saved from Japanese imperialism only to fall under Communist control. I have always thought that the American interest in China owed more to missionary than to economic connections; nevertheless, the interest in China was deep and genuine.

There were few Pacific isolationists and it can plausibly be asserted that it was not only formally but really the determination to protect the "freedom of China" that brought America into the Second World War. Seeing China pass under Communist control, seeing the uprooting of a century of missionary effort, the quenching of a century of missionary hopes was an embittering and a blinding experience. It blinded many Americans to the fact that there are more than three Chinese for each American and no natural law determines that the United States can or could determine the fate of China. To "lose China" was to lose something that had never been possessed. Yet the sense of loss was reasonable and human, the sense of danger is not totally unreasonable now, and possibly will be much less unreasonable in the future.

If China is to be communized, transformed, deprived of its ancient weaknesses as well as its ancient virtues, this may be a greater event in the history of the world than even the Russian Revolution and one removing a great part of the human race from the American influence and leadership so confidently counted on in 1945. Here the American paradox is most bitter. For it was American victory, by eliminating Japanese power, that made possible the Communist victory in China. To have dropped the atomic bomb, to have risked that guilt, to produce such a result, this is irony unbearable. This is a world that no American wished to make but for which the United States must take some responsibility. If the American sense that the world is uncontrollable, not subject to reason and not necessarily moving in the direction of liberty and human betterment, has any one root it is in the great deception of China.

That deception was reinforced by the experience of the Korean War. To the average American, no war could be more innocent in origin, more worthy in object. Yet it was a war full of disillusionment. It involved a temporary but humiliating American defeat at the hands of those Chinese who had already inflicted a political defeat on the United States by their conquest of the Nationalists. Fought in the name of the United Nations, it was a war whose burden fell overwhelmingly on the Americans and for most of the members of the United Nations the motto was obviously "Let Sam do it." And it was a war settled in an unsatisfactory way.

Americans brought up to believe in what I once called "the illusion of American omnipotence" found it painful to accept and hard to believe that a settlement could mean less than a complete American triumph. Was it for this that tens of thousands of Americans had died in Korea as, before them, hundreds of thousands had died in the Pacific? This was a world unintelligible to millions of honest men and women. It was natural that they should seek an explanation in cries of "treason." And if that was not enough, there was the further resource of seeing a world in which the United States alone did its duty, and if that world was in a bad way the fault lay entirely elsewhere.

Nor was this the only disillusionment. It was natural to see in the newly liberated nations children eager to come to school to the great pioneer in the cause of freedom, the great exemplar of the more abundant life. Yet everywhere eager pupils went to another school, not only in China but in other parts of Asia and Africa. The ending of the old imperialism did not necessarily give the United States a set of friendly, grateful, and admiring pupils. At most it gave the opportunity to compete in what often seemed a rigged market for the friendship and tolerance of the newly liberated peoples. It was even a shock to learn that in some liberated countries, like India, the old masters preserved in some minds more prestige than the new allies.

Far from finding a world ready to follow the American lead, the American people found, even in Latin America, a world that was ready to shop and bargain and hesitate as to which of the rival world leaders to follow. And even when the American people won the support or docility of the governments where the competition for adherence was keenest, it did not follow that they had won the most active elements of the population. To their horror and usually to their justified horror the American people found the tag of "imperialist" pinned to the coattails of Uncle Sam, and in the war for men's minds the American way did not always win. The old identification of liberty in the sense of freedom from foreign rule with liberty in the sense of freedom from domestic tyranny was no longer firm or even customary.

All over the world liberty in the first sense warred with liberty in the second, a war that was often waged to the loss of the United States, which offered not authoritarian leadership but the more complicated way to self-rule. Were the common peoples of the world so blinded by nationalist passion, so ill-equipped to work democracy, American style, that the United States must give up the old hope of being automatically the natural leader of nations rightly struggling to be free? That there should be any question, that there should be any contest between so obviously tyrannical a system as Russian communism and the time-tried and inevitably beneficent system proclaimed to a candid world in 1776 was an affront to the spirit of '76 and to the American belief in an intelligible and manageable world.

And when, in addition to the too often successful competition offered by new societies that prostituted the name of freedom and democracy, there was suddenly flashed across the heavens proof that the other competition in material achievement was open too, the American whose history had been so fortunate, who until this century and until this generation, had never had to consider the limits of American power, was forced to reconsider his national situation. At the moment when mankind was on the edge of adventuring into space, the old, familiar world seemed less familiar, less homely, more in danger of self-destruction than ever. And now it could no longer be doubted by even the most obstinate that of that old, dangerous, and ill-ordered world the United States was at last and finally a part. It is a world the Americans never made but have to live in.

✦

D. W. BROGAN Born in Scotland in 1900, he was educated at Glasgow, Oxford, and Harvard, and has long been professor of political science at Cambridge University. A frequent visitor to the United States, many of his books and articles deal with American government and history.

"*A World They Never Made*" (1959) The tight organization and simple diction and syntax make a complex subject clear and orderly. The author, while admonitory and controversial, avoids being patronizing or offensive.

✦

1. *To what extent is American resentment against the rest of the world still justified? 2. Could a similar article about Russia be written by a sympathizer with Communism?*

KINGSLEY DAVIS

Population

Just as the nation-state is a modern phenomenon, so is the explosive increase of the human population. For hundreds of millenniums *Homo sapiens* was a sparsely distributed animal. As long as this held true man could enjoy a low mortality in comparison to other species and could thus breed slowly in relation to his size. Under primitive conditions, however, crowding tended to raise the death rates from famine, disease and warfare. Yet man's fellow mammals even then might well have voted him the animal most likely to succeed. He had certain traits that portended future dominance: a wide global dispersion, a tolerance for a large variety of foods (assisted by his early adoption of cooking) and a reliance on group co-operation and socially transmitted techniques. It was only a matter of time before he and his kind would learn how to live together in communities without paying the penalty of high death rates.

Man remained sparsely distributed during the neolithic revolution, in spite of such advances as the domestication of plants and animals and the invention of textiles and pottery. Epidemics and pillage still held him back, and new kinds of man-made disasters arose from erosion, flooding and crop failure. Indeed, the rate of growth of the world population remained low right up to the 16th and 17th centuries.

Then came a spectacular quickening of the earth's human increase. Between 1650 and 1850 the annual rate of increase doubled, and by the 1920's it had doubled again. After World War II, in the decade from 1950 to 1960, it took another big jump. The human population is now growing at a rate that is impossible to sustain for more than a moment of geologic time.

Since 1940 the world population has grown from about 2.5 billion to 3.2 billion. This increase, within 23 years, is more than the *total* estimated population of the earth in 1800. If the human population were to continue to grow at the rate of the past decade, within 100 years it would be multiplied sixfold.

Projections indicate that in the next four decades the growth will be even more rapid. The United Nations' "medium" projections give a rate during the closing decades of this century high enough, if continued, to multiply the world population sevenfold in 100 years. These projections are based on the assumption that the changes in mortality and fertility in regions in various stages of development will be roughly like those of the recent past. They do not, of course, forecast the actual population, which may turn out to be a billion or two greater than that projected for the year 2000 or to be virtually nil. So far the UN projections, like most others in recent decades, are proving conservative. In 1960 the world population was 75 million greater than the figure given by the UN's "high" projection (published in 1958 and based on data up to 1955).

In order to understand why the revolutionary rise of world population has occurred, we cannot confine ourselves to the global trend, because this trend is a summation of what is happening in regions that are at any one time quite different with respect to their stage of development. For instance, the first step in the demographic evolution of modern nations—a decline in the death rate—began in northwestern Europe long before it started elsewhere. As a result, although population growth is now slower in this area than in the rest of the world, it was here that the unprecedented upsurge in human numbers began. Being most advanced in demographic development, northwestern Europe is a good place to start in our analysis of modern population dynamics.

In the late medieval period the average life expectancy in England, according to life tables compiled by the historian J. C. Russell, was about 27 years. At the end of the 17th century and during most of the 18th it was about 31 in England, France and Sweden, and in the first half of the 19th century it advanced to 41.

The old but reliable vital statistics from Denmark, Norway and Sweden show that the death rate declined erratically up to 1790, then steadily and more rapidly. Meanwhile the birth rate remained remarkably stable (until the latter part of the 19th century). The result was a marked increase in the excess of births over deaths, or what demographers call "natural increase." In the century from about 1815 until World War I the average annual increase in the three Scandinavian countries was 11.8 per 1,000 —nearly five times what it had been in the middle of the 18th century, and sufficient to triple the population in 100 years.

For a long time the population of northwestern Europe showed little reaction to this rapid natural increase. But when it came, the reaction was emphatic; a wide variety of responses occurred, all of which tended to reduce the growth of the population. For example, in the latter part of the 19th century people began to emigrate from Europe by the millions, mainly to America, Australia and South Africa. Between 1846 and 1932 an estimated 27 million people emigrated overseas from Europe's 10 most advanced countries. The three Scandinavian countries alone sent out 2.4 million, so that in 1915 their combined population was 11.1 million instead of the 14.2 million it would otherwise have been.

In addition to this unprecedented exodus there were other responses, all of which tended to reduce the birth rate. In spite of opposition from church and state, agitation for birth control began and induced abortions became common. The age at marriage rose. Childlessness became frequent. The result was a decline in the birth rate that eventually overtook the continuing decline in the death rate. By the 1930's most of the industrial European countries had age-specific fertility rates so low that, if the rates had continued at that level, the population would eventually have ceased to replace itself.

In explaining this vigorous reaction one gets little help from two popular clichés. One of these—that population growth is good for business—would hardly explain why Europeans were so bent on stopping population growth. The other—that numerical limitation comes from the threat of poverty because "population always presses on the means of subsistence"—is factually untrue. In every one of the industrializing countries of Europe economic growth outpaced population growth. In the United Kingdom, for example, the real per capita income increased 2.3 times between the periods 1855–1859 and 1910–1914. In Denmark from 1770 to 1914 the rise of the net domestic product in constant prices was two and a half times the natural increase rate; in Norway and Sweden from the 1860's to 1914 it was respectively 1.4 and 2.7 times the natural increase rate. Clearly the strenuous efforts to lessen population growth were due to some stimulus other than poverty.

The stimulus, in my view, arose from the clash between new opportunities on the one hand and larger families on the other. The modernizing society of northwestern Europe necessarily offered new opportunities to people of all classes: new ways of gaining wealth, new means of rising socially, new symbols of status. In order to take advantage of those opportunities, however, the individual and his children required education, special skills, capital and mobility—none of which was facilitated by an improvident marriage or a large family. Yet because mortality was being reduced (and reduced more successfully in the childhood than in the adult ages) the size of families had become potentially larger than before. In Sweden, for instance, the mortality of the period 1755–1775 allowed only 6.1 out of every 10 children born to reach the age of 10, whereas the mortality of 1901–1910 allowed 8.5 to survive to that age. In order to avoid the threat of a large family to his own and his children's socioeconomic position, the individual tended to postpone or avoid marriage and to limit reproduction within marriage by every means available. Urban residents had to contend particularly with the cost and inconvenience of young children in the city. Rural families had to adjust to the lack of enough land to provide for new marriages when the children reached marriageable age. Land had become less available not only because of the plethora of families with numerous youths but also because, with modernization, more capital was needed per farm and because the old folks, living longer, held on to the property. As a result farm youths postponed marriage, flocked to the cities or went overseas.

In such terms we can account for the paradox that, as the progressive European nations became richer, their population growth slowed down. The process of economic development itself provided the motives for curtailment of reproduction, as the British sociologist J. A. Banks has made clear in his book *Prosperity and Parenthood*. We can see now that in all modern nations the long-run trend is one of low mortality, a relatively modest rate of reproduction and slow population growth. This is an efficient demographic system that allows such countries, in spite of their "maturity," to continue to advance economically at an impressive speed.

Naturally the countries of northwestern Europe did not all follow an identical pattern. Their stages differed somewhat in timing and in the pattern of preference among the various means of population control. France, for example, never attained as high a natural increase as Britain or Scandinavia did. This was not due solely to an earlier decline in the birth rate, as is often assumed, but also to a slower decline in the death rate. If we historically substitute the Swedish death rate for the French, we revise the natural increase upward by almost the same amount as we do by substituting the Swedish birth rate. In accounting for the early and easy drop in French fertility one recalls that France, already crowded in the 18th century and in the van of intellectual radicalism and sophistication, was likely to have a low threshold for the adoption of abortion and contraception. The death rate, however, remained comparatively high because France did not keep economic pace with her more rapidly industrializing neighbors. As a result the relatively small gap between births and deaths gave France a slower growth in population and a lesser rate of emigration.

Ireland also has its own demographic history, but like France it differs from the other countries in emphasis rather than in kind. The emphasis in Ireland's escape from human inflation was on emigration, late marriage and permanent celibacy. By 1891 the median age at which Irish girls married was 28 (compared with 22 in the U.S. at that date); nearly a fourth of the Irish women did not marry at all, and approximately a third of all Irish-born people lived outside of Ireland. These adjustments, begun with the famine of the 1840's and continuing with slight modifications until today, were so drastic that they made Ireland the only modern nation to experience an absolute decline in population. The total of 8.2 million in 1841 was reduced by 1901 to 4.5 million.

The Irish preferences among the means of population limitation seem to come from the island's position as a rural region participating only indirectly in the industrial revolution. For most of the Irish, land remained the basis for respectable matrimony. As land became inaccessible to young people they postponed marriage. In doing so they were not discouraged by their parents who wished to keep control of the land or by their religion. Their Catholicism, which they embraced with exceptional vigor both because they were rural and because it was a rallying point for Irish nationalism as against the Protestant English, placed a high value on celibacy. The clergy, furthermore, were powerful enough to exercise strict control over courtship and thus to curtail illicit pregnancy and romance as factors leading to marriage. They were also able to exercise exceptional restraint on abortion and contraception. Although birth control was practiced to some extent, as evidenced by a decline of fertility within marriage, its influence was so small as to make early marriage synonymous with a large family and therefore to be avoided. Marriage was also discouraged by the ban on divorce and by the lowest participation of married women in the labor force to be found in Europe. The country's failure to industrialize meant that the normal exodus from farms to cities was at the same time an exodus from Ireland itself.

Ireland and France illustrate contrasting variations on a common theme. Throughout northwestern Europe the population upsurge resulting from the fall in death rates brought about a multiphasic reaction that eventually reduced the population growth to a modest pace. The main force behind this response was not poverty or hunger but the desire of the people involved to preserve or improve their social standing by grasping the opportunities offered by the newly emerging industrial society.

Is this an interpretation applicable to the history of any industrialized country, regardless of traditional culture? According to the evidence the answer is yes. We might expect it to be true, as it currently is, of the countries of southern and eastern Europe that are finally industrializing. The crucial test is offered by the only nation outside the European tradition to become industrialized: Japan. How closely does Japan's demographic evolution parallel that of northwestern Europe?

If we superpose Japan's vital-rate curves on those of Scandinavia half a century earlier, we see a basically similar, although more rapid, development. The reported statistics, questionable up to 1920 but good after that, show a rapidly declining death rate as industrialization took hold after World War I. The rate of natural increase during the period from 1900 to 1940 was almost exactly the same as Scandinavia's between 1850 and 1920, averaging 12.1 per 1,000 population per year compared with Scandinavia's 12.3. And Japan's birth rate, like Europe's, began to dip until it was falling faster than the death rate, as it did in Europe. After the usual baby boom following World War II the decline in births was precipitous, amounting to 50 per cent from 1948 to 1960—perhaps the swiftest drop in reproduction that has ever occurred in an entire nation. The rates of childbearing for women in various ages are so low that, if they continued indefinitely, they would not enable the Japanese population to replace itself.

In thus slowing their population growth have the Japanese used the same means as the peoples of northwestern Europe did? Again, yes. Taboo-ridden Westerners have given disproportionate attention to two features of the change—the active role played by the Japanese government and the widespread resort to abortion—but neither of these disproves the similarity. It is true that since the war the Japanese government has pursued a birth-control policy more energetically than any government ever has before. It is also clear, however, that the Japanese people would have reduced their childbearing of their own accord. A marked decline in the reproduction rate had already set in by 1920, long before there was a government policy favoring this trend.

As for abortion, the Japanese are unusual only in admitting its extent. Less superstitious than Europeans about this subject, they keep reasonably good records of abortions, whereas most of the other countries have no accurate data. According to the Japanese records, registered abortions rose from 11.8 per 1,000 women of childbearing age in 1949 to a peak of 50.2 per 1,000 in 1955. We have no reliable historical information from Western countries, but we do know from many indirect indications that induced abortion played a tremendous role in the reduction of the birth rate in western Europe from 1900 to 1940, and that it still plays a considerable role. Furthermore, Christopher Tietze of the National Committee for Maternal Health has assembled records that show that in five eastern European countries where abortion has been legal for some time the rate has shot up recently in a manner strikingly similar to Japan's experience. In 1960–1961 there were 139 abortions for every 100 births in Hungary, 58 per 100 births in Bulgaria, 54 in Czechoslovakia and 34 in Poland. The countries of eastern Europe are in a developmental stage comparable to that of northwestern Europe earlier in the century.

Abortion is by no means the sole factor in the decline of Japan's birth rate. Surveys made since 1950 show the use of contraception before that date, and increasing use thereafter. There is also a rising frequency of sterilization. Furthermore, as in Europe earlier, the Japanese are postponing marriage. The proportion of girls under 20 who have ever married fell from 17.7 per cent in 1920 to 1.8 per cent in 1955. In 1959 only about 5 per cent of the Japanese girls marrying for the first time were under 20, whereas in the U.S. almost half the new brides (48.5 per cent in the registration area) were that young.

Finally, Japan went through the same experience as western Europe in another respect—massive emigration. Up to World War II Japan sent millions of emigrants to various regions of Asia, Oceania and the Americas.

In short, in response to a high rate of natural increase brought by declining mortality, Japan reacted in the same ways as the countries of northwestern Europe did at a similar stage. Like the Europeans, the Japanese limited their population growth in their own private interest and that of their children in a developing society, rather than from any fear of absolute privation or any concern with overpopulation in their homeland. The nation's average 5.4 per cent annual growth in industrial output from 1913 to 1958 exceeded the performance of European countries at a similar stage.

As our final class of industrialized countries we must now consider the frontier group—the U.S., Canada, Australia, New Zealand, South Africa and Russia. These countries are distinguished from those of northwestern Europe and Japan by their vast wealth of natural resources in relation to their populations; they are the genuinely affluent nations. They might be expected to show a demographic history somewhat different from that of Europe. In certain particulars they do, yet the general pattern is still much the same.

One of the differences is that the riches offered by their untapped resources invited immigration. All the frontier industrial countries except Russia received massive waves of emigrants from Europe. They therefore had a more rapid population growth than their industrializing predecessors had experienced. As frontier countries with great room for expansion, however, they were also characterized by considerable internal migration and continuing new opportunities. As a result their birth rates remained comparatively high. In the decade from 1950 to 1960, with continued immigration, these countries grew in population at an average rate of 2.13 per cent a year, compared with 1.76 per cent for the rest of the world. It was the four countries with the sparsest settlement (Canada, Australia, New Zealand and South Africa), however, that accounted for this high rate; in the U.S. and the U.S.S.R. the growth rate was lower—1.67 per cent per year.

Apparently, then, in pioneer industrial countries with an abundance of resources population growth holds up at a higher level than in Japan or northwestern Europe because the average individual feels it is easier for himself and his children to achieve a respectable place in the social scale. The immigrants attracted by the various opportunities normally begin at a low level and thus make the status of natives relatively better. People marry earlier and have slightly larger families. But this departure from the general pattern for industrial countries appears to be only temporary.

In the advanced frontier nations, as in northwestern Europe, the birth rate began to fall sharply after 1880, and during the depression of the 1930's it was only about 10 per cent higher than in Europe. Although the postwar baby boom has lasted longer than in other advanced countries, it is evidently starting to subside now, and the rate of immigration has diminished. There are factors at work in these affluent nations that will likely limit their population growth. They are among the most urbanized countries in the world, in spite of their low average population density. Their birth rates are extremely sensitive to business fluctuations and social changes. Furthermore, having in general the world's highest living standards, their demand for resources, already staggering, will become fantastic if both population and per capita consumption continue to rise rapidly, and their privileged position in the world may become less tolerated.

Let us shift now to the other side of the population picture: the nonindustrial, or underdeveloped, countries.

As a class the nonindustrial nations since 1930 have been growing in population about twice as fast as the industrial ones. This fact is so familiar and so taken for granted that its irony tends to escape us. When we think of it, it is astonishing that the world's most impoverished nations, many of them already overcrowded by any standard, should be generating additions to the population at the highest rate.

The underdeveloped countries have about 69 per cent of the earth's adults—and some 80 per cent of the world's children. Hence the demographic situation itself tends to make the world constantly more underdeveloped, or impoverished, a fact that makes economic growth doubly difficult.

How can we account for the paradox that the world's poorest regions are producing the most people? One is tempted to believe that the underdeveloped countries are simply repeating history: that they are in the same phase of rapid growth the West experienced when it began to industrialize and its death rates fell. If that is so, then sooner or later the developing areas will limit their population growth as the West did.

It is possible that this may prove to be true in the long run. But before we accept the comforting thought we should take a close look at the facts as they are.

In actuality the demography of the nonindustrial countries today differs in essential respects from the early history of the present industrial nations. Most striking is the fact that their rate of human multiplication is far higher than the West's ever was. The peak of the industrial nations' natural increase rarely rose above 15 per 1,000 population per year; the highest rate in Scandinavia was 13, in England and Wales 14, and even in Japan it was slightly less than 15. True, the U.S. may have hit a figure of 30 per 1,000 in the early 19th century, but if so it was with the help of heavy immigration of young people (who swelled the births but not the deaths) and with the encouragement of an empty continent waiting for exploitation.

In contrast, in the present underdeveloped but often crowded countries the natural increase per 1,000 population is everywhere extreme. In the decade from 1950 to 1960 it averaged 31.4 per year in Taiwan, 26.8 in Ceylon, 32.1 in Malaya, 26.7 in Mauritius, 27.7 in Albania, 31.8 in Mexico, 33.9 in El Salvador and 37.3 in Costa Rica. These are not birth rates; they are the *excess* of births over deaths! At an annual natural increase of 30 per 1,000 a population will double itself in 23 years.

The population upsurge in the backward nations is apparently taking place at an earlier stage of development—or perhaps we should say *un*development—than it did in the now industrialized nations. In Britain, for instance, the peak of human multiplication came when the country was already highly industrialized and urbanized, with only a fifth of its working males in agriculture. Comparing four industrial countries at the peak of their natural increase in the 19th century (14.1 per 1,000 per year) with five nonindustrial countries during their rapid growth in the 1950's (32.2 per 1,000 per year), I find that the industrial countries were 38.5 per cent urbanized and had 27.9 per cent of their labor force in manufacturing, whereas now the nonindustrial countries are 29.4 per cent urbanized and have only 15.1 per cent of their people in manufacturing. In short, today's nonindustrial populations are growing faster and at an earlier stage than was the case in the demographic cycle that accompanied industrialization in the 19th century.

As in the industrial nations, the main generator of the population upsurge in the underdeveloped countries has been a fall in the death rate. But their resulting excess of births over deaths has proceeded faster and farther, as a comparison of Ceylon in recent decades with Sweden in the 1800's shows.

In most of the underdeveloped nations the death rate has dropped with record speed. For example, the sugar-growing island of Mauritius in the Indian Ocean within an eight-year period after the war raised its average life expectancy from 33 to 51—a gain that took Sweden 130 years to achieve. Taiwan within two decades has increased its life expectancy from 43 to 63; it took the U.S. some 80 years to make this improvement for its white population. According to the records in 18 underdeveloped countries, the crude death rate has dropped substantially in each decade since 1930; it fell some 6 per cent in the 1930's and nearly 20 per cent in the 1950's, and according to the most recent available figures the decline in deaths is still accelerating.

The reasons for this sharp drop in mortality are in much dispute. There are two opposing theories. Many give the credit to modern medicine and public health measures. On the other hand, the public health spokesmen, rejecting the accusation of complicity in the world's population crisis, belittle their own role and maintain that the chief factor in the improvement of the death rate has been economic progress.

Those in the latter camp point out that the decline in the death rate in northwestern Europe followed a steadily rising standard of living. Improvements in diet, clothing, housing and working conditions raised the population's resistance to disease. As a result many dangerous ailments disappeared or subsided without specific medical attack. The same process, say the public health people, is now at work in the developing countries.

On the other side, most demographers and economists believe that economic conditions are no longer as important as they once were in strengthening a community's health. The development of medical science has provided lifesaving techniques and medicines that can be transported overnight to the most backward areas. A Stone Age people can be endowed with a low 20th-century death rate within a few years, without waiting for the slow process of economic development or social change. International agencies and the governments of the affluent nations have been delighted to act as good Samaritans and send out public health missionaries to push disease-fighting programs for the less developed countries.

The debate between the two views is hard to settle. Such evidence as we have indicates that there is truth on both sides. Certainly the newly evolving countries have made economic progress. Their economic advance, however, is not nearly rapid enough to account for the very swift decline in their death rates, nor do they show any clear correlation between economic growth and improvement in life expectancy. For example, in Mauritius during the five-year period from 1953 to 1958 the per capita income fell by 13 per cent, yet notwithstanding this there was a 36 per cent drop in the death rate. On the other hand, in the period between 1945 and 1960 Costa Rica had a 64 per cent increase in the per capita gross national product and a 55 per cent decline in the death rate. There seems to be no consistency—no significant correlation between the two trends when we look at the figures country by country. In 15 underdeveloped countries for which such figures are available we find that the decline in death rate in the 1950's was strikingly uniform (about 4 per cent per year), although the nations varied greatly in economic progress—from no improvement to a 6 per cent annual growth in per capita income.

Our tentative conclusion must be, therefore, that the public health people are more efficient than they admit. The billions of dollars spent in public health work for underdeveloped areas has brought down death rates, irrespective of local economic conditions in these areas. The programs instituted by outsiders to control cholera, malaria, plague and other diseases in these countries have succeeded. This does not mean that death control in underdeveloped countries has become wholly or permanently independent of economic development but that it has become temporarily so to an amazing degree.

Accordingly the unprecedented population growth in these countries bears little relation to their economic condition. The British economist Colin G. Clark has contended that rapid population growth stimulates economic progress. This idea acquires plausibility from the association between human increase and industrialization in the past and from the fact that in advanced countries today the birth rate (but not the death rate) tends to fluctuate with business conditions. In today's underdeveloped countries, however, there seems to be little or no visible connection between economics and demography.

In these countries neither births nor deaths have been particularly responsive to economic change. Some of the highest rates of population growth ever known are occurring in areas that show no commensurate economic advance. In 34 such countries for which we have data, the correlation between population growth and economic gain during the 1950's was negligible, and the slight edge was on the negative side: −.2. In 20 Latin-American countries during the period from 1954 to 1959, while the annual gain in per capita gross domestic product fell from an average of 2 per cent to 1.3 per cent, the population growth rate *rose* from 2.5 to 2.7 per cent per year.

All the evidence indicates that the population upsurge in the underdeveloped countries is not helping them to advance economically. On the contrary, it may well be interfering with their economic growth. A surplus of labor on the farms holds back the mechanization of agriculture. A rapid rise in the number of people to be maintained uses up income that might otherwise be utilized for long-term investment in education, equipment and other capital needs. To put it in concrete terms, it is difficult to give a child the basic education he needs to become an engineer when he is one of eight children of an illiterate farmer who must support the family with the produce of two acres of ground.

By definition economic advance means an increase in the amount of product per unit of human labor. This calls for investment in technology, in improvement of the skills of the labor force and in administrative organization and planning. An economy that must spend a disproportionate share of its income in supporting the consumption needs of a growing population—and at a low level of consumption at that—finds growth difficult because it lacks capital for improvements.

A further complication lies in the process of urbanization. The shifts from villages and farmsteads to cities is seemingly an unavoidable and at best a painful part of economic development. It is most painful when the total population is skyrocketing; then the cities are bursting both from their own multiplication and from the stream of migrants from the villages. The latter do not move to cities because of the opportunities there. The opportunities are few and unemployment is prevalent. The migrants come, rather, because they are impelled by the lack of opportunity in the crowded rural areas. In the cities they hope to get something—a menial job, government relief, charities of the rich. I have recently estimated that if the population of India increases at the rate projected for it by the UN, the net number of migrants to cities between 1960 and 2000 will be of the order of 99 to 201 million, and in 2000 the largest city will contain between 36 and

66 million inhabitants. One of the greatest problems now facing the governments of underdeveloped countries is what to do with these millions of penniless refugees from the excessively populated countryside.

Economic growth is not easy to achieve. So far, in spite of all the talk and the earnest efforts of underdeveloped nations, only one country outside the northwestern European tradition has done so: Japan. The others are struggling with the handicap of a population growth greater than any industrializing country had to contend with in the past. A number of them now realize that this is a primary problem, and their governments are pursuing or contemplating large-scale programs of birth-limitation. They are receiving little help in this matter, however, from the industrial nations, which have so willingly helped them to lower their death rates.

The Christian nations withhold this help because of their official taboos against some of the means of birth-limitation (although their own people privately use all these means). The Communist nations withhold it because limitation of population growth conflicts with official Marxist dogma (but Soviet citizens control births just as capitalist citizens do, and China is officially pursuing policies calculated to reduce the birth rate).

The West's preoccupation with the technology of contraception seems unjustified in view of its own history. The peoples of northwestern Europe utilized all the available means of birth limitation once they had strong motives for such limitation. The main question, then, is whether or not the peoples of the present underdeveloped countries are likely to acquire such motivation in the near future. There are signs that they will. Surveys in India, Jamaica and certain other areas give evidence of a growing desire among the people to reduce the size of their families. Furthermore, circumstances in the underdeveloped nations today are working more strongly in this direction than they did in northwestern Europe in the 19th century.

As in that earlier day, poverty and deprivation alone are not likely to generate a slowdown of the birth rate. But personal aspirations are. The agrarian peoples of the backward countries now look to the industrialized, affluent fourth of the world. They nourish aspirations that come directly from New York, Paris and Moscow. No more inclined to be satisfied with a bare subsistence than their wealthier fellows would be, they are demanding more goods, education, opportunity and influence. And they are beginning to see that many of their desires are incompatible with the enlarged families that low mortality and customary reproduction are giving them.

They live amid a population density far greater than existed in 19th-century Europe. They have no place to which to emigrate, no beckoning continents to colonize. They have rich utopias to look at and industrial models to emulate, whereas the Europeans of the early 1800's did not know where they were going. The peoples of the underdeveloped, overpopulated countries therefore seem likely to start soon a multiphasic limitation of births such as began to sweep through Europe a century ago. Their governments appear ready to help them. Government policy in these countries is not quibbling over means or confining itself to birth-control technology; its primary task is to strengthen and accelerate the peoples' motivation for reproductive restraint.

Meanwhile the industrial countries also seem destined to apply brakes to their population growth. The steadily rising level of living, multiplied by the still growing numbers of people, is engendering a dizzying rate of consumption. It is beginning to produce painful scarcities of space, of clean water, of clean air and of quietness. All of this may prompt more demographic moderation than these countries have already exercised.

❦

KINGSLEY DAVIS   Born in 1908 in Texas, educated at Harvard, and now a professor of sociology at the University of California at Berkeley, he is a frequently published expert on problems of demography.

"Population" (1963) Straightforward, comprehensive, clear, and circumstantial, this article exemplifies the functional use of facts and quantitative analyses to support a controversial interpretation and conclusion.

❦

1. What is the author's basic attitude toward contraception? 2. In what ways is this essay optimistic? in what ways pessimistic?

C. NORTHCOTE PARKINSON

Parkinson's Law or the Rising Pyramid

Work expands so as to fill the time available for its completion. General recognition of this fact is shown in the proverbial phrase "It is the busiest man who has time to spare." Thus, an elderly lady of leisure can spend the entire day in writing and dispatching a postcard to her niece at Bognor Regis. An hour will be spent in finding the postcard, another in hunting for spectacles, half an hour in a search for the address, an hour and a quarter in composition, and twenty minutes in deciding whether or not to take an umbrella when going to the mailbox in the next street. The total effort that would occupy a busy man for three minutes all told may in this fashion leave another person prostrate after a day of doubt, anxiety, and toil.

Granted that work (and especially paperwork) is thus elastic in its demands on time, it is manifest that there need be little or no relationship between the work to be done and the size of the staff to which it may be assigned. A lack of real activity does not, of necessity, result in leisure. A lack of occupation is not necessarily revealed by a manifest idleness. The thing to be done swells in importance and complexity in a direct ratio with the time to be spent. This fact is widely recognized, but less attention has been paid to its wider implications, more especially in the field of public administration. Politicians and taxpayers have assumed (with occasional phases of doubt) that a rising total in the number of civil servants must reflect a growing volume of work to be done. Cynics, in questioning this belief, have imagined that the multiplication of officials must have left some of them idle or all of them able to work for shorter hours. But this is a matter in which faith and doubt seem equally misplaced. The fact is that the number of the officials and the quantity of the work are not related to each other at all. The rise in the total of those employed is governed by Parkinson's Law and would be much the same whether the volume of the work were to increase, diminish, or even disappear. The importance of Parkinson's Law lies in the fact that it is a law of growth based upon an analysis of the factors by which that growth is controlled.

The validity of this recently discovered law must rest mainly on statistical proofs, which will follow. Of more interest to the general reader is the explanation of the factors underlying the general tendency to which this law gives definition. Omitting technicalities (which are numerous) we may distinguish at the outset two motive forces. They can be represented for the present purpose by two almost axiomatic statements, thus: (1) "An official wants to multiply subordinates, not rivals" and (2) "Officials make work for each other."

To comprehend Factor 1, we must picture a civil servant, called A, who finds himself overworked. Whether this overwork is real or imaginery is immaterial, but we should observe in passing, that A's sensation (or illusion) might easily result from his own decreasing energy: a normal symptom of middle age. For this real or imagined overwork there are, broadly speaking, three possible remedies. He may resign; he may ask to halve the work with a colleague called B; he may demand the assistance of two subordinates, to be called C and D. There is probably no instance in history, however, of A choosing any but the third alternative. By resignation he would lose his pension rights. By having B appointed, on his own level in the hierarchy, he would merely bring in a rival for promotion to W's vacancy when W (at long last) retires. So A would rather have C and D, junior men, below him. They will add to his consequence and, by dividing the work into two categories, as between C and D, he will have the merit of being the only man who comprehends them both. It is essential to realize at this point that C and D are, as it were, inseparable. To appoint C alone would have been impossible. Why? Because C, if by himself, would divide the work with A and so assume almost the equal status that has been refused in the first instance to B; a status the more emphasized if C is A's only possible successor. Subordinates must thus number two or more, each being thus kept in order by fear of the other's promotion. When C complains in turn of being overworked (as he certainly will) A will, with the concurrence of C, advise the appointment of two assistants to help C. But he can then avert internal friction only by advising the appointment of two more assistants to help D, whose position is much the same. With this recruitment of E, F, G, and H the promotion of A is now practically certain.

Seven officials are now doing what one did before. This is where Factor 2 comes into operation. For these seven make so much work for each other that all are fully occupied and A is actually working harder than ever. An incoming document may well come before each of them in turn. Official E decides that it falls within the province of F, who places a draft reply before C, who amends it drastically before consulting D, who asks G to deal with it. But G goes on leave at this point, handing the file over to H, who drafts a minute that is signed by D and returned to C, who revises his draft accordingly and lays the new version before A.

What does A do? He would have every excuse for signing the thing unread, for he has many other matters on his mind. Knowing now that he is to succeed W next year, he has to decide whether C or D should succeed to his own office. He had to agree to G's going on leave even if not yet strictly entitled to it. He is worried whether H should not have gone instead, for reasons of health. He has looked pale recently—partly but not solely because of his domestic troubles. Then there is the business of F's special increment of salary for the period of the conference and E's application for transfer to the Ministry of Pensions. A has heard that D is in love with a married typist and that G and F are no longer on speaking terms—no one seems to know why. So A might be tempted to sign C's draft and have done with it. But A is a conscientious man. Beset as he is with problems created by his colleagues for themselves and for him—created by the mere fact of these officials' existence—he is not the man to shirk his duty. He reads through the draft with care, deletes the fussy paragraphs added by C and H, and restores the thing back to the form preferred in the first instance by the able (if quarrelsome) F. He corrects the English—none of these young men can write grammatically—and finally produces the same reply he would have written if officials C to H had never been born. Far more people have taken far longer to produce the same result. No one has been idle. All have done their best. And it is late in the evening before A finally quits his office and begins the return journey to Ealing. The last of the office lights are being turned off in the gathering dusk that marks the end of another day's administrative toil. Among the last to leave, A reflects with bowed shoulders and a wry smile that late hours, like gray hairs, are among the penalties of success.

From this description of the factors at work the student of political science will recognize that administrators are more or less bound to multiply. Nothing has yet been said, however, about the period of time likely to elapse between the date of A's appointment and the date from which we can calculate the pensionable service of H. Vast masses of statistical evidence have been collected and it is from a study of this data that Parkinson's Law has been deduced. Space will not allow of detailed analysis but the reader will be interested to know that research began in the British Navy Estimates. These were chosen because the Admiralty's responsibilities are more easily measureable than those of, say, the Board of Trade. The question is merely one of numbers and tonnage. Here are some typical figures. The strength of the Navy in 1914 could be shown as 146,000 officers and men, 3249 dockyard officials and clerks, and 57,000 dockyard workmen. By 1928 there were only 100,000 officers and men and only 62,439 workmen, but the dockyard officials and clerks by then numbered 4558. As for warships, the strength in 1928 was a mere fraction of what it had been in 1914—fewer than 20 capital ships in commission as compared with 62. Over the same period the Admiralty officials had increased in number from 2000 to 3569, providing (as was remarked) "a magnificent navy on land." These figures are more clearly set forth in tabular form.

ADMIRALTY STATISTICS

Year	Capital ships in commission	Officers and men in R.N.	Dockyard workers	Dockyard officials and clerks	Admiralty officials
1914	62	146,000	57,000	3249	2000
1928	20	100,000	62,439	4558	3569
Increase or Decrease	−67.74%	−31.5%	+9.54%	+40.28%	+78.45%

The criticism voiced at the time centered on the ratio between the numbers of those available for fighting and those available only for administration. But that comparison is not to the present purpose. What we have to note is that the 2000 officials of 1914 had become the 3569 of 1928; and that this growth was unrelated to any possible increase in their work. The Navy during that period had diminished in point of fact, by a third in men and two-thirds in ships. Nor, from 1922 onward, was its strength even expected to increase; for its total of ships (unlike its total of officials) was limited by the Washington Naval Agreement of that year. Here we have then a 78 per cent increase over a period of fourteen years; an average of 5.6 per cent increase a year on the earlier total. In fact, as we shall see, the rate of increase was not as regular as that. All we have to consider, at this stage, is the percentage rise over a given period.

Can this rise in the total number of civil servants be accounted for except on the assumption that such a total must always rise by a law governing its growth? It might be urged at this point that the period under discussion was one of rapid development in naval technique. The use of the flying machine was no longer confined to the eccentric. Electrical devices were being multiplied and elaborated. Submarines were tolerated if not approved.

Engineer officers were beginning to be regarded as almost human. In so revolutionary an age we might expect that storekeepers would have more elaborate inventories to compile. We might not wonder to see more draughtsmen on the payroll, more designers, more technicians and scientists. But these, the dockyard officials, increased only by 40 per cent in number when the men of Whitehall increased their total by nearly 80 per cent. For every new foreman or electrical engineer at Portsmouth there had to be two more clerks at Charing Cross. From this we might be tempted to conclude, provisionally, that the rate of increase in administrative staff is likely to be double that of the technical staff at a time when the actually useful strength (in this case, of seamen) is being reduced by 31.5 per cent. It has been proved statistically, however, that this last percentage is irrelevant. The officials would have multiplied at the same rate had there been no actual seamen at all.

It would be interesting to follow the further progress by which the 8118 Admiralty staff of 1935 came to number 33,788 by 1954. But the staff of the Colonial Office affords a better field of study during a period of imperial decline. Admiralty statistics are complicated by factors (like the Fleet Air Arm) that make comparison difficult as between one year and the next. The Colonial Office growth is more significant in that it is more purely administrative. Here the relevant statistics are as follows:

1935	1939	1943	1947	1954
372	450	817	1139	1661

Before showing what the rate of increase is, we must observe that the extent of this department's responsibilities was far from constant during these twenty years. The colonial territories were not much altered in area or population between 1935 and 1939. They were considerably diminished by 1943, certain areas being in enemy hands. They were increased again in 1947, but have since then shrunk steadily from year to year as successive colonies achieve self-government. It would be rational to suppose that these changes in the scope of Empire would be reflected in the size of its central administration. But a glance at the figures is enough to convince us that the staff totals represent nothing but so many stages in an inevitable increase. And this increase, although related to that observed in other departments, has nothing to do with the size—or even the existence—of the Empire. What are the percentages of increase? We must ignore, for this purpose, the rapid increase in staff which accompanied the diminution of responsibility during World War II. We should note rather, the peacetime rates of increase: over 5.24 per cent between 1935 and 1939, and 6.55 per cent between 1947 and 1954. This gives an average increase of 5.89 per cent each year, a percentage markedly similar to that already found in the Admiralty staff increase between 1914 and 1928.

Further and detailed statistical analysis of departmental staffs would be inappropriate in such a work as this. It is hoped, however, to reach a tentative conclusion regarding the time likely to elapse between a given official's first appointment and the later appointment of his two or more assistants.

Dealing with the problem of pure staff accumulation, all our researches so far completed point to an average increase of 5.75 per cent per year. This fact established, it now becomes possible to state Parkinson's Law in mathematical form: In any public administrative department not actually at war, the staff increase may be expected to follow this formula—

$$x = \frac{2k^m + l}{n}$$

k is the number of staff seeking promotion through the appointment of subordinates; l represents the difference between the ages of appointment and retirement; m is the number of man-hours devoted to answering minutes within the department; and n is the number of effective units being administered. x will be the number of new staff required each year. Mathematicians will realize, of course, that to find the percentage increase they must multiply x by 100 and divide by the total of the previous year, thus:

$$\frac{100 \ (2k^m + l)}{yn}\%$$

where y represents the total original staff. This figure will invariably prove to between 5.17 per cent and 6.56 per cent, irrespective of any variation in the amount of work (if any) to be done.

The discovery of this formula and of the general principles upon which it is based has, of course, no political value. No attempt has been made to inquire whether departments *ought* to grow in size. Those who hold that this growth is essential to gain full employment are fully entitled to their opinion. Those who doubt the stability of an economy based upon reading each other's minutes are equally entitled to theirs. It would probably be premature to attempt at this stage any inquiry into the quantitative ratio that should exist between the administrators and the administered. Granted, however, that a maximum ratio exists, it should soon be possible to ascertain by formula how many years will elapse before that ratio, in any given community will be reached. The forecasting of such a result will again have no political value. Nor can it be sufficiently emphasized that Parkinson's Law is a purely scientific discovery, inapplicable except in theory to the politics of the day. It is not the business of the botanist to eradicate the weeds. Enough for him if he can tell us just how fast they grow.

✦

C. Northcote Parkinson   Born in England in 1909, educated at Cambridge and London Universities, a specialist in Asian affairs, he has written widely on historical and economic topics. He has also taught history at several universities, among them Malaya. He learned something about administration serving in the British War Office in World War II.

"Parkinson's Law or the Rising Pyramid" (1957) This essay is apparently straightforward and very scientific—complete with formulae and statistical tables. But despite its deadpan surface, it is a fine parody as well as an incisive if indirect commentary on modern society.

✦

1. *What are the devices by which the author tries to secure your unquestioning agreement with him?* 2. *On the basis of your own experience, give an example of Parkinson's Law.*

SUSANNE K. LANGER

Man and Animal: The City and the Hive

Within the past five or six decades, the human scene has probably changed more radically than ever before in history. The outward changes in our own setting are already an old story: the disappearance of horse-drawn vehicles, riders, children walking to school, and the advent of the long, low, powerful Thing in their stead; the transformation of the mile-wide farm into a ticktacktoe of lots, each sprouting a split-level dream home. These are the obvious changes, more apparent in the country than in the city. The great cities have grown greater, brighter, more mechanized, but their basic patterns seem less shaken by the new power and speed in which the long industrial revolution culminates.

The deepest change, however, is really a change in our picture of mankind, and that is most spectacular where mankind is teeming and concentrated—in the city. Our old picture of human life was a picture of local groups, each speaking its mother tongue, observing some established religion, following its own customs. It might be a civilized community or a savage tribe, but it had its distinct traditions. And in it were subdivisions, usually families, with their more special local ties and human relations.

Today, natural tribes and isolated communities have all but disappeared. The ease and speed of travel, the swift economic changes that send people in search of new kinds of work, the two wars that swept over all boundaries, have wiped out most of our

This essay originally appeared in *The Antioch Review* and is reprinted by permission of the copyright holders, The Antioch Press.

traditions. The old family structure is tottering. Society tends to break up into new and smaller units—in fact, into its ultimate units, the human individuals that compose it.

This atomization of society is most obvious in a great cosmopolitan city. The city seems to be composed of millions of unrelated individuals, each scrambling for himself, yet each caught in the stream of all the others.

Discerning eyes saw this a hundred years ago, especially in industrial cities, where individuals from far or near came to do what other individuals from far or near had also come to do— each a cog in the new machine. Most of the cogs had no other relation to each other. And ever since this shake-up in society began, a new picture of society has been in the making—the picture of *human masses*, brought together by some outside force, some imposed function, into a superpersonal unit—masses of people, each representing an atom of "manpower" in a new sort of organism, the industrial state.

The idea of the state as a higher organism—the state as a superindividual—is old. But our conception of such a state is new, because our industrial civilization, which begets our atomized society, is new. The old picture was not one of masses driven by some imposed economic power, or any other outside power. The superindividual was a rational being, directed by a mind within it. The guardians of the state, the rulers, were its mind. Plato described the state as "the man writ large." Hobbes, two thousand years later, called it "Leviathan," the great creature. A city-state like ancient Athens or Sparta might be "a man writ large," but England was too big for that. It was the big fish in the big pond. The mind of Hobbes's fish was perhaps subhuman, but it was still single and sovereign in the organism.

Another couple of centuries later, Rudyard Kipling, faced with a democratic, industrialized civilization, called his allegory of England, "The Mother Hive." Here, a common will, dictated by complicated instincts, replaced even Leviathan's mind; each individual was kept in line by the blind forces of the collective life.

The image of the hive has had a great success as an ideal of collaborative social action. Every modern utopia (except the completely wishful Shangri-La) reflects the beehive ideal. Even a statesman of highest caliber, Jan Smuts, has praised it as a pattern for industrial society. Plato's personified state and Hobbes's sea monster impress us as fantasies, but the hive looks like more than a poetic figure; it seems really to buzz around us.

I think the concept of the state as a collective organism, composed of multitudes of little workers, guided by social forces that none of the little workers can fathom, and accomplishing some greater destiny, is supported by a factor other than our mechanized industry; that other factor is a momentous event in our intellectual history: the spread of the theory of evolution.

First biologists, then psychologists, and finally sociologists and moralists have become newly aware that man belongs to the animal kingdom. The impact of the concept of evolution on scientific discovery has been immense, and it has not stopped at laboratory science; it has also produced some less sober and sound inspirations. The concept of continuous animal evolution has made most psychologists belittle the differences between man and his nonhuman relatives, and led some of them, indeed, to think of *Homo sapiens* as just one kind of primate among others, like the others in all essential respects—differing from apes and monkeys not much more than they differ from species to species among themselves. Gradually the notion of the human animal became common currency, questioned only by some religious minds. This in turn has made it natural for social theorists with scientific leanings to model their concepts of human society on animal societies, the anthill and the beehive.

Perhaps it were well, at this point, to say that I myself stand entirely in the scientific camp. I do not argue against any religious or even vitalistic doctrines; such things are not arguable. I speak not *for*, but *from*, a naturalist's point of view, and anyone who does not share it can make his own reservations in judging what I say.

Despite man's zoological status, which I wholeheartedly accept, there is a deep gulf between the highest animal and the most primitive normal human being: a difference in mentality that is fundamental. It stems from the development of one new process in the human brain—a process that seems to be entirely peculiar to that brain: the use of *symbols for ideas*. By "symbols" I mean all kinds of signs that can be used and understood whether the things they refer to are there or not. The word "symbol" has, unfortunately, many different meanings for different people. Some people reserve it for mystic signs, like Rosicrucian symbols; some mean by it *significant images,* such as Keats's "Huge cloudy symbols of a high romance"; some use it quite the opposite way and speak of "mere symbols," meaning empty gestures, signs that have lost their meanings; and some, notably logicians, use the term for mathematical signs, marks that constitute a code, a brief, concise language. In their sense, ordinary words are symbols, too. Ordinary language is a symbolism.

When I say that the distinctive function of the human brain is the use of symbols, I mean any and all of these kinds. They are all different from signs that animals use. Animals interpret signs, too, but only as pointers to actual things and events, cues to action or expectation, threats and promises, landmarks and ear-marks in the world. Human beings use such signs, too, but above all they use symbols—especially words—to think and talk about things that are neither present nor expected. The words convey *ideas,* that may or may not have counterparts in actuality. This power of thinking *about* things expresses itself in language, imagination, and speculation—the chief products of human mentality that animals do not share.

Language, the most versatile and indispensable of all symbolisms, has put its stamp on all our mental functions, so that I think they always differ from even their closest analogues in animal life. Language has invaded our feeling and dreaming and action, as well as our reasoning, which is really a product of it. The greatest change wrought by language is the increased scope of awareness in speech-gifted beings. An animal's awareness is always of things in its own place and life. In human awareness, the present, actual situation is often the least part. We have not only memories and expectations; we have *a past* in which we locate our memories, and *a future* that vastly overreaches our own anticipations. Our past is a story, our future a piece of imagination. Likewise our ambient is a place in a wider, symbolically conceived place, the universe. We live in *a world.*

This difference of mentality between man and animal seems to me to make a cleft between them almost as great as the division between animals and plants. There is continuity between the orders, but the division is real nevertheless. Human life differs radically from animal life. By virtue of our incomparably wider awareness, of our power of envisagement of things and events beyond any actual perception, we have acquired needs and aims that animals do not have; and even the most savage human society, having to meet those needs and implement those aims, is not really comparable to any animal society. The two may have some analogous functions, but the essential structure must be different, because man and beast live differently in every way.

Probably the profoundest difference between human and animal needs is made by one piece of human awareness, one fact that is not present to animals, because it is never learned in any direct experience: that is our foreknowledge of death. The fact that we ourselves must die is not a simple and isolated fact. It is built on a wide survey of facts that discloses the structure of history as a succession of overlapping brief lives, the patterns of youth and age, growth and decline; and above all that, it is built on the logical insight that *one's own life is a case in point*. Only a creature that can think symbolically *about* life can conceive of its own death. Our knowledge of death is part of our knowledge of life.

What, then, do we—all of us—know about life?

Every life that we know is generated from other life. Each living thing springs from some other living thing or things. Its birth is a process of new individuation, in a life stream whose beginning we do not know.

Individuation is a word we do not often meet. We hear about individuality, sometimes spoken in praise, sometimes as an excuse for someone's being slightly crazy. We hear and read about "the individual," a being that is forever adjusting, like a problem child, to something called "society." But how does individuality arise? What makes an individual? A fundamental, biological process of *individuation*, that marks the life of every stock, plant or animal. Life is a series of individuations, and these can be of various sorts, and reach various degrees.

Most people would agree, offhand, that every creature lives its life and then dies. This might, indeed, be called a truism. But, like some other truisms, it is not true. The lowest forms of life, such as the amoebae, normally (that is, barring accidents) do not die. When they grow very large and might be expected to lay eggs, or in some other way raise a family, they do no such thing; they divide, and make two small ones ready to grow. Well now, where is the old one? It did not die. But it is gone. Its individuation was only an episode in the life of the stock, a phase, a transient form that changed again. Amoebae are individuated in space—they move and feed as independent, whole organisms— but in time they are not self-identical individuals. They do not generate young ones while they themselves grow old; they grow old and *become* young ones.

All the higher animals, however, are final individuations that end in death. They spring from a common stock, but they do not merge back into it. Each one is an end. Somewhere on its way toward death it usually produces a new life to succeed it, but its own story is finished by death.

That is our pattern, too. Each human individual is a culmination of an inestimably long line—its ancestry—and each is destined to die. The living stock is like a palm tree, a trunk composed of its own past leaves. Each leaf springs from the trunk, unfolds, grows, and dies off; its past is incorporated in the trunk, where new life has usually arisen from it. So there constantly are ends, but the stock lives on, and each leaf has that whole life behind it.

The momentous difference between us and our animal cousins is that they do not know they are going to die. Animals spend their lives avoiding death, until it gets them. They do not know it is going to. Neither do they know that they are part of a greater life, but pass on the torch without knowing. Their aim, then, is simply to keep going, to function, to escape trouble, to live from moment to moment in an endless Now.

Our power of symbolic conception has given us each a glimpse of himself as one final individuation from the great human stock. We do not know when or what the end will be, but we know that there will be one. We also envisage a past and future, a stretch of time so vastly longer than any creature's memory, and a world so much richer than any world of sense, that it makes our time in that world seem infinitesimal. This is the price of the great gift of symbolism.

In the face of such uncomfortable prospects (probably conceived long before the dawn of any religious ideas), human

beings have evolved aims different from those of any other creatures. Since we cannot have our fill of existence by going on and
on, we want to have *as much life as possible* in our short span. If
our individuation must be brief, we want to make it complete; so
we are inspired to think, act, dream our desires, create things,
express our ideas, and in all sorts of ways make up by concentration what we cannot have by length of days. We seek the greatest
possible individuation, or development of personality. In doing
this, we have set up a new demand, not for mere continuity of
existence, but for *self-realization.* That is a uniquely human aim.

But obviously, the social structure could not arise on this principle alone. Vast numbers of individualists realizing themselves
with a vengeance would not make up an ideal society. A small
number might try it; there is a place, far away from here, called
the Self-Realization Golden World Colony. But most of us have
no golden world to colonize. You can only do that south of Los
Angeles.

Seriously, however, an ideal is not disposed of by pointing out
that it cannot be implemented under existing conditions. It may
still be a true ideal; and if it is very important we may have to
change the conditions, as we will have to for the ideal of world
peace. If complete individuation were really the whole aim of
human life, our society would be geared to it much more than it
is. It is not the golden world that is wanting, but something else;
the complete individualist is notoriously not the happy man, even
if good fortune permits his antics.

The fact is that *the greatest possible individuation* is usually
taken to mean, "as much as is possible without curtailing the
rights of others." But that is not the real measure of how much is
possible. The measure is provided in the individual himself, and
is as fundamental as his knowledge of death. It is the other part
of his insight into nature—his knowledge of life, of the great un-
broken stream, the life of the stock from which his individuation stems.

One individual life, however rich, still looks infinitesimal; no
matter how much self-realization is concentrated in it, it is a tiny
atom—and we don't like to be tiny atoms, not even hydrogen
atoms. We need more than fullness of personal life to counter our
terrible knowledge of all it implies. And we have more; we have

our history, our commitments made for us before we were born, our relatedness to the rest of mankind. The counterpart of individuation from the great life of the stock is our rootedness in that life, our involvement with the whole human race, past and present.

Each person is not only a free, single end, like the green palm leaf that unfolds, grows in a curve of beauty, and dies in its season; he is like the whole palm leaf, the part inside the trunk, too. He is the culmination of his entire ancestry, and *represents* that whole human past. In his brief individuation he is an *expression* of all humanity. That is what makes each person's life sacred and all-important. A single ruined life is the bankruptcy of a long line. This is what I mean by the individual's involvement with all mankind.

All animals are unconsciously involved with their kind. Heredity governs not only their growth, color, and form, but their actions, too. They carry their past about with them in everything they do. But they do not know it. They don't need to, because they never could lose it. Their involvement with the greater life of the race is implicit in their limited selfhood.

Our knowledge that life is finite, and, in fact, precarious and brief, drives us on to greater individuation than animals attain. Our mental talents have largely freed us from that built-in behavior called instinct. The scope of our imagination gives each of us a separate world, and a separate consciousness, and threatens to break the instinctual ties of brotherhood that make all the herrings swim into one net, and all the geese turn their heads at the same moment. Yet we cannot afford to lose the feeling of involvement with our kind; for if we do, personal life shrinks up to nothingness.

The sense of involvement is our social sense. We have it by nature, originally just as animals do, and just as unconsciously. It is the direct feeling of needing our own kind, caring what happens. Social sense is an instinctive sense of being somehow one with all other people—a feeling that reflects the rootedness of our existence in a human past. Human society rests on this feeling. It is often said to rest on the need of collaboration, or on domination of the weak by the strong, or some other circumstance, but I think such theories deal with its modes, and ignore

its deeper structure; at the bottom of it is the feeling of involvement, or social sense. If we lose that, no coercion will hold us to
our duties, because they do not feel like commitments, and no
achievements will matter, because they are doomed to be snuffed
out with the individual, without being laid to account in the
continuity of life.

Great individual development, such as human beings are driven
by their intellectual insights to seek, does of course always
threaten to break the bonds of direct social involvement, that
give animal life its happy unconscious continuity. When the
strain gets hard, we have social turmoil, anarchy, irresponsibility,
and in private lives the sense of loneliness and infinite smallness
that lands some people in nihilism and cynicism, and leads others
to existentialism or less intellectual cults.

It is then that social philosophers look on animal societies as
models for human society. There is no revolt, no strike, no competition, no anti-Anything party, in a beehive. As Kipling, fifty years
or more ago, represented his British utopia, which he called the
Mother Hive, that ideal state had a completely co-operative
economy, an army that went into action without a murmur, each
man with the same impulse the moment an enemy threatened to
intrude, and a populace of such tribal solidarity that it would
promptly run out any stranger that tried to become established in
the state and disrupt its traditions. Any native individual that
could not fit into the whole had to be liquidated; the loss was
regrettable, but couldn't be helped, and would be made up.

Yet the beehive really has no possible bearing on human affairs,
for it owes its harmonious existence to the fact that its members
are *incompletely individuated*, even as animals go. None of them
performs all of a creature's essential functions: feeding, food
getting, nest building, mating, and procreating. The queen has
to be fed and tended; she has only procreative functions. She
doesn't even bring up her own children; they have nurses. The
drones are born and reared only as her suitors, and when the
romance is finished they are killed, like proper romantic heroes.
The building, nursing, food getting, and fighting are done by
sterile females who cannot procreate, amazons who do all their
own housework. So there is not only division of labor, but division
of organs, functional and physical incompleteness. This direct

involvement of each bee with the whole lets the hive function with an organic rhythm that makes its members appear wonderfully socialized. But they are really not socialized at all, any more than the cells in our tissues are socialized; they are associated, by being unindividuated.

That is as far away from a human ideal as one can get. We need, above all, a world in which we can realize our capacities, develop and act as personalities. That means giving up our instinctive patterns of habit and prejudice, our herd instincts. Yet we need the emotional security of the greater, continuous life—the awareness of our involvement with all mankind. How can we eat that cake, and have it too?

The same mental talent that makes us need so much individuation comes to the rescue of our social involvement: I mean the peculiarly human talent of holding ideas in the mind by means of symbols. Human life, even in the simplest forms we know, is shot through and through with *social symbols*. All fantastic beliefs in a great ancestor are symbolic of the original and permanent life of the stock from which every individual life stems. The totem, the hero, the sacred cow, these are the most elementary social symbols. With a maturer view of the world, and the development of religious ideas, the symbolic image of man is usually taken up into the greater view of a divine world order and a moral law. We are sons of Adam and daughters of Eve. If Adam and Eve were simply some human couple supposed to have lived in the Near East before it was so difficult, this would be an odd way of speaking; we don't ordinarily refer to our neighbor's children as Mr. Brown's boys and Mrs. Brown's girls. But Adam is Man, and Eve is Woman (the names even mean that): and among us transient little mites, every man is Man, every woman is Woman. That is the source of human dignity, the sense of which has to be upheld at all levels of social life.

Most people have some religious ritual that supports their knowledge of a greater life, but even in purely secular affairs we constantly express our faith in the continuity of human existence. Animals provide lairs or nests for their immediate offspring. Man builds for the future—often for nothing else. His earliest great buildings were not mansions, but monuments. And not only physical edifices, but above all laws and institutions are intended for the future, and often justified by showing that they have a precedent, or are in accord with the past. They are conveniences of their day, but symbols of more than their day. They are symbols of society, and of each individual's inalienable membership in society.

What, then, is the measure of our possible individuation, without loss of social sense? It is the power of social symbolism. We can give up our actual, instinctual involvements with our kind just to the extent that we can replace them by symbolic ones. This is the prime function of social symbols, from a handshake, to the assembly of robed judges in a Supreme Court. In protocol and ritual, in the investment of authority, in sanctions and honors, lies our security against loss of involvement with mankind; in such bonds lies our freedom to be individuals.

It has been said that an animal society, like a beehive, is really an organism, and the separate bees its organic parts. I think this statement requires many reservations, but it contains some truth. The hive is an organic structure, a superindividual, something like an organism. A human city, however, is an *organization*. It is above all a symbolic structure, a mental reality. Its citizens are the whole and only individuals. They are not a "living mass," like a swarm of semi-individuated bees. The model of the hive has brought with it the concept of human masses, to be cared for in times of peace, deployed in times of war, educated for use or sacrificed for the higher good of their state. In the specious analogy of animal and human society, the hive and the city, lies, I think, the basic philosophical fallacy of all totalitarian theory, even the most sincere and idealistic—even the thoroughly noble political thought of Plato.

We are like leaves of the palm tree, each deeply embedded in the tree, a part of the trunk, each opening to the light in a final, separate life. Our world is a human world, organized to implement our highest individuation. There may be ten thousand of us working in one factory. There are several millions of us living in a city like New York. But we are not the masses; we are the public.

ʳ

Susanne K. Langer   Born in New York in 1895, educated at Radcliffe
and the University of Vienna, Professor Langer is a productive, controversial, and probing philosopher, with a special interest in aesthetics
and linguistics.

"Man and Animal: The City and the Hive" (1958) The author skillfully uses metaphor and analogy, and, in addition, she analyzes how
metaphoric and symbolic conceptions have made man what he is.
The argument is deep and far ranging, yet it consistently avoids the
irrelevant, the wishy-washy, and the jargon of overspecialization.

ʳ

*1. According to this essay, how and why is the individual involved with
all mankind? 2. Is the author's use of metaphor and simile effective?
3. In what ways is a city a "symbolic structure"?*

JACQUES BARZUN

Myths for Materialists

The Anglo-Americans of the twentieth century complained that they had no myths. Their poets, critics and scholars kept bewailing this supposed lack and some even tried to supply it by artificial drafts upon the Irish, Greek or Oriental mythologies. Modern investigation, however, points to the familiar truth that the men of that restless culture were calling for something they already had. Myth, in fact, so pervaded their lives that they could not see it for what it was.

The proof of this statement rests chiefly on the finds recently made in a great hollow formed below the Manhattan schist, probably during the Big (or subatomic) Depression of 1999. Under the usual pile of rubbish in this vast and naturally airtight enclosure, excavation has revealed a group of small buildings, with some adjoining structures shortly to be described; and within the best preserved of these buildings, a large room virtually undamaged. This room may have been the library of a club, or alternatively—for the indications are ambiguous—a dentist's waiting room. In either event, the discovery remains the most significant since that of the lost continent itself. For although the books add little or nothing to our knowledge, the large mass of magazines dating from the middle years of the century constitutes a unique, illuminating, and priceless collection.

Reprinted by permission of the author.

I hasten to add that in putting this high value upon it, I have in mind not the reading matter which presumably satisfied the contemporary readers, but the much greater bulk of pictorial representations, often accompanied by text, which resemble earlier fragments identified by the symbol ADVT. Scholars have disputed at length over the exact meaning of this device. I can now, I believe, settle the principal doubts and establish—or at least confidently advance—a fairly complete theory of the subject. Those pictures, that text, enshrine the mythology of the twentieth century. After examining and comparing some seven thousand pieces, I am in a position to sketch in broad strokes the religious thoughts and the moral feelings evoked by that body of myths.[1]

I may at once explain that I draw my assurance from the curious structures which I referred to as adjoining the buildings recently found. Collapsed though these structures now are, it is clear that they were once meant to stand upright as panels of great size, occupying open spaces set apart to afford the widest visibility. All this suggests a religious consecration of both the site and the structure. On the face of these panels (often marked Outdoor Advt) were the same colored images as in the periodicals, but of heroic proportions and usually accompanied by some pithy aphorism. The number of such dedicated placards in a relatively small area like the one examined justifies my belief that we have in these words and pictures literally the revealed religion of the twentieth century.

It is normal in any culture for the commonest beliefs to be tacit and for the meaning of symbols to be so obvious as never to give rise to any glossary. From the outset, then, we face the double enigma of those four letters ADVT. What was their ordinary meaning and what their ultimate significance? The three main hypotheses regarding the first question are that the mark stands for (1) Advertising, (2) Advantage, and (3) Adventitious. Not the least startling conclusion I have come to is that the symbol denotes all three ideas. There is no discrepancy among them, even though historically the first meaning was the

[1] More exactly, that *mytho-pinaco-prosopopoeia*.

most usual. In twentieth century usage, "advertise" was a verb derived from the character of the Bitch-Goddess of Appearance, whose sacred name is now lost. The four letters stood for something like "Behold Me"—whence the plausible but false etymology of "advert eyes."

Without at first suspecting it, we touch here the central dogma in the Anglo-Americans' religious system. What they called their "modern" civilization was built on the preponderance of one physical sense over all the others, the sense of sight. Their science was not, as with us, the whole of knowledge, but only such knowledge as could be brought within range of the eye, directly or through instruments. They believed only in what they could measure, that is, what they could lay along a ruler, or between two hairlines, or could otherwise visually place. No competent student of their age can deny that they displayed extraordinary ingenuity in achieving this universal reduction of Being to the grasp of a single faculty.

But this monomania entailed an ascetic drying up of the inner life in every member of the culture. It was a prodigal expense of spirit for which ordinary life had to supply emotional compensation. Hence the need for, and the slow creation of, the vast mythology known as Advertising. An "ad"—as it came to be called in demotic speech—was simply the power of things made into pictures. Through the eye was given what actual life denied—beauty, strength, leisure, love, and personal distinction.

"Objects," as one contemporary philosopher confessed, "change their usual faces with the myth maker's emotions."[2] How much did he know of the origin and results of this transformation in the familiar things about him? We cannot tell, but in his day mind control through icons was well-nigh omnipotent. For example, by collating scattered references in the ancient literature with the newly found "ads," it is clear that just at the moment when the myth makers began to invoke the supernatural power of citrus to sustain and embellish existence, technological improvements were depriving the fruit of its natural color, taste and chance of ripening. At the very time when the sense of life as a whole was being atomized into a series of "processes," the

2 Cassirer.

mythology was verbally making up for the deficiency by a poetical iteration having Life as its theme. "Vital" became a magic word, as for example in an ad referring to the various kinds of popcorn eaten at breakfast: "Be sure you get the *vital* outer covering of wheat."

About the same period also, the mysterious substances called Vitamins—precious if measured by cost and complex if judged by their name—became the object of an official cult created jointly by mythologers and medicine men. To carry out the myth, Vitamins were chosen by symbolic letters and were weighed in thousands of "life-giving units." A last example will show how unremitting was this grasping after a runaway sense of well-being. Ten, twenty, thirty times a day, the Anglo-Americans were reminded of their need for vigor, for youth, for a "lift" by drug or weed—the worship of Pep. Initiated by one of the national heroes, Ponce de Leon, this quest was originally for a fountain in the south (*soda-fountain*). Many claimed to have found it and "advertised" to that effect; bottled drinks and packaged foods bore the magic syllable. "To be full of Pep" was equivalent to our "enthusiastic" or possessed by the god—the rare state then known in full as *pepsicola.*

We must now turn from the concept to the embodiment, the pictures. What strikes the unprejudiced observer at once is the overwhelming emphasis on womanhood—presumably as the inexhaustible fount of human life—and on the situation of sexual approach as the characteristic moment in that life. If one did not know the ways of myth makers, their habit of juxtaposing incompatibles for the sake of a higher truth, one would suppose that the Anglo-Americans were unable to do anything without a member of the opposite sex in a state of provocative or compliant amorousness. In their iconography, seductiveness and sheeps' eyes invariably accompany eating, working, and riding, securing food, clothing, and shelter, listening to music or averting constipation.

An important corollary was that suggestive effects of nudity and drapery were limited, perhaps by law, to the portrayal of women. In all the seven thousand documents examined there occurs not a single instance of Father Paul's Pills showing him in tights, nor of the Chesterfield girl wearing a cassock. Despite this

rigid esthetic, based on the complementary traits of the sexes as
regards display, all objects whatever acquired an erotic component. The motive is clear enough: the artificial search for life
through objects can only be kept at high pitch by associating
the objects themselves with the strongest of desires. Advertising
maxims were explicit enough: "Look sweeter in a sweater," "Use
the soap with sex appeal," etc.

This mythopoeic principle did not, however, rely solely on the
mating instinct. It employed two others, closely related—vanity
and devotion to the Mother. This last, which goes back very far
in the western tradition, was in its latest form singularly debased.
Though I am certain that the best literary and pictorial talent of
America went into this highly revered and highly paid art of
mythography, all the efforts of these creative artists did not succeed in making The Mothers interesting. The type remained
domestic and sentimental. One has only to think of the earlier
school of Madonna makers, or of the medieval poet von Goethe-
Faust, to see the difference.

The decline may well have been due to some obscure physical
cause: the American myth-mother is always depicted as frail,
grey-haired, with glasses and a senile rictus. Yet by a strange
contradiction, the American maiden or young matron is almost
always represented as nature makes her during the months of
lactation. This is an improbability—or a religious mystery—which
I do not pretend to have fathomed.

Contrary to the feeling of all mankind about ancestors, the
second appeal, directed at personal vanity, occupies a much
larger place than mother worship. Yet the anomaly disappears
when we understand the democratic paradox of competition
within equality: everyone has a mother; not everyone has a
Packard.[3] Moreover, mass production tended to make any class
of objects (as of men) virtually identical; some kind of mythical
individuality had to be imparted to them in hopes of its transfer
to the mass man. More and more, the social self came to depend
on the constant tonic of acquiring these specially wrapped goods,
these "superheterogene" articles.

I cannot agree with a famous critic of that epoch, Veblen, who
spoke of "conspicuous consumption" and attendant waste as the

[3] Highly upholstered locomotive.

mainspring of "modern" behavior. He described, it seems to me, an earlier age, that of kings and nobles, who translated power into munificence. The common man, on the contrary, receives direct satisfaction from objects, and for the reason I gave earlier: that the goddess ADVT consecrates matter by guaranteeing (1) secret worth and (2) miraculous origin. This is in keeping with all we know about myth. The medicine man infuses the magic into the familiar thing; whence the American advertising formulas, "A Wonderful Buy" and "It's Different," i.e., supernatural. A fuller text of the best period informs us, over a beguiling triptych, "Not just a fur coat, but an important aid to gracious living. It will give your morale a lift, *as well as impress your friends.*" (Italics mine.) No distinction between direct and indirect help to self-esteem could be clearer, and as it happens, the distinction was noted even at the time by the author of the satiric poem, "Civilizoo." As he tersely put it: "Women think fur beauty,/ Scholars, books knowledge." Here was no showing off, but simple faith in the fetish.

It would be tedious to enumerate the myriad forms of the faith: they equal the number of consumable articles. Some, however, lent themselves to the arousing of fear preparatory to flattery. To be soothed by possession of the fetish, the citizen must be first alarmed by a dramatization of evil—halitosis, falling hair, teeth, garters, B. O. (undecipherable), as well as by the ever-present threat of Wrong Choice.

In this connection I may instance the farthest reach of magic power found in our documents. As with us, the Anglo-American word for "spirits" has a double meaning, for alcohol makes man cheerful and enterprising. But the ancients' impressionable souls seem to have drawn virtue not alone from the contents of the bottle; they were affected by the label upon it, which conferred tone or talents on the buyer. Thus a celebrated whisky was normally advertised as being "For Men of Decision." One would have thought that the thing needed was a whisky for men of *In*decision, but doubtless the poet was using the rhetorical figure known as hypallage—taking the result for the action. In a like manner, medicines, food and personal attire were, whenever possible, held up as proved fetishes.

In discussing any mythology, however "vital," one must consider the treatment accorded to the subject of death. At first, I

believed that the ancients ignored it. I knew, to be sure, of a few
covert eulogies of funeral parlors, but it was evident that the aim
here was still to make the living comfortable. Then it occurred
to me that the previously noted tendency to portray happy results
without regard to probability might hold a clue to my problem.
And it happened that I had on my hands a series of absolutely
inexplicable ads. Putting two and two together gave me what I
was looking for.

My unexplained series consisted of simple but beautiful com-
positions depicting entire families sitting about the fire in smooth
white uniforms, deceptively like our own suits of underwear. The
faces, suggesting the school of Puvis de Chavannes, are full of
benignity and repose. The atmosphere, too, is unusual—hardly
any luxuries, no hint of the muscular strain, due to toothache or
dandruff, financial or scientific anxiety, which meets us elsewhere.
More significant still, all marks of sex have disappeared. Young
and old seem beyond self-consciousness, or indeed consciousness
of any kind. I conclude that we are logically and mythologically
bound to accept these beatific groups as showing us the way the
ancients represented death.[4] I have in fact found one marked
"After the Last Supper," but the words are pencilled in and may
lack authority.

If we did not know how uncommon was the belief in an after-
life during the twentieth and twenty-first centuries, one could
entertain the alternative that these classical figures were meant
for angels. But mature reflection rules out this hypothesis; I will
at most concede that they may have been Supermen, in the very
special condition of immobility. Since all other icons show action,
or at least animation, I find it far easier to believe that this sober
grouping, these firm outlines, are the work of the religious artist
contemplating death. Under conditions then prevailing, it happened more and more frequently that whole families died simultaneously. Their friends coming to pay their last visit, without any
hope of reunion hereafter, would find them posed by the under-
taker's art in familiar attitudes, clad in ritual white—in fact in
that one-piece knitted suit as advertised (with or without buttons)

[4] We find the same serenity in the users of certain soap flakes. This coincidence suggests that the flakes procured euthanasia. One brand was significantly called Lux.

which would match the wreath of lilies and the silk-lined coffin. Over the abyss of centuries, one feels a catch in the throat at the thought of these once-living men, in whose desperate symbolism the white of snow, fitting like a new skin, meant death and peace.

Yet despite this symbol of hope, each year in midwinter—on December 25 to be exact—there occurred a nation-wide panic about the renewal of life. It may have come down from the old fear that the earth would not bear in spring. If so, with urbanization and technological farming the fear shifted from the earth to the self. Wearied by a routine divorced from nature, the citizen began to question his own survival. "Who and what am I, why so pale and listless?" Early November saw him sitting before a sun-lamp to cure the paleness; the end of the month would see him, and particularly his wife, storming the shops.

It was a saturnalia of devotion to the goddess ADVT. The vernacular name Splurge indeed suggests a baptismal rite—to immerse oneself and wallow in things and be made new by contact. Life was goods after all. By an historical irony, the Anglo-Americans associated this feast with the short-lived founder of Christianity, who always showed the greatest alacrity in leaving his coat in another's hands, and who died possessed of one garment and three nails. His worshippers nonetheless celebrated his birth in a smothering of cloaks, scarfs, ties, silks, baubles and furs. This fact proves again that myth and religion are uncertain allies, but it also enables us to feel the pathos of that puzzling lyric in the American Anthology:

> The first thing to turn green in Spring
> Is the Christmas jewelry.

That "shopping" on these regular occasions was an essential part of mental health is naturally assumed by the advertisers. But the practical proof of the assumption was never more striking than in the serious incidents of the so-called Reconversion Period of the mid-forties. Drained of goods by war, the people nearly perished. They starved, not in their bodies but in their imaginations: six years virtually without the consolation of ads were to them as the suspension of the sacraments would be to us. The shops, though bare, were haunted by women as by insects seeking

their prey, while the entire population grew irritable, distem-
pered, antisocial. Women fought over pylon hose (i.e., leg coverings) and men committed suicide for lack of telegrams. Diaries
tell us that those who by luck secured even a single object—an
icebox or a full-tailed shirt—showed the restorative effect immediately. It was at the worst of these bad times that a laconic
sage summed up the mood in the famous phrase, "Money no
Object."

Such is, in rough outline, the mythology of the Anglo-Americans
as far as archeological research can reconstruct it. I reserve the
right to give a fuller account at some later time and to make it
more vivid, though I trust not more persuasive, by the addition
of plates in color. Meanwhile it may help to settle any lingering
doubts if I conclude with a few words on the historical link between the faith in ADVT, on the one hand, and the powerful
class of medicine men, on the other.

What distinguishes ADVT from all other great creeds is that
its beginnings were perfectly natural and its final form completely
miraculous. But at all times it was entangled with established
religions. We know that the Greeks, almost as soon as they
learned to write, began to inscribe curses on sheets of lead, which
were then placed in their temples to call down the vengeance of
the god on the person so advertised.

In the early Middle Ages, the public crier could be hired for
any sort of advertising and it is on record that new religious
dogmas were sometimes entrusted to his powers of publicity.
Throughout every period, the marriage market made use of
kindred devices and called on the gods to further and sanctify
the deed. With the advent of the daily printed sheet, about the
middle of the eighteenth century, the real cult of ADVT begins.
Dr. Samuel Johnson, an early anthropologist, complains in 1759
of abuses then coming into practice: "It is become necessary to
gain attention by magnificence of promises and by eloquence
sometimes sublime, sometimes pathetic . . ." and it is "a moral
question" whether advertisers do not "play too wantonly with our
passions."[5]

But the junction of all the elements into what I ventured to

[5] *The Idler*, No. 40.

call a *mytho-pinaco-prosopopoeia* (fable in pictures personifying things) came at the end of Dr. Johnson's century, when a medicine man of Bristol, Dr. Joseph Fry, had the revelation that his Maker had chosen him to extend the business of importing cocoa, and had ordained the means. He carried out this injunction in a small way at first, then on a national scale; himself boasting that he was the first man, not indeed to import cocoa; but to import the idea of a *signed guarantee on each and every package* into the distribution of goods. From him were descended the brothers Smith, Lydia Pinkham, and other eponymous figures worthy to rank with Beowulf.

In time, the signed guarantee became superfluous. A strong assertion in print, with an illustration lending color to it, sufficed to make converts. The suffering martyrs to a cough became willing martyrs to *Rem*, the well-named. But an overextension of this true church nearly caused its undoing: too many rival assertions neutralized one another. New guarantees were needed, fuller of Authority than manufacturers could command. They appealed, and not in vain, to a new class of medicine men, the laboratory testers.[6] Their success was shown by the fact that in a short time all advertising emanated from a few Oratories and Laboratories, keeping up, for appearance's sake, a pretended competition among products.

In the final phase, the tester was simply symbolized by a white coat, a piece of apparatus, and the look of a seer. Behind him, invisible but using him and his device, was the newest type of Thaumaturgist, to whom no miracles were impossible. I refer to the Expert in Public Relations. He was believed capable of making fraud innocuous, starvation pleasant, and wars remote. It was rumored that such a man had once succeeded in making the public take an interest in the curriculum of a university. But this exaggeration can be dismissed.

Heretics could now and then be found who tried to undermine the common faith. But their small numbers can be inferred from the fact that they were never molested. They might deride mythadology, calling its effect "the massage of the mass age,"

---

[6] "A medicine man sits on a deerskin when he makes medicine. He puts herbs in a can, adds water and blows bubbles through a straw to purify it."—From a contemporary account.

the larger body of believers could ignore them and sincerely continue their search for myth. Perhaps this was as it should be, for myth will move mankind most when they do not call it so, and what men find indispensable, they preserve. The conveniences of life, as their name implies, are matters of convention; so Chesterfield must forever repeat "They Satisfy," though things in themselves do not. But things enhanced by art and color, sex and slogans, did give the illusions of a lotus-eating life to the men of the strange civilization I have described. The role of ADVT was to suffuse visible matter with invisible virtues, adding to bread the nutrition it had lost and to stone or steel the warmth it had never had.

✦

JACQUES BARZUN   Born in France in 1907, he came to the United States in 1919. After graduating from Columbia University he became a professor of history there, and is now Dean of the Graduate School. He has written widely on modern culture and the problems of higher education.

"Myths for Materialists" (1946)   In a style that is obviously scholarly, the author parodies the pedant, thus adding to the humor of his "reconstruction" of our materialistic myths. By his chronological fiction and an argument based on analogue, hypothesis, and induction, he views our culture in an amusing but devastating way.

✦

1. *Would the author's conclusions be different if his "evidence" consisted of current television commercials? 2. What are the basic attitudes he is satirizing? 3. What contribution do his footnotes make?*

WILLIAM FAULKNER

On Privacy—the American Dream: What Happened to It

This was the American Dream: a sanctuary on the earth for individual man: a condition in which he could be free not only of the old established closed-corporation hierarchies of arbitrary power which had oppressed him as a mass, but free of that mass into which the hierarchies of church and state had compressed and held him individually thralled and individually impotent.

A dream simultaneous among the separate individuals of men so asunder and scattered as to have no contact to match dreams and hopes among the old nations of the Old World which existed as nations not on citizenship but subjectship, which endured only on the premise of size and docility of the subject mass; the individual men and women who said as with one simultaneous voice: "We will establish a new land where man can assume that every individual man—not the mass of men but individual men—has inalienable right to individual dignity and freedom within a fabric of individual courage and honorable work and mutual responsibility."

Not just an idea, but a condition: a living human condition designed to be co-eval with the birth of America itself, engendered, created, and simultaneous with the very air and word

America, which at that one stroke, one instant, should cover the whole earth with one simultaneous suspiration like air or light. And it was, it did: radiating outward to cover even the old weary repudiated still-thralled nations, until individual men everywhere, who had no more than heard the name, let alone knew where America was, could respond to it, lifting up not only their hearts but the hopes too which until now they did not know—or anyway dared not remember—that they possessed.

A condition in which every man would not only not be a king, he wouldn't even want to be one. He wouldn't even need to bother to need to be the equal of kings because now he was free of kings and all their similar congeries; free not only of the symbols but of the old arbitrary hierarchies themselves which the puppet-symbols represented—courts and cabinets and churches and schools—to which he had been valuable not as an individual but only as that integer, his value compounded in that immutable ratio to his sheer mindless numbers, that animal increase of his will-less and docile mass.

The dream, the hope, the condition which our forefathers did not bequeath to us, their heirs and assigns, but rather bequeathed us, their successors, to the dream and the hope. We were not even given the chance then to accept or decline the dream, for the reason that the dream already owned and possessed us at birth. It was not our heritage because we were its, we ourselves heired in our successive generations to the dream by the idea of the dream. And not only we, their sons born and bred in America, but men born and bred in the old alien repudiated lands, also felt that breath, that air, heard that promise, that proffer that there was such a thing as hope for individual man. And the old nations themselves, so old and so long-fixed in the old concepts of man as to have thought themselves beyond all hope of change, making oblation to that new dream of that new concept of man by gifts of monuments and devices to mark the portals of that inalienable right and hope:

"There is room for you here from about the earth, for all ye individually homeless, individually oppressed, individually unindividualized."

A free gift left to us by those who had mutually travailed and individually endured to create it; we, their successors, did not

even have to earn, deserve it, let alone win it. We did not even
need to nourish and feed it. We needed only to remember that,
living, it was therefore perishable and must be defended in its
crises. Some of us, most of us perhaps, could not have proved by
definition that we knew exactly what it was. But then, we didn't
need to: who no more needed to define it than we needed to
define that air we breathed or that word, which, the two of them,
simply by existing simultaneously—the breathing of the American air which made America—together had engendered and
created the dream on that first day of America as air and motion
created temperature and climate on the first day of time.

Because that dream was man's aspiration in the true meaning
of the word aspiration. It was not merely the blind and voiceless
hope of his heart: it was the actual inbreathe of his lungs, his
lights, his living and unsleeping metabolism, so that we actually
lived the Dream. We did not live *in* the dream: we lived the
Dream itself, just as we do not merely live *in* air and climate, but
we live Air and Climate; we ourselves individually representative
of the Dream, the Dream itself actually audible in the strong
uninhibited voices which were not afraid to speak cliché at. the
very top of them, giving to the cliché-avatars of "Give me liberty
or give me death" or "This to be self-evident that all individual
men were created equal in one mutual right to freedom" which
had never lacked for truth anyway, assuming that hope and
dignity and truth, a validity and immediacy absolving them even
of cliché.

That was the Dream: not man created equal in the sense that
he was created black or white or brown or yellow and hence
doomed irrevocably to that for the remainder of his days—or
rather, not doomed with equality but blessed with equality, himself lifting no hand but instead lying curled and drowsing in the
warm and airless bath of it like the yet-wombed embryo; but
liberty in which to have an equal start at equality with all other
men, and freedom in which to defend and preserve that equality
by means of the individual courage and the honorable work and
the mutual responsibility. Then we lost it. It abandoned us, which
had supported and protected and defended us while our new
nation of new concepts of human existence got a firm enough

foothold to stand erect among the nations of the earth, demanding nothing of us in return save to remember always that, being alive, it was therefore perishable and so must be held always in the unceasing responsibility and vigilance of courage and honor and pride and humility. It is gone now. We dozed, slept, and it abandoned us. And in that vacuum now there sound no longer the strong loud voices not merely unafraid but not even aware that fear existed, speaking in mutual unification of one mutual hope and will. Because now what we hear is a cacophony of terror and conciliation and compromise babbling only the mouth-sounds, the loud and empty words which we have emasculated of all meaning whatever—freedom, democracy, patriotism—with which, awakened at last, we try in desperation to hide from ourselves that loss.

Something happened to the Dream. Many things did. This, I think, is a symptom of one of them.

About ten years ago a well known literary critic and essayist, a good friend of long standing, told me that a wealthy widely circulated weekly pictorial magazine had offered him a good price to write a piece about me—not about my work or works, but about me as a private citizen, an individual. I said No, and explained why: my belief that only a writer's works were in the public domain, to be discussed and investigated and written about, the writer himself having put them there by submitting them for publication and accepting money for them; and therefore he not only would but must accept whatever the public wished to say or do about them from praise to burning. But that, until the writer committed a crime or ran for public office, his private life was his own; and not only had he the right to defend his privacy, but the public had the duty to do so since one man's liberty must stop at exactly the point where the next one's begins; and that I believed that anyone of taste and responsibility would agree with me.

But the friend said No. He said:

"You are wrong. If I do the piece, I will do it with taste and responsibility. But if you refuse me, sooner or later someone will do it who will not bother about taste or responsibility either, who will care nothing about you or your status as a writer, an artist, but only as a commodity: merchandise: to be sold, to increase circulation, to make a little money."

"I don't believe it," I said. "Until I commit a crime or announce for office, they can't invade my privacy after I ask them not to."

"They not only can," he said, "but once your European reputation gets back here and makes you financially worth it, they will. Wait and see."

I did. I did both. Two years ago, by mere chance during a talk with an editor in the house which publishes my books, I learned that the same magazine had already set on foot the same project which I had declined eight years before; I don't know whether the publishers were formally notified or if they just heard about it by chance too, as I did. I said No again, recapitulating the same reasons which I still believed were not even arguable by anyone possessing the power of the public press, since the qualities of taste and responsibility would have to be inherent in that power for it to be valid and allowed to endure. The editor interrupted.

"I agree with you," he said. "Besides, you don't need to give me reasons. The simple fact that you don't want it done is enough. Shall I attend to it for you?" So he did, or tried to. Because my critic friend was still right. Then I said:

"Try them again. Say 'I ask you: please don't.'" Then I submitted the same I *ask you: please don't* to the writer who was to do the piece. I don't know whether he was a staff writer designated to the job, or whether he volunteered for it, or perhaps himself sold his employers on the idea. Though my recollection is that his answer implied, "I've got to, if I refuse they will fire me," which is probably correct, since I got the same answer from a staff-member of another magazine on the same subject.

And if that was so, if the writer, a member of the craft he served, was victim too of that same force of which I was victim— that irresponsible use which is therefore misuse and which in its turn is betrayal, of that power called Freedom of the Press which is one of the most potent and priceless of the defenders and preservers of human dignity and rights—then the only defense left me was to refuse to co-operate, have anything to do with the project at all. Though by now I knew that that would not save me, that nothing I could do would stop them.

Perhaps they—the writer and his employer—didn't believe me, could not believe me. Perhaps they dared not believe me. Perhaps it is impossible now for any American to believe that anyone not hiding from the police could actually not want, as a free gift, his name and photograph in any printed organ, no matter how base or modest or circumscribed in circulation. Though perhaps the matter never reached this point: that both of them—the publisher and the writer—knew from the first, whether I did or not, that the three of us, the two of them and their victim, were all three victims of that fault (in the sense that the geologist uses the term) in our American culture which is saying to us daily: "Beware!" the three of us faced as one not with an idea, a principle of choice between good and bad taste or responsibility or lack of it, but with a fact, a condition in our American life before which all three of us were (at that moment) helpless, at that moment doomed.

So the writer came with his group, force, crew, and got his material where and how he could and departed and published his article. But that's not the point. The writer is not to be blamed since, empty-handed, he would (if my recollection is right) have been fired from the job which deprived him of the right to choose between good and bad taste. Nor the employer either, since to hold his (the employer's) precarious own in a craft can compel even him, head and chief of one of its integral components, to serve the mores of the hour in order to survive among his rival ones.

It's not what the writer said, but that he said it. That he—they —published it, in a recognized organ which, to be and remain recognized, functions on the assumption of certain inflexible standards; published it not only over the subject's protests but with complete immunity to them; an immunity not merely assumed to itself by the organ but an immunity already granted in advance by the public to which it sold its wares for a profit. The terrifying (not shocking; we cannot be shocked by it since we permitted its birth and watched it grow and condoned and validated it and even use it individually for our own private ends at need) thing is that it could have happened at all under those conditions. That it could have happened at all with its subject not even notified in advance. And even when he, the victim, was warned by accident in advance, he was still completely helpless to prevent it. And even after it was done, the victim had no recourse whatever since, unlike sacrilege and obscenity, we have no laws against bad taste, perhaps because in a democracy the majority of the people who make the laws don't recognize bad taste when they see it, or perhaps because in our democracy bad taste has been converted into a marketable and therefore taxable and therefore lobbyable commodity by the merchandising federations which at the same simultaneous time create the market (not the appetite: that did not need creating: only pandering to) and the product to serve it, and bad taste by simple solvency was purified of bad taste and absolved. And even if there had been grounds for recourse, the matter would still have remained on the black side of the ledger since the publisher could charge the judgment and costs to operating loss and the increased sales from the publicity to capital investment.

The point is that in America today any organization or group, simply by functioning under a phrase like Freedom of the Press or National Security or League Against Subversion, can postulate to itself complete immunity to violate the individualness—the individual privacy lacking which he cannot be an individual and lacking which individuality he is not anything at all worth the having or keeping—of anyone who is not himself a member of some organization or group numerous enough or rich enough to frighten them off. That organization will not be of writers, artists, of course; being individuals, not even two artists could ever confederate, let alone enough of them. Besides, artists in America don't have to have privacy because they don't need to be artists as far as America is concerned. America doesn't need artists because they don't count in America; artists have no more place in American life than the employers of the weekly pictorial magazine staffwriters have in the private life of a Mississippi novelist.

But there are the other two occupations which are valuable to American life, which require, demand privacy in order to endure, live. These are science and the humanities, the scientists and the humanitarians: the pioneers in the science of endurance and mechanical craftsmanship and self-discipline and skill like Colonel Lindbergh who was compelled at last to repudiate it by the nation and culture one of whose mores was an inalienable right to violate his privacy instead of an inviolable duty to defend it, the nation which assumed an inalienable right to abrogate to itself the glory of his renown yet which had neither the power to protect his children nor the responsibility to shield his grief; the pioneers in the simple science of saving the nation like Dr. Oppenheimer who was harassed and impugned through those same mores until all privacy was stripped from him and there remained only the qualities of individualism whose possession we boast since they alone differ us from animals—gratitude for kindness, fidelity to friendship, chivalry toward women, and the capacity to love—before which even his officially vetted harassers were impotent, turning away themselves (one hopes) in shame, as though the whole business had had nothing whatever to do with loyalty or disloyalty or security or insecurity, but was simply to batter and strip him completely naked of the privacy lacking which he could never have become one of that handful of individuals capable of serving the nation at a moment when apparently nobody else was, and so reduce him at last to one more identityless integer in that identityless anonymous unprivacied mass which seems to be our goal.

And even that is only a point of departure. Because the sickness itself goes much further back. It goes back to that moment in our history when we decided that the old simple moral verities over which taste and responsibility were the arbiters and controls, were obsolete and to be discarded. It goes back to that moment when we repudiated the meaning which our fathers had stipulated for the words "liberty" and "freedom," on and by and to which they founded us as a nation and dedicated us as a people, ourselves in our time keeping only the mouth-sounds of them. It goes back to the moment when we substituted license in the place of liberty—license for any action which kept within the proscription of laws promulgated by confederations of the practitioners of the license and the harvesters of the material benefits. It goes back to that moment when in place of freedom we substituted immunity for any action to any recourse, provided merely that the act be performed beneath the aegis of the empty mouth-sound of freedom.

At which instant truth vanished too. We didn't abolish truth; even we couldn't do that. It simply quit us, turned its back on us, not in scorn nor even contempt nor even (let us hope) despair. It just simply quit us, to return perhaps when whatever it will be —suffering, national disaster, maybe even (if nothing else will serve) military defeat—will have taught us to prize truth and pay any price, accept any sacrifice (oh yes, we are brave and tough too; we just intend to put off having to be as long as possible) to regain and hold it again as we should never have let it go: on its own compromiseless terms of taste and responsibility. Truth— that long clean clear simple undeviable unchallengeable straight and shining line, on one side of which black is black and on the other white is white, has now become an angle, a point of view having nothing to do with truth nor even with fact, but depending solely on where you are standing when you look at it. Or rather —better—where you can contrive to have him standing whom you are trying to fool or obfuscate when he looks at it.

Across the board in fact, a parlay, a daily triple: truth and free- dom and liberty. The American sky which was once the topless empyrean of freedom, the American air which was once the living breath of liberty, are now become one vast down-crowding pressure to abolish them both, by destroying man's individuality as a man by (in that turn) destroying the last vestige of privacy without which man cannot be an individual. Our very architec- ture itself has warned us. Time was when you could see neither from inside nor outside through the walls of our houses. Time is when you can see from inside out though still not from outside in through the walls. Time will be when you can do both. Then privacy will indeed be gone; he who is individual enough to want it even to change his shirt or bathe in, will be cursed by one universal American voice as subversive to the American way of life and the American flag.

If (by that time) walls themselves, opaque or not, can still stand before that furious blast, that force, that power rearing like a thunder-clap into the American zenith, multiple-faced yet mutually conjunctived, bellowing the words and phrases which we have long since emasculated of any significance or meaning other than as tools, implements, for the further harassment of the private individual human spirit, by their furious and immunized high priests: "Security." "Subversion." "Anti-Communism." "Chris- tianity." "Prosperity." "The American Way." "The Flag."

With odds at balance (plus a little fast footwork now and then of course) one individual can defend himself from another

individual's liberty. But when powerful federations and organizations and amalgamations like publishing corporations and religious sects and political parties and legislative committees can
absolve even one of their working units of the restrictions of moral
responsibility by means of such catch-phrases as "Freedom" and
"Salvation" and "Security" and "Democracy," beneath which
blanket absolution the individual salaried practitioners are themselves freed of individual responsibility and restraint, then let us
beware. Then even people like Dr. Oppenheimer and Colonel
Lindbergh and me (the weekly magazine staff-writer too if he
really was compelled to choose between good taste and starvation) will have to confederate in our turn to preserve that privacy
in which alone the artist and scientist and humanitarian can
function.

Or to preserve life itself, breathing; not just artists and scientists
and humanitarians, but the parents by law or biology of doctors
of osteopathy too. I am thinking of course of the Cleveland doctor
convicted recently of the brutal slaying of his wife, three of whose
parents—his wife's father and his own father and mother—with
one exception did not even outlive that trial regarding which the
Press itself, which kept the sorry business on most of the nation's
front pages up to the very end, is now on record as declaring that
it was overcovered far beyond its value and importance.

I am thinking of the three victims. Not the convicted man: he
will doubtless live a long time yet; but of the three parents, two
of whom died—one of them anyway—because, to quote the Press
itself, "he was wearied of life," and the third one, the mother, by
her own hand, as though she had said, *I can bear no more of this.*

Perhaps they died solely because of the crime, though one
wonders why the coincidence of their deaths was not with the
commission of the murder but with the publicity of the trial. And
if it was not solely because of the tragedy itself that one of the
victims was "wearied of life" and another obviously said, *I can
bear no more*—if they had more than that one reason to relinquish
and even repudiate life, and the man was guilty as the jury said
he was, just what medieval witchhunt did that power called
Freedom of the Press, which in any civilized culture must be
accepted as that dedicated paladin through whose inflexible rec-
titude truth shall prevail and justice and mercy be done, con-

done and abet that the criminal's very progenitors be eliminated from the earth in expiation of his crime? And if he was innocent as he said he was, what crime did that champion of the weak and the oppressed itself participate in? Or (to repeat) not the artist. America has not yet found any place for him who deals only in things of the human spirit except to use his notoriety to sell soap or cigarettes or fountain pens or to advertise automobiles and cruises and resort hotels, or (if he can be taught to contort fast enough to meet the standards) in radio or moving pictures where he can produce enough income tax to be worth attention. But the scientist and the humanitarian, yes: the humanitarian in science and the scientist in the humanity of man, who might yet save that civilization which the professionals at saving it—the publishers who condone their own battening on man's lust and folly, the politicians who condone their own trafficking in his stupidity and greed, and the churchmen who condone their own trading on his fear and superstition—seem to be proving that they can't.

*

WILLIAM FAULKNER   Born in Mississippi in 1897, died in 1962; in 1950 he won the Nobel Prize for Literature, and it is very likely that he is America's outstanding twentieth-century novelist.

"On Privacy—the American Dream: What Happened to It" (1955) The style is Faulknerian, the argument vigorous. The author's diction is mixed, ranging from the colloquial to the pedantic. He employs common rhetorical and syntactical devices in a highly uncommon way: series, parallel constructions, repetitive figures—all within a fragment; the piling up of parallel fragments to give the effect of impetuosity; complex parenthetical insertions; distorted images; and strongly accentuated rhythms, along with unusual punctuation.

*

1. *In what ways is this essay's interpretation of American history valid? in what ways invalid?* 2. *What are Faulkner's implications in regard to freedom of the press?* 3. *Does his style make his argument more or less convincing?*

DIANA TRILLING

The Death of Marilyn Monroe

It was on a Sunday morning in August, 1962, now almost a year
ago, that Marilyn Monroe, aged 36, was found dead in the bed-
room of her home in Los Angeles, her hand on the telephone as
if she had just received or, far more likely, been about to make a
call. On the night table next to her bed stood a formidable array
of medicines, among them a bottle that had held 25 Nembutal
pills, now empty. Two weeks later a team of psychiatrists, appointed by the state in conformity with Californian law, brought
in its report on the background and circumstances of her death,
declaring it a suicide. There had, of course, never been any suggestion of foul play. The death was clearly self-inflicted, a climax
of extended mental suffering. In fact, it was soon revealed that on
Saturday evening Marilyn Monroe had made an emergency call
to the psycho-analyst who had been treating her for acute sleep-
lessness, her anxieties and depression, and that he had paid her a
visit. But the formal psychiatric verdict had to do with the highly
technical question of whether the overdose of barbiturates was
purposeful or accidental: had Marilyn Monroe *intended* to kill
herself when she took the 25 sleeping pills? The jury of experts
now ruled it was purposeful: she had wanted to die.

It is an opinion, or at least a formulation, that can bear, I believe, a certain amount of modification. Obviously, I'm not pro-
posing that Marilyn Monroe's death was accidental in the sense

that she took so large a dose of pills with no knowledge of their lethal properties. But I think it would be more precise to call this kind of death incidental rather than purposeful—incidental to the desire to escape the pain of living. I am not a psychiatrist and I never knew Marilyn Monroe, but it seems to me that a person can want to be released from consciousness without seeking actual death; that someone can want to stop living without wishing to die. And this is my feeling about Marilyn Monroe; that even when she had spoken of "wanting to die" she really meant that she wanted to end her suffering, not her life. She wanted to destroy consciousness rather than herself. Then, having taken the pills, she realised she might never return from the sleep she craved so passionately and reached for the phone for help.

But this is, of course, only speculation, and more appropriately engaged in by the medical profession than by the layman. For the rest of us, the motives surrounding Marilyn Monroe's suicide fade in importance before the all-encompassing reality of the act itself: Marilyn Monroe terminated her life. While the medical experts pondered the delicate difference between accident and suicide, the public recognised that the inevitable had at last occurred: Marilyn Monroe had killed herself. Shocked and grieved as everyone was, no one was at all surprised that she had died by her own hand, because for some years now the world had been prepared for just some such tragic outcome to one of the extraordinary careers of our time.

The potentiality of suicide or, at any rate, the threat of extreme mental breakdown had been, after all, conveyed to us by virtually every news story about Marilyn Monroe of recent years. I don't mean that it had been spelled out that she would one day take her life or otherwise go off the deep psychic end. But no one seemed able to write about her without reassuring us that despite her instability and the graveness of her emotional problems, she was still vital and eager, still, however precariously, a going concern. Marilyn Monroe was an earnest, ambitious actress, determined to improve her skill; Marilyn Monroe had failed in several marriages but she was still in pursuit of fulfilment in love; Marilyn Monroe had several times miscarried but she still looked forward to having children; Marilyn Monroe was seriously engaged in psycho-analysis; Marilyn Monroe's figure was better than ever; she was learning to be prompter; she was coping, or was struggling to cope, with whatever it was that had intervened in the making of her last picture—so, on the well-worn track, ran all the news stories. Even what may have been her last interview to appear in print (by the time it came out, she was already dead) sounded the same dominant chord of hopefulness, telling us of a Marilyn Monroe full of confidence that she would improve her acting and find her roles, and that between the two therapies, hard work and psycho-analysis, she would achieve the peace of mind that had for so long eluded her.

Where there is this much need for optimism, surely there is great peril, and the public got the message. But what is striking is the fact that throughout this period of her mounting difficulties, with which we were made so familiar, the popular image re-mained intact. Whatever we were told of her weak hold on life, we retained our image of Marilyn Monroe as the very embodi-ment of life energy. I think my response to her death was the common one: it came to me with the impact of a personal depri-vation but I also felt it as I might a catastrophe in history or in nature; there was less in life, there was less of life, because she had ceased to exist. In her loss life itself had been injured.

In my own instance, it happens that she was already an estab-lished star before I knew her as anything except the latest pin-up girl. There is always this shield of irony some of us put up be-tween ourselves and any object of popular adulation, and I had made my dull point of snubbing her pictures. Then one evening I chanced on a television trailer for *Bus Stop*, and there she was. I'm not even sure I knew whom I was seeing on the screen, but a light had gone on in the room. Where everything had been grey there was all at once an illumination, a glow as of something be-yond the ordinarily human. It was a remarkable moment, of a kind I don't recall having had with any other actress, and it has its place with certain rare, cherished experiences of art such as my youthful remembrance of Pavlova, the most perfect of performing artists, whose control of her body was like a radiance, or even the quite recent experience of seeing some photographs of Nijinsky in motion. Marilyn Monroe was in motion, too, which is important, since no still picture could quite catch her electric quality; in posed pictures the redundancy of flesh was what first imposed itself, dimming one's perception of its peculiar aliveness, of the translucence that infused body with spirit. In a moment's flash of light, the ironies with which I had resisted this sex idol, this object of an undifferentiating public taste, dropped from me never to be restored.

But mine was a minority problem; the world had long since recognised Marilyn Monroe's unique gift of physical being and responded to it as any such gift of life demands. From the start of her public career it had acknowledged the genius of biology or chemistry or whatever it was that set this young woman apart from the general kind. And once it had admitted her magic, nothing it was to learn of her "morbidity" could weigh against the conviction that she was alive in a way not granted the rest of us, or, more accurately, that she communicated such a charge of vitality as altered our imagination of life, which is of course the whole job and wonder of art.

Since her death it has occurred to me that perhaps the reason we were able to keep these two aspects in which we knew Marilyn Monroe—her life affirmation and her impulse to death—in such discreet balance was that they never presented themselves to us as mutually exclusive but, on the contrary, as two intimately related, even expectable, facets of her extraordinary endowment. It is as if the world that loved Marilyn Monroe understood that her superabundant biology had necessarily to provoke its own restraint, that this is the cruel law by which nature, or at least nature within civilisation, punishes those of us who ask too much of life or bring too much to life. We are told that when one of the senses is defective, nature frequently provides a compensation in one of the other senses; the blind often hear better than the seeing, or have a sharper sense of touch. What we are not told but perhaps understand nonetheless is the working of nature's system of negative compensation—the price we pay for gift; the revenge that life seems so regularly to take upon distinction. Certainly our awareness of the more, the "plus," in Marilyn Monroe prepared us for some sort of minus. The fact that this young woman whose biological gift was so out of the ordinary was in mental pain seemed to balance the ledger. And one can speculate that had we not known of her emotional suffering, we would have been prepared for some other awful fate for her—an airplane disaster, maybe, or a deforming illness. So superstition may be thought of as an accurate reading of the harder rules of life.

And yet it is difficult to suppose the gods could be all that jealous. Had Marilyn Monroe not been enough punished in childhood to ensure her against further misfortune? Once this poor, forlorn girl had been so magically brought into her own, the most superstitious of us had the right to ask happiness for her ever after. It was impossible to think of Marilyn Monroe except as Cinderella. The strange power of her physical being seemed best explained and justified by the extreme circumstances of her early life—the illegitimate birth, the mad mother, the orphanage and near-mad foster homes, the rape by one of her early guardians. If there was no good fairy in Marilyn Monroe's life and no Prince Charming, unless Hollywood, this didn't rob her story of its fairy-book miraculousness; it merely assimilated to the old tale our newer legend of the self-made hero or heroine. Grace Kelly had had her good Philadelphia family to pave her path and validate her right to a crown. But Marilyn Monroe reigned only by virtue of her beauty and her determination to be raised out of the squalor and darkness, and to shine in the full, the fullest, light. It is scarcely a surprise that the brighter her radiance, the more we listened for the stroke of midnight that would put a limit on such transcendence.

But it was not only the distance Marilyn Monroe had travelled from her unhappy beginnings that represented for us a challenge of reality, to be punished by reality. If her gift is to be regarded not as that of the stage or screen, which I think it primarily was not, but as the gift of biology, she was among those who are greatly touched with power; she was of the true company of artists. And her talent was so out of the range of the usual that we were bound to feel of it that it was not to be contained in society as we know it; therefore it proposed its own dissolution. Like any great artistic gift, Marilyn Monroe's power of biology was explosive, a primitive and savage force. It had, therefore and inevitably, to be a danger both to herself and to the world in which it did its work. All art is fierce in the measure that it matters, finally, and in its savagery it chooses either to push against society, against the restrictions that hedge it in, or against the artist himself. And no doubt it is the incapacity of most human beings to sustain this inordinate pressure that accounts for the fact that the artist is an exception in any civilised population. To mediate between the assault upon oneself and upon society, to keep alive in the battle and come out more or less intact, is a giant undertaking in which the native endowment of what we call talent is probably but a small element.

Among the very few weapons available to the artist in this monstrous struggle, naïveté can be the most useful. But it is not at all my impression that Marilyn Monroe was a naïve person. I think she was innocent, which is very different. To be naïve is to be simple or stupid on the basis of experience, and Marilyn Monroe was far from stupid; no one who was stupid could have been so quick to turn her wit against herself, or to manage the ruefulness with which she habitually replied to awkward questioning. To be innocent is to suffer one's experience without being able to learn self-protection from it; as if will-lessly, innocence is at the mercy of experience, unable to mobilise counterforces to fortune.

Of Ernest Hemingway, for example, I feel much as I do of Marilyn Monroe, that he was unable to marshal any adequate defence against the painful events of his childhood, and this despite his famous toughness and the courage he could call upon in war, in hunting, in all the dangerous enterprises that seduced him. He was an innocent man, not a naïve man, though not always intelligent. Marilyn Monroe offers us a similar paradox. Even while she symbolised an extreme of experience, of sexual knowingness, she took each new circumstance of life, as it came to her or as she sought it, like a new-born babe. And yet this was what made her luminous—her innocence. The glow was not rubbed off her by her experience of the ugliness of life because finally, in some vital depth, she had been untouched by it.

From the psychiatrist's point of view, too much innocence, a radical disproportion between what has happened to a person and what he has absorbed from his experience, is a symptom, and alarming. It can indicate a rude break in his connection with himself, and if he is in treatment, it suggests a difficult cure, since, in emotional logic, he will probably be as impervious to the therapy as to the events through which he has passed, and yet without any mitigation of suffering. In the creative spheres, an excess of innocence unquestionably exercises an enormous fascination on us; it produces the purity of expression which leads us to say of an artistic creation or performance that it is "out of this world." But the psychiatric judgment has to pick its way on tiptoe between the gift and the pathology. What constitutes a person's art may eventually spell his emotional undoing.

I can suppose of Marilyn Monroe that she was peculiarly elusive to the psychiatrists or analysts who tried to help her, that emotionally speaking she presented herself to them as a kind of blank page on which nothing had been written, failing to make the connection between herself and them even as she pleaded for it. And yet disconnection was at the heart of her gift, it defined her charm for the world, much as Hemingway's dissociation from his own experience was determinative of his gift.

For several decades, scores of writers have tried to imitate Hemingway's style: the flexibility and purity of his prose, the bright, cogent distance he was able to put between himself and the object under examination. But none has succeeded. And I believe this is because his prose was, among many other things, a direct report of the unbridgeable distance between external reality and his emotions. Just so, Marilyn Monroe was inimitable. Hollywood, Broadway, the night-clubs: they all regularly produce their quota of sex queens, but the public takes them and leaves them, or doesn't really take them; the world is not enslaved as it was by Marilyn Monroe because none but Marilyn Monroe could suggest such a purity of sexual delight. The boldness with which she could parade herself and yet never be gross, her sexual flamboyance and bravado which yet breathed an air of mystery and even reticence, her voice which carried such ripe overtones of erotic excitement and yet was the voice of a shy child—these complications were integral to her gift. And they described a young woman trapped in some never-never land of unawareness.

What I imply here, of course, is a considerable factitiousness in Marilyn Monroe as a sexual figure. Certainly the two or three men I've known who met her in "real life" were agreed on her lack of direct sexual impact; she was sweet and beautiful and lovely, yes, but somehow not at all the arousing woman they had expected. The nature of true sexuality is most difficult to define; so much of what we find sexually compelling has its source in fantasies that have little to do with the primary sexual instinct. Especially in the case of a movie star we enter a realm where dream and biology make their easiest merger. The art of acting is the art of *performing as if*, and the success of this feat of suggestion depends upon the degree to which it speaks to some fantasy of the onlookers.

Marilyn Monroe spoke to our dreams as much as to our animal nature, but in a most unusual way. For what she appealed to was our determination to be rid of fantasy and to get down to the rock-bottom actuality. She gratified our wish to confront our erotic desires without romance, without diversion. And working within a civilisation like ours, in which sexuality is so surrounded with restraints and fears and prohibitons, she perhaps came as close as possible to giving us the real thing. But she didn't give us the real thing; she merely acted as if she were giving it to us. She glamourised sexuality to the point at which it lost its terrors for us; and maybe it was this veil that she raised to sexual reality that permitted women, no less than men, to respond to her so generously. Instinctively, I think, women understood that this seemingly most sexual of female creatures was no threat to them.

The myth of Marilyn Monroe was thus even more of a myth than we realised, for this girl who was supposed to release us from our dreams into sexual actuality was in all probability not actual even to herself. Least of all could she have been sexually actual to herself and at the same time such a marvellous public performer of sex, such a conscious artist of sex. And we can conjecture that it was this deep alienation from her own feelings, including her sexual feeling, that enabled her to sustain the disorder of her early years even as long and as well as she did, and to speak of her awful childhood so simply and publicly. For most of us, the smallest "shame" in our past must be kept locked from others. We prefer that the least menacing of skeletons remains in the closet lest our current image of ourselves be violated by their emergence into the open. But Marilyn Monroe had no need for such reserves. She told the public the most gruesome facts of her personal history, for all the world as if we on the outside were worthy of such confidences—except that in some odd, generous response to her innocence, we exceeded ourselves in her instance and didn't take the advantage of her that we might have. Judged from the point of view of what we require of the artist, that he have the will and fearlessness to rise above the conventions which bind those of us with less gift, Marilyn Monroe's candour about her early life was something to be celebrated. But from another point of view her frankness was a warning that the normal barriers of self-protection were down or non-existent, leaving her grievously exposed to the winds of circumstance.

And indeed the very word "exposed" is a keyword in the pattern of her life. She was an actress and she exposed her person and her personality to the public gaze. She was an exposed human being who told the truth about herself too readily, too publicly. And more than most actresses, she exposed her body, with but inadequate understanding of what this involved. We recall, for instance, the awkward little scandal about her having once posed naked for a calendar and the bewildered poise, the really untoward innocence and failure of comprehension, with which she met the dismay of her studio, as if to say, "But that was me yesterday when I needed money. That isn't me to-day; to-day I have money." Just as to-day and yesterday were discontinuous with each other, she was discontinuous with herself, held together, one feels, only and all too temporarily by her success.

And this success was perhaps more intimately connected with her awareness of her physical appeal that we always understood. It may well have been the fact that she was so much and so admiringly in the public eye that gave Marilyn Monroe the largest part of her sense of a personal identity. Not long before her death, we now discover, she had herself photographed in the nude, carefully editing the many pictures as if to be certain she left the best possible record for posterity. The photographs leave, however, a record only of wasted beauty, at least of the famous body—while Marilyn Monroe's face is lovely as ever, apparently unscarred by her intense suffering, her body looked ravaged and ill, already drained of life. Recently the pictures have been published in an expensive magazine devoted to erotica. If their high price, prohibitive to the general buyer, could be interpreted as a precaution against their being too easily available to a sensation-seeking audience, the restraint was not really necessary. At the last, the nude Marilyn Monroe could excite no decent viewer to anything but the gentlest pity, and some terror.

But even before this ultimate moment the public success had been threatened. The great career was already failing. There had not been a Marilyn Monroe movie for a long time, and the last film she had worked on had had to be halted because she was unable to appear. And there was no private life to fall back upon, not even the formal structure of one: no marriage, no family, apparently not even friends. One had come, indeed, to think of her as the loneliest of people, so that it was not without bitterness that, on her death, one discovered that it was not only oneself who had wished to help her but many other strangers, especially women to whose protectiveness her extreme vulnerability spoke so directly. But we were the friends of whom she knew nothing, and among the people she knew it would seem that real relationships were out of reach across the desert emptiness that barricades whoever is out of touch with his feelings. One thinks of her that last evening of her life, alone and distraught, groping for human comfort and finding nothing but those endless bottles of medicine, and one confronts a pathos worse than tragedy.

Certainly it strains justice as well as imagination that the world's most glamorous woman should have been alone, with no date, on a Saturday night—for it was, in fact, a Saturday night when she killed herself. On other nights but Saturday, we are allowed our own company. Saturday night is when all American boys and girls must prove themselves sexually. This is when we must be "out," out in the world where we can be seen among the sexually chosen. Yet the American girl who symbolised sexual success for all of us spent her last Saturday night alone in despair. Every man in the country would have wanted to date Marilyn Monroe, or so he would say, but no man who knew her did.

Or, contemplating her loneliness, we think of her funeral, which contrived to give her the peace and privacy that had so strenuously eluded her throughout her life, yet by its very restraint and limited attendance reminded us of the limitations of her actual connection with the world. Joe DiMaggio, who had been

her husband for a few brief months earlier in her career, was the
chief mourner. It was DiMaggio to whom, she had told us, it was
impossible to be married because he had no conversation; at
meals, instead of talking to her, he read the papers or looked at
television. The more recent husband, *with* conversation, was not
present, no doubt for his own inviolable reasons, but it was sad-
dening. I do not know what, if anything, was read at the service,
but I'd like to think it was of an elevated and literary kind, such
as might be read at the funeral of a person of the first intellectual
rank.

For of the cruelties directed at this young woman even by the
public that loved her, it seems to me that the most biting, and
unworthy of the supposedly enlightened people who were particularly guilty of it, was the mockery of her wish to be educated,
or thought educated. Granting our right to be a bit confused when
our sex idol protests a taste for Dostoevsky, surely the source of
our discomfort must yet be located in our suspicions of Dostoevsky's worth for us and in our own sexual unease rather than in
Marilyn Monroe. For what our mockery signifies is our disbelief
that anyone who has enough sexuality needs to read Dostoevsky.
The notion that someone with Marilyn Monroe's sexual advantages could have wanted anything except to make love robbed us
of a prized illusion, that enough sexual possibility is enough
everything.

I doubt that sex was enough anything for Marilyn Monroe,
except the means for advancing herself in the world. One of the
touching revelations of her early life was her description of how
she discovered that somehow she was sexually different from other
girls her age: the boys all whistled at her and crowded to her like
bears to honey, so she came to realise that she must have something special about her, which she could use to rise above her poor
circumstances. Her sexual awareness, that is, came to her from
outside herself. It would be my guess that it remained outside her
always, leaving a great emptiness, where a true sexuality would
have supplied her with a sense of herself as a person with connection and content.

This void she tried to fill in every way available, with worldly
goods, with fame and public attention and marriage, and also in
ways that turned out to be unavailable, like children and domes-

ticity—nothing could be more moving than the eagerness with which she seized upon a Jewish mother-in-law, even upon Jewish ceremonials and cooking, as if in the home life of her last husband's people she would find the secret of emotional plenitude. She also tried to fill her emptiness with books and learning. How mean-spirited can we be, to have denied her whatever might have added to her confidence that she was really a solid person and not just an uninhabited body?

And that she had the intellectual capacity for education there can be no question, had it but been matched with emotional capacity. No one without a sharp native intelligence could have spoofed herself as gracefully as she did or parried reporters with such finesse. If we are to judge by her interviews, she was as singularly lacking in the endemic off-stage dullness of actors and actresses, the trained courtesy and charm that is only another boring statement of their self-love, as she was deficient in the established defences of her profession: one recalls no instance of even implied jealousy of her colleagues or of censure of others— directors, script-writers, husbands—for her own failures. Her generosity of spirit, indeed, was part of the shine that was on her. But unfortunately it spared everyone but herself; she had never studied self-justification. To herself she was not kind. She made fun of herself and of all that she had to go on in life: her biology. Certainly this added to her lovableness but it cut from under her the little ground that she could call her own. When she exhibited her sexual abundance with that wonderful, gay exaggeration of hers, or looked wide-eyed upon the havoc she wrought, it was her way of saying, "Don't be afraid. I don't take myself seriously so you don't have to take me seriously either." Her talent for comedy, in other words, was a public beneficence but a personal depredation, for, far more than most people, she precisely needed the assurance that she weighed in the scheme of human life, that she had substance and reality, that she had all the qualifications that make for a person we take seriously. Herself a supplicant, she gave us comfort. Herself a beggar, she distributed alms.

At her death, several writers of goodwill who undertook to deal with the tragedy of her suicide blamed it on Hollywood. In the industry that had made millions from her and in the methods by which Hollywood had exploited her, they found the explanation of her failed life; they wrote about her as the sacrificial lamb on the altar of American vulgarity and greed. I share their disgust with Hollywood and I honour their need to isolate Marilyn Monroe from the nastiness that fed on her, but I find it impossible to believe that this girl would have been an iota better off were Hollywood to have been other than what we all know it to be, a madness in our culture.

The self-destructiveness that Marilyn Monroe carried within her had not been put there by the "system," however overbearing in its ugliness. Just as her sweetness was her own, and immune to the influences of Hollywood, her terrors were also her own. They were not implanted in her, though undoubtedly they were increased, by the grandiosity of being a star. Neither for better nor worse, I feel, was she essentially falsified or distorted by her public role, though she must often have suffered cruelly from the inescapability of the public glare. In fact, it would be my conjecture that had she never gone into the movies and become rich and world-famous, her troubled spirit would long since have had its way with her. She would have been equally undone, and sooner, and with none of the many alleviations and compensations that she must have known in these years of success.

This doesn't mean that I don't think she was a "victim." But she was not primarily a victim of Hollywood commercialism, or exploitation, or of the inhumanity of the press. She was not even primarily a victim of the narcissistic inflation that so regularly attends the grim business of being a great screen personality. Primarily she was a victim of her gift, a biological victim, a victim of life itself. It is one of the excesses of contemporary thought that we like to blame our very faulty culture for tragedies that are inherent in human existence—at least, inherent in human existence in civilisation. I think Marilyn Monroe was a tragedy of civilisation, but this is something quite else again from, and even more poignant than, being a specifically American tragedy.

✦

DIANA TRILLING   Born in New York, a graduate of Radcliffe, she is a successful editor, critic, and essayist.

"The Death of Marilyn Monroe" (1963) In a strong, feminine voice the author substantiates her account with intelligent intuitions. At the same time, she does not disguise the fact that her conjectures, though tentative and groping, potentially concern all of us.

✦

1. *What is the connection between innocence and suicide?* 2. *Could Marilyn Monroe's story be made into a classic tragedy? a Shakespearean tragedy? a Shavian tragicomedy? a serious movie?*

LOUIS KRONENBERGER

Our Unhappy Happy Endings

Any enterprising young American with his fortune to make might consider setting up in a small way as a manufacturer of rose-colored glasses. The market for them is great already, and said to be increasing; there is even, I gather, a particular market for rose-colored glasses that can also increase astigmatism or induce myopia. And people have been told that soon they can have a pair that not only softens the landscape but also blots part of it out.

For the world (as who does not know) has grim sights to offer today and may be offering grimmer ones tomorrow. Any moment, for example, there may be earth satellites galore, though no longer any earth. And together with frightening things to see, there are all the new facilities for seeing them more clearly: what with the light shed by sociology in one place, and science in another, and medicine in a third, truth—or at any rate the exposure of error and the collapse of illusion—everywhere confronts us. And not every one likes this; the liking for Truth, let alone the dedicated search for it, is not extensive. Truth is a luxury item, not a mass-consumed commodity; and if the truth about the world is never in great demand, how much less—despite the influence of the Freuds—is the truth about oneself. Actually, people will clutch at the truth about what a cruel, cold, dog-eat-dog world this is as an excuse for turning their backs on the truth about themselves; but this, if it lessens their feeling of guilt, still leaves them uneasy: they would rather turn their backs on both things.

I am speaking for the most part of the situation in America, which differs from that of Europe. Unlike Europe, America has for a long time lived in a prospering present, with the sense of an even more prosperous future. There have been depressions; but materially, the American dream has been nourished by America's waking hours. Given such a Land of Plenty, is it not perforce a Land of Promise as well? In a country where any one can become president, every one will dream of becoming president—if not of the U.S., then at least of U.S. Steel. In a country, again, where making money is so much a national talent that 2 x 2 can overnight just as easily be 4000 as 4, a sense of realism is not likely to prevail. In America the facts of life, as borne out by reams of statistics, by thousands of careers, are every bit as resplendent as the fantasies. In spite of periodic depressions and of world events, the happy ending has become a reigning American myth because it is demonstrably no myth at all. Things may differ in a Europe of collapsing economies, violent usurpations, bombed-out and blood-stained recollections, weary bones and protesting bellies. There the sense of reality is far more insistent; there, one always built castles in Spain from living in France. Or, struggling in Poland or Ireland, one looked to America as a real-life solution; there, escapism involved an actual escape. With us, it is rarely even a genuine transcendence; it is the merest transference; it more and more means TV glimpses not of castles in Spain but of penthouses on Park Avenue, not of fairyland but of twenty-times-our-own-income land: if we are perhaps the most unrealistic of nations today, we are at the same time perhaps the least romantic.

In a land like ours, of such unquestionable—and unquestioned —plenty, with most people not many escapist visions of their own are needed; nor, in a land of incessant sales talks, are very many allowed. Wildly escapist as we are in our thought processes, we are just as timidly so in what we project. It is all peculiarly recognizable, local, life-sized escapism, a matter of Cadillacs and mink coats, of flood-lighted swimming pools and soft-lighted boudoirs, of executive suites and headwaiter salaams; it is a world, in fact, where pushbuttons do virtually everything that magic carpets once did. Even our daydreams have a way of carrying price tags and including commercials. With ours the most advertised as well as affluent of existences, we tend less and less toward moonlit mysterious romanticizings and more and more toward high-priced vicarious living. I know all the fine things TV has done and is capable of doing, what an education it can be for the young, and what a blessing for the old, and what a godsend for the house-bound; all the same, it seems to me the greatest cultural calamity in this country's history. And not, as might be supposed, because it has so cut down on reading and reflection, or become a vicious drug-like habit—true and bad though both things are; but rather because it has so enormously increased our escapist instincts while so crucially cheapening our escapist symbols. Instead of magic casements opening on a faery world—which even the movies in some degree provided—television offers authentic close-ups of affluent real life, authentic lowdowns on luxurious highlife. Its happy endings are not of the old fairy-prince sort, or so very often of Boy-Meets-Girl; they are of a you-too-can-play variety all too often concerned not with romance or heroism or *gloire*, but with give-away merchandise and quiz-show hauls and commercialized competitions, with people leaping to dangerous ephemeral fame or to ruinously surtaxed fortune, the sort of thing you look at on Tuesday and by Friday week may very well be competing for yourself.

The old daydreams, I would think, were healthier in kind and less harmful in effect: even the victims of the old gilded twaddle seldom mistook it for truth. Such stuff, indeed, wore the magic cloak of impossibility. Today's daydreams do not; they don't need a miracle to come true, all they need is a break. At the same time, in a world of candid-camera intimacy and of owner-authorized closeups and of spotlighted keyholes, all sense of distance has been annihilated, hence the enchantment lent by distance has vanished. For one reluctant Garbo there are a thousand palpitant publicity seekers. The highly possible daydreams, the do-it-yourself happy endings, have a plausible real-life air; but just because they make us so competitive, they themselves become more compulsive. They are not just part of our dreaming, they are part of our thinking. And all this, for another reason too, may very well be in our blood. Since the United States itself constitutes the greatest success story in the history of nations, the success story is part of our heritage, has everywhere colored our psychology. And we have come to equate it with happiness, partly because we pretty much believe there can be no happy ending without material success, partly because we tell ourselves that *with* material success, we can reorder and elevate our lives. The very reassuring idea in all this is that once you have money, you can quite truthfully affirm that money isn't everything.

If, as I have said, mass-mind daydreams are not too difficult of fulfillment in a thriving democracy, then the very dreaming will be along fulfillable lines. Hence our nationally nursed happy ending has followed the success story rather than the self-development or the heroic-achievement or the love-in-a-cottage story (indeed this last, in an atmosphere with the slightest sophistication, is apt to involve a snicker). To be sure, we do respond to an ending that combines a higher self with a bigger income; but "All for love and the world well lost"—or all for country, or for God—seems a little excessive as well as unreal. We exult in something not only more down-to-earth but also more just-around-the-corner, more local-boy-makes-good. Our Van Cliburns delight us not just because they are so talented, or even so Texan, but because of how sensationally their talent pays off.

Now, if the good thing about an immensely affluent democracy is how often it lets dreams come true, the not so good thing is that far more people will go in for such dreams than can ever fulfill them; and the not much better thing is that, with so many people competing, even for the winners there must be frightful tensions and ruthless techniques. There is no secret to any of this: it is all too well known that the happy ending in America can involve very unhappy preliminaries, that the photo finish we dote on is often the photo finish of a rat race. Nor are the unhappy preliminaries the kind of trumped-up snags and romantical setbacks they once were: mass-medium fiction today often sticks quite close to real life, to un-Tarkingtonian adolescence, to un-Derring-Do sensationalism, to the realistic headaches that follow marriage, not the romantic heartaches that precede it. The story, *except for the happy ending*, is often all too plausible, identifiable, disturbing—a genuine problem play or novel. It knows the real score, regardless of its last-minute fictional home-run. Indeed, it knows the real score so well that the home-run is less an old-fashioned sop than a present-day necessity. For we are neurotically haunted today by the imminence, and by the ignominy, of failure. We know at how frightening a cost one *succeeds:* to fail is something too awful to think about.

This is the most unwholesome, the most degrading aspect of our life today: that the harshly competitive terms, the overwhelmingly materialistic standards of success—as most Americans would define success—rob failure of all distinction and even all dignity. The happy ending is so much needed because the unhappy ending is so genuinely painful—a matter of being squeezed out, sucked dry, looked down on, pushed under, thrown on the scrap heap, smuggled into a sanitarium. And so succeed we must, at all cost—even if it means being a *dead* millionaire at fifty.

The need for such happy endings is, I would suggest, a symptom of an anxiety-ridden culture ("One way of getting an idea of our fellow-countrymen's miseries," said George Eliot, "is to go look at their pleasures"); certainly a symptom of something more acquiescent than affirmative. At any rate, it would seem no accident that during ages of great human adventurousness, of great humanistic advancement, of great creative drive—a Periclean Athens or an Elizabethan England—tragedy has always flourished and been prized, life has been looked at unflinchingly for what it is, yet has at the same time seemed more than life-sized. The heroic downfall had something exultant, not shoddy or self-pitying about it; and just as the protagonists of great tragic drama spurned comfortable solutions, so their audiences needed no last-minute consolations. "Those nations are happy," Lord Acton remarked, "which do not resent the complexity of life."

There are, of course, good happy endings as well as bad ones, but surely they are of a kind that in some way expresses happiness rather than glibly promises it. What seems to me so disquieting is that our current happy endings rarely have to do with happiness itself. They emphasize not the victory but the spoils. They reveal people not profiting by their own mistakes but capitalizing on other people's. They show people not rising above their surroundings but coming to terms with them. It would seem that there is very little nobility left, even in America's daydreams.

✓

Louis Kronenberger   Born in Cincinnati in 1904, he is well known as a teacher, lecturer, librarian, editor, writer, and critic.

"Our Unhappy Happy Endings" (1964) This is a wide-ranging subject that the author progressively brings into sharper focus. His use of analogies is functional; his sentence rhetoric, energetic and varied; and his tone, if usually caustic, contains a note of regret.

✓

1. *How might you refute the author's conclusions?* 2. *In what ways does this essay move forward, rather than merely repeat itself?*

Stranger in the Village

From all available evidence no black man had ever set foot in this tiny Swiss village before I came. I was told before arriving that I would probably be a "sight" for the village; I took this to mean that people of my complexion were rarely seen in Switzerland, and also that city people are always something of a "sight" outside of the city. It did not occur to me—possibly because I am an American—that there could be people anywhere who had never seen a Negro.

It is a fact which cannot be explained on the basis of the inaccessibility of the village. The village is very high, but it is only four hours from Milan and three hours from Lausanne. It is true that it is virtually unknown. Few people making plans for a holiday would elect to come here. On the other hand, the villagers are able, presumably, to come and go as they please—which they do: to another town at the foot of the mountain, with a population of approximately five thousand, the nearest place to see a movie or go to the bank. In the village there is no movie house, no bank, no library, no theater; very few radios, one jeep, one station wagon; and, at the moment, one typewriter, mine, an invention which the woman next door to me here had never seen. There are about six hundred people living here, all Catholic—I conclude this from the fact that the Catholic church is open all year round, whereas the Protestant chapel, set off on a hill a little removed

From *Notes of a Native Son* by James Baldwin. Reprinted by permission of the Beacon Press, copyright © 1953, 1955 by James Baldwin.

from the village, is open only in the summertime when the tourists arrive. There are four or five hotels, all closed now, and four or five *bistros,* of which, however, only two do any business during the winter. These two do not do a great deal, for life in the village seems to end around nine or ten o'clock. There are a few stores, butcher, baker, *épicerie,* a hardware store, and a money-changer—who cannot change travelers' checks, but must send them down to the bank—an operation which takes two or three days. There is something called the *Ballet Haus,* closed in the winter and used for God knows what, certainly not ballet, during the summer. There seems to be only one schoolhouse in the village, and this for the quite young children; I suppose this to mean that their older brothers and sisters at some point descend from these mountains in order to complete their education—possibly, again, to the town just below. The landscape is absolutely forbidding, mountains towering on all four sides, ice and snow as far as the eye can reach. In this white wilderness, men and women and children move all day, carrying washing, wood, buckets of milk or water, sometimes skiing on Sunday afternoons. All week long boys and young men are to be seen shoveling snow off the rooftops, or dragging wood down from the forest in sleds.

The village's only real attraction, which explains the tourist season, is the hot spring water. A disquietingly high proportion of these tourists are cripples, or semi-cripples, who come year after year—from other parts of Switzerland, usually—to take the waters. This lends the village, at the height of the season, a rather terrifying air of sanctity, as though it were a lesser Lourdes. There is often something beautiful, there is always something awful, in the spectacle of a person who has lost one of his faculties, a faculty he never questioned until it was gone, and who struggles to recover it. Yet people remain people, on crutches or indeed on deathbeds; and wherever I passed, the first summer I was here, among the native villagers, or among the lame, a wind passed with me—of astonishment, curiosity, amusement, and outrage. That first summer I stayed two weeks and never intended to return. But I did return in the winter, to work; the village offers, obviously, no distractions whatever and has the further advantage of being extremely cheap. Now it is winter again, a year later, and I am here again. Everyone in the village knows my name, though they scarcely ever use it, knows that I come from America—though, this, apparently, they will never really believe: black men come from Africa—and everyone knows that I am the friend of the son of a woman who was born here, and that I am staying in their chalet. But I remain as much a stranger today as I was the first day I arrived, and the children shout *Neger! Neger!* as I walk along the streets.

It must be admitted that in the beginning I was far too shocked to have any real reaction. In so far as I reacted at all, I reacted by trying to be pleasant—it being a great part of the American Negro's education (long before he goes to school) that he must make people "like" him. This smile-and-the-world-smiles-with-you routine worked about as well in this situation as it had in the situation for which it was designed, which is to say that it did not work at all. No one, after all, can be liked whose human weight and complexity cannot be, or has not been, admitted. My smile was simply another unheard-of phenomenon which allowed them to see my teeth—they did not, really, see my smile and I began to think that, should I take to snarling, no one would notice any difference. All of the physical characteristics of the Negro which had caused me, in America, a very different and almost forgotten pain were nothing less than miraculous—or infernal—in the eyes of the village people. Some thought my hair was the color of tar, that it had the texture of wire, or the texture of cotton. It was jocularly suggested that I might let it all grow long and make myself a winter coat. If I sat in the sun for more than five minutes some daring creature was certain to come along and gingerly put his fingers on my hair, as though he were afraid of an electric shock, or put his hand on my hand, astonished that the color did not rub off. In all of this, in which it must be conceded there was the charm of genuine wonder and in which there was certainly no element of intentional unkindness, there was yet no suggestion that I was Human: I was simply a living wonder.

I knew that they did not mean to be unkind, and I know it now; it is necessary, nevertheless, for me to repeat this to myself each time that I walk out of the chalet. The children who shout *Neger!* have no way of knowing the echoes this sound raises in me. They are brimming with good humor and the more daring swell with pride when I stop to speak with them. Just the same, there are days when I cannot pause and smile, when I have no heart to play with them; when, indeed, I mutter sourly to myself, exactly as I muttered on the streets of a city these children have never seen, when I was no bigger than these children are now: *Your* mother was a *nigger.* Joyce is right about history being a nightmare— but it may be the nightmare from which no one *can* awaken. People are trapped in history and history is trapped in them.

There is a custom in the village—I am told it is repeated in many villages—of "buying" African natives for the purpose of converting them to Christianity. There stands in the church all year round a small box with a slot for money, decorated with a black figurine, and into this box the villagers drop their francs. During the *carnaval* which precedes Lent, two village children have their faces blackened—out of which bloodless darkness their blue eyes shine like ice—and fantastic horsehair wigs are placed on their blond heads; thus disguised, they solicit among the villagers for money for the missionaries in Africa. Between the box in the church and the blackened children, the village "bought" last year six or eight African natives. This was reported to me with pride by the wife of one of the *bistro* owners and I was careful to express astonishment and pleasure at the solicitude shown by the village for the souls of black folks. The *bistro* owner's wife beamed with a pleasure far more genuine than my own and seemed to feel that I might now breathe more easily concerning the souls of at least six of my kinsmen.

I tried not to think of these so lately baptized kinsmen, of the price paid for them, or the peculiar price they themselves would pay, and said nothing about my father, who having taken his own conversion too literally, never, at bottom, forgave the white world (which he described as heathen) for having saddled him with a Christ in whom, to judge at least from their treatment of him, they themselves no longer believed. I thought of white men arriving for the first time in an African village, strangers there, as I am a stranger here, and tried to imagine the astounded populace touching their hair and marveling at the color of their skin. But there is a great difference between being the first white man to be seen by Africans and being the first black man to be seen by whites. The white man takes the astonishment as tribute, for he arrives to conquer and to convert the natives, whose inferiority in relation to himself is not even to be questioned; whereas I, without a thought of conquest, find myself among a people whose culture controls me, has even, in a sense, created me, people who have cost me more in anguish and rage than they will ever know, who yet do not even know of my existence. The astonishment with which I might have greeted them, should they have stumbled into my African village a few hundred years ago, might have rejoiced their hearts. But the astonishment with which they greet me today can only poison mine.

And this is so despite everything I may do to feel differently, despite my friendly conversations with the *bistro* owner's wife, despite their three-year-old son who has at last become my friend, despite the *saluts* and *bonsoirs* which I exchange with people as I walk, despite the fact that I know that no individual can be taken to task for what history is doing, or has done. I say that the culture of these people controls me—but they can scarcely be held responsible for European culture. America comes out of Europe, but these people have never seen America, nor have most of them seen more of Europe than the hamlet at the foot of their mountain. Yet, they move with an authority which I shall never have, and they regard me, quite rightly, not only as a stranger in their village but as a suspect latecomer, bearing no credentials, to everything they have—however unconsciously—inherited.

For this village, even were it incomparably more remote and incredibly more primitive, is the West, the West onto which I have been so strangely grafted. These people cannot be, from the point of view of power, strangers anywhere in the world: they have made the modern world, in effect, even if they do not know it. The most illiterate among them is related, in a way that I am not, to Dante, Shakespeare, Michelangelo, Aeschylus, Da Vinci, Rembrandt, and Racine; the cathedral at Chartres says something to them which it cannot say to me, as indeed would New York's Empire State Building, should anyone here ever see it. Out of their hymns and dances come Beethoven and Bach. Go back a few centuries and they are in their full glory—but I am in Africa, watching the conquerors arrive.

The rage of the disesteemed is personally fruitless, but it is also absolutely inevitable; this rage, so generally discounted, so little understood even among the people whose daily bread it is, is one of the things that makes history. Rage can only with difficulty, and never entirely, be brought under the domination of the intelligence and is therefore not susceptible to any arguments whatever. This is a fact which ordinary representatives of the *Herrenvolk*, having never felt this rage and being unable to imagine it, quite fail to understand. Also, rage cannot be hidden, it can only be dissembled. This dissembling deludes the thoughtless and strengthens rage, and adds, to rage, contempt. There are, no doubt as many ways of coping with the resulting complex of tensions as there are black men in the world, but no black man can hope ever to be entirely liberated from this internal warfare—rage, dissembling, and contempt having inevitably accompanied his first realization of the power of white men. What is crucial here is that, since white men represent in the black man's world so heavy a weight, white men have for black men a reality which is far from being reciprocal; and hence all black men have toward white men an attitude which is designed, really, either to rob the white man of the jewel of his naïveté, or else to make it cost him dear.

The black man insists, by whatever means he finds at his disposal, that the white man cease to regard him as an exotic rarity and recognize him as a human being. This is a very charged and difficult moment, for there is a great deal of will power involved in the white man's naïveté. Most people are not naturally reflective any more than they are naturally malicious, and the white man prefers to keep the black man at a certain human remove because it is easier for him thus to preserve his simplicity and avoid being called to account for crimes committed by his forefathers, or his neighbors. He is inescapably aware, nevertheless, that he is in a better position in the world than black men are, nor can he quite put to death the suspicion that he is hated by black men therefore. He does not wish to be hated, neither does he wish to change places, and at this point in his uneasiness he can scarcely avoid having recourse to those legends which white men have created about black men, the most usual effect of which is that the white man finds himself enmeshed, so to speak, in his own language which describes hell, as well as the attributes which lead one to hell, as being as black as night.

Every legend, moreover, contains its residuum of truth, and the root function of language is to control the universe by describing it. It is of quite considerable significance that black men remain, in the imagination, and in overwhelming numbers in fact, beyond the disciplines of salvation; and this despite the fact that the West has been "buying" African natives for centuries. There is, I should hazard, an instantaneous necessity to be divorced from this so visibly unsaved stranger, in whose heart, moreover, one cannot guess what dreams of vengeance are being nourished; and, at the same time, there are few things on earth more attractive than the idea of the unspeakable liberty which is allowed the unredeemed. When, beneath the black mask, a human being begins to make himself felt one cannot escape a certain awful wonder as to what kind of human being it is. What one's imagination makes of other people is dictated, of course, by the laws of one's own personality and it is one of the ironies of black-white relations that, by means of what the white man imagines the black man to be, the black man is enabled to know who the white man is.

I have said, for example, that I am as much a stranger in this village today as I was the first summer I arrived, but this is not quite true. The villagers wonder less about the texture of my hair than they did then, and wonder rather more about me. And the fact that their wonder now exists on another level is reflected in their attitudes and in their eyes. There are the children who make those delightful, hilarious, sometimes astonishingly grave over-tures of friendship in the unpredictable fashion of children; other children, having been taught that the devil is a black man, scream in genuine anguish as I approach. Some of the older women never pass without a friendly greeting, never pass, indeed, if it seems that they will be able to engage me in conversation; other women look down or look away or rather contemptuously smirk. Some of the men drink with me and suggest that I learn how to ski— partly, I gather, because they cannot imagine what I would look like on skis—and want to know if I am married, and ask questions about my *métier*. But some of the men have accused *le sale nègre* —behind my back—of stealing wood and there is already in the eyes of some of them that peculiar, intent, paranoiac malevolence which one sometimes surprises in the eyes of American white men when, out walking with their Sunday girl, they see a Negro male approach.

There is a dreadful abyss between the streets of this village and the streets of the city in which I was born, between the children who shout *Neger!* today and those who shouted *Nigger!* yester-day—the abyss is experience, the American experience. The syl-lable hurled behind me today expresses, above all, wonder; I am a stranger here. But I am not a stranger in America and the same syllable riding on the American air expresses the war my presence has occasioned in the American soul.

For this village brings home to me this fact: that there was a day, and not really a very distant day, when Americans were scarcely Americans at all but discontented Europeans, facing a great unconquered continent and strolling, say, into a marketplace and seeing black men for the first time. The shock this spectacle afforded is suggested, surely, by the promptness with which they decided that these black men were not really men but cattle. It is true that the necessity on the part of the settlers of the New World of reconciling their moral assumptions with the fact—and the necessity—of slavery enhanced immensely the charm of this idea, and it is also true that this idea expresses, with a truly American bluntness, the attitude which to varying extents all masters have had toward all slaves.

But between all former slaves and slave-owners and the drama which begins for Americans over three hundred years ago at Jamestown, there are at least two differences to be observed. The American Negro slave could not suppose, for one thing, as slaves in past epochs had supposed and often done, that he would ever be able to wrest the power from his master's hands. This was a supposition which the modern era, which was to bring about such vast changes in the aims and dimensions of power, put to death; it only begins, in unprecedented fashion, and with dreadful im-plications, to be resurrected today. But even had this supposition persisted with undiminished force, the American Negro slave could not have used it to lend his condition dignity, for the reason that this supposition rests on another: that the slave in exile yet remains related to his past, has some means—if only in memory—of revering and sustaining the forms of his former life, is able, in short, to maintain his identity.

This was not the case with the American Negro slave. He is unique among the black men of the world in that his past was taken from him, almost literally, at one blow. One wonders what on earth the first slave found to say to the first dark child he bore. I am told that there are Haitians able to trace their ancestry back to African kings, but any American Negro wishing to go back so far will find his journey through time abruptly arrested by the signature on the bill of sale which served as the entrance paper for his ancestor. At the time—to say nothing of the circumstances—of the enslavement of the captive black man who was to become the American Negro, there was not the remotest possibility that he would ever take power from his master's hands. There was no reason to suppose that his situation would ever change, nor was there, shortly, anything to indicate that his situation had ever been different. It was his necessity, in the words of E. Franklin Frazier, to find a "motive for living under American culture or die." The identity of the American Negro comes out of this extreme situation, and the evolution of this identity was a source of the most intolerable anxiety in the minds and the lives of his masters.

For the history of the American Negro is unique also in this: that the question of his humanity, and of his rights therefore as a human being, became a burning one for several generations of Americans, so burning a question that it ultimately became one of those used to divide the nation. It is out of this argument that the venom of the epithet *Nigger!* is derived. It is an argument which Europe has never had, and hence Europe quite sincerely fails to understand how or why the argument arose in the first place, why its effects are so frequently disastrous and always so unpredictable, why it refuses until today to be entirely settled. Europe's black possessions remained—and do remain—in Europe's colonies, at which remove they represented no threat whatever to European identity. If they posed any problem at all for the European conscience, it was a problem which remained comfortingly abstract: in effect, the black man, *as a man,* did not exist for Europe. But in America, even as a slave, he was an inescapable part of the general social fabric and no American could escape having an attitude toward him. Americans attempt until today to make an abstraction of the Negro, but the very nature of these abstractions reveals the tremendous effects the presence of the Negro has had on the American character.

When one considers the history of the Negro in America it is of the greatest importance to recognize that the moral beliefs of a person, or a people, are never really as tenuous as life—which is not moral—very often causes them to appear; these create for them a frame of reference and a necessary hope, the hope being that when life has done its worst they will be enabled to rise above themselves and to triumph over life. Life would scarcely be bearable if this hope did not exist. Again, even when the worst has been said, to betray a belief is not by any means to have put oneself beyond its power; the betrayal of a belief is not the same thing as ceasing to believe. If this were not so there would be no moral standards in the world at all. Yet one must also recognize that morality is based on ideas and that all ideas are dangerous— dangerous because ideas can only lead to action and where the action leads no man can say. And dangerous in this respect: that confronted with the impossibility of remaining faithful to one's beliefs, and the equal impossibility of becoming free of them, one can be driven to the most inhuman excesses. The ideas on which American beliefs are based are not, though Americans often seem to think so, ideas which originated in America. They came out of Europe. And the establishment of democracy on the American continent was scarcely as radical a break with the past as was the necessity, which Americans faced, of broadening this concept to include black men.

This was, literally, a hard necessity. It was impossible, for one thing, for Americans to abandon their beliefs, not only because these beliefs alone seemed able to justify the sacrifices they had endured and the blood that they had spilled, but also because these beliefs afforded them their only bulwark against a moral chaos as absolute as the physical chaos of the continent it was their destiny to conquer. But in the situation in which Americans found themselves, these beliefs threatened an idea which, whether or not one likes to think so, is the very warp and woof of the heritage of the West, the idea of white supremacy.

Americans have made themselves notorious by the shrillness and the brutality with which they have insisted on this idea, but they did not invent it; and it has escaped the world's notice that those very excesses of which Americans have been guilty imply a certain, unprecedented uneasiness over the idea's life and power, if not, indeed, the idea's validity. The idea of white supremacy rests simply on the fact that white men are the creators of civiliza- tion (the present civilization, which is the only one that matters;

all previous civilizations are simply "contributions" to our own) and are therefore civilization's guardians and defenders. Thus it was impossible for Americans to accept the black man as one of themselves, for to do so was to jeopardize their status as white men. But not so to accept him was to deny his human reality, his human weight and complexity, and the strain of denying the over-whelmingly undeniable forced Americans into rationalizations so fantastic that they approached the pathological.

At the root of the American Negro problem is the necessity of the American white man to find a way of living with the Negro in order to be able to live with himself. And the history of this problem can be reduced to the means used by Americans—lynch law and law, segregation and legal acceptance, terrorization and concession—either to come to terms with this necessity, or to find a way around it, or (most usually) to find a way of doing both these things at once. The resulting spectacle, at once foolish and dreadful, led someone to make the quite accurate observation that "the Negro-in-America is a form of insanity which overtakes white men."

In this long battle, a battle by no means finished, the unfore-seeable effects of which will be felt by many future generations, the white man's motive was the protection of his identity; the black man was motivated by the need to establish an identity. And despite the terrorization which the Negro in America en-dured and endures sporadically until today, despite the cruel and totally inescapable ambivalence of his status in his country, the battle for his identity has long ago been won. He is not a visitor to the West, but a citizen there, an American; as American as the Americans who despise him, the Americans who fear him, the Americans who love him—the Americans who became less than themselves, or rose to be greater than themselves by virtue of the fact that the challenge he represented was inescapable. He is per-haps the only black man in the world whose relationship to white men is more terrible, more subtle, and more meaningful than the relationship of bitter possessed to uncertain possessor. His survival depended, and his development depends, on his ability to turn his peculiar status in the Western world to his own advantage and, it may be, to the very great advantage of that world. It remains for him to fashion out of his experience that which will give him sustenance, and a voice.

The cathedral at Chartres, I have said, says something to the people of this village which it cannot say to me; but it is important to understand that this cathedral says something to me which it cannot say to them. Perhaps they are struck by the power of the spires, the glory of the windows; but they have known God, after all, longer than I have known him, and in a different way, and I am terrified by the slippery bottomless well to be found in the crypt, down which heretics were hurled to death, and by the obscene, inescapable gargoyles jutting out of the stone and seeming to say that God and the devil can never be divorced. I doubt that the villagers think of the devil when they face a cathedral because they have never been identified with the devil. But I must accept the status which myth, if nothing else, gives me in the West before I can hope to change the myth.

Yet, if the American Negro has arrived at his identity by virtue of the absoluteness of his estrangement from his past, American white men still nourish the illusion that there is some means of recovering the European innocence, of returning to a state in which black men do not exist. This is one of the greatest errors Americans can make. The identity they fought so hard to protect has, by virtue of that battle, undergone a change: Americans are as unlike any other white people in the world as it is possible to be. I do not think, for example, that it is too much to suggest that the American vision of the world—which allows so little reality, generally speaking, for any of the darker forces in human life, which tends until today to paint moral issues in glaring black and white—owes a great deal to the battle waged by Americans to maintain between themselves and black men a human separation which could not be bridged. It is only now beginning to be borne in on us—very faintly, it must be admitted, very slowly, and very much against our will—that this vision of the world is dangerously inaccurate, and perfectly useless. For it protects our moral high-mindedness at the terrible expense of weakening our grasp of reality. People who shut their eyes to reality simply invite their own destruction, and anyone who insists on remaining in a state of innocence long after that innocence is dead turns himself into a monster.

The time has come to realize that the interracial drama acted out on the American continent has not only created a new black man, it has created a new white man, too. No road whatever will lead Americans back to the simplicity of this European village where white men still have the luxury of looking on me as a stranger. I am not, really, a stranger any longer for any American alive. One of the things that distinguishes Americans from other people is that no other people has ever been so deeply involved in the lives of black men, and vice versa. This fact faced, with all its implications, it can be seen that the history of the American Negro problem is not merely shameful, it is also something of an achievement. For even when the worst has been said, it must also be added that the perpetual challenge posed by this problem was always, somehow, perpetually met. It is precisely this black-white experience which may prove of indispensable value to us in the world we face today. This world is white no longer, and it will never be white again.

✦

JAMES BALDWIN   Born in New York in 1924; a successful novelist, essayist, and playwright, he is probably today's leading literary spokesman for the American Negro.

"Stranger in the Village" (1955) This essay has a complex and subtle organization out of which an involved and extensive argument emerges. The style is generally restrained, but there are sections that are lyrical and impassioned. The variations in syntax and diction orchestrate the shifts in subject and attitude.

✦

1. What, according to Baldwin, are the main differences between European and American history? 2. Is he consistent in what he says about isolation? 3. What is the rationale behind the organization of this essay?

HARRISON E. SALISBURY

The Shook-Up Kids

I met Smokey on the first night that I spent in Schroeder's candy store. It was cold on the Brooklyn streets that February evening. The temperature stood at eighteen or twenty and the wind was brisk. It seemed to me that Brooklyn, or at least the places the kids hung out, was always colder than anywhere else. In such weather the corner is no fun. The few youngsters who turned out came inside the candy store. They played the juke, riffled through the rack of comic books and peered, from time to time, through the frosted window into the street.

As the boys straggled into the candy store a street club worker introduced me to them. I was impressed by the limp handshake each gave me and I asked the worker about it. He laughed.

"They don't know you," he said. "They aren't sure whether you are a friend or enemy. They shake hands—but not very strongly because they don't know how far to trust you."

After three or four meetings I noticed that the handclasps were growing firmer. I had won a measure of their uncertain confidence.

Smokey was a little different from the start. Possibly, being a leader, he had more self-confidence. At any rate his grip was almost normal. We exchanged only a few words that evening. I noticed that he was dressed better than most of his companions.

He wore a warm tan toggle coat and black beret on which he had pinned a tufted ornament. The radiators in the candy store didn't give much heat so he kept his coat on all evening. His smile was easy but I could see it wash off his face when he stepped into a corner to confer with his lieutenants. The other boys deferred to Smokey. Several times he flipped a hand at a boy. The youngster stepped up quickly, Smokey whispered a word or two in his ear and the boy hurried off, obviously carrying an order to someone or delivering a message.

Many gang members are deficient in intelligence. They may never have ventured beyond a few blocks from their homes. Sometimes, they are so illiterate that they cannot ride the subway because they cannot read the names of the stations. I have met boys who could not articulate their words and had difficulty in using speech. They did not seem to be able to fit words to ideas. I was puzzled to know how they communicated with each other.

Smokey, on the other hand, was a boy whom you would notice in any group. I liked him from my first meeting. He had an air of assurance and authority that was unmistakable. He talked easily and his mind was quick. Not that he did well in school. Several weeks later I had a long discussion with him.

"I do all right in school," he said. "Of course, I could do much better if I put my mind to it. All I do is pass. I could be an honor student. That's no crap. But you know how it is. The boys are always suggesting—you do this, you do that. So you don't have the courage of your convictions. You are per-suaded."

Smokey laughed wryly.

"I was per-suaded today," he said. "Some of the Chaplains had a bottle in school. If I'm a little fuzzy it's because we were drinking all day."

The Chaplains and the Cobras are enemies, but the boys do not usually carry their quarrels to school.

"I couldn't refuse to drink with them," he explained. "I couldn't punk out. I had to show them that the Cobras could drink better than the Chaplains."

When Smokey got to talking he had few inhibitions and he discussed himself and his problems with considerable insight. I found that street youngsters reacted to serious questions with serious answers. When they are convinced that you are sincere they reveal a pathetic eagerness to talk about themselves. It is not often that they encounter an adult who really cares what their life is like. Probably 95 per cent of them come from broken families or families in name only. They get neither understanding nor interest at home. Home life is apt to be a compound of neglect, curses, beatings and drink. This did not hold true for Smokey, nor many other gang leaders. These boys are superior to their comrades and their homes are usually superior. Smokey had a good family, a warm family. His father and mother had been strict in bringing him up, possibly too strict. But they were concerned about his welfare and they loved him. In his way Smokey was concerned about them, too. He loved his mother and regarded his father with a mixture of respect and affection.

Smokey said he was seventeen. He was born in Florida but he was brought north when he was so small that he did not remember it. He had a young brother and three younger sisters. The other children were doing well in school. If Smokey could help it his brother would not get mixed up in the gang. He himself never jitterbugged until he was thirteen or fourteen. Then he was drafted by the Cobra Juniors.

"I wish I could of stayed out," he says now. "But there is no real alternative. If you stay out they beat you up. Maybe you complain to a policeman. What is he going to do about it? Maybe he gets the guys who did it. But what about the next time? He can't keep it from happening again. So you might as well join."

Smokey was seriously worried about his future. He insisted that he hated and feared street fighting.

"People don't understand," he said. "I would much rather not bop. Nobody wants to bop. It isn't any fun to bop. If you are going down on somebody your heart is going to beat faster. You don't know what will happen. You may be killed. Or you may kill someone. Nobody knows. If anyone goes down and isn't afraid it just means he don't know what he's doing."

At seventeen Smokey was thinking a great deal about the gang and what it implied. He was thinking about getting out.

"I'll be through with school in June," he said. "I figure on going in the Army. I know it's about time for me to be giving up the gang. So far I've been very lucky. Very lucky. So far I've never been hurt. And I've never hurt anyone." (In street language "hurt" means to kill or seriously wound.) "But this can't go on forever. I don't want to get arrested. I don't want to get involved in killing someone. But if this goes on someone will get killed. On one side or another. You never know. It can be you."

Smokey had definite ambitions. The ordinary gang member does not. He often has no perspective beyond the street. He counts it an achievement just to get through today or this week or this month. He can see no further.

"Would you think it funny if I said that my real ambition was to become a policeman?" Smokey asked. "I don't know whether I can be now. But I know that I want to stay out of jail and I want to get out of this."

Smokey discussed his mother and father with deep feeling. It would be terrible if he caused them trouble. They thought so much of him. His father was a machinist. He had a good job. His parents did not know he was in a bopping club. They suspected. But they weren't sure.

"There isn't anything that would hurt me more," Smokey said, "than to cause them worry or trouble, to be arrested or to get into some kind of trouble like that. That's where there's a conflict. Between what you should do and what you want to do."

When he spoke of his gang Smokey revealed the nature of this conflict clearly.

"I love every one of them!" he said of the gang. "Well, I mean I like them. I would do anything for those boys. A leader has to have a sense of responsibility for his men. Like right now. There's all kinds of police in the district. I give my men orders. Not to walk around more than two or three together. It's too dangerous. Don't start anything. The cops are just waiting to pick you up."

I wondered how Smokey was going to resolve the conflict between his feelings for his family and for his gang. Perhaps it was beyond his powers to resolve. Perhaps life would have to resolve it for him.

Smokey had a job as a messenger boy with a firm in Manhattan. He was going "almost steady" with a girl who had moved out of the neighborhood.

Looking to the future he said: "After I am through the service —if I get in the service—maybe I'll get married. Maybe I'll have to get married. But then I don't want to come back here. By that time the Little People will be running the club. I want to be far away and out of it. Because if I come back here I'll still be in it. The bopping will still be going on. It won't change. And it's that way all over the city."

Again and again I encountered among the gangs this conviction of the inevitability of conflict on the streets. To these youngsters it seemed a pattern of existence that would go on forever.

It was early March when I had that conversation with Smokey. Six weeks passed before I heard anything more about him. What I heard was not pleasant. A lot had happened in those six weeks. But nothing good.

A few days after our talk Smokey had been arrested on a charge of assault and extortion. He had beaten up a boy and taken money from him. This was serious. It was made more serious by the fact that Smokey was already on probation. The jerry-built structure of Smokey's life started to collapse immediately. The truth about his gang activity could no longer be concealed from his parents. His father had to get a lawyer to defend Smokey and obtain his release on bail. This put his father into debt by $300. Even so, the chances were good that the court would send Smokey up for a term in reformatory.

When the housing project manager heard of Smokey's arrest he gave the family an eviction notice. At the end of two months they must move. Where they would find a new place they had no idea. But certainly it would cost $200 or $300 key money—another trip to the loan shark.

Because he was in jail for a week Smokey lost his job.

Because it no longer seemed to make any difference Smokey quit school.

His girl, only fifteen, discovered that she was pregnant. Smokey said he didn't care. He stopped going with her and started running around with other girls.

This is all that has happened to Smokey so far. It is a good bet that other bad things are coming. He is drinking more now. Without school, without work, without his girl, with his parents disturbed and angry, with the threat of prison hanging over him, Smokey is retreating from the world. Drink and the gang provide a temporary escape. But his leadership of the gang is not as assured as it was a few months ago. He is belligerent, ready to fight anyone. The gang is getting into more and more trouble.

Only a miracle can save Smokey now. But in the world of the street boy miracles are even more rare than they are in our world. What has happened to Smokey is more than a bitter personal tragedy. It is symbolic of the fate which awaits most of Smokey's comrades. Smokey is exceptional only because he has more intelligence, more ability. He has, however, a fatal weakness—the need and desire for the adulation of his fellows. In another environment this might have spurred him to classroom success or athletic triumph. But in Smokey's neighborhood there is only one place where a boy can star. That is the street.

The street is the only life which Seven Up knows. He is an undersized youngster of sixteen with scars on his forehead and on the back of his closely clipped head—battle wounds. He was brought to New York seven years ago from a South Carolina farm. His parents died soon thereafter. Seven Up has been passed from hand to hand ever since. One distant relative after another. No one wanted him. Now he lives with an elderly aunt who is on relief. The old lady is barely able to move about. She makes no attempt to care for Seven Up.

Seven Up is a member of the Cobras. He wears a dirty gray jacket that needs mending. He has a quick smile and a twisted sense of humor. His poverty is complete. He is often hungry. There are days when he goes all day without food. He can read simple words in big type. He can write his name. Otherwise he is illiterate.

There is no one to whom Seven Up has the slightest importance except the Cobras. The school is happier when he does not show up. His aunt is past any interest in him. No one cares what happens to Seven Up. He often injects the phrase "if I live" or "if I don't die" into his conversation. It seems natural. Like many desperately poor, desperately deprived youngsters he is famous for one thing—"heart." This brings affection and acclaim from his gang. They are his world and if he can win their warmth by defying the adult world, well, the price is cheap to Seven Up. Anyone in his situation, I suspect, would feel the same. It is hard to think what society has done for Seven Up which would warrant his feeling toward it any respect, duty or obligation.

Chocolate might be Seven Up's brother, his situation is so similar. He belongs to a Bedford-Stuyvesant gang. He is sixteen, a short youngster with a faraway gleam in his eye. He has been in state institutions several times. He came out recently and certainly will return soon—if he is not killed first. This boy is more illiterate than Seven Up. In the words of a friend "he couldn't read 'New York' if the letters were as big as a truck." He is drunk from early morning until late at night. He probably uses narcotics. His mental condition is dubious. But he has heart to a suicidal degree. Chocolate is past the point where he can really recognize danger, if, indeed, he ever had any clear conception of the risks he has taken. He is, in the understatement of a social worker "a very sick boy." Nothing good will ever happen to Chocolate. There is really no reason why he should not court death. It could not possibly be more unkind to him than life has been.

Pepito isn't as shook-up as Chocolate. Not yet. But he is only fourteen. At his present pace he will be lucky to reach sixteen. When I saw Pepito in the playroom of the community center I did not guess that he smoked marijuana. Nor would I have thought that he sniffed heroin occasionally. His hair is plastered over his forehead in a Sal Mineo cowlick and his face has a babyish quality. His eyes are brown and sulky and he looks like a spoiled younger brother as he plays table tennis—quick, active, alert and a little edgy. I did not pick him as one of the most shook-up members of the Silver Arrows. But the boys agreed that he was. He was on probation for shoplifting and narrowly had escaped being picked up for purse snatching. Almost every evening he walked into the community house, munching a slab of pastry he had swiped off a bakery truck. No one in the neighborhood would turn in Pepito for such petty thievery. They knew how often he went without meals.

When I met Pepito he was living with a grandmother on relief. She could not manage him. He seldom bothered to go to school. Even within the gang he was quarrelsome and irresponsible. But the gang valued him. He had heart. He would do things no other boy would dare. He would sound a cop on the beat and run away laughing. In a rumble he was like a wildcat.

Pepito knew nothing of the world beyond his neighborhood. He "read" the pictures in comic books and was enchanted with the gunplay of cowboy movies.

Soon after I met Pepito he was taken by his father to live up in the Bronx. I thought this might get the boy off to a fresh start. For a short time it seemed that it had. Pepito came back to his old hangout, saying the life in the Bronx was terrible, the kids were no good, there was nothing to do. But a few weeks later he turned up tougher and more self-confident than ever. Two friends, leather-jacket lads like himself, came with him. He told his old gang that things were not so bad in the Bronx after all. "Come up and see our club sometimes," he said. "We got some good bops."

Pepito's life in the Bronx had gotten back on the same tracks it followed in Brooklyn. The progression is hard to change.

There is nothing to distinguish the Chimp from any other overgrown eighteen-year-old high school boy. He sits in the candy store with a Coke in front of him. There are five boys in all, crowded into a booth built for four. All are drinking Cokes. Across from them are four girls, drinking sodas. It is the kind of scene you can see in any town of America, any day of the week around nine of an evening. It would make a good cover for the *Saturday Evening Post*. The girls have pony-tail hairdos which they keep inspecting in the wall mirror. Most of the boys have butch haircuts. The boys are talking among themselves but they keep eying the girls. Several boys and several girls wear white-and maroon school sweaters.

These boys are Rovers. Most Rovers are Italian or Irish although there is one Negro member and two Puerto Ricans. The Chimp is one of the leadership clique even though his status is not too high. The Chimp, unfortunately, has a tendency to "punk out" when the fighting gets tough. His uncle was a famous Brooklyn gangster whose name made many headlines. His father, his uncles, his brothers all work on the docks.

The Chimp is a good deal brighter than most of his companions. He is more intelligent than his record indicates. He was expelled from parochial school. He did no better in public high school. He skipped the last year by getting a fake doctor's certificate of ill health. He worked instead.

But the Chimp understands more about himself than most gang youngsters. He realizes that bravery is not his long suit. When I met him he was about to be inducted into the Army. Army induction in this neighborhood is an occasion—presents from parents, going-away parties and a grand all-night liquor party the evening before reporting.

The Chimp was looking forward to getting into the Army. "I hope the Army will make a man of me," he said. He meant he hoped it would cure his lack of nerve. Also he hoped it would lead him away from the docks. He did not want to follow in the footsteps of his father and uncles. His chief interests were quite different—jazz, dancing (he has won several competitions) and hi-fi. Like most of his group he likes *Confidential* magazine. Reading about the scandalous conduct of persons who are well known or important makes the Chimp feel that he has done nothing very bad. "So what have I ever done?" he says. "Geez, I never stole anything big. These people—they get away with murder and I do mean murder."

He watches the horror movies on the television late late shows and tries to catch Dick Clark's late-afternoon TV rock 'n' roll show from Philadelphia. A New York radio station with a disc jockey who caters to candy-store cliques is a favorite of his. He and other adolescents telephone in messages all evening long. "Greetings from the gang in the Kandy Kitchen of Delmar Avenue," "Al of 159th Street, the Bronx, sends his regards to the boys and girls at Joe's Candy Store," "Christine wishes a big hello to the bunch on the Bronx Concourse." On at least one occasion these broadcasts have been used for inter-gang communication—to set up arrangements for a rumble.

The Chimp and his friends spend more time looking at television than do the Cobras or Arrows. Last summer they watched a TV play which told how the Communists had gained control of a corporation and used their power to wreck the company and throw a lot of people out of jobs. When the Chimp's good friend, Steve, lost his job in the merger of a steel firm he knew the answer.

"The Commies must of got ahold of that company," Steve says. "It's happening every day now. Lookit all the unemployed there are."

Steve doesn't mind unemployment. He gets his benefits. He describes himself now as "a free air inspector." He says he is too busy to work. There is some truth in that. If he got a job he would not have so much time to spend at the candy store.

The Chimp makes no secret of the fact that he hopes to leave the neighborhood someday. A psychologist might say that the Chimp is revolting against his family and the whole waterfront environment of violence and brutality. This may be so. But few youngsters in this area escape. The normal evolution is from participation in the teen-age Rovers to participation in adult gangs on the docks—from little crime and juvenile violence to big crime and adult violence.

"Sometimes, guys come to work on the docks," the Chimp says sagely. "They hope to make money, save it and get away and go into business. But they never make it. How can they? Where else can you earn that kind of dough?"

This is a bitter lesson which the Chimp himself probably will learn. His hopes for utilizing the Army as a bridge out of his environment overlooked one important fact. The Chimp had a police record. After all the parties, all the presents, all the drinking the Chimp came back to the block less than a month later. He only lasted in the Army long enough for the electronic computors to turn up his larceny conviction.

I think that only one among the young people in the candy store that night had a reasonable chance of breaking the pattern. This was Maureen, a tall mature brunette of eighteen. She talked very frankly and looked you in the eye as she talked. She was in her last year of parochial high school. She wanted to go to college. "But not with the sisters, thank you," she laughed. "I've had twelve years with them. They are very nice and all that but enough is enough. I'm going upstate. To a teachers' college."

The girl sitting next to Maureen was called Flora. She was a blonde with wide eyes and heavily painted lips. She didn't pay any attention to Maureen's talk. There was a bridge of freckles over her nose and traces of a tan. Flora had only been back home two weeks from Florida. She went there with a married man who kept her a month and then put her on a bus for home. No one thought the worse of Flora for this. She had come right back to the candy store. If a boy wanted to take her out in his car that was fine. If another boy wanted her when they got back that was okay, too. She was just sitting around, waiting for something to turn up. Maybe another man who would like to take her to Florida. Or possibly California. It didn't really make any difference.

Maureen did not disapprove of Flora. If Flora wanted to go with men that was Flora's business. It just wasn't Maureen's style, that was all. Nor was Maureen like Annabella, the dark-haired Italian girl with ruby cheeks who sat across from her. Annabella had a single-track mind. She wanted a boy to go steady with, a boy who had a job and who wanted to get married. Annabella wanted to get married. Nothing else made the slightest difference. When she went out with boys she didn't let them fool around. Not unless they wanted to get married. Some girls said she was foolish. That wasn't the way to get a boy. Let him make love. Get pregnant. When the baby was coming he would have to marry you. Maybe the girls were right. So far Annabella wasn't sure. If she didn't get a boy this year maybe she would change her tactics. She would see.

Maureen laughed at Annabella.

"Go steady if you want to," she said. "Go ahead and get married. Have your babies. As for me, I'm not going steady. There's not a boy in the world I would go steady with. First, I'm going to college. Maybe I'll meet somebody there. One thing I'll tell you, I'm going to get out of this dump. And never come back."

It will take a year or two to test Maureen's determination. But she had a better chance of success than the boys. Her parents were backing her. Her father earned enough money on the docks to send her to school. He was not a heavy drinker. Maureen was a strong, tough girl. If a boy used filthy language, and the boys liked to use obscenity before girls, Maureen told him off in the same words. She knew them all. If a boy got rough with her she knew where to hit him so it would hurt most.

I did not meet many youngsters of Maureen's tenacity but I did not meet a single gang leader who did not say that he wanted to break out of the pattern of street life. I think the boys are sincere in this. The difficulty lies in their ignorance of how to go about it and their lack of strength to cope with stubborn reality.

This seemed to be the case with Tommy, the leader of one branch of the Chaplains. Tommy told me that he was almost seventeen but I would have guessed his age at fourteen. He is a thin, birdlike youngster with a muscle on the side of his face that twitches nervously. He does not dress like a bop. He wears a neat felt hat, tan windbreaker, red sweater, neat dark tie, white shirt, ordinary black shoes. He was busy collecting money from his members when I met him.

"We're going to buy some sweaters," he said. "They'll have 'C' on them—'C' for Casanova not Chaplains. Do you think the police will believe it when we say 'C' is for Casanova?"

I doubted very much if the police or anyone else would believe such a story.

Tommy was born in Georgia and has been back there for summer vacations. He didn't like it because the "people are too old-fashioned." By this he meant that he was made to go to bed at ten o'clock.

Tommy does not get along well with his parents. His mother, father and brother work. There is no lack of money in the home. They live in public housing. The family is gone all day and Tommy is supposed to take care of the house. He gets an allowance of $1.75 a week. This is far more than any of his gang comrades receives. But he is not satisfied.

"That's just enough for bubble gum," he says, in contempt. He would rather skip the allowance if he could get out of housework. He receives passing grades but doesn't like school. His favorite subject, he says with a sneer, is "lunch."

"What do you like to read?" I asked him.

"Nothin'," he replied. "I don't like to read."

"What do you like to do?"

"Sit."

"Just sit?"

"Just sit."

He was sardonic about his ambitions. "What do I want to do in life?" he asked. "Stay alive. Some people say I won't live so long."

This was not just adolescent bravado. Tommy had nine stiches taken in his scalp after an encounter with the Bishops on New

Year's Eve. "I was drunk," he said. "I got careless. But we made
it up to them."

Tommy likes very few things in his life. He dislikes his home,
his school, the neighborhood (he would like to live in a house in
the country) and the gang. He does not like sports. Football is
too rough. He doesn't follow baseball. He couldn't think of any
heroes, neither prize fighters nor soldiers. Like all gang kids he
is ready to risk his life in combat with knife or gun but he won't
go out to fight in the rain. He doesn't want to spoil his clothes.
He has never owned a cat or dog. He would like to work in an
office where "it is clean and you can dress nice." He is another
boy who looks to the Army as a possible escape from the vicious
circle of his life. When I asked if he'd rather there were no gangs
he said: "Oh, yes! Then, we'd be able to go everywhere freely
and keep all strangers off our turf."

Why didn't he like strangers?

"Because," he said, with a small boy's petulance, "one night
one would come down. The next night there would be two. And
the next night three and pretty soon they'd be all over the place."

Perhaps the most impressive gang leader whom I met was
Vincent, the slender Puerto Rican leader of the Silver Arrows.
Vincent is seventeen. He looks a little like an Aztec prince, his
black hair combed in a massive crest and his head carried high.
When Vincent came from Puerto Rico in 1949 his family first
settled in Manhattan on the edge of East Harlem. He likes Brooklyn much better for a reason which any street boy would understand.

"I hate Manhattan," Vincent said, shuddering. "Those square
blocks! You walk into a block—they can jap you anywhere. There
is no way out of them. Once you are in a block you have to go to
the end. You can't escape. It is terrible!"

Vincent thinks Brooklyn is wonderful:

"All those curved streets, going this way and that way. You
can always run somewhere. You can get away."

Security, security, security. This is close to the surface of almost
everything the youngsters do or say. Want of security is what
leads them into the gang and want of security is what keeps them
in this dangerous limbo.

Vincent was introduced to street fighting by the Italian boys in
the neighborhood into which his family first moved. They beat

him up many times. Finally, he joined their gang. When he came to Brooklyn his street experience enabled him to take leadership of the Puerto Rican boys in Whitman Houses.

It had been Vincent's hope that he might become an aviation mechanic. He was enrolled in Aviation High School and did fair work there. But he quit school the day before his graduation when he learned that because he had a police record he could not get a certificate. Vincent is bitter over this. He was charged with stealing a pistol from a National Guard Armory and he says the charge was false.

"That's the way it starts," he said. "I've seen it happen many times. The police blame you for something you didn't do. You get a record. They send you away. So, then, the kid comes back and he says, 'Well, I'm going to do something and get a record of my own. At least then if I'm sent up it will be for something I did myself.'"

When that happens, Vincent says, there is no holding a youngster. He will go on and on and on until finally he is caught and sent back to prison. I think he is right about this. Even among the small sampling of youngsters whom I got to know it seemed to me that the number who were falsely accused by the police was about as great as those who were justly accused. This was a source of great bitterness. One reason for this, of course, is that boys do not come forward and admit their guilt even when a friend is held for the crime which they committed.

There is also a certain resignation to fate. Vincent, for example, was given an opportunity for legal assistance in reopening the question of his high school certificate. But he never bothered to get in touch with the lawyer. He didn't really believe it would be of any use.

Vincent comes from a big poor family. He lives with his mother and father and eight brothers and sisters. The family has been on relief for several years. Vincent is the only one who is involved with gangs.

"I'm the only bad one," he says, almost shame-faced. "My mother knows that I fight. She asks me what I am doing and I tell her. I tell her I only fight when I have to. For some good reason. She does not like this but she understands this. I do not like it either. But what is there to do? That is the way it is."

Now that his chance of getting a job as an aviation mechanic has vanished Vincent doesn't know what to do. He worked for a while in a machine shop but he had to get up so early and travel so far that he quit.

"I don't know," he said. "I don't know what there is for me to do. The only thing I want to do I can't do. So it doesn't make much difference."

Vincent says that he bears no grudges against the boys with whom he fights "except for a few." He says he would like a permanent cool but "they don't have it that way." He doesn't think the police can stop the fighting.

"The trouble with the police is the way they look at you," he says. "We are standing on the corner. The cop comes along. He tells you to move along. If he treated you like you were people— but he doesn't. He has that hard look. I just can't stand to have cops look at me like that."

Vincent, like his comrades, feels that there will be no end to street fighting.

"The only way to stop it would be for you to be free to go anywhere in the city and nobody would touch you," he said. "Then there would be no fighting. But somebody will always interfere. One fellow will start it and then it is on again. That's the way it is."

Vincent had come uptown to have dinner in a restaurant with me where we could talk with a freedom that was not possible in the candy store or community house. We finished our coffee and went out into the brisk air of an early March evening. I walked a little way with Vincent and stood with him while he waited for his bus. The sky was clear and the stars were sparkling dust against the dark space of the universe. We stood a moment and then Vincent boarded his bus, back to the housing project and the Arrows, back to his turf and his narrow island of security. I turned and headed for the subway back to Manhattan. No policeman gave me any hard looks and I was free to go anywhere I wanted to in the city. I wondered whether it was really beyond the ability of a rich city like New York to make the streets as safe and free for boys like Vincent as they were for me.

✦

HARRISON E. SALISBURY   Born in Minneapolis in 1908, he worked for the United Press, then as Moscow correspondent for the *New York Times*, for which he still writes. He is the author of four books, three of them on Russia, the fourth on "the shook-up generation," from which this is a chapter. In modified form, this book was originally a series of articles in the *Times*.

"The Shook-Up Kids" (1958) Employing brief case histories, on-the-spot authorities, interviews, and dramatic incidents to comprise the matter of this essay, the author achieves an organic narrative the chief purpose of which is expository. It is an example of journalistic writing at its best, and it says far more than appears at first glance.

✦

1. In what ways is this account relevant to your own group? 2. How does the author himself seem to have changed as a result of these experiences?

FRED DICKENSON

How to Iron a Telephone Book

If you have been putting off ironing your telephone book, you need no longer hesitate. I can tell you how it's done. I recently ironed the Manhattan Directory—all eighteen hundred and thirty-six pages. This stimulating adventure had its beginning when our electric dishwasher accidentally turned itself on—a little caprice caused, we later found out, by a short in some inscrutable automatic control. Nobody was home except our beagle, Lucky. There were no dishes in the machine, but these details are really irrelevant. What *is* important is that the top was up. Dishwashers are not supposed to turn themselves on, in the first place, and, in the second place, there are all sorts of safety devices that shut them off when the cover is raised, but apparently a short circuit takes care of this safeguard nonsense easily.

We live in Chappaqua, thirty-two miles north of New York City. My wife was at the supermarket, the children were in school, and I was at my office, in New York, when our dishwasher started automatically flooding the kitchen. When my wife returned home and opened the kitchen door, she was met by a cloud of steam and by the beagle, who, although slightly parboiled, was still able to fly. He set a new dash record from kitchen door to driveway, and vanished under our car.

My wife turned off the machine and settled down at the telephone, first calling the repairman, who said that the dishwasher

Reprinted by permission; © 1959 The New Yorker Magazine, Inc. This selection originally appeared in *The New Yorker*, January 17, 1959.

could not possibly have turned itself on by accident. Then she called me. "The kitchen looks like one of those Kentucky caves" was the picturesque way she put it. "Water is dripping from the ceiling. I never saw so much water in my life. I found a double boiler full of water inside a closed cabinet."

By the time I got home that night, the paper on the kitchen walls and ceiling had dried, leaving only a faint fragrance of old paste, and everything else had been emptied or mopped up. The only important damage was to our precious new 1958–59 Manhattan Telephone Directory. Both the Manhattan and the Westchester telephone books, which nestle on a shelf near the dishwasher (it now sullenly refused to do *anything*), were sopping. I must explain that, as residents of Chappaqua, we are entitled only to the Westchester County book. This, I knew, we could have replaced by simply calling the phone company. But a Manhattan book can only be obtained free in the suburbs by borrowing it from one's own office in the city when nobody is looking, and hauling it all the way home on the train. It had taken me two years to find the exact moment when this nervy maneuver could be executed. And now, within a few weeks, the fruit of my endeavors was a sodden mass.

"Maybe it will dry out by itself," I said hopefully the next morning. "We'll leave it as it is."

A week later, the book had swollen to almost twice its normal size and was threatening to force the phone itself off the shelf. A quick flip—or flop—through the pages showed them to be as wet as ever.

"We'll dry it in the oven," my wife said brightly. "If you can make bricks that way, you certainly ought to be able to dry a telephone book. I'd say about two hundred and fifty degrees, so it won't get too well done on the outside."

The oven was turned on, and we slipped the book in tenderly. Five hours later, you still couldn't get a fork into it. It steamed merrily but damply, and now we were alarmed to notice that it was beginning to wrinkle. We took it out and set it on a window sill to cool.

"There's only one thing to do," my wife said. "We've got to iron it. How many pages are there?"

I looked. "One thousand eight hundred and thirty-six."

She made a rapid calculation. We have three teen-age daughters. The beagle, of course, could not be counted upon. "That means three hundred and sixty-seven pages each," she said.

What we did not realize was that teen-age daughters cannot be counted upon, either, especially when it comes to ironing telephone books. They simply do not seem to grasp the challenge. When they came home from school, my wife told them gaily, "Tonight we are all going to take turns ironing the telephone book!"

They regarded her steadily, with that terrible candor of the teen-ager, and asked for a repeat. When the full import of her plan struck home, the response was loud and negative—so negative, in fact, that I, in disgust, said I would do the entire job, all by myself. I expected a chorus of protests to greet this suggestion. I was wrong. Ironing is woman's work, but, for some reason, all the ladies in my family seemed to take the attitude that ironing a telephone book is a masculine undertaking, like carpentry or car washing.

Pioneering this little-known field, I believe I picked up a few pointers that should be passed on to those who may come after. First of all, when you are ironing a telephone book the size of the Manhattan Directory, it is important that you be properly dressed. I chose sneakers, tennis socks, brown chino trousers, and a T shirt. Although I ironed in the evenings, I found that even a cool basement laundry room heats up long before you have completed a hundred pages, and I was grateful that I had had the foresight to select an outfit that provided maximum comfort and freedom of movement.

The heat dial of the iron should be set for Cotton. Rayon is not hot enough, and Linen is apt to scorch around the edges, particularly if you get to watching for lady chiropractors, Arabian delicatessens, and the like.

Begin at the back. For some reason, it helps to think of yourself as on page 1836, rather than page 1. I will never again see a Manhattan Directory without recalling the ZzzyZzy Ztamp Ztudioz Co., the last entry in the book, and the first your iron touches under the circumstances.

You may sit down while ironing, but only during the earlier stages. I used my workbench stool for a while, but I soon found that as the ironed pages grew higher, it was increasingly difficult to exert sufficient downward pressure to smooth out the more stubborn wrinkles.

Dismiss from your mind any time-saving ideas that may occur to you. It is impossible to iron a wet telephone book quickly and still maintain a high standard of workmanship. There is no use trying to iron more than one page at a time. Purely in the interests of science, and not because of any weakening in my resolve, I tried this short cut as early as the "T"s, taking first four pages, then three, and finally settling for two, but the bottom one will not dry. (In the course of this experiment, I kept the iron on one page too long, and was warned just in time by a tiny spiral of smoke. A half column of Thompsons in my book are now the color of toast.)

And don't think you can speed things up by holding the wet pages in one hand and flipping them down one by one, as needed. It won't work. The moisture causes the pages to stick together, and they have to be separated, with both hands, which means, of course, that you have to put the iron down nine hundred and eighteen times.

For one wild moment, along about the mid-"O"s, I considered using the mangle (*"They laughed when I sat down at the mangle, but . . ."*), and I did take a brief respite to study the machine. You operate a mangle with your knees, of course, and this would have been a welcome change, for my hand had begun to cramp around the handle of the iron. However, it was obvious that I would have to hold the book, feed in one page at a time, and release the roller at precisely the right instant. The danger of tearing the pages was too great, and I went back to hand labor, comforting myself with the thought that the best places always advertise that type of work.

Since there are no short cuts to success in this rather special field, I suggest that you allow at least two nights for the job. I ended my first ironing session around 2 A.M. The next evening was almost a complete loss. Just as I was starting on the "K"s, some friends asked us over, and my wife was too embarrassed—as well she might have been—to say that we couldn't go because I was down in the cellar ironing the telephone book. The upshot was that I had to change out of my ironing costume and play games for the rest of the evening. I finally finished the job at one-fifteen the following night.

Ironing the Manhattan Directory is not mentally stimulating. From time to time, my wife would come down to see how I was doing, or one of the children would call down the stairs to ask me for information about ancient Egyptian civilization. The dog also came to visit, nervously sniffing the unusual mixture of steam, paper, and ink. But even with occasional visitors the hours do not fly by, and I suggest that you try to think of yourself as on a scenic tour of the glittering metropolis. On my magic iron, I glided through the West Side Zuckermans, passed the Yale Club and the Woolworth Bldg., and appreciated for the first time the sprawling bureaucracy of the United States Government— "WEATHER BUR." through "ADVISORY GROUP ON ELECTRON TUBES." There was the United Nations (Yugoslavia through Afghanistan), Trinity Church, the Stork Club, the Smiths (seven and a half pages of them), and the Original Crispy Pizza Crust Co. My iron smoothed the furrowed brows of Merrill Lynch Pierce Fenner & Smith, paused at Luchow's, pressed on to the Joneses (only four pages of them), and dropped into El Morocco for a nightcap. The whole vast panorama of Manhattan (smelling only slightly of hot paper) passed before me, until finally I ironed the last wrinkle from Page 1—"Emergency Calls."

A cautionary note: When ironing a telephone book, you will find that several beers not only enhance the tour but also diminish the importance of any little burns or muscular aches picked up along the way. The quantity of beer consumed must be carefully regulated. I erred on the side of generosity the first evening, and by the time I reached the "Mc"s, I noticed that the quality of my work had deteriorated. In fact, I had to sprinkle the "McD"s and iron them all over again.

1

FRED DICKENSON   Born in 1909, he makes his living—in his own words "sometimes comfortably, often precariously"—as a free-lance writer. He has contributed to newspapers and magazines, and written a mystery novel and the text for a comic strip.

"*How to Iron a Telephone Book*" (1959) A parody of a process analysis, this essay also offers an oblique commentary on suburbia. It features both understatement and hyperbole, and it dramatically uses the incongruous to produce a narrative that is gay but not entirely frivolous.

1

1. What are the main things satirized in this essay? 2. What devices does the author employ to evoke laughter?

E. B. WHITE

A Slight Sound at Evening

Allen Cove, Summer, 1954

In his journal for July 10–12, 1841, Thoreau wrote: "A slight sound at evening lifts me up by the ears, and makes life seem inexpressibly serene and grand. It may be in Uranus, or it may be in the shutter." The book into which he later managed to pack both Uranus and the shutter was published in 1854, and now, a hundred years having gone by, *Walden,* its serenity and grandeur unimpaired, still lifts us up by the ears, still translates for us that language we are in danger of forgetting, "which all things and events speak without metaphor, which alone is copious and standard."

Walden is an oddity in American letters. It may very well be the oddest of our distinguished oddities. For many it is a great deal too odd, and for many it is a particular bore. I have not found it to be a well-liked book among my acquaintances, although usually spoken of with respect, and one literary critic for whom I have the highest regard can find no reason for anyone's giving *Walden* a second thought. To admire the book is, in fact, something of an embarrassment, for the mass of men have an indistinct notion that its author was a sort of Nature Boy.

I think it is of some advantage to encounter the book at a period in one's life when the normal anxieties and enthusiasms and rebellions of youth closely resemble those of Thoreau in that spring of 1845 when he borrowed an ax, went out to the woods, and began to whack down some trees for timber. Received at such a juncture, the book is like an invitation to life's dance, assuring the troubled recipient that no matter what befalls him in the way of success or failure he will always be welcome at the party—that the music is played for him, too, if he will but listen and move his feet. In effect, that is what the book is—an invitation, unengraved; and it stirs one as a young girl is stirred by her first big party bid. Many think it a sermon; many set it down as an attempt to rearrange society; some think it an exercise in nature-loving; some find it a rather irritating collection of inspirational puffballs by an eccentric show-off. I think it none of these. It still seems to me the best youth's companion yet written by an American, for it carries a solemn warning against the loss of one's valuables, it advances a good argument for travelling light and trying new adventures, it rings with the power of positive adoration, it contains religious feeling without religious images, and it steadfastly refuses to record bad news. Even its pantheistic note is so pure as to be noncorrupting—pure as the flute-note blown across the pond on those faraway summer nights. If our colleges and universities were alert, they would present a cheap pocket edition of the book to every senior upon graduating, along with his sheepskin, or instead of it. Even if some senior were to take it literally and start felling trees, there could be worse mishaps: the ax is older than the Dictaphone and it is just as well for a young man to see what kind of chips he leaves before listening to the sound of his own voice. And even if some were to get no farther than the table of contents, they would learn how to name eighteen chapters by the use of only thirty-nine words and would see how sweet are the uses of brevity.

If Thoreau had merely left us an account of a man's life in the woods or if he had simply retreated to the woods and there recorded his complaints about society, or even if he had contrived to include both records in one essay, *Walden* would probably not have lived a hundred years. As things turned out, Thoreau, very likely without knowing quite what he was up to, took man's relation to Nature and man's dilemma in society and man's capacity for elevating his spirit and he beat all these matters together, in a wild free interval of self-justification and delight, and produced an original omelette from which people can draw nourishment in a hungry day. *Walden* is one of the first of the vitamin-enriched American dishes. If it were a little less good than it is, or even a little less queer, it would be an abominable book. Even as it is, it will continue to baffle and annoy the literal mind and all those who are unable to stomach its caprices and imbibe its theme. Certainly the plodding economist will continue to have rough going if he hopes to emerge from the book with a clear system of economic thought. Thoreau's assault on the Concord society of the mid-nineteenth century has the quality of a modern Western: he rides into the subject at top speed, shooting in all directions. Many of his shots ricochet and nick him on the rebound, and throughout the melee there is a horrendous cloud of inconsistencies and contradictions, and when the shooting dies down and the air clears, one is impressed chiefly by the courage of the rider and by how splendid it was that somebody should have ridden in there and raised all that ruckus.

When he went to the pond, Thoreau struck an attitude and did so deliberately, but his posturing was not to draw the attention of others to him but rather to draw his own attention more closely to himself. "I learned this at least by my experiment: that if one advances confidently in the direction of his dreams, and endeavors to live the life which he has imagined, he will meet with a success unexpected in common hours." The sentence has the power to resuscitate the youth drowning in his sea of doubt. I recall my exhilaration upon reading it, many years ago, in a time of hesitation and despair. It restored me to health. And now in 1954 when I salute Henry Thoreau on the hundredth birthday of his book, I am merely paying off an old score—or an installment on it.

In his journal for May 3–4, 1838—Boston to Portland—he wrote: "Midnight—head over the boat's side—between sleeping and waking—with glimpses of one or more lights in the vicinity of Cape Ann. Bright moonlight—the effect heightened by seasickness." The entry illuminates the man, as the moon the sea on that night in May. In Thoreau the natural scene was heightened, not depressed, by a disturbance of the stomach, and nausea met its match at last. There was a steadiness in at least one passenger if there was none in the boat. Such steadiness (which in some would be called intoxication) is at the heart of *Walden*—confidence, faith, the discipline of looking always at what is to be seen, undeviating gratitude for the life-everlasting that he found growing in his front yard. "There is nowhere recorded a simple and irrepressible satisfaction with the gift of life, any memorable praise of God." He worked to correct that deficiency. *Walden* is his acknowledgment of the gift of life. It is the testament of a man in a high state of indignation because (it seemed to him) so few ears heard the uninterrupted poem of creation, the morning wind that forever blows. If the man sometimes wrote as though all his readers were male, unmarried, and well-connected, it is because he gave his testimony during the callow years, and, for that matter, never really grew up. To reject the book because of the immaturity of the author and the bugs in the logic is to throw away a bottle of good wine because it contains bits of the cork.

Thoreau said he required of every writer, first and last, a simple and sincere account of his own life. Having delivered himself of this chesty dictum, he proceeded to ignore it. In his books and even in his enormous journal, he withheld or disguised most of the facts from which an understanding of his life could be drawn. *Walden*, subtitled "Life in the Woods," is not a simple and sincere account of a man's life, either in or out of the woods; it is an account of a man's journey into the mind, a toot on the trumpet to alert the neighbors. Thoreau was well aware that no one can alert his neighbors who is not wide-awake himself, and he went to the woods (among other reasons) to make sure that he would stay awake during his broadcast. What actually took place during the years 1845–47 is largely unrecorded, and the reader is excluded from the private life of the author, who supplies almost no gossip about himself, a great deal about his neighbors and about the universe.

As for me, I cannot in this short ramble give a simple and sincere account of my own life, but I think Thoreau might find it instructive to know that this memorial essay is being written in a house that, through no intent on my part, is the same size and shape as his own domicile on the pond—about ten by fifteen, tight, plainly finished, and at a little distance from my Concord. The house in which I sit this morning was built to accommodate a boat, not a man, but by long experience I have learned that in most respects it shelters me better than the larger dwelling where my bed is, and which, by design, is a manhouse not a boathouse. Here in the boathouse I am a wilder and, it would appear, a healthier man, by a safe margin. I have a chair, a bench, a table, and I can walk into the water if I tire of the land. My house fronts a cove. Two fishermen have just arrived to spot fish from the air—an osprey and a man in a small yellow plane who works for the fish company. The man, I have noticed, is less well equipped than the hawk, who can dive directly on his fish and carry it away, without telephoning. A mouse and a squirrel share the house with me. The building is, in fact, a multiple dwelling, a semidetached affair. It is because I am semidetached while here that I find it possible to transact this private business with the fewest obstacles.

There is also a woodchuck here, living forty feet away under the wharf. When the wind is right, he can smell my house; and when the wind is contrary, I can smell his. We both use the wharf for sunning, taking turns, each adjusting his schedule to the other's convenience. Thoreau once ate a woodchuck. I think he felt he owed it to his readers, and that it was little enough, considering the indignities they were suffering at his hands and the dressing-down they were taking. (Parts of *Walden* are pure scold.) Or perhaps he ate the woodchuck because he believed every man should acquire strict business habits, and the woodchuck was destroying his market beans. I do not know. Thoreau had a strong experimental streak in him. It is probably no harder to eat a woodchuck than to construct a sentence that lasts a hundred years. At any rate, Thoreau is the only writer I know who prepared himself for his great ordeal by eating a woodchuck; also the only one who got a hangover from drinking too much water. (He was drunk the whole time, though he seldom touched wine or coffee or tea.)

Here in this compact house where I would spend one day as deliberately as Nature if I were not being pressed by the editor of a magazine, and with a woodchuck (as yet uneaten) for neighbor, I can feel the companionship of the occupant of the pondside cabin in Walden woods, a mile from the village, near the Fitchburg right of way. Even my immediate business is no barrier between us: Thoreau occasionally batted out a magazine piece, but was always suspicious of any sort of purposeful work that cut into his time. A man, he said, should take care not to be thrown off the track by every nutshell and mosquito's wing that falls on the rails.

There had been much guessing as to why he went to the pond. To set it down to escapism is, of course, to misconstrue what happened. Henry went forth to battle when he took to the woods, and *Walden* is the report of a man torn by two powerful and opposing drives—the desire to enjoy the world (and not be derailed by a mosquito wing) and the urge to set the world straight. One cannot join these two successfully, but sometimes, in rare cases, something good or even great results from the attempt of the tormented spirit to reconcile them. Henry went forth to battle, and if he set the stage himself, if he fought on his own terms and with his own weapons, it was because it was his nature to do things differently from most men, and to act in a cocky fashion. If the pond and the woods seemed a more plausible site for a house than an in-town location, it was because a cowbell made for him a sweeter sound than a churchbell. *Walden*, the book, makes the sound of a cowbell, more than a churchbell, and proves the point, although both sounds are in it, and both remarkably clear and sweet. He simply preferred his churchbell at a little distance.

I think one reason he went to the woods was a perfectly simple and commonplace one—and apparently he thought so, too. "At a certain season of our life," he wrote, "we are accustomed to consider every spot as the possible site of a house." There spoke the young man, a few years out of college, who had not yet broken away from home. He hadn't married, and he had found no job that measured up to his rigid standards of employment, and like any young man, or young animal, he felt uneasy and on the defensive until he had fixed himself a den. Most young men, of course, casting about for a site, are content merely to draw apart from their kinfolks. Thoreau, convinced that the greater part of what his neighbors called good was bad, withdrew from a great deal more than family: he pulled out of everything for a while, to serve everybody right for being so stuffy, and to try his own prejudices on the dog.

The house-hunting sentence above, which starts the chapter called "Where I Lived, and What I Lived For," is followed by another passage that is worth quoting here because it so beautifully illustrates the offbeat prose that Thoreau was master of, a prose at once strictly disciplined and wildly abandoned. "I have surveyed the country on every side within a dozen miles of where I live," continued this delirious young man. "In imagination I have bought all the farms in succession, for all were to be bought, and I knew their price. I walked over each farmer's premises, tasted his wild apples, discoursed on husbandry with him, took his farm at his price, at any price, mortgaging it to him in my mind; even put a higher price on it—took everything but a deed of it—took his word for his deed, for I dearly love to talk—cultivated it, and him too to some extent, I trust, and withdrew when I had enjoyed it long enough, leaving him to carry it on." A copy-desk man would get a double hernia trying to clean up that sentence for the management, but the sentence needs no fixing, for it perfectly captures the meaning of the writer and the quality of the ramble.

"Wherever I sat, there I might live, and the landscape radiated from me accordingly." Thoreau, the home-seeker, sitting on his hummock with the entire State of Massachusetts radiating from him, is to me the most humorous of the New England figures, and *Walden* the most humorous of the books, though its humor is almost continuously subsurface and there is nothing deliberately funny anywhere, except a few weak jokes and bad puns that rise to the surface like the perch in the pond that rose to the sound of the maestro's flute. Thoreau tended to write in sentences, a feat not every writer is capable of, and *Walden* is, rhetorically speaking, a collection of certified sentences, some of them, it would now appear, as indestructible as they are errant. The book is distilled from the vast journals, and this accounts for its intensity: he picked out bright particles that pleased his eye, whirled them in the kaleidoscope of his content, and produced the pattern that has endured—the color, the form, the light.

On this its hundredth birthday, Thoreau's *Walden* is pertinent and timely. In our uneasy season, when all men unconsciously seek a retreat from a world that has got almost completely out of hand, his house in the Concord woods is a haven. In our culture of gadgetry and the multiplicity of convenience, his cry "Simplicity, simplicity, simplicity!" has the insistence of a fire alarm. In the brooding atmosphere of war and the gathering radioactive storm, the innocence and serenity of his summer afternoons are enough to burst the remembering heart, and one gazes back upon that pleasing interlude—its confidence, its purity, its deliberateness—with awe and wonder, as one would look upon the face of a child asleep.

"This small lake was of most value as a neighbor in the intervals of a gentle rain-storm in August, when, both air and water being perfectly still, but the sky overcast, midafternoon had all the serenity of evening, and the wood-thrush sang around, and was heard from shore to shore." Now, in the perpetual overcast in which our days are spent, we hear with extra perception and deep gratitude that song, tying century to century.

I sometimes amuse myself by bringing Henry Thoreau back to life and showing him the sights. I escort him into a phone booth and let him dial Weather. "This is a delicious evening," the girl's voice says, "when the whole body is one sense, and imbibes delight through every pore." I show him the spot in the Pacific where an island used to be, before some magician made it vanish. "We know not where we are," I murmur. "The light which puts out our eyes is darkness to us. Only that day dawns to which we are awake." I thumb through the latest copy of *Vogue* with him. "Of two patterns which differ only by a few threads more or less of a particular color," I read, "the one will be sold readily, the other lie on the shelf, though it frequently happens that, after the lapse of a season, the latter becomes the most fashionable." Together we go outboarding on the Assabet, looking for what we've lost—a hound, a bay horse, a turtledove. I show him a distracted farmer who is trying to repair a hay baler before the thunder shower breaks. "This farmer," I remark, "is endeavoring to solve the problem of a livelihood by a formula more complicated than the problem itself. To get his shoestrings he speculates in herds of cattle."

I take the celebrated author to Twenty-One for lunch, so the waiters may study his shoes. The proprietor welcomes us. "The gross feeder," remarks the proprietor, sweeping the room with his arm, "is a man in the larva stage." After lunch we visit a classroom in one of those schools conducted by big corporations to teach their superannuated executives how to retire from business without serious injury to their health. (The shock to men's systems these days when relieved of the exacting routine of amassing wealth is very great and must be cushioned.) "It is not necessary," says the teacher to his pupils, "that a man should earn his living by the sweat of his brow, unless he sweats easier than I do. We are determined to be starved before we are hungry."

I turn on the radio and let Thoreau hear Winchell beat the red hand around the clock. "Time is but the stream I go a-fishing in," shouts Mr. Winchell, rattling his telegraph key. "Hardly a man takes a half hour's nap after dinner, but when he wakes he holds up his head and asks, 'What's the news?' If we read of one man robbed, or murdered, or killed by accident, or one house burned, or one vessel wrecked, or one steamboat blown up, or one cow run over on the Western Railroad, or one mad dog killed, or one lot of grasshoppers in the winter—we need never read of another. One is enough."

I doubt that Thoreau would be thrown off balance by the fantastic sights and sounds of the twentieth century. "The Concord nights," he once wrote, "are stranger than the Arabian nights." A four-engined airliner would merely serve to confirm his early views on travel. Everywhere he would observe, in new shapes and sizes, the old predicaments and follies of men—the desperation, the impedimenta, the meanness—along with the visible capacity for elevation of the mind and soul. "This curious world which we inhabit is more wonderful than it is convenient; more beautiful than it is useful; it is more to be admired and enjoyed than used." He would see that today ten thousand engineers are busy making sure that the world shall be convenient even if it is destroyed in the process, and others are determined to increase its usefulness even though its beauty is lost somewhere along the way.

At any rate, I'd like to stroll about the countryside in Thoreau's company for a day, observing the modern scene, inspecting today's snowstorm, pointing out the sights, and offering belated apologies for my sins. Thoreau is unique among writers in that those who admire him find him uncomfortable to live with—a regular hairshirt of a man. A little band of dedicated Thoreauvians would be a sorry sight indeed: fellows who hate compromise and have compromised, fellows who love wildness and have lived tamely, and at their side, censuring them and chiding them, the ghostly figure of this upright man, who long ago gave corroboration to impulses they perceived were right and issued warnings against the things they instinctively knew to be their enemies. I should hate to be called a Thoreauvian, yet I wince every time I walk into the barn I'm pushing before me, seventy-five feet by forty, and the author of *Walden* has served as my conscience through the long stretches of my trivial days.

Hairshirt or no, he is a better companion than most, and I would not swap him for a soberer or more reasonable friend even if I could. I can reread his famous invitation with undiminished excitement. The sad thing is that not more acceptances have been received, that so many decline for one reason or another, pleading some previous engagement or ill health. But the invitation stands. It will beckon as long as this remarkable book stays in print—which will be as long as there are August afternoons in the intervals of a gentle rainstorm, as long as there are ears to catch the faint sounds of the orchestra. I find it agreeable to sit here this morning, in a house of correct proportions, and hear across a century of time his flute, his frogs, and his seductive summons to the wildest revels of them all.

E. B. WHITE   Born in Mount Vernon, New York in 1899, he has been a journalist, editor, and free-lance writer. Among his many literary productions are children's books, poems, and several collections of essays.

"A Slight Sound at Evening" (1954)   The rhetoric and style are mixed: though simple on the surface, they move back and forth between the lyrical and the declarative, the personal and the impersonal, the angry and the easy-going, the warmly appreciative and the detachedly objective, the humorous and the serious, the past and the present. The author's admiration for Thoreau is evident in both what he says and how he says it.

1. *What do White and Thoreau have in common?* 2. *To what is this essay an invitation?* 3. *How does it try to make you accept that invitation?*

JOHN KENNETH GALBRAITH

The Decline of the Machine

I

Those who guide our worries on large issues regularly ask us to ponder man's losing competition with the machine. On the assembly lines he is being replaced by automatic machinery which is regulated and instructed by electronic controls. If the resulting product is a consumer item it has almost certainly been designed to minimize both the effort and intelligence required of its user. Not even the question of whether people will want it has been left entirely to judgment. This has been ascertained by market surveys and insured by advertising and both, perhaps, were analyzed with the aid of an electronic computer, sometimes too ambitiously called an electronic brain.

The tendency to dispense with men and intelligence is held to go far beyond the consumer gadgets. The unmanned missile is about to replace the old-fashioned hand-operated bomber. In the near future, according to enthusiasts, unmanned missiles will take flight to intercept other unmanned missiles which will prevent these from intercepting other automated missiles. The operation will be handled under contract by IBM. If the globe were larger or the explosions smaller the prospect would be not unattractive. The machines having taken over, men would all be noncombatants. The charm of war has always been greatest for those whose role was to guide it from a certain distance.

These visions of the triumph of the machine can be multiplied endlessly. We do not take them quite seriously for we do not

From *The Liberal Hour* by John Kenneth Galbraith. Copyright © by John Kenneth Galbraith. Reprinted by permission of Houghton Mifflin Company.

really believe that we are being replaced, and our instinct is sound. If there is a competition between man and machine, man is winning it—not for at least two centuries has his position been so strong compared with the apparatus with which he works.

And the fact that this is the age of ascendant man, not triumphant machine, has practical consequences. If machines are the decisive thing, then the social arrangements by which we increase our physical plant and equipment will be of first importance. But if it is men that count, then our first concern must be with arrangements for conserving and developing personal talents. It will be these on which progress will depend. Should it happen, moreover, that for reasons of antiquated design our society does well in supplying itself with machines and badly in providing itself with highly improved manpower, there would be cause for concern. There is such cause, for that, precisely, is our situation.

But first, what is the evidence that men have been gaining on machines—that skill and intelligence have become more important in what we call economic progress than capital plant and equipment?

II

The change is most prominently reflected in the changed position of the owner or supplier of physical capital. For a half century he has been a man of steadily declining prestige and importance. Once it was taken for granted that ownership of an industrial enterprise—the ownership of the capital assets or a substantial share of them—gave a man a decisive voice in its direction. So it was with Ford, Carnegie, the elder Rockefeller, Commodore Vanderbilt, and John Jacob Astor. And to be a source of capital, as in the case of the elder Morgan, insured an almost equal power over the enterprise. It also insured a considerable position in the community. Indeed, it was because the provision of capital conveyed such power that the system was called capitalism.

Now the ownership of capital, or the capacity to supply it, accords no such power. Few large corporations are now run by their owners; those like Du Pont where, for many generations, a talented family has had a decisive influence on the enterprise it owns, are becoming a rarity. Typically the power lies with the professional managers. These make elaborate obeisance to the stockholders. But they select the Board of Directors, which the stockholders then dutifully elect, and in equally solemn ritual the Board then selects the management that selected it. In some cases, for example the Standard Oil Company of New Jersey, once dominated by the first Rockefeller, the Board consists exclusively of managers selected by the managers who were selected by the Board.

There are a number of reasons for the rise of the professional manager, but by far the most important is that ownership of capital has come to count for much less than ownership of ability, knowledge, and brains. The man of ability could get the capital; the man who had capital and was devoid of other qualification had become pretty much a hopeless case. (Even to give away his money would eventually require the services of a professional.) The relatively impecunious but better-trained, more intelligent, more determined, or politically more adept managers have almost everywhere taken over. Once in office it is only rarely that the owners of capital can dislodge them.

Nor is this a misfortune for the companies in question. Some of the worst cases of corporate misfortune in recent times have been those in which the owners of the capital have managed to use their power to keep the professionals out. In the thirties and early forties the elder Henry Ford used his power as the sole owner of the Ford Motor Company to remain in command. It is now freely acknowledged that the company suffered severely as a result. Following his death the management was professionalized and much improved. The great merchandising house of Montgomery Ward under Sewell Avery provided a parallel example. Control and direction of a large company by a capitalist has become, indeed, a rather risky affair. He may try to do what can only be done well by a professionally qualified group of diverse and specialized talent.

III

But though it is most visible at the top, the shift in the comparative importance of men and capital is perceptible throughout the modern industrial enterprise. The procedures by which the large and successful enterprise raises funds for new plant and equipment are orderly and predictable. And, depending on circumstances, there is a considerable range of choice—earnings can be withheld, there can be resort to banks, or securities can be sold. A great deal of pompous ritual attends this process, but for the large and successful firm this signifies neither uncertainty nor difficulty but only that we have considerable respect for money and expect large sums to be handled with decent ceremony.

There is no similar certainty in the procedures by which even the most successful concern supplies itself with talent. It must send its emissaries to participate in the annual talent hunt, and if the most imposing men still go to the money markets, the most eloquent go to the colleges. The bag is always uncertain and frequently inadequate. If a successful firm is contemplating a considerable expansion it will almost certainly worry more about where to find the men than where to get the money.

And the change is reflected in the fears and apprehensions of the community at large. We wonder whether we are investing as much as we should in physical capital; we hear that the Soviets, who in our time have largely replaced conscience as the stern small voice of duty, are doing much more. But there is more everyday concern about the state of our schools and colleges. Are they doing properly by our children? Where can we find the resources to enable them to do better? Increasingly we are wondering about the adequacy of our output of highly trained and educated people.

This shows itself in a very practical way. Every family knows that the automobile industry is equipped to supply it with a new car almost on a moment's notice. Such is the admirable condition of our physical plant. But it cannot be at all sure there will be a place for all the children in a good college. Even the automobile executive may wonder where he can get his boy in. Such is the contrasting state of our facilities for human development.

IV

The forces back of the change in the relative position of man as compared with capital are not new. Some of them, curiously enough, are those which, at first glance, seem to suggest the ascendancy of the machine.

The classical trinity of productive factors were land (including natural resources), labor (broadly defined to include both physical and intellectual effort), and capital. All production was seen as resulting from the combination of these factors in one form or another and in one proportion or another. Some economists have questioned whether there was much difference between land and capital goods—both support man's efforts to produce things, and many economists have insisted on adding as a fourth factor of production entrepreneurship or the human effort which was devoted to organizing and managing the other three factors. Subject to these modifications and a few quibbles, the classical delineation of productive agents is still accepted and, indeed, is deeply imbedded in economic thought.

All production requires all three (or all four) factors and in this sense all are equally vital. But the importance attached to the different factors has changed remarkably in the last hundred and fifty years. At the beginning of the last century—the formative years of modern economics—land seemed peculiarly important. Population was growing. Europe and Asia seemed very crowded. The vast fertile spaces of the Americas, Australia, and Africa were but slightly appreciated. The effect of modern agricultural techniques on production per acre was, of course, beyond view. Both Ricardo and Malthus, two of the towering figures in the history of economic ideas, concluded that, in different ways, man's fate would be largely decided by the relentless pressure of population on limited land. Labor being abundant, perhaps excessively so, it seemed far less important than land. Capital, though important, also lacked the life-and-death significance of the land supply. Land was the factor of greatest prestige.

As the nineteenth century passed, capital gained rapidly to a position of dominance in the trinity. The new world added enormously to the supply of land. The decisive question was its development and for this ports, steamships, roads, railroads, farmsteads, and farm equipment were needed. The land was there; the labor came almost automatically; but the more capital the greater the pace of progress.

This emphasis on capital was reinforced by the nature of industrial advance during the last century. It consisted not of the invention of a great number of new techniques but the spread of a relatively small number of spectacularly important ones. Thus, textile manufacture became a factory industry. Steam power was applied to manufacturing, transport, and mining to replace power from men, animals, falling water, or wind. Iron and steel became plentiful and cheap and thus available for many new uses.

These inventions resulted, so far as anyone could tell, from a combination of accident, inspiration, and genius. Men like James Watt, Benjamin Franklin, and Eli Whitney could not be cultivated, and while they might under some circumstances be protected by the patent office, that was about all that could be done to foster technological progress.

But if little could be done to stimulate inventions, much could be done about putting them to use. Savings could be stimulated by exhortations to thrift—and even more by a system of ethics and religion which assured the diligent, abstemious, and self-denying man esteem in this world and salvation in the next. Investment could be encouraged by stable government and laws which assured investors that profits would be theirs to enjoy. Looking rationally at the thing that was subject to wise policy, economists came to measure progress by the proportion of the nation's income that, each year, was saved and invested.

v

Investment in physical capital is still a prime measure of progress but it is an obsolescent one. More and more progress is coming to depend on the quality rather than the quantity of the capital equipment in use and on the intelligence and skill of those who use it.

There are reasonably good figures to go on. Between the early seventies of the last century and the decade 1944–53, according to calculations made under the auspices of the National Bureau of Economic Research, the net output of the American economy increased by an average of 3.5 per cent a year. Less than half of this (1.7 per cent) is explained by increases in the supply of capital and labor.[1] The rest was the result of improvements in

[1] These figures have been most thoughtfully interpreted by Professor Theodore Schultz to whom all who discuss these matters are in debt. See his "Investment in Man: An Economist's View," *Social Service Review*, XXXIII, No. 2, June 1959.

capital equipment—technological advance—and improvements in the working force, including, of course, its leadership and direction. The *share* in the advance attributable to technological improvement and to the improved skill and ability of workers, technicians, and managers has been increasing.

But both technological advance and improved skills and abilities are the product of personal development. Machines do not improve themselves; this is still the work of highly improved men. And most technological advance is now the result not of the accident of inspiration or genius but of highly purposeful effort. Once we had to wait for the accidental appearance of Edisons and Wrights. Now through education and organized effort in a laboratory or experimental shop we get something approaching the same results from much more common clay.

So it comes to this. We now get the larger part of our industrial growth not from more capital investment but from improvements in men and improvements brought about by highly improved men. And this process of technological advance has become fairly predictable. We get from men pretty much what we invest in them. So now in its turn, after land and after capital, labor— highly improved labor to be sure—has come to the center of the stage. Investment in personal development is therefore at least as useful as an index of progress as investment in physical capital. It could be more valuable. This is the kind of change which solemn men of self-confessed soundness of judgment will continue to resist; the familiar is always defended with much more moral fervor just before it becomes foolish.

What then of our practical accommodation to this new urgency of investment in personal development?

VI

At first glance our position would seem to be quite good. We have been reaping large gains from the application of trained intelligence to our economic life. This is the fruit of one of the world's pioneer experiments in public education. Surely our advantage will continue.

We cannot be so optimistic. Until the last century learning and even literacy were the badges of privilege. They had always been reserved to the favored few. Accordingly learning was a symbol of equality—a symbol that our grandparents, determined to establish their claim to full equality, were not disposed to overlook. Hence the free elementary schools, high schools, the Land Grant College system, and the remarkable number and variety of other institutions of higher (and not excessively high) learning.

This system was adequate, even admirable, so long as education was a socially provided service designed to insure (though it had other purposes too) rough equality of opportunity. It has ceased to be sufficient as education has become a form of investment.

The test of what a community should spend on a social service is what it can afford—what it believes it can spare from other forms of consumption. The test of investment, by contrast, is what will pay for itself. We apply the investment test as a matter of course to physical capital and even the commonplace terminology reflects the different attitudes; while we "invest" in physical capital, we "spend" for education.

The investment test is far the more generous of the two—that is to say, it sanctions much larger outlays. It implies an aggressive canvass of all possible uses of funds to see what will pay off at a profit. To find new ways of investing at a profit is to prove one's enterprise. One of the most familiar theorems of accepted economics is that, subject to some lags and irregularities, investment in physical capital will occur whenever marginal return exceeds the marginal cost; that is, whenever the return to additional investment is sufficient to cover the added cost including interest and some allowance for risk.

The test of what can be afforded, by contrast, invokes far more frugal attitudes. The outlay, even if it is for education, is vaguely self-indulgent. If we wish it—if we wish our children to have the prestige and satisfactions and opportunities from learning— we must measure the cost against other important alternatives. Virtue resides not in finding ways of investing more but in finding ways of spending less. The community honors the man who is identified with economy. These attitudes remain even though, as we have seen, the outlays economized may yield as large a return (perhaps larger) as those for physical capital.

Investment in personal development is also handicapped by the lack of a close relationship of outlay with the resulting benefit. A chemical company invests in a new plant because it knows it will get the higher earnings. If it invests in the education of a young chemist it has no similar assurance that it will get a return from its outlay. The fellow may decide to become an artist or a farmer, or he may go faithlessly to work for a competitor.

One can see by a simple illustration what the kind of firm relationship of cost to benefit that exists for physical capital would do for investment in personal development if it existed there. Imagine an arrangement by which promising youngsters, when halfway through high school, were indentured for life to a corporation. The corporation would then be responsible for all further education and would be assured of their services for life. Performance of the companies tomorrow, it would soon be evident, would depend on the quality of the postulant executives, scientists, and other specialists being selected and trained today. The quality of this group would become a matter of major concern. It would be under the eye of accomplished educators. Money would start flowing into it. Investment fund managers would send scouts to seek information on its quality. If one of the larger oil companies found that the schools and colleges available for training its oncoming geologists and engineers were inadequate, it would obviously have to take steps to remedy the situation—perhaps by establishing its own. Otherwise, in a few years, it would be outclassed by the companies with better talent. One can easily imagine bond issues by backward companies to develop stronger technical echelons. The result would be a substantial and possibly an astronomical increase in outlays for personal development—all justified by the resulting profit. All this would be the result of giving the corporation a firm lien on the individual's services and thus on the return on the money it spends on him. It has such a lien on a machine; the example only makes human beings as privileged, for purposes of investment, as are machines.

The final reason for thinking that our arrangements for investing in personal development are deficient is that the Soviets have, technically speaking, superior ones. They begin with all resources under public control; hence, there is no problem in transferring those to be devoted to personal development from private to public use. And outlays for physical capital and those for personal development are items in the same huge budget. The returns from one type of investment can be measured against the returns from the other. There is no inherent reason why physical capital should have a preference as in our case. The result is that the U.S.S.R., by our standards still a comparatively poor country, treats its schools, research and training institutes, universities, and adult and worker education with a generosity which impresses all Western visitors. These outlays, needless to say, not old-fashioned expansion of physical capital, were decisive for launching the Sputniks and for landing their successor on the moon.

VII

We cannot solve the problem of personal investment by indenturing our youngsters at a tender age to a corporation. And we should not expect the kindly corporation to rise to the rescue with large voluntary grants for education. Time has already been wasted on this notion. The problem is far too serious to be left to the conscience of those with a particular willingness to spend the stockholder's money.

Most likely we will solve the problem by making fuller and better use of the familiar instruments of public finance. We must see spending for personal development not as a cost but as an opportunity. Then we must make sure that we are taxing ourselves sufficiently to exploit this opportunity. That the Federal Government must play a role is elementary. It has access to fiscal resources that are inherently far greater than those of states and localities; now that education has become an investment rather than a social service, these resources are indispensable. It is also the unit of government with responsibility for national development and growth. There is at least a likelihood that investment in personal development is a better guarantee of national power than some of our military expenditures.[2]

We need also to review our attitudes toward state and local taxation. In a poor country there are sound reasons for reluctance in taxing objects of everyday consumption in order to have more public services and amenities. But we are not a poor country and personal development has become not a service but an investment. So states and localities should no longer hesitate to use sales and

[2] We must see too that waste, including that of the athletic circuses, is brought under control. It is not only indefensible in itself; it brings investment in human development into disrepute.

excise taxes (as an addition to and not as a substitute for others) to pay for schools and universities. And liberals, in particular, should not be too indignant when this is proposed.

There is another way of putting provision for personal development on a par with capital development that we should consider. We assume that a corporation, either by withholding from earnings or by resort to the capital market, will take responsibility for improving and expanding its own physical plant. The pressure for voluntary contributions by corporations to education reflects, no doubt, a feeling that there is a similar responsibility for personal development. Corporations are the largest employers of trained talent. They reap the rewards from employing such people. Why shouldn't they pay a part of the cost of training this talent?

Perhaps they should. Voluntary contributions will always be inequitable as well as inadequate. Conscience can readily be assuaged by a small contribution and the levy falls only on those with a social view of the corporation. But a special tax for education and training would encounter no similar objection. Levied as a percentage of total payroll—executive, scientific, skilled and unskilled—it would be roughly proportioned to the quantity and quality of the people employed. Thus it would be related to benefit from past investment in personal development; and it would mean that the company was assuming its rough share of the cost of replacing with improved talent the skilled workers, technicians, scientists, and executives that it employs. Initially the tax would presumably be borne in the form of higher prices by the consumers of the product. Ultimately the better talent would bring better methods, improved efficiency, and hence lower prices. It would be self-liquidating for it supports a profitable investment.

Corporations are now at great pains to explain that their prices must include provision for earnings sufficient to replace and expand their physical capital. This, they regularly assure their public, means that production will continue and be more efficient in the future. But, as the National Bureau figures show, we have more to gain from improving the quality of people. So a levy for this purpose would be an even better bargain.

Maybe there are other ways of augmenting the flow of resources into personal development. In a society that is changing we dare not assume that we have thought the last thoughts on any such subject. For man has not retreated before the machine; rather the machine has become desperately dependent on the improvement of man. And our economy is still arranged to supply machines rather than to improve men.

1

JOHN KENNETH GALBRAITH   Born in Canada, he is now a professor of economics at Harvard. He has held many responsible positions with the federal government, among them that of Ambassador to India, and he has written several popular books on social and economic problems.

"The Decline of the Machine" (1960) The approach is straightforward and thorough, but so lucid and unpedantic that it avoids dullness. Nor is the author at all patronizing. Well-developed paragraphs display the best of workaday rhetoric and a diction that is colloquial, forceful, and lively.

1

1. *What are this essay's implications for the college curriculum? for graduate education?* 2. *Is the light touch appropriate to the argument?*

Eclipse

I went out into the backyard and the usually roundish spots of dappled sunlight underneath the trees were all shaped like feathers, crescent in the same direction, from left to right. Though it was five o'clock on a summer afternoon, the birds were singing good-bye to the day, and their merged song seemed to soak the strange air in an additional strangeness. A kind of silence prevailed. Few cars were moving on the streets of the town. Of my children only the baby dared come into the yard with me. She wore only underpants, and as she stood beneath a tree, bulging her belly toward me in the mood of jolly flirtation she has grown into at the age of two, her bare skin was awash with pale crescents. It crossed my mind that she might be harmed, but I couldn't think how. *Cancer?*

The eclipse was to be over 90 percent in our latitude and the newspapers and television for days had been warning us not to look at it. I looked up, a split-second Prometheus, and looked away. The bitten silhouette of the sun lingered redly on my retinas. The day was half-cloudy, and my impression had been of the sun struggling, amid a furious knotted huddle of black and silver clouds, with an enemy too dreadful to be seen, with an eater as ghostly and hungry as time. Every blade of grass cast a long bluish-brown shadow, as at dawn.

My wife shouted from behind the kitchen screen door that as long as I was out there I might as well burn the wastepaper. She darted from the house, eyes downcast, with the wastebasket, and darted back again, leaving the naked baby and me to wander up through the strained sunlight to the wire trash barrel. After my forbidden peek at the sun, the flames dancing transparently from the blackening paper—yesterday's Boston *Globe*, a milk carton, a Hi-Ho cracker box—seemed dimmer than shadows, and in the teeth of all the warnings I looked up again. The clouds seemed bunched and twirled as if to plug a hole in the sky, and the burning afterimage was the shape of a near-new moon, horns pointed down. It was gigantically unnatural, and I lingered in the yard under the vague apprehension that in some future life I might be called before a cosmic court to testify to this assault. I seemed to be the sole witness. The town around my yard was hushed, all but the singing of the birds, who were invisible. The feathers under the trees had changed direction, and curved from right to left.

Then I saw my neighbor sitting on her porch. My neighbor is a widow, with white hair and brown skin; she has in her yard an aluminum-and-nylon-net chaise longue on which she lies at every opportunity, head back, arms spread, prostrate under the sun. Now she hunched dismally on her porch steps in the shade, which was scarcely darker than the light. I walked toward her and hailed her as a visitor to the moon might salute a survivor of a previous expedition. "How do you like the eclipse?" I called over the fence that distinguished our holdings on this suddenly lunar earth.

"I don't like it," she answered, shading her face with a hand. "They say you shouldn't go out in it."

"I thought it was just you shouldn't look at it."

"There's something in the rays," she explained, in a voice far louder than it needed to be, for silence framed us. "I shut all the windows on that side of the house and had to come out for some air."

"I think it'll pass," I told her.

"Don't let the baby look up," she warned, and turned away from talking to me, as if the open use of her voice exposed her more fatally to the rays.

Superstition, I thought, walking back through my yard, clutching my child's hand as tightly as a good-luck token. There was no question in her touch. Day, night, twilight, noon were all wonders to her, unscheduled, free from all bondage of prediction. The sun was being restored to itself and soon would radiate influence as brazenly as ever—and in this sense my daughter's blind trust was vindicated. Nevertheless, I was glad that the eclipse had passed, as it were, over her head; for in my own life I felt a certain assurance evaporate forever under the reality of the sun's disgrace.

JOHN UPDIKE   Born in Shillington, Pennsylvania in 1932, he is one of America's leading writers of poems, novels, short stories, and essays.

"Eclipse" (1963) The imagery is vivid, the diction rich, the style at once stripped and lyrical. The result is both graphic and haunting.

1. *In what ways do the contrasts between neighbor, mother, father, and child contribute to the meaning and effect of this description?* 2. *What is that meaning?* 3. *What is that effect?*

Creative Possibilities

JOSEPH WOOD KRUTCH

The Colloid and the Crystal

That first real snow . . . was soon followed by a second. Over the radio the weatherman talked lengthily about cold masses and warm masses, about what was moving out to sea and what wasn't. Did Benjamin Franklin, I wondered, know what he was starting when it first occurred to him to trace by correspondence the course of storms? From my stationary position the most reasonable explanation seemed to be simply that winter had not quite liked the looks of the landscape as she first made it up. She was changing her sheets.

Another forty-eight hours brought one of those nights ideal for frosting the panes. When I came down to breakfast, two of the windows were almost opaque and the others were etched with graceful, fernlike sprays of ice which looked rather like the impressions left in rocks by some of the antediluvian plants, and they were almost as beautiful as anything which the living can achieve. Nothing else which has never lived looks so much as though it were actually informed with life.

I resisted, I am proud to say, the almost universal impulse to scratch my initials into one of the surfaces. The effect, I knew, would not be an improvement. But so, of course, do those less virtuous than I. That indeed is precisely why they scratch. The impulse to mar and to destroy is as ancient and almost as nearly universal as the impulse to create. The one is an easier way than the other of demonstrating power. Why else should anyone not hungry prefer a dead rabbit to a live one? Not even those horrible Dutch painters of bloody still—or shall we say stilled?—lifes can have really believed that their subjects were more beautiful dead.

Indoors it so happened that a Christmas cactus had chosen this moment to bloom. Its lush blossoms, fuchsia-shaped but pure red rather than magenta, hung at the drooping ends of strange, thick stems and outlined themselves in blood against the glistening background of the frosty pane—jungle flower against frostflower; the warm beauty that breathes and lives and dies competing with the cold beauty that burgeons, not because it wants to, but merely because it is obeying the laws of physics which require that crystals shall take the shape they have always taken since the world began. The effect of red flower against white tracery was almost too theatrical, not quite in good taste perhaps. My eye recoiled in shock and sought through a clear area of the glass the more normal out-of-doors.

On the snow-capped summit of my bird-feeder a chickadee pecked at the new-fallen snow and swallowed a few of the flakes which serve him in lieu of the water he sometimes sadly lacks when there is nothing except ice too solid to be picked at. A downy woodpecker was hammering at a lump of suet and at the coconut full of peanut butter. One nuthatch was dining while the mate waited his—or was it her?—turn. The woodpecker announces the fact that he is a male by the bright red spot on the back of his neck, but to me, at least, the sexes of the nuthatch are indistinguishable. I shall never know whether it is the male or the female who eats first. And that is a pity. If I knew, I could say, like the Ugly Duchess, "and the moral of that is . . ."

But I soon realized that at the moment the frosted windows were what interested me most—especially the fact that there is no other natural phenomenon in which the lifeless mocks so closely the living. One might almost think that the frostflower had got the idea from the leaf and the branch if one did not know how inconceivably more ancient the first is. No wonder that enthusiastic biologists in the nineteenth century, anxious to conclude that there was no qualitative difference between life and chemical processes, tried to believe that the crystal furnished the link, that its growth was actually the same as the growth of a living organism. But excusable though the fancy was, no one, I think, believes anything of the sort today. Protoplasm is a colloid and the colloids are fundamentally different from the crystalline substances. Instead of crystallizing they jell, and life in its simplest known form is a shapeless blob of rebellious jelly rather than a crystal eternally obeying the most ancient law.

No man ever saw a dinosaur. The last of these giant reptiles was dead eons before the most dubious half-man surveyed the world about him. Not even the dinosaurs ever cast their dim eyes upon many of the still earlier creatures which preceded them. Life changes so rapidly that its later phases know nothing of those which preceded them. But the frostflower is older than the dinosaur, older than the protozoan, older no doubt than the enzyme or the ferment. Yet it is precisely what it has always been. Millions of years before there were any eyes to see it, millions of years before any life existed, it grew in its own special way, crystallized along its preordained lines of cleavage, stretched out its pseudo-branches and pseudo-leaves. It was beautiful before beauty itself existed.

We find it difficult to conceive a world except in terms of purpose, of will, or of intention. At the thought of the something without beginning and presumably without end, of something which is, nevertheless, regular though blind, and organized without any end in view, the mind reels. Constituted as we are it is easier to conceive how the slime floating upon the waters might become in time Homo sapiens than it is to imagine how so complex a thing as a crystal could have always been and can always remain just what it is—complicated and perfect but without any meaning, even for itself. How can the lifeless even obey a law?

To a mathematical physicist I once confessed somewhat shame-facedly that I had never been able to understand how inanimate nature managed to follow so invariably and so promptly her own laws. If I flip a coin across a table, it will come to rest at a certain point. But before it stops at just that point, many factors must be taken into consideration. There is the question of the strength of the initial impulse, of the exact amount of resistance offered by the friction of that particular table top, and of the density of the air at the moment. It would take a physicist a long time to work out the problem and he could achieve only an approximation at that. Yet presumably the coin will stop exactly where it should. Some very rapid calculations have to be made before it can do so, and they are, presumably, always accurate.

And then, just as I was blushing at what I supposed he must regard as my folly, the mathematician came to my rescue by informing me that Laplace had been puzzled by exactly the same fact. "Nature laughs at the difficulties of integration," he remarked —and by "integration" he meant, of course, the mathematician's word for the process involved when a man solves one of the differential equations to which he has reduced the laws of motion.

When my Christmas cactus blooms so theatrically a few inches in front of the frost-covered pane, it also is obeying laws but obeying them much less rigidly and in a different way. It blooms at about Christmastime because it has got into the habit of doing so, because, one is tempted to say, it wants to. As a matter of fact it was, this year, not a Christmas cactus but a New Year's cactus, and because of this unpredictability I would like to call it "he," not "it." His flowers assume their accustomed shape and take on their accustomed color. But not as the frostflowers follow their predestined pattern. Like me, the cactus has a history which stretches back over a long past full of changes and developments. He has not always been merely obeying fixed laws. He has resisted and rebelled; he has attempted novelties, passed through many phases. Like all living things he has had a will of his own. He has made laws, not merely obeyed them.

"Life," so the platitudinarian is fond of saying, "is strange." But from our standpoint it is not really so strange as those things which have no life and yet nevertheless move in their predestined orbits and "act" though they do not "behave." At the very least one ought to say that if life is strange there is nothing about it more strange than the fact that it has its being in a universe so astonishingly shared on the one hand by "things" and on the other by "creatures," that man himself is both a "thing" which obeys the laws of chemistry or physics and a "creature" who to some extent defies them. No other contrast, certainly not the contrast between the human being and the animal, or the animal and the plant, or even the spirit and the body, is so tremendous as this contrast between what lives and what does not.

To think of the lifeless as merely inert, to make the contrast merely in terms of a negative, is to miss the real strangeness. Not the shapeless stone which seems to be merely waiting to be acted upon but the snowflake or the frostflower is the true representative of the lifeless universe as opposed to ours. They represent plainly, as the stone does not, the fixed and perfect system of organization which includes the sun and its planets, includes therefore this earth itself, but against which life has set up its seemingly puny opposition. Order and obedience are the primary characteristics of that which is not alive. The snowflake eternally obeys its one and only law: "Be thou six pointed"; the planets their one and only: "Travel thou in an ellipse." The astronomer can tell where the North Star will be ten thousand years hence; the botanist cannot tell where the dandelion will bloom tomorrow.

Life is rebellious and anarchial, always testing the supposed immutability of the rules which the nonliving changelessly accepts. Because the snowflake goes on doing as it was told, its story up to the end of time was finished when it first assumed the form which it has kept ever since. But the story of every living thing is still in the telling. It may hope and it may try. Moreover, though it may succeed or fail, it will certainly change. No form of frostflower ever became extinct. Such, if you like, is its glory. But such also is the fact which makes it alien. It may melt but it cannot die.

If I wanted to contemplate what is to me the deepest of all mysteries, I should choose as my object lesson a snowflake under a lens and an amoeba under the microscope. To a detached observer—if one can possibly imagine any observer who *could* be detached when faced with such an ultimate choice—the snowflake would certainly seem the "higher" of the two. Against its intricate glistening perfection one would have to place a shapeless, slightly turbid glob, perpetually oozing out in this direction or that but not suggesting so strongly as the snowflake does, intelligence and plan. Crystal and colloid, the chemist would call them, but what an inconceivable contrast those neutral terms

imply! Like the star, the snowflake seems to declare the glory of
God, while the promise of the amoeba, given only perhaps to
itself, seems only contemptible. But its jelly holds, nevertheless,
not only its promise but ours also, while the snowflake represents
some achievement which we cannot possibly share. After the
passage of billions of years, one can see and be aware of the
other, but the relationship can never be reciprocal. Even after
these billions of years no aggregate of colloids can be as beautiful
as the crystal always was, but it can know, as the crystal cannot,
what beauty is.

Even to admire too much or too exclusively the alien kind of
beauty is dangerous. Much as I love and am moved by the grand,
inanimate forms of nature, I am always shocked and a little
frightened by those of her professed lovers to whom landscape is
the most important thing, and to whom landscape is merely a
matter of forms and colors. If they see or are moved by an animal
or flower, it is to them merely a matter of a picturesque completion and their fellow creatures are no more than decorative details. But without some continuous awareness of the two great
realms of the inanimate and the animate there can be no love of
nature as I understand it, and what is worse, there must be a sort
of disloyalty to our cause, to us who are colloid, not crystal. The
pantheist who feels the oneness of all living things, I can understand; perhaps indeed he and I are in essential agreement. But
the ultimate All is not one thing, but two. And because the alien
half is in its way as proud and confident and successful as our
half, its fundamental difference may not be disregarded with im-
punity. Of us and all we stand for, the enemy is not so much
death as the not-living, or rather that great system which succeeds
without ever having had the need to be alive. The frostflower is
not merely a wonder; it is also a threat and a warning. How
admirable, it seems to say, not living can be! What triumphs mere
immutable law can achieve!

Some of Charles Pierce's strange speculations about the possibility that "natural law" is not law at all but merely a set of
habits fixed more firmly than any habits we know anything about
in ourselves or in the animals suggest the possibility that the snowflake was not, after all, always inanimate, that it merely surren-
dered at some time impossibly remote the life which once

achieved its perfect organization. Yet even if we can imagine such a thing to be true, it serves only to warm us all the more strongly against the possibility that what we call the living might in the end succumb also to the seduction of the immutably fixed.

No student of the anthill has ever failed to be astonished either into admiration or horror by what is sometimes called the perfection of its society. Though even the anthill can change its ways, though even ant individuals—ridiculous as the conjunction of the two words may seem—can sometimes make choices, the perfection of the techniques, the regularity of the habits almost suggest the possibility that the insect is on its way back to inanition, that, vast as the difference still is, an anthill crystallizes somewhat as a snowflake does. But not even the anthill, nothing else indeed in the whole known universe is so perfectly planned as one of these same snowflakes. Would, then, the ultimately planned society be, like the anthill, one in which no one makes plans, any more than a snowflake does? From the cradle in which it is not really born to the grave where it is only a little deader than it always was, the ant-citizen follows a plan to the making of which he no longer contributes anything.

Perhaps we men represent the ultimate to which the rebellion, begun so long ago in some amoeba-like jelly, can go. And perhaps the inanimate is beginning the slow process of subduing us again. Certainly the psychologist and the philosopher are tending more and more to think of us as creatures who obey laws rather than as creatures of will and responsibility. We are, they say, "conditioned" by this or by that. Even the greatest heroes are studied on the assumption that they can be "accounted for" by something outside themselves. They are, it is explained, "the product of forces." All the emphasis is placed, not upon that power to resist and rebel which we were once supposed to have, but upon the "influences" which "formed us." Men are made by society, not society by men. History as well as character "obeys laws." In their view, we crystallize in obedience to some dictate from without instead of moving in conformity with something within.

And so my eye goes questioningly back to the frosted pane. While I slept the graceful pseudo-fronds crept across the glass, assuming, as life itself does, an intricate organization. "Why live," they seem to say, "when we can be beautiful, complicated, and orderly without the uncertainty and effort required of a living thing? Once we were all that was. Perhaps some day we shall be all that is. Why not join us?"

Last summer no clod or no stone would have been heard if it had asked such a question. The hundreds of things which walked and sang, the millions which crawled and twined were all having their day. What was dead seemed to exist only in order that the living might live upon it. The plants were busy turning the in-organic into green life and the animals were busy turning that green into red. When we moved, we walked mostly upon grass. Our pre-eminence was unchallenged.

On this winter day nothing seems so successful as the frost-flower. It thrives on the very thing which has driven some of us indoors or underground and which has been fatal to many. It is having now its hour of triumph, as we before had ours. Like the cactus flower itself, I am a hothouse plant. Even my cats gaze dreamily out of the window at a universe which is no longer theirs.

How are we to resist, if resist we can? This house into which I have withdrawn is merely an expedient and it serves only my mere physical existence. What mental or spiritual convictions, what will to maintain to my own kind of existence can I assert? For me it is not enough merely to say, as I do say, that I shall resist the invitation to submerge myself into a crystalline society and to stop planning in order that I may be planned for. Neither is it enough to go further, as I do go, and to insist that the most important thing about a man is not that part of him which is "the product of forces" but that part, however small it may be, which enables him to become something other than what the most accomplished sociologist, working in conjunction with the most accomplished psychologist, could predict that he would be.

I need, so I am told, a faith, something outside myself to which I can be loyal. And with that I agree, in my own way. I am on what I call "our side," and I know, though vaguely, what I think that is. Wordsworth's God had his dwelling in the light of setting suns. But the God who dwells there seems to me most probably the God of the atom, the star, and the crystal. Mine, if I have one, reveals Himself in another class of phenomena. He makes the grass green and the blood red.

✓

JOSEPH WOOD KRUTCH Born in 1893 in Knoxville, Tennessee, a teacher of English literature and of journalism, as well as a scholar, editor, critic, and essayist, Professor Krutch has long been a prolific and versatile author.

"The Colloid and the Crystal" (1950) A sensitive observer here brings coincidental experiences into an organized, sequential pattern to produce an argument that is at first indirect, then increasingly direct, in a sense thereby duplicating the creative process he is describing. The style mixes the straightforward declarative and the haunting lyrical, the localized and the eternal, the simple and the profound in such a way that the essay is at once a scientific treatise and prose poem.

✓

1. *What are the seductions of the lifeless? 2. What are the social and political implications of this essay? 3. In what ways does its organization lead up to and support the conclusion?*

J. BRONOWSKI

The Creative Mind

I

On a fine November day in 1945, late in the afternoon, I was
landed on an airstrip in Southern Japan. From there a jeep was
to take me over the mountains to join a ship which lay in Nagasaki Harbour. I knew nothing of the country or the distance before us. We drove off; dusk fell; the road rose and fell away, the
pine woods came down to the road, straggled on and opened
again. I did not know that we had left the open country until
unexpectedly I heard the ship's loudspeakers broadcasting dance
music. Then suddenly I was aware that we were already at the
centre of damage in Nagasaki. The shadows behind me were the
skeletons of the Mitsubishi factory buildings, pushed backwards
and sideways as if by a giant hand. What I had thought to be
broken rocks was a concrete power house with its roof punched
in. I could now make out the outline of two crumpled gasometers;
there was a cold furnace festooned with service pipes; otherwise
nothing but cockeyed telegraph poles and loops of wire in a bare
waste of ashes. I had blundered into this desolate landscape as
instantly as one might wake among the craters of the moon. The
moment of recognition when I realized that I was already in
Nagasaki is present to me as I write, as vividly as when I lived it.

Reprinted by permission of Julian Messner, Division of Pocket Books, Inc.,
from *Science and Human Values* by J. Bronowski. Copyright © 1956 by
J. Bronowski.

I see the warm night and the meaningless shapes; I can even remember the tune that was coming from the ship. It was a dance tune which had been popular in 1945, and it was called "Is You Is Or Is You Ain't Ma Baby?"

. . . [T]he moment I have recalled was a universal moment; what I met was, almost as abruptly, the experience of mankind. On an evening like that evening, some time in 1945, each of us in his own way learned that his imagination had been dwarfed. We looked up and saw the power of which we had been proud loom over us like the ruins of Nagasaki.

The power of science for good and for evil has troubled other minds than ours. We are not here fumbling with a new dilemma; our subject and our fears are as old as the tool-making civilizations. Men have been killed with weapons before now: what happened at Nagasaki was only more massive (for 40,000 were killed there by a flash which lasted seconds) and more ironical (for the bomb exploded over the main Christian community in Japan). Nothing happened in 1945 except that we changed the scale of our indifference to man; and conscience, in revenge, for an instant became immediate to us. Before this immediacy fades in a sequence of televised atomic tests, let us acknowledge our subject for what it is: civilization face to face with its own implications. The implications are both the industrial slum which Nagasaki was before it was bombed, and the ashy desolation which the bomb made of the slum. And civilization asks of both ruins, "Is You Is Or Is You Ain't Ma Baby?"

II

The man whom I imagine to be asking this question, wrily with a sense of shame, is not a scientist; he is civilized man. It is of course more usual for each member of civilization to take flight from its consequences by protesting that others have failed him. Those whose education and perhaps tastes have confined them to the humanities protest that the scientists alone are to blame, for plainly no mandarin ever made a bomb or an industry. The scientists say, with equal contempt, that the Greek scholars and the earnest explorers of cave paintings do well to wash their hands of blame; but what in fact are they doing to help direct the society whose ills grow more often from inaction than from error?

This absurd division reached its *reductio ad absurdum*, I think, when one of my teachers, G. H. Hardy, justified his great life work on the ground that it could do no one the least harm—or the least good.[1]* But Hardy was a mathematician; will humanists really let him opt out of the conspiracy of scientists? Or are scientists in their turn to forgive Hardy because, protest as he might, most of them learned their indispensable mathematics from his books?

There is no comfort in such bickering. When Shelley pictured science as a modern Prometheus who would wake the world to a wonderful dream of Godwin, he was alas too simple. But it is as pointless to read what has happened since as a nightmare. Dream or nightmare, we have to live our experience as it is, and we have to live it awake. We live in a world which is penetrated through and through by science, and which is both whole and real. We cannot turn it into a game simply by taking sides.

And this make-believe game might cost us what we value most: the human content of our lives. The scholar who disdains science may speak in fun, but his fun is not quite a laughing matter. To think of science as a set of special tricks, to see the scientist as the manipulator of outlandish skills—this is the root of the poison mandrake which flourishes rank in the comic strips. There is no more threatening and no more degrading doctrine than the fancy that somehow we may shelve the responsibility for making the decisions of our society by passing it to a few scientists armoured with a special magic. This is another dream, the dream of H. G. Wells, in which the tall elegant engineers rule, with perfect benevolence, a humanity which has no business except to be happy. To H. G. Wells this was a dream of heaven—a modern version of the idle, harp-resounding heaven of other childhood pieties. But in fact it is the picture of a slave society, and should make us shiver whenever we hear a man of sensibility dismiss science as someone else's concern. The world today is made, it is powered by science; and for any man to abdicate an interest in science is to walk with open eyes towards slavery. . . .

III

There is a likeness between the creative acts of the mind in art and in science. Yet, when a man uses the word science in such

---

* The notes for this essay appear at the end.

a sentence, it may be suspected that he does not mean what the headlines mean by science. Am I about to sidle away to those riddles in the Theory of Numbers which Hardy loved, or to the heady speculations of astrophysicists, in order to make claims for abstract science which have no bearing on its daily practice?

I have no such design. My purpose is to talk about science as it is, practical and theoretical. I define science as the organization of our knowledge in such a way that it commands more of the hidden potential in nature. What I have in mind therefore is both deep and matter of fact; it reaches from the kinetic theory of gases to the telephone and the suspension bridge and medicated toothpaste. It admits no sharp boundary between knowledge and use. There are of course people who like to draw a line between pure and applied science; and oddly, they are often the same people who find art unreal. To them, the word useful is a final arbiter, either for or against a work; and they use this word as if it can mean only what makes a man feel heavier after meals.

There is no sanction for confining the practice of science in this or another way. True, science is full of useful inventions. And its theories have often been made by men whose imagination was directed by the uses to which their age looked. Newton turned naturally to astronomy because it was the subject of his day, and it was so because finding one's way at sea had long been a practical preoccupation of the society into which he was born. It should be added, mischievously, that astronomy also had some standing because it was used very practically to cast horoscopes. (Kepler used it for this purpose; in the Thirty Years' War he cast the horoscope of Wallenstein which wonderfully told his character, and he predicted a universal disaster for 1634 which proved to be the murder of Wallenstein.[2])

In a setting which is more familiar, Faraday worked all his life to link electricity with magnetism because this was the glittering problem of his day; and it was so because his society, like ours, was on the lookout for new sources of power. Consider a more modest example today: the new mathematical methods of automatic control, a subject sometimes called cybernetics, have been developed now because this is a time when communication and control have in effect become forms of power.[3] These inventions have been directed by social needs, and they are useful inventions; yet it was not their usefulness which dominated and set light to the minds of those who made them. Neither Newton nor Faraday, nor yet Professor Norbert Wiener, spent their time in a scramble for patents.

What a scientist does is compounded of two interests: the interest of his time and his own interest. In this his behaviour is no different from any other man's. The need of the age gives its shape to scientific progress as a whole. But it is not the need of the age which gives the individual scientist his sense of pleasure and of adventure, and that excitement which keeps him working late into the night when all the useful typists have gone home at five o'clock. He is personally involved in his work, as the poet is in his, and as the artist is in the painting. Paints and painting too must have been made for useful ends; and language was developed, from whatever beginnings, for practical communication. Yet you cannot have a man handle paints or language or the symbolic concepts of physics, you cannot even have him stain a microscope slide, without instantly waking in him a pleasure in the very language, a sense of exploring his own activity. This sense lies at the heart of creation.[4]

IV

The sense of personal exploration is as urgent, and as delightful, to the practical scientist as to the theoretical. Those who think otherwise are confusing what is practical with what is humdrum. Good humdrum work without originality is done every day by everyone, theoretical scientists as well as practical, and writers and painters too, as well as truck drivers and bank clerks. Of course the unoriginal work keeps the world going; but it is not therefore the monopoly of practical men. And neither need the practical man be unoriginal. If he is to break out of what has been done before, he must bring to his own tools the same sense of pride and discovery which the poet brings to words. He cannot afford to be less radical in conceiving and less creative in designing a new turbine than a new world system.

And this is why in turn practical discoveries are not made only by practical men. As the world's interest has shifted, since the Industrial Revolution, to the tapping of new springs of power, the theoretical scientist has shifted his interests too. His speculations about energy have been as abstract as once they were about astronomy; and they have been profound now as they were then, because the man loved to think. The Carnot cycle and the dynamo grew equally from this love, and so did nuclear physics and the German V weapons and Kelvin's interest in low temperatures. Man does not invent by following either use or tradition; he does not invent even a new form of communication by calling a conference of communication engineers. Who invented the television set? In any deep sense, it was Clerk Maxwell who foresaw the existence of radio waves, and Heinrich Hertz who proved it, and J. J. Thomson who discovered the electron. This is not said in order to rob any practical man of the invention, but from a sad sense of justice; for neither Maxwell nor Hertz nor J. J. Thomson would take pride in television just now.

Man masters nature not by force but by understanding. This is why science has succeeded where magic failed: because it has looked for no spell to cast over nature. The alchemist and the magician in the Middle Ages thought, and the addict of comic strips is still encouraged to think, that nature must be mastered by a device which outrages her laws. But in four hundred years since the Scientific Revolution we have learned that we gain our ends only *with* the laws of nature; we control her only by understanding her laws. We cannot even bully nature by any insistence that our work shall be designed to give power over her. We must be content that power is the by-product of understanding. So the Greeks said that Orpheus played the lyre with such sympathy that wild beasts were tamed by the hand on the strings. They did not suggest that he got this gift by setting out to be a lion tamer.

v

What is the insight with which the scientist tries to see into nature? Can it indeed be called either imaginative or creative? To the literary man the question may seem merely silly. He has been taught that science is a large collection of facts; and if this is true, then the only seeing which scientists need do is, he supposes, seeing the facts. He pictures them, the colourless professionals of science, going off to work in the morning into the universe in a neutral, unexposed state. They then expose themselves like a photographic plate. And then in the darkroom or laboratory they develop the image, so that suddenly and startlingly it appears, printed in capital letters, as a new formula for atomic energy.

Men who have read Balzac and Zola are not deceived by the claims of these writers that they do no more than record the facts. The readers of Christopher Isherwood do not take him literally when he writes "I am a camera." Yet the same readers solemnly carry with them from their schooldays this foolish picture of the scientist fixing by some mechanical process the facts of nature. I have had of all people a historian tell me that science is a collection of facts, and his voice had not even the ironic rasp of one filing cabinet reproving another.

It seems impossible that this historian had ever studied the beginnings of a scientific discovery. The Scientific Revolution can be held to begin in the year 1543 when there was brought to Copernicus, perhaps on his deathbed, the first printed copy of the book he had written about a dozen years earlier. The thesis of this book is that the earth moves round the sun. When did Copernicus go out and record this fact with his camera? What appearance in nature prompted his outrageous guess? And in what odd sense is this guess to be called a neutral record of fact?

Less than a hundred years after Copernicus, Kepler published (between 1609 and 1619) the three laws which describe the paths of the planets. The work of Newton and with it most of our mechanics spring from these laws. They have a solid, matter of fact sound. For example, Kepler says that if one squares the year of a planet, one gets a number which is proportional to the cube of its average distance from the sun. Does anyone think that such a law is found by taking enough readings and then squaring and cubing everything in sight? If he does then, as a scientist, he is doomed to a wasted life; he has as little prospect of making a scientific discovery as an electronic brain has.

It was not this way that Copernicus and Kepler thought, or that scientists think today. Copernicus found that the orbits of the planets would look simpler if they were looked at from the sun and not from the earth. But he did not in the first place find this by routine calculation. His first step was a leap of imagination— to lift himself from the earth, and put himself wildly, speculatively into the sun.[5] "The earth conceives from the sun," he wrote; and "the sun rules the family of stars." We catch in his mind an image, the gesture of the virile man standing in the sun, with arms outstretched, overlooking the planets. Perhaps Copernicus took the picture from the drawings of the youth with outstretched arms which the Renaissance teachers put into their books on the proportions of the body. Perhaps he had seen Leonardo's drawings of his loved pupil Salai. I do not know. To me, the gesture of Copernicus, the shining youth looking outward from the sun, is still vivid in a drawing which William Blake in 1780 based on all these: the drawing which is usually called "Glad Day."[6]

Kepler's mind, we know, was filled with just such fanciful analogies; and we know what they were. Kepler wanted to relate the speeds of the planets to the musical intervals. He tried to fit the five regular solids into their orbits. None of these likenesses worked, and they have been forgotten; yet they have been and they remain the stepping stones of every creative mind. Kepler felt for his laws by way of metaphors, he searched mystically for likenesses with what he knew in every strange corner of nature. And when among these guesses he hit upon his laws, he did not think of their numbers as the balancing of a cosmic bank account, but as a revelation of the unity in all nature. To us, the analogies by which Kepler listened for the movement of the planets in the music of the spheres are far-fetched.[7] Yet are they more so than the wild leap by which Rutherford and Bohr in our own century found a model for the atom in, of all places, the planetary system?

VI

No scientific theory is a collection of facts. It will not even do to call a theory true or false in the simple sense in which every fact is either so or not so. The Epicureans held that matter is made of atoms two thousand years ago and we are now tempted to say that their theory was true. But if we do so we confuse their notion of matter with our own. John Dalton in 1808 first saw the structure of matter as we do today, and what he took from the ancients was not their theory but something richer, their image: the atom. Much of what was in Dalton's mind was as vague as the Greek notion, and quite as mistaken. But he suddenly gave life to the new facts of chemistry and the ancient theory together, by fusing them to give what neither had: a coherent picture of how matter is linked and built up from different kinds of atoms. The act of fusion is the creative act.

All science is the search for unity in hidden likenesses. The search may be on a grand scale, as in the modern theories which try to link the fields of gravitation and electro-magnetism. But we do not need to be browbeaten by the scale of science. There are discoveries to be made by snatching a small likeness from the air too, if it is bold enough. In 1935 the Japanese physicist Yukawa wrote a paper which can still give heart to a young scientist. He took as his starting point the known fact that waves of light can sometimes behave as if they were separate pellets. From this he reasoned that the forces which hold the nucleus of an atom together might sometimes also be observed as if they were solid pellets. A schoolboy can see how thin Yukawa's analogy is, and his teacher would be severe with it. Yet Yukawa without a blush calculated the mass of the pellet he expected to see, and waited. He was right; his meson was found, and a range of other mesons, neither the existence nor the nature of which had been suspected before. The likeness had borne fruit.

The scientist looks for order in the appearances of nature by exploring such likenesses. For order does not display itself of itself; if it can be said to be there at all, it is not there for the mere looking. There is no way of pointing a finger or a camera at it; order must be discovered and, in a deep sense, it must be created. What we see, as we see it, is mere disorder.

This point has been put trenchantly in a fable by Professor Karl Popper. Suppose that someone wished to give his whole life to science. Suppose that he therefore sat down, pencil in hand, and for the next twenty, thirty, forty years recorded in notebook after notebook everything that he could observe. He may be supposed to leave out nothing: today's humidity, the racing results, the level of cosmic radiation and the stock market prices and the look of Mars, all would be there. He would have compiled the most careful record of nature that has ever been made; and, dying in the calm certainty of a life well spent, he would of course leave his notebooks to the Royal Society. Would the Royal Society thank him for the treasure of a lifetime of observation? It would not. The Royal Society would treat his notebooks exactly as the English bishops have treated Joanna Southcott's box. It would refuse to open them at all, because it would know without looking that the notebooks contain only a jumble of disorderly and meaningless items.

Science finds order and meaning in our experience, and sets about this in quite a different way. It sets about it as Newton did in the story which he himself told in his old age, and of which the school-books give only a caricature. In the year 1665, when Newton was twenty-two, the plague broke out in southern England, and the University of Cambridge was closed. Newton therefore spent the next eighteen months at home, removed from traditional learning, at a time when he was impatient for knowledge and, in his own phrase, "I was in the prime of my age for invention." In this eager, boyish mood, sitting one day in the garden of his widowed mother, he saw an apple fall. So far the books have the story right; we think we even know the kind of apple; tradition has it that it was a Flower of Kent. But now they miss the crux of the story. For what struck young Newton at the sight was not the thought that the apple must be drawn to the earth by gravity; that conception was older than Newton. What struck him was the conjecture that the same force of gravity, which reaches to the top of the tree, might go on reaching out beyond the earth and its air, endlessly into space. Gravity might reach the moon: this was Newton's new thought; and it might be gravity which holds the moon in her orbit. There and then he calculated what force from the earth (falling off as the square of the distance) would hold the moon, and compared it with the known force of gravity at tree height. The forces agreed; Newton says laconically, "I found them answer pretty nearly." Yet they agreed only nearly: the likeness and the approximation go together, for no likeness is exact. In Newton's sentence modern science is full grown.

It grows from a comparison. It has seized a likeness between two unlike appearances; for the apple in the summer garden and the grave moon overhead are surely as unlike in their movements as two things can be. Newton traced in them two expressions of a single concept, gravitation: and the concept (and the unity) are in that sense his free creation. The progress of science is the discovery at each step of a new order which gives unity to what had long seemed unlike. Faraday did this when he closed the link between electricity and magnetism. Clerk Maxwell did it when he linked both with light. Einstein linked time with space, mass with energy, and the path of light past the sun with the flight of a bullet; and spent his dying years in trying to add to these like-nesses another, which would find a single imaginative order be-tween the equations of Clerk Maxwell and his own geometry of gravitation.

VIII

When Coleridge tried to define beauty, he returned always to one deep thought: beauty, he said, is "unity in variety."[8] Science is nothing else than the search to discover unity in the wild va-riety of nature—or more exactly, in the variety of our experience. Poetry, painting, the arts are the same search, in Coleridge's phrase, for unity in variety. Each in its own way looks for like-nesses under the variety of human experience. What is a poetic image but the seizing and the exploration of a hidden likeness, in holding together two parts of a comparison which are to give depth each to the other? When Romeo finds Juliet in the tomb, and thinks her dead, he uses in his heart-breaking speech the words,

Death that hath suckt the honey of thy breath.

The critic can only haltingly take to pieces the single shock which this image carries. The young Shakespeare admired Marlowe, and Marlowe's Faustus had said of the ghostly kiss of Helen of Troy that it sucked forth his soul. But that is a pale image; what Shakespeare has done is to fire it with the single word honey. Death is a bee at the lips of Juliet, and the bee is an insect that stings; the sting of death was a commonplace phrase when Shake-speare wrote. The sting is there, under the image; Shakespeare has packed it into the word honey; but the very word rides powerfully over its own undertones. Death is a bee that stings other people, but it comes to Juliet as if she were a flower; this is the moving thought under the instant image. The creative mind speaks in such thoughts.

The poetic image here is also, and accidentally, heightened by the tenderness which town dwellers now feel for country ways. But it need not be; there are likenesses to conjure with, and images as powerful, within the man-made world. The poems of Alexander Pope belong to this world. They are not countrified, and therefore readers today find them unemotional and often artificial. Let me then quote Pope: here he is in a formal satire face to face, towards the end of his life, with his own gifts. In eight lines he looks poignantly forward towards death and back to the laborious years which made him famous.

> Years foll'wing Years, steal something ev'ry day,
> At last they steal us from our selves away;
> In one our Frolicks, one Amusements end,
> In one a Mistress drops, in one a Friend:
> This subtle Thief of Life, this paltry Time,
> What will it leave me, if it snatch my Rhime?
> If ev'ry Wheel of that unweary'd Mill
> That turn'd ten thousand Verses, now stands still.

The human mind had been compared to what the eighteenth century called a mill, that is to a machine, before; Pope's own idol Bolingbroke had compared it to a clockwork. In these lines the likeness goes deeper, for Pope is thinking of the ten thousand Verses which he had translated from Homer: what he says is sad and just at the same time, because this really had been a mechanical and at times a grinding task.[9] Yet the clockwork is present in the image too; when the wheels stand still, time for Pope will stand still for ever; we feel that we already hear, over the horizon, Faust's defiant reply to Mephistopheles, which Goethe had not yet written—"let the clock strike and stop, let the hand fall, and time be at an end."

> Werd ich zum Augenblicke sagen:
> Verweile doch! du bist so schön!
> Dann magst du mich in Fesseln schlagen,
> Dann will ich gern zugrunde gehn!
> Dann mag die Totenglocke schallen,
> Dann bist du deines Dienstes frei,
> Die Uhr mag stehn, der Zeiger fallen,
> Es sei die Zeit für mich vorbei![10]

I have quoted Pope and Goethe because their metaphor here is not poetic; it is rather a hand reaching straight into experience and arranging it with new meaning. Metaphors of this kind need not always be written in words. The most powerful of them all is simply the presence of King Lear and his Fool in the hut of a man who is shamming madness, while lightning rages outside. Or let me quote another clash of two conceptions of life, from a modern poet. In his later poems W. B. Yeats was troubled by the feeling that in shutting himself up to write, he was missing the active pleasures of life; and yet it seemed to him certain that the man who lives for these pleasures will leave no lasting work behind him. He said this at times very simply, too:

> The intellect of man is forced to choose
> Perfection of the life, or of the work.

This problem, whether a man fulfils himself in work or in play, is of course more common than Yeats allowed; and it may be more commonplace. But it is given breadth and force by the images in which Yeats pondered it.

> Get all the gold and silver that you can,
> Satisfy ambition, or animate
> The trivial days and ram them with the sun,
> And yet upon these maxims meditate:
> All women dote upon an idle man
> Although their children need a rich estate;
> No man has ever lived that had enough
> Of children's gratitude or woman's love.[11]

The love of women, the gratitude of children: the images fix two philosophies as nothing else can. They are tools of creative thought, as coherent and as exact as the conceptual images with which science works: as time and space, or as the proton and the neutron.

IX

The discoveries of science, the works of art are explorations—more, are explosions, of a hidden likeness. The discoverer or the artist presents in them two aspects of nature and fuses them into one. This is the act of creation, in which an original thought is born, and it is the same act in original science and original art. But it is not therefore the monopoly of the man who wrote the poem or who made the discovery. On the contrary, I believe this view of the creative act to be right because it alone gives a meaning to the act of appreciation. The poem or the discovery exists in two moments of vision: the moment of appreciation as much as that of creation; for the appreciator must see the movement, wake to the echo which was started in the creation of the work. In the moment of appreciation we live again the moment when the creator saw and held the hidden likeness. When a simile takes us aback and persuades us together, when we find a juxtaposition in a picture both odd and intriguing, when a theory is at once fresh and convincing, we do not merely nod over someone else's work. We re-enact the creative act, and we ourselves make the discovery again. At bottom, there is no unifying likeness there until we too have seized it, we too have made it for ourselves.

How slipshod by comparison is the notion that either art or science sets out to copy nature. If the task of the painter were to copy for men what they see, the critic could make only a single judgement: either that the copy is right or that it is wrong. And if science were a copy of fact, then every theory would be either right or wrong, and would be so for ever. There would be nothing left for us to say but this is so, or is not so. No one who has read a page by a good critic or a speculative scientist can ever again think that this barren choice of yes or no is all that the mind offers.

Reality is not an exhibit for man's inspection, labelled, "Do not touch." There are no appearances to be photographed, no experiences to be copied, in which we do not take part. We re-make nature by the act of discovery, in the poem or in the theorem. And the great poem and the deep theorem are new to every reader, and yet are his own experiences, because he himself re-creates them. They are the marks of unity in variety; and in the instant when the mind seizes this for itself, in art or in science, the heart misses a beat.

NOTES

[1] This is the argument in Hardy's delightful small book *A Mathematician's Apology* (Cambridge 1940). The title of the book and its date, soon after the outbreak of war, suggest that it was prompted by the same distress at the visible misuse of science that has prompted my book. Hardy was a great mathematician, and he was also (under his restrained manner) a man of passionate human and social sympathies.

[2] Wallenstein, the great Catholic general in this religious war, was born at the conjunction of Jupiter and Saturn. There is a conjunction of these two planets when they appear to change places repeatedly: in the language of astrology, when they "play." This rare conjunction has accompanied a num-

ber of historic events, for historic events are always plentiful. It occurred
about the time of the birth of Christ, and also when the Protestant king
William of Orange came to England in the Glorious Revolution of 1688.
The same conjunction of Jupiter and Saturn occurred in 1940, and I will
quote a poem which I wrote about it in that year.

> Jupiter and Saturn played.
> The age was broken and re-made.
> A rocket rose from Bethlehem.
> Christ marched with the Orangemen;
> Till, diving, the exploding light
> Struck today, and charred it white.
>
> The rocket roars and plunges out.
> Saturn and Jupiter turn about.
> No child again shall put to shame
> The gunsights trained on Bethlehem;
> While ice-cap, omen, march to birth
> The orbit of the screaming earth.

[3] At the time of the Scientific Revolution in the sixteenth century, and
for two centuries after it, most self-made men got their wealth by trade (in
which I include the support of trade by insurance and banking), and often
by oversea trade. As *The Merchant of Venice* reminds us, this is how the
great fortunes in North Italy, in Holland and in England were made. It was
therefore natural that science in these two centuries was agog with problems of trade, and particularly of navigation. The Industrial Revolution in
the eighteenth century shifted the source of wealth from trade to manufacture; and manufacture has needed more and more mechanical energy.
Science has therefore been preoccupied in the last two centuries with problems which centre on energy—practical problems from the heat engine to
the electro-magnetic field, and theoretical problems from thermodynamics
to atomic structure. Now that we are in sight of having as much energy as
we can need, the interest of scientists is moving from the generation of
energy to its control, and particularly to the automatic control of power
processes, whose tools are the valve, the semi-conductor and the computer.
A characteristic invention of the Scientific Revolution was the telescope, of
which Galileo heard from Holland, and which he presented to the Doge
after a demonstration in the port of Venice in the presence of the Senate in
1609. The characteristic invention of the Industrial Revolution was the
power machine which does the routine work of the human muscle. The
characteristic invention of the second Industrial Revolution through which
we are passing is the control mechanism which does the routine work of the
human brain.

[4] As an example, consider the practice of mathematics. Mathematics is in
the first place a language in which we discuss those parts of the real world
which can be described by numbers or by similar relations of order. But
with the workaday business of translating the facts into this language there
naturally goes, in those who are good at it, a pleasure in the activity itself.
They find the language richer than its bare content; what is translated comes
to mean less to them than the logic and the style of saying it; and from these
overtones grows mathematics as a literature in its own right. Mathematics in
this sense, pure mathematics, is a form of poetry, which has the same rela-

tion to the prose of practical mathematics as poetry has to prose in any other language. This element of poetry, the delight in exploring the medium for its own sake, is an essential ingredient in the creative process.

[5] This has now been admirably documented by Thomas S. Kuhn in *The Copernican Revolution* (Harvard 1957). As he shows, from the Neoplatonist elements in the new humanism "some Renaissance scientists, like Copernicus, Galileo, and Kepler, seem to have drawn two decidedly un-Aristotelian ideas: a new belief in the possibility and importance of discovering simple arithmetic and geometric regularities in nature, and a new view of the sun as the source of all vital principles and forces in the universe." Kuhn draws particular attention to the influence of the "symbolic identification of the sun and God" in the *Liber de Sole* of Marsilio Ficino, a central figure in the humanist and Neoplatonist academy of Florence in the fifteenth century. The subject has also been attractively discussed recently by Arthur Koestler in *The Sleepwalkers* (London 1959).

[6] The derivation of Blake's drawing from the Renaissance studies, by Leonardo and others, of the Vitruvian proportions and mathematical harmonies of the human figure is also discussed by Sir Kenneth Clark in *The Nude* (London 1956).

[7] The music of the spheres was itself a mathematical conception, which had been invented by Pythagoras in the sixth century B.C. Pythagoras taught that the distances between the heavenly bodies match the length of the strings that sound the different musical notes. It was deduced that the spheres that carry the heavenly bodies make music as they turn.

[8] In one of the places in which Coleridge put forward this definition, the essays *On the Principles of Genial Criticism* (which Coleridge thought "the best things he had ever written"), he traced it back to Pythagoras: "The safest definition, then, of Beauty, as well as the oldest, is that of Pythagoras: THE REDUCTION OF MANY TO ONE."

[9] Pope was near the end of his career, and his friends Gay and Arbuthnot were already dead, when he published these lines in 1737. (They expand a thought from Horace, and his surviving friend Swift was particularly moved by them.) Twenty-five years earlier, as a young man in *The Rape of the Lock,* Pope had pictured the mill as a happy symbol in the ritual of the coffee-table.

> For lo! the Board with Cups and Spoons is crown'd,
> The Berries crackle, and the Mill turns round.

As the eighteenth century moved on, the image of the mill became more menacing in the minds of poets, until Blake in 1804 wrote of "dark Satanic Mills." In part the change kept step with the progress of the Industrial Revolution, which Blake, for example, felt very sensitively. But in the main what the romantic poets feared was the new vision of nature as a machine, which Newton's great reputation had imposed. Blake meant by the Satanic Mills not a factory but the imperturbable cosmic mechanism which was now imagined to drive the planets round their orbits. Blake used the words "abstract," "Newtonian" and "Satanic" with the same meaning, to describe a machinery that seemed to him opposed to organic life; and he wrote, "A Machine is not a Man nor a Work of Art; it is destructive of Humanity & of Art; the word Machination." Goethe, who did original work in biology, also disliked Newton's view of science; like other poets of the time, he felt that it turned the world into a clockwork. Yet at the same time religious apologists like

William Paley in his *Evidences of Christianity* were using the same analogy to prove that the world, like a clock, must have an intelligent designer. Thus the symbol of the clockwork, and (as T. S. Ashton has pointed out) a new sense of time in general, were critical in the thought of those who lived through the Industrial Revolution.

10 The greatest satire of the First World War, Karl Kraus's *Die Letzten Tage der Menschheit*, contains a moving echo of these lines, which bears on what I have written in the preceding note. In one poem Kraus describes the machine-made murders of modern war as observed by a man *Mit der Uhr in der Hand*—that is, watch in hand. I quote two verses.

> Dort ist ein Mörser. Ihm entrinnt der arme Mann,
> der ihn erfand. Er schützt sich in dem Graben.
> Weil Zwerge Riesen überwältigt haben,
> seht her, die Uhr die Zeit zum Stehen bringen kann!

> Wie viel war's an der Zeit, als jenes jetzt geschah?
> Schlecht sieht das Aug, das giftige Gase beizen.
> Doch hört das Ohr, die Uhr schlug eben dreizehn.
> Unsichtig Wetter kommt, der Untergang ist nah.

11 This verse comes from the poem "Vacillation," and I have quoted it as Yeats first printed it, for example in *The Winding Stair and other poems*. In his *Collected Poems* soon after, Yeats left out the word "or" in the second line. No doubt the change improves the metre; but since I am here concerned with the contrast between the two images in Yeats's mind, I have given his original text.

—

J. BRONOWSKI   Born in England in 1908, he has been a teacher, civil servant in both research and administrative positions, and prolific author, having written a play, many essays and articles, and books on science and literature. "The Creative Mind" was first presented as a lecture at the Massachusetts Institute of Technology in 1953, then, after several reprintings, made into the first chapter of his *Science and Human Values.*

"*The Creative Mind*" (1956) The author employs a dramatic opening to set up his theme. His subsequent argument is carefully ordered and expanded. It displays a strong sense of beginning, middle, and end, as well as a neat structuring of paragraphs. The essay also illustrates the functional use of such rhetorical devices as parallel constructions, rhetorical questions, and repetitive figures, along with pertinent quotations from a broad spectrum of literature.

—

1. In what ways is the "act of fusion," rather than the act of fission, creative? 2. How does your own work in science support or refute the author's analysis of how the creative mind operates?

L E H R

Albert Camus: Philosopher of Limits

The writers of contemporary existential literature portray man and
the universe as odd-shaped pieces in some gigantic, meaningless
puzzle. Deprived of teleological significance, the human creature
is condemned, without hope of escape, to a barren and aimless
existence. And the universe, devoid of cosmological design, is but
a spinning mass of confusion. Hence, the existential protagonist
is a metaphysical misfit, groping blindly in a black world.

Albert Camus, though included in the school of contemporary
existentialism, differs radically from his colleagues who equate the
irrational character of the universe with the character of man.
Camus agrees that the universe is irrational, but that is as far as
he is willing to go. Man, he discovers, is both rational and meaningful, manifesting the qualities of a benevolent human nature.
Separating man from his universe by virtue of this rationality,
Camus argues that human life can have value and purpose,
though the chaotic universe stands in powerful refutation. In
reality, then, man and the universe are antithetically related giving
the age-worn struggle between good and evil the form of rational
man versus irrational nature; and the good life must be lived not
in harmony but in defiance of the natural order of things.

In *The Plague,* nature puts mankind to the test, challenging
with its ubiquitous weapon of death the existence of basic human
goodness. The irrational and unjust universe is admittedly over-

Reprinted from *Modern Fiction Studies,* Vol. X, No. 3 (Autumn 1964), by
permission of the author and the Purdue Research Foundation.

powering, yet its violent outrage cannot destroy the inherent human virtue revealed in Dr. Rieux's observation that "there are more things in men to admire than to despise."[1] The tenacity of human compassion, despite such impossible odds, substantiates the worth of man and offers him hope for a valuable existence, even in the antagonistic universe. Camus writes, "I continue to believe that this world has no higher meaning. But I know that something in it has meaning and that is man, because he is the only being to insist upon having it. This world has at least the truth of man and our task is to give him his reasons to oppose destiny itself."[2]

I

Camus' search for these reasons begins with an ontological examination of what he alarmingly labels the "Absurd." Through the frightened eyes of Camus' hero, the world is seen as a terrible monster to be faced unaided and alone. A God that might have helped with an offer of salvation, is silent. If life on this earth were but an obstacle in the road to a better life, the plague of this world could be more easily endured. But without the comfort of this belief, existence assumes a different dimension. Bereft of such salvation, life is defined in terms of the existential rather than the ideal, and Caligula's discovery becomes pathetically real: "Men die," he laments, "and they are not happy."[3] Death, rather than being a beginning, is the end of the road to happiness. Thus man cannot wait to escape the evils of the world but must find his happiness within the limits of his finite existence. "At this point in his effort," says Camus, "man is confronted with the irrational. He feels within him a desire for happiness and for reason. The absurd is born of this confrontation between the human appeal and the unreasonable silence of the world."[4] Camus does not say the silent, non-rational world is itself absurd. Neither is man, pathetic though he is, absurd. What is absurd is the contradictory combination of this rational man in a non-rational world. Camus says that "the Absurd is not in man . . . nor in the world, but in their

---

[1] Albert Camus, *La Peste* (Paris, 1947), p. 247. Translations from Camus are my own.
[2] Albert Camus, *Lettres à un Ami Allemand* (Paris, 1948), p. 74.
[3] Albert Camus, *Le Malentendu/Caligula* (Paris, 1947), p. 111.
[4] Albert Camus, *Le Mythe de Sisyphe* (Paris, 1942), pp. 44–45.

presence together."[5] Turning from the supernatural to the existential, from the infinite to the finite, man is faced with the seemingly impossible predicament of searching for rational meaning in an irrational world. This, says Camus, is the Absurd, "the confrontation of this irrational [world] and of the desperate desire for clarity whose call resounds in the depths of man."[6]

II

Man-in-the-world, then, is Absurd and Camus examines two possible ways to resolve this absurdity. The first is suicide. If the world is cold and unfriendly, perhaps existence is not worth the struggle. If there is no purpose or reason behind the apparent chaos, why should man suffer the burden of his daily toil? He can jump off this spinning ball and put an end to the game. Camus handles this primary dilemma in *The Myth of Sisyphus*, which he says was written to resolve the "one truly serious philosophical problem: suicide. To judge whether life is or is not worth living, is to answer the fundamental question of philosophy."[7] Camus argues in this polemic that suicide cannot be ethically justified, and his purpose is to show that even in an empty universe where God is absent if not dead, suicide cannot be condoned.

Working toward this conclusion, Camus finds that "everything begins with lucid indifference."[8] The first reaction to the testimony of experience that life is without design or purpose is to become indifferent to this traditional requirement. A "who cares" attitude develops in response to the failures of philosophy, religion, and science to explain and account for existence. If the security of knowing is forever denied, and the world gyrates without direction, and nature's death sentence mocks our endeavors, who cares?

This mood of indifference, this feeling of apathetic despondency is most clearly portrayed in *The Stranger*. Meursault's indifference to everything: to love, to life, and particularly to death (his mother's, his victim's, and his own) is overwhelming. The day after his mother's funeral, Meursault goes swimming and finds a girl he had once known. From the water they're off to a film

5 *Mythe*, p. 48.
6 *Mythe*, p. 37.
7 *Mythe*, p. 15.
8 *Mythe*, p. 131.

comedy and from there to his place for the night. On the following
evening, the events of the weekend pass through his mind: "I
thought how Sundays always drag by, that mother was now
buried, that I was about to go back to work, and how, actually,
nothing had changed."[9] To the despondent, who is insensitive to
the irrationality of the universe, who agrees with Meursault that
"life is not worth living,"[10] suicide is a real possibility. And as
man's existence in the world constitutes the Absurd, by eliminating that component, the Absurd would be destroyed. "To destroy
one of its terms," Camus states, "is to destroy it entirely. There can
be no absurd outside of the human mind. Thus, as with all things,
the absurd ends with death."[11] Killing oneself, however, destroys
the Absurd for that individual only; the Absurd will continue as
long as there are men. Suicide then merely escapes the problem;
it does not solve it.

But the dispassionate individual at Meursault's stage of development is not concerned with destroying the Absurd. Life is insignificant and meaningless for him, but he is not frustrated by it and
demands no explanations or justifications. His depravity, however,
can be only short-lived, for as it was his intellect that showed him
the world's emptiness, so it is his intellect that will dislodge him
from his apathy. Through the voice of Cherea, the sage of
Caligula's court, Camus states firmly his belief in man's basic
rational nature: "One cannot live without rationality."[12] And this
inherent aspect of human character will disquiet the sterile existence typified by Meursault and demand some other response to
the Absurd.

III

If self-destruction is an unsatisfactory answer to the Absurd,
another possibility, non-corporeal, is what Camus calls "philosophical suicide." The Absurd, in part, depends upon a universe
devoid of reason. If man can postulate a reason, if he can attribute purpose and design to the world, then the Absurd would
be destroyed. But once again man's rational nature would be
violated. If reality is not *in fact* as it appears to human reason,

[9] Albert Camus, *L'Etranger* (Paris, 1942), p. 39.
[10] *L'Etranger,* p. 160.
[11] *Mythe,* p. 49.
[12] *Caligula,* p. 131.

then the existential is illusion, reducing the irrational to merely a failing of the human mind. This transcends human reason in favor of a higher intellect which is denotative of religious epistomology. In this connection, Camus cites Chestov, who says, "'The only true solution . . . is precisely where there is no solution for human judgement. Otherwise, what need would we have of God? One turns toward God in order to obtain the impossible. As for the possible, men suffice.'" Camus points out that when "Chestov discovers the fundamental absurdity of all existence, he does not at all say, 'Here is the absurd,' but 'Here is God. . . .'"[13] This is what Camus means by philosophical suicide. Philosophy demands that reality be explained in terms of logic and reason—these are the tools of philosophy. Therefore, the believer abandons philosophy when he accepts on enigmatic authority what philosophically he must only discover through reason.

Suicide, whether physical or philosophical, is an unsatisfactory answer to the Absurd. Physical suicide does not resolve the Absurd; it merely escapes it. Philosophical suicide destroys the Absurd only by forsaking human rationality. Both refuse to acknowledge man's rational capabilities to cope with the problem of existence. The former turns its back to the world, and the latter attempts to destroy the Absurd by ignoring the human rationality that defines it. Thus physical and philosophical suicide do not face life squarely, and the authentic individual is denied either exit. Camus believes that within man's reach, there is another alternative, one that will accept the truth of the human predicament. This alternative is implicit in the epigram that opens *The Myth:* "'O my soul, do not aspire to immortal life, but exhaust the realm of the possible.'"[14]

IV

And openly I dedicated my heart to the grave and suffering earth, and often, in the sacred night, I promised to love it faithfully, until death, without fear, with its heavy burden of fatality, and to despise none of its enigmas. Thus I bound myself to it with a mortal tie.[15]

[13] *Mythe*, pp. 52–53.
[14] Pindare, $3°$ *Pythique*, in *Mythe*, p. 9.
[15] This passage, quoted from Hölderlin's *The Death of Empedocles*, opens *The Rebel* and sets the theme, in Albert Camus, *L'Homme Révolté* (Paris, 1951), p. 9.

The Absurd is man's existential reality. It is not altered by suicide; it must not be ignored by a leap of faith. Thus the question
is no longer how to resolve the Absurd, but how to live authen-
tically within it. Camus contends that once it is accepted, the
Absurd can be the existential "cogito," for it exists as a concrete
fact and can thus serve as an epistemological foundation and a
metaphysical point of departure. Camus states that whereas the
Absurd is usually taken as a conclusion, he considers it a starting
point, and he startles his reader with paradoxical statements
such as, "It was previously a question of knowing if life had to
have meaning in order to be lived. It is apparent here to the
contrary that it will be lived so much the better if it has no
meaning."[16]

But if the Absurd continues, so must the tension it creates.
Nature will forever be man's dire antagonist. Rebellion, then, is
the ethical key to authenticity, for the human being must resist
his environment to maintain his identity. In the words of Camus,
"In order to exist, man must rebel."[17]

Analysis of rebellion discloses the universal dimension implicit
in its meaning. It becomes evident that the whole human race
faces the same dilemma. Camus defines the rebel as one who acts
"in the name of a value, yet confused, but which he feels, at least,
he holds in common with all men."[18] The rebel realizes at this
point that existence is Absurd for every rational individual and
hence he no longer sees the human tragedy as a solitary struggle.
"In absurd experience," says Camus, "suffering is individual. From
the beginning of a movement of rebellion, it is known to be collective, the experience of all. . . . It founds the first value on all of
humanity." And the maxim: In order to exist, man must rebel,
becomes, "I rebel, therefore we exist."[19]

The first form of revolt Camus terms "metaphysical rebellion,"
and he defines it as "the movement in which man rises up in pro-

[16] *Mythe,* p. 76.
[17] *Révolté,* p. 35.
[18] *Révolté,* p. 28.
[19] *Révolté,* p. 36. Camus uses the word "absurd" in its normal denotative
sense of irrational as well as in the specific meaning he has assigned to it.
The "absurd experience" or the "absurd man" that he speaks of here and
elsewhere is simply that unreflective life or that individual who, like
Meursault, lives without reason.

test against his condition and the whole creation."[20] This protest is against the irrational universe that challenges human significance. Born in the Absurd, the rebel can turn to no God who, being responsible for existence, can explain the mystery of this life and sympathize with complaints about it. The rebel is denied theological metaphysics which promises recognition of the self, reward for the will, and an eternity of dreams fulfilled in a heaven where justice is done and death overcome. The fulfillment of these dreams must come, if at all, from man himself. He must look, not to another life, but to this one; not to greater powers, but to the limit of his own.

Illustrating an early stage in metaphysical rebellion is the romantic "dandy." The dandy's reaction to theological estrangement is to live life with abandon, reasoning that without God to govern his behavior, the affairs of life are without limits. The dandy's attitude, writes Camus, is that the "individual who must die is at least glorious before he disappears, and this grandeur is his justification."[21] But this attitude is invalid, for it disregards the purpose of rebellion. Dandyism merely exploits the Absurd to the immediate advantage of the individual, and in the end, offers no meaningful way of life to satisfy the human quest for significance.

As an example of the more mature metaphysical rebel, Camus picks Dostoevsky's Ivan Karamazov. Ivan insists humanity is innocent and affirms that the death sentence which hangs over man is unjust. He argues that if evil is essential to divine creation, he cannot accept its salvation. " 'If the suffering of children,' says Ivan, 'serves to make up the sum of sorrow necessary to the acquisition of truth, I affirm now and henceforth that this truth is not worth such a price.' "[22] Ivan cannot reconcile the contradiction of a benevolent creator and a grief-ridden creation. He will not compromise with God; the evil and suffering that he witnesses in the world cannot be explained away nor ignored. As a metaphysical rebel he wants *All or Nothing*. " 'All the knowledge in the world' " he says, " 'is not worth a child's tears.' "[23]

[20] *Révolté,* p. 39.
[21] *Révolté,* p. 72.
[22] *Révolté,* p. 77.
[23] *Révolté,* p. 78.

In addition, Ivan refuses salvation if only on the individual level. Reflecting the universal compassion of rebellion (I rebel, therefore we exist), Ivan throws in with the damned, for he recognizes that if he alone were saved, suffering would continue until all were saved. His individual salvation would not destroy suffering; it would merely escape it as suicide escapes the Absurd and the dandy escapes his social responsibility. Thus, "one step more, and from the *All or Nothing*, we come to *Everyone or No One*."[24]

With Ivan's position, the history of contemporary nihilism begins. Though Ivan did not deny God, he refused Him. It was not a question of whether God existed but whether to accept His authority in any case. But for the nihilists, this was not enough. In their bitterness they "transformed the 'even if you exist' into 'you do not deserve to exist,' therefore 'you do not exist.' "[25] With God thus dethroned, the nihilists contended that man could be his own God. It is up to man to create the standard of conduct and in the minds of the nihilists this meant that with their newly acquired infinite power, *Everything is Permitted*. With this deduction, however, the metaphysical rebel fell into a self-destroying dilemma. He began by refusing to accept the evil in the world out of compassion for his fellow man. But, through his logic, he ended by permitting everything, which opened the way for man-made atrocities to add to the sorrow of the world. Summing up the rebel's fate thus far, Camus says, "To the crimes of the irrational, man, on an earth that he knows is henceforth solitary, is going to add the crimes of reason moving toward the supremacy of men. To the 'I rebel, therefore we exist,' he adds, contemplating prodigious plans and even the death of rebellion: 'and we are alone.' "[26]

V

"Actually," Tarrou said simply, "what interests me is to know how to become a saint."

"But you don't believe in God."

"Exactly. How to be a saint without God, that is the only concrete problem I know today."

[24] *Révolté*, p. 78.
[25] *Révolté*, pp. 130–31.
[26] *Révolté*, p. 132.

. . . "Perhaps," the doctor answered, "but you know, I feel more fellowship with the vanquished than with the saints. I don't care much for heroism and saintliness, I guess. What interests me is to be a man."[27]

The rebel, as God and "alone" in the universe, begins to create his own world. In the name of mankind, he takes up the fight against oppressors of human freedom, justifying his crimes by the ominous principle *Everything is Permitted*. This is the transformation into a second type of rebellion which Camus calls "historical rebellion." The rebel, now a bloodthirsty revolutionary, protests against the history of human malignity. Beginning in Russia in the nineteenth century, this revolutionism made its attack upon absolute monarchy (The Regicides), reasoning that if there is no God, there can be no divine right of kings. But the corrupting, unlimited power distorted the rebel's principles, turning rebellion into terrorism though the goal was professed to be the triumph of human dignity. Says Camus, "The terrorists without doubt want first to destroy, to make absolutism totter under the shock of bombs. But by its death, at least, they aim at recreating a community of justice and love, and thus to resume a mission that the Church has betrayed. In reality, the terrorists want to create a Church from where one day will spring the new God."[28]

But the new Church was not coming. Terrorism persisted, culminating in Fascism (The Irrational Terror) and Communism (The Rational Terror) in the twentieth century, about which Camus judges: "One would think that an age which, in fifty years, uproots, enslaves, or kills seventy million human beings should be above all condemned."[29]

The criminal mind of the contemporary world has logically deduced, from the premises of Absurdity and Rebellion, the justification of murder. Camus, however, questions "if we have the right to kill a fellow human being or to allow him to be killed."[30] If murder were a valid consequence of the human condition, then there must exist a higher value to which man may be

---

[27] *Peste,* pp. 204–05.
[28] *Révolté,* pp. 207–08.
[29] *Révolté,* p. 14.
[30] *Révolté,* p. 14.

sacrificed. That is to say, if Communism, for example, argues that for the good of its end homicide is legitimate, then what it is stating is that the absolute ideal of History has a higher value than individual man. Camus denies the validity of this argument. Man began, in the Absurd, with the belief that he embodied the only value in existence. He learned through analysis of philosophical suicide, that this condition cannot be altered without denying human rationality.

The error of the historical rebel lies in the deduction that *Everything is Permitted.* Acting upon this error, the rebel evolved rebellion into revolution, committing crimes that equaled, perhaps surpassed, the evils of the irrational universe. He wanted to become God and enjoy the power of infinite freedom, but Camus believes, "The freedom of each finds its limits in that of others; no one has a right to absolute freedom."[31] The rebel must never lose sight of the Absurd which stands as a constant reminder that existence is dependent upon, and limited to, the finite, and that therefore the limits of human reason, space, and time are the bounds of authentic existence. Thus the rebel must follow what Camus sees to be "the only original rule of life today: to learn to live and to die, and, in order to be a man, to refuse to be a god."[32]

Camus' Philosophy of Limits defines existence and therefrom derives individual authenticity (The Myth of Sisyphus) and universal ethics (The Myth of Prometheus). It gives the fundamental question of philosophy a positive answer: In the Absurd, life *is* worth living. This theory of value, underscoring all of Camus' writings, is ironically punctuated by his own life which ended abruptly in irrational catastrophe. It was as though to say in deed as he does in words: In this troubled world, man's only hope is to keep the Absurd alive.

[31] Albert Camus, *Resistance, Rebellion and Death,* trans. Justin O'Brien (London, 1960), p. 74.
[32] *Révolté,* p. 377.

✦

Lehr The author identifies himself as "a devoted student of existential philosophy." This article was written in Paris, where he went "to explore contemporary French contributions and developments" in existentialism.

"Albert Camus: Philosopher of Limits" (1964) The organization and style are so direct and unequivocal that a highly complex topic is made intelligible. The approach is objective and comprehensive, and the author skillfully uses appropriate quotations to fill out and substantiate his analysis.

✦

1. *What are the philosophical and political implications of Camus' sentence, "I rebel, therefore we exist?"* 2. *What pre-twentieth-century authors, if any, might be considered existentialists?*

Why I Write

From a very early age, perhaps the age of five or six, I knew that when I grew up I should be a writer. Between the ages of about seventeen and twenty-four I tried to abandon this idea, but I did so with the consciousness that I was outraging my true nature and that sooner or later I should have to settle down and write books.

I was the middle child of three, but there was a gap of five years on either side, and I barely saw my father before I was eight. For this and other reasons I was somewhat lonely, and I soon developed disagreeable mannerisms which made me unpopular throughout my schooldays. I had the lonely child's habit of making up stories and holding conversations with imaginary persons, and I think from the very start my literary ambitions were mixed up with the feeling of being isolated and undervalued. I knew that I had a facility with words and a power of facing unpleasant facts, and I felt that this created a sort of private world in which I could get my own back for my failure in everyday life. Nevertheless the volume of serious—*i.e.* seriously intended—writing which I produced all through my childhood and boyhood would not amount to half a dozen pages. I wrote my first poem at the age of four or five, my mother taking it down to dictation. I cannot remember anything about it except that it was about a tiger and the tiger had "chair-like teeth"—a good enough phrase, but I fancy the poem was a plagiarism of Blake's "Tiger, Tiger." At eleven when the war of 1914–18 broke out, I wrote a patriotic poem which was printed in the local newspaper, as was another, two years later, on the death of Kitchener. From time to time, when I was a bit older, I wrote bad and usually unfinished "nature poems" in the Georgian style. I also, about twice, attempted a short story which was a ghastly failure. That was the total of the would-be serious work that I actually set down on paper during all those years.

However, throughout this time I did in a sense engage in literary activities. To begin with there was the made-to-order stuff which I produced quickly, easily and without much pleasure to myself. Apart from school work, I wrote *vers d'occasion*, semi-comic poems which I could turn out at what now seems to me astonishing speed—at fourteen I wrote a whole rhyming play, in imitation of Aristophanes, in about a week—and helped to edit school magazines, both printed and in manuscript. These magazines were the most pitiful burlesque stuff that you could imagine, and I took far less trouble with them than I now would with the cheapest journalism. But side by side with all this, for fifteen years or more, I was carrying out a literary exercise of a quite different kind: this was the making up of a continuous "story" about myself, a sort of diary existing only in the mind. I believe this is a common habit of children and adolescents. As a very small child I used to imagine that I was, say, Robin Hood, and picture myself as the hero of thrilling adventures, but quite soon my "story" ceased to be narcissistic in a crude way and became more and more a mere description of what I was doing and the things I saw. For minutes at a time this kind of thing would be running through my head: "He pushed the door open and entered the room. A yellow beam of sunlight, filtering through the muslin curtains, slanted on to the table, where a matchbox, half open, lay beside the inkpot. With his right hand in his pocket he moved across to the window. Down in the street a tortoiseshell cat was chasing a dead leaf," etc., etc. This habit continued till I was about twenty-five, right through my non-literary years. Although I had to search, and did search, for the right words, I seemed to be making this descriptive effort almost against my will, under a kind of compulsion from outside. The "story" must, I suppose, have reflected the styles of the various writers I admired at different ages, but so far as I remember it always had the same meticulous descriptive quality.

When I was about sixteen I suddenly discovered the joy of mere words, *i.e.* the sounds and associations of words. The lines from *Paradise Lost*—

> "So hee with difficulty and labour hard
> Moved on: with difficulty and labour hee,"

which do not now seem to me so very wonderful, sent shivers down my backbone; and the spelling "hee" for "he" was an added pleasure. As for the need to describe things, I knew all about it already. So it is clear what kind of books I wanted to write, in so far as I could be said to want to write books at that time. I wanted to write enormous naturalistic novels with unhappy endings, full of detailed descriptions and arresting similes, and also full of purple passages in which words were used partly for the sake of their sound. And in fact my first completed novel, *Burmese Days*, which I wrote when I was thirty but projected much earlier, is rather that kind of book.

I give all this background information because I do not think one can assess a writer's motives without knowing something of his early development. His subject matter will be determined by the age he lives in—at least this is true in tumultuous, revolutionary ages like our own—but before he ever begins to write he will have acquired an emotional attitude from which he will never completely escape. It is his job, no doubt, to discipline his temperament and avoid getting stuck at some immature stage, or in some perverse mood: but if he escapes from his early influences altogether, he will have killed his impulse to write. Putting aside the need to earn a living, I think there are four great motives for writing, at any rate for writing prose. They exist in different degrees in every writer, and in any one writer the proportions will vary from time to time, according to the atmosphere in which he is living. They are:

(1) Sheer egoism. Desire to seem clever, to be talked about, to be remembered after death, to get your own back on grown-ups who snubbed you in childhood, etc., etc. It is humbug to pre-

tend that this is not a motive, and a strong one. Writers share this characteristic with scientists, artists, politicians, lawyers, soldiers, successful businessmen—in short, with the whole top crust of humanity. The great mass of human beings are not acutely selfish. After the age of about thirty they abandon individual ambition—in many cases, indeed, they almost abandon the sense of being individuals at all—and live chiefly for others, or are simply smothered under drudgery. But there is also the minority of gifted, wilful people who are determined to live their own lives to the end, and writers belong in this class. Serious writers, I should say, are on the whole more vain and self-centered than journalists, though less interested in money.

(2) Aesthetic enthusiasm. Perception of beauty in the external world, or, on the other hand, in words and their right arrangement. Pleasure in the impact of one sound on another, in the firmness of good prose or the rhythm of a good story. Desire to share an experience which one feels is valuable and ought not to be missed. The aesthetic motive is very feeble in a lot of writers, but even a pamphleteer or a writer of textbooks will have pet words and phrases which appeal to him for nonutilitarian reasons; or he may feel strongly about typography, width of margins, etc. Above the level of a railway guide, no book is quite free from aesthetic considerations.

(3) Historical impulse. Desire to see things as they are, to find out true facts and store them up for the use of posterity.

(4) Political purpose—using the word "political" in the widest possible sense. Desire to push the world in a certain direction, to alter other people's idea of the kind of society that they should strive after. Once again, no book is genuinely free from political bias. The opinion that art should have nothing to do with politics is itself a political attitude.

It can be seen how these various impulses must war against one another, and how they must fluctuate from person to person and from time to time. By nature—taking your "nature" to be the state you have attained when you are first adult—I am a person in whom the first three motives would outweigh the fourth. In a peaceful age I might have written ornate or merely descriptive books, and might have remained almost unaware of my political loyalties. As it is I have been forced into becoming a sort of

pamphleteer. First I spent five years in an unsuitable profession
(the Indian Imperial Police, in Burma), and then I underwent
poverty and the sense of failure. This increased my natural hatred
of authority and made me for the first time fully aware of the
existence of the working classes, and the job in Burma had given
me some understanding of the nature of imperialism: but these
experiences were not enough to give me an accurate political
orientation. Then came Hitler, the Spanish civil war, etc. By the
end of 1935 I had still failed to reach a firm decision. I remember
a little poem that I wrote at that date, expressing my dilemma:

> A happy vicar I might have been
> Two hundred years ago,
> To preach upon eternal doom
> And watch my walnuts grow;
>
> But born, alas, in an evil time,
> I missed that pleasant haven,
> For the hair has grown on my upper lip
> And the clergy are all clean-shaven.
>
> And later still the times were good,
> We were so easy to please,
> We rocked our troubled thoughts to sleep
> On the bosoms of the trees.
>
> All ignorant we dared to own
> The joys we now dissemble;
> The greenfinch on the apple bough
> Could make my enemies tremble.
>
> But girls' bellies and apricots,
> Roach in a shaded stream,
> Horses, ducks in flight at dawn,
> All these are a dream.
>
> It is forbidden to dream again;
> We maim our joys or hide them;
> Horses are made of chromium steel
> And little fat men shall ride them.
>
> I am the worm who never turned,
> The eunuch without a harem;
> Between the priest and the commissar
> I walk like Eugene Aram;

And the commissar is telling my fortune
While the radio plays,
But the priest has promised an Austin Seven,
For Duggie always pays.

I dreamed I dwelt in marble halls,
And woke to find it true;
I wasn't born for an age like this;
Was Smith? Was Jones? Were you?

The Spanish war and other events in 1936–7 turned the scale and thereafter I knew where I stood. Every line of serious work that I have written since 1936 has been written, directly or indirectly, *against* totalitarianism and *for* democratic socialism, as I understand it. It seems to me nonsense, in a period like our own, to think that one can avoid writing of such subjects. Everyone writes of them in one guise or another. It is simply a question of which side one takes and what approach one follows. And the more one is conscious of one's political bias, the more chance one has of acting politically without sacrificing one's aesthetic and intellectual integrity.

What I have most wanted to do throughout the past ten years is to make political writing into an art. My starting point is always a feeling of partisanship, a sense of injustice. When I sit down to write a book, I do not say to myself, "I am going to produce a work of art." I write it because there is some lie that I want to expose, some fact to which I want to draw attention, and my initial concern is to get a hearing. But I could not do the work of writing a book, or even a long magazine article, if it were not also an aesthetic experience. Anyone who cares to examine my work will see that even when it is downright propaganda it contains much that a full-time politician would consider irrelevant. I am not able, and I do not want, completely to abandon the world-view that I acquired in childhood. So long as I remain alive and well I shall continue to feel strongly about prose style, to love the surface of the earth, and to take a pleasure in solid objects and scraps of useless information. It is no use trying to suppress that side of myself. The job is to reconcile my ingrained likes and dislikes with the essentially public, non-individual activities that this age forces on all of us.

It is not easy. It raises problems of construction and of language, and it raises in a new way the problem of truthfulness. Let me give just one example of the cruder kind of difficulty that arises. My book about the Spanish civil war, *Homage to Catalonia*, is, of course, a frankly political book, but in the main it is written with a certain detachment and regard for form. I did try very hard in it to tell the whole truth without violating my literary instincts. But among other things it contains a long chapter, full of newspaper quotations and the like, defending the Trotskyists who were accused of plotting with Franco. Clearly such a chapter, which after a year or two would lose its interest for any ordinary reader, must ruin the book. A critic whom I respect read me a lecture about it. "Why did you put in all that stuff?" he said. "You've turned what might have been a good book into journalism." What he said was true, but I could not have done otherwise. I happened to know, what very few people in England had been allowed to know, that innocent men were being falsely accused. If I had not been angry about that I should never have written the book.

In one form or another this problem comes up again. The problem of language is subtler and would take too long to discuss. I will only say that of late years I have tried to write less picturesquely and more exactly. In any case I find that by the time you have perfected any style of writing, you have always outgrown it. *Animal Farm* was the first book in which I tried, with full consciousness of what I was doing, to fuse political purpose and artistic purpose into one whole. I have not written a novel for seven years, but I hope to write another fairly soon. It is bound to be a failure, every book is a failure, but I do know with some clarity what kind of book I want to write.

Looking back through the last page or two, I see that I have made it appear as though my motives in writing were wholly public-spirited. I don't want to leave that as the final impression. All writers are vain, selfish and lazy, and at the very bottom of their motives there lies a mystery. Writing a book is a horrible, exhausting struggle, like a long bout of some painful illness. One would never undertake such a thing if one were not driven on by some demon whom one can neither resist nor understand. For all one knows that demon is simply the same instinct that makes a baby squall for attention. And yet it is also true that one can write nothing readable unless one constantly struggles to efface one's own personality. Good prose is like a window pane. I cannot say with certainty which of my motives are the strongest, but I know which of them deserve to be followed. And looking back through my work, I see that it is invariably where I lacked a *political* purpose that I wrote lifeless books and was betrayed into purple passages, sentences without meaning, decorative adjectives and humbug generally.

*

GEORGE ORWELL   Born in India in 1903, died in 1950, Orwell had a strenuous and adventurous life, including service with the Imperial Police in Burma, living in poverty in Paris, and being wounded while fighting for the Loyalists in the Spanish Civil War. He is well known as a novelist (especially for *1984*) and as an incisive journalist and essayist.

"Why I Write" (1947) Lucidly organized and written in a restrained style, this essay conveys a sense of honesty and depth in the author's relation to himself and to the tumultuous world in which he lived.

*

1. *In what ways is Orwell's poem a good summary of the entire essay?*
2. *If you were to become a writer, how might your motives differ from his?*

E. M. FORSTER

Art for Art's Sake

An address delivered before the
American Academy of Arts and Letters in New York

I believe in art for art's sake. It is an unfashionable belief, and
some of my statements must be of the nature of an apology. Fifty
years ago I should have faced you with more confidence. A writer
or a speaker who chose "Art for Art's Sake" for his theme fifty
years ago could be sure of being in the swim, and could feel so
confident of success that he sometimes dressed himself in
esthetic costumes suitable to the occasion—in an embroidered
dressing-gown, perhaps, or a blue velvet suit with a Lord Faunt-
leroy collar; or a toga, or a kimono, and carried a poppy or a lily
or a long peacock's feather in his mediaeval hand. Times have
changed. Not thus can I present either myself or my theme today.
My aim rather is to ask you quietly to reconsider for a few
minutes a phrase which has been much misused and much
abused, but which has, I believe, great importance for us—has,
indeed, eternal importance.

Now we can easily dismiss those peacock's feathers and other
affectations—they are but trifles—but I want also to dismiss a
more dangerous heresy, namely the silly idea that only art matters, an idea which has somehow got mixed up with the idea of
art for art's sake, and has helped to discredit it. Many things,
besides art, matter. It is merely one of the things that matter, and
high though the claims are that I make for it, I want to keep them

in proportion. No one can spend his or her life entirely in the creation or the appreciation of masterpieces. Man lives, and ought to live, in a complex world, full of conflicting claims, and if we simplified them down into the esthetic he would be sterilised. Art for art's sake does not mean that only art matters, and I would also like to rule out such phrases as "The Life of Art," "Living for Art," and "Art's High Mission." They confuse and mislead.

What does the phrase mean? Instead of generalising, let us take a specific instance—Shakespeare's *Macbeth*, for example, and pronounce the words, "*Macbeth* for *Macbeth's* sake." What does that mean? Well, the play has several aspects—it is educational, it teaches us something about legendary Scotland, something about Jacobean England, and a good deal about human nature and its perils. We can study its origins, and study and enjoy its dramatic technique and the music of its diction. All that is true. But *Macbeth* is furthermore a world of its own, created by Shakespeare and existing in virtue of its own poetry. It is in this aspect *Macbeth* for *Macbeth's* sake, and that is what I intend by the phrase "art for art's sake." A work of art—whatever else it may be—is a self-contained entity, with a life of its own imposed on it by its creator. It has internal order. It may have external form. That is how we recognise it.

Take for another example that picture of Seurat's which I saw two years ago in Chicago—"*La Grande Jatte*." Here again there is much to study and to enjoy: the pointillism, the charming face of the seated girl, the nineteenth-century Parisian Sunday sunlight, the sense of motion in immobility. But here again there is something more; "*La Grande Jatte*" forms a world of its own, created by Seurat and existing by virtue of its own poetry: "*La Grande Jatte*" pour "*La Grande Jatte*": *l'art pour l'art*. Like *Macbeth* it has internal order and internal life.

It is to the conception of order that I would now turn. This is important to my argument, and I want to make a digression, and glance at order in daily life, before I come to order in art.

In the world of daily life, the world which we perforce inhabit, there is much talk about order, particularly from statesmen and politicians. They tend, however, to confuse order with orders, just as they confuse creation with regulations. Order, I suggest, is something evolved from within, not something imposed from without; it is an internal stability, a vital harmony, and in the social and political category it has never existed except for the convenience of historians. Viewed realistically, the past is really a series of *dis*orders, succeeding one another by discoverable laws, no doubt, and certainly marked by an increasing growth of human interference, but disorders all the same. So that, speaking as a writer, what I hope for today is a disorder which will be more favourable to artists than is the present one, and which will provide them with fuller inspirations and better material conditions. It will not last—nothing lasts—but there have been some advantageous disorders in the past—for instance, in ancient Athens, in Renaissance Italy, eighteenth-century France, periods in China and Persia—and we may do something to accelerate the next one. But let us not again fix our hearts where true joys are not to be found. We were promised a new order after the first world war through the League of Nations. It did not come, nor have I faith in present promises, by whomsoever endorsed. The implacable offensive of Science forbids. We cannot reach social and political stability for the reason that we continue to make scientific discoveries and to apply them, and thus to destroy the arrangements which were based on more elementary discoveries. If Science would discover rather than apply—if, in other words, men were more interested in knowledge than in power—mankind would be in a far safer position, the stability statesmen talk about would be a possibility, there could be a new order based on vital harmony, and the earthly millennium might approach. But Science shows no signs of doing this: she gave us the internal combustion engine, and before we had digested and assimilated it with terrible pains into our social system, she harnessed the atom, and destroyed any new order that seemed to be evolving. How can man get into harmony with his surroundings when he is constantly altering them? The future of our race is, in this direction, more unpleasant than we care to admit, and it has sometimes seemed to me that its best chance lies through apathy, uninventiveness, and inertia. Universal exhaustion might promote that Change of Heart which is at present so briskly recommended from a thousand pulpits. Universal exhaustion would certainly be a new experience. The human race has never undergone it, and is still too perky to admit that it may be coming and might result in a sprouting of new growth through the decay.

I must not pursue these speculations any further—they lead me too far from my terms of reference and maybe from yours. But I do want to emphasise that order in daily life and in history, order in the social and political category, is unattainable under our present psychology.

Where is it attainable? Not in the astronomical category, where it was for many years enthroned. The heavens and the earth have become terribly alike since Einstein. No longer can we find a reassuring contrast to chaos in the night sky and look up with George Meredith to the stars, the army of unalterable law, or listen for the music of the spheres. Order is not there. In the entire universe there seem to be only two possibilities for it. The first of them—which again lies outside my terms of reference— is the divine order, the mystic harmony, which according to all religions is available for those who can contemplate it. We must admit its possibility, on the evidence of the adepts, and we must believe them when they say that it is attained, if attainable, by prayer. "O thou who changest not, abide with me," said one of its poets. *"Ordina questo amor, o tu che m'ami,"* said another: "Set love in order, thou who lovest me." The existence of a divine order, though it cannot be tested, has never been disproved.

The second possibility for order lies in the esthetic category, which is my subject here: the order which an artist can create in his own work, and to that we must now return. A work of art, we are all agreed, is a unique product. But why? It is unique not because it is clever or noble or beautiful or enlightened or original or sincere or idealistic or useful or educational—it may embody any of those qualities—but because it is the only material object in the universe which may possess internal harmony. All the others have been pressed into shape from outside, and when their mould is removed they collapse. The work of art stands up by itself, and nothing else does. It achieves something which has often been promised by society, but always delusively. Ancient Athens made a mess—but the *Antigone* stands up. Renaissance Rome made a mess—but the ceiling of the Sistine got painted. James I made a mess—but there was *Macbeth*. Louis XIV—but there was *Phèdre*. Art for art's sake? I should just think so, and more so than ever at the present time. It is the one orderly product which our muddling race has produced. It is the cry of a thousand sentinels, the echo from a thousand labyrinths; it is the lighthouse which cannot be hidden: *c'est le meilleur témoignage que nous puissions donner de notre dignité*. *Antigone* for *Antigone's* sake, *Macbeth* for *Macbeth's*, "*La Grande Jatte*" *pour* "*La Grande Jatte*."

If this line of argument is correct, it follows that the artist will tend to be an outsider in the society to which he has been born, and that the nineteenth-century conception of him as a Bohemian was not inaccurate. The conception erred in three particulars: it postulated an economic system where art could be a full-time job, it introduced the fallacy that only art matters, and it overstressed idiosyncrasy and waywardness—the peacock-feather aspect— rather than order. But it is a truer conception than the one which prevails in official circles on my side of the Atlantic—I don't know about yours: the conception which treats the artists as if he were a particularly bright government advertiser and encourages him to be friendly and matey with his fellow citizens, and not to give himself airs.

Estimable is mateyness, and the man who achieves it gives many a pleasant little drink to himself and to others. But it has no traceable connection with the creative impulse, and probably acts as an inhibition on it. The artist who is seduced by mateyness may stop himself from doing the one thing which he, and he alone, can do—the making of something out of words or sounds or paint or clay or marble or steel or film which has internal harmony and presents order to a permanently disarranged planet. This seems worth doing, even at the risk of being called uppish by journalists. I have in mind an article which was published some years ago in the London *Times*, an article called "The Eclipse of the Highbrow," in which the "Average Man" was exalted, and all contemporary literature was censured if it did not toe the line, the precise position of the line being naturally known to the writer of the article. Sir Kenneth Clark, who was at that time director of our National Gallery, commented on this pernicious doctrine in a letter which cannot be too often quoted. "The poet and the artist," wrote Clark, "are important precisely because they are not average men; because in sensibility, intelligence, and power of invention they far exceed the average."

These memorable words, and particularly the words "power of invention," are the Bohemian's passport. Furnished with it, he slinks about society, saluted now by a brickbat and now by a penny, and accepting either of them with equanimity. He does not consider too anxiously what his relations with society may be, for he is aware of something more important than that—namely the invitation to invent, to create order, and he believes he will be better placed for doing this if he attempts detachment. So round and round he slouches, with his hat pulled over his eyes, and maybe with a louse in his beard, and—if he really wants one —with a peacock's feather in his hand.

If our present society should disintegrate—and who dare prophesy that it won't?—this old-fashioned and démodé figure will become clearer: the Bohemian, the outsider, the parasite, the rat—one of those figures which have at present no function either in a warring or a peaceful world. It may not be dignified to be a rat, but many of the ships are sinking, which is not dignified either—the officials did not build them properly. Myself, I would sooner be a swimming rat than a sinking ship—at all events I can look around me for a little longer—and I remember how one of us, a rat with particularly bright eyes called Shelley, squeaked out, "Poets are the unacknowledged legislators of the world," before he vanished into the waters of the Mediterranean.

What laws did Shelley propose to pass? None. The legislation of the artist is never formulated at the time, though it is sometimes discerned by future generations. He legislates through creating. And he creates through his sensitiveness and his power to impose form. Without form the sensitiveness vanishes. And form is as important today, when the human race is trying to ride the whirlwind, as it ever was in those less agitating days of the past, when the earth seemed solid and the stars fixed, and the discoveries of science were made slowly, slowly. Form is not tradition. It alters from generation to generation. Artists always seek a new technique, and will continue to do so as long as their work excites them. But form of some kind is imperative. It is the surface crust of the internal harmony, it is the outward evidence of order.

My remarks about society may have seemed too pessimistic, but I believe that society can only represent a fragment of the human spirit, and that another fragment can only get expressed through art. And I wanted to take this opportunity, this vantage ground, to assert not only the existence of art, but its pertinacity. Looking back into the past, it seems to me that that is all there has ever been: vantage grounds for discussion and creation, little vantage grounds in the changing chaos, where bubbles have been blown and webs spun, and the desire to create order has found temporary gratification, and the sentinels have managed to utter their challenges, and the huntsmen, though lost individually, have heard each other's calls through the impenetrable wood, and the lighthouses have never ceased sweeping the thankless seas. In this pertinacity there seems to me, as I grow older, something more and more profound, something which does in fact concern people who do not care about art at all.

In conclusion, let me summarise the various categories that have laid claim to the possession of Order.

(1) The social and political category. Claim disallowed on the evidence of history and of our own experience. If man altered psychologically, order here might be attainable; not otherwise.

(2) The astronomical category. Claim allowed up to the present century, but now disallowed on the evidence of the physicists.

(3) The religious category. Claim allowed on the evidence of the mystics.

(4) The esthetic category. Claim allowed on the evidence of various works of art, and on the evidence of our own creative impulses, however weak these may be, or however imperfectly they may function. Works of art, in my opinion, are the only objects in the material universe to possess internal order, and that is why, though I don't believe that only art matters, I do believe in Art for Art's Sake.

E. M. FORSTER   Born in England in 1879, he studied at Cambridge and was early associated with the so-called Bloomsbury Group. Though not a prolific writer, he has produced several novels, a biography, two volumes of short stories and two of essays. His *A Passage to India* (1924) is one of the great novels of the twentieth century.

"Art for Art's Sake" (1949) In this convincing exposition of an osten-sibly unfashionable position the author manages, without loss of seri-ousness or conviction, to retain the light touch. He is expert and un-selfconscious in scattering relevant literary allusions, and throughout one can hear the urbane voice of the experienced novelist and man of the world.

1.*Why should the artist be a bohemian? 2. How does Forster achieve an air of casualness, of non-solemnity, in this highly serious essay?*

WAYNE C. BOOTH

Telling and Showing

AUTHORITATIVE "TELLING" IN EARLY NARRATION

One of the most obviously artificial devices of the storyteller is
the trick of going beneath the surface of the action to obtain a
reliable view of a character's mind and heart. Whatever our ideas
may be about the natural way to tell a story, artifice is unmistakably present whenever the author tells us what no one in
so-called real life could possibly know. In life we never know
anyone but ourselves by thoroughly reliable internal signs, and
most of us achieve an all too partial view even of ourselves. It
is in a way strange, then, that in literature from the very beginning we have been told motives directly and authoritatively
without being forced to rely on those shaky inferences about
other men which we cannot avoid in our own lives.

"There was a man in the land of Uz, whose name was Job; and
that man was perfect and upright, one that feared God, and es-
chewed evil." With one stroke the unknown author has given us
a kind of information never obtained about real people, even
about our most intimate friends. Yet it is information that we
must accept without question if we are to grasp the story that
is to follow. In life if a friend confided his view that *his* friend
was "perfect and upright," we would accept the information with
qualifications imposed by our knowledge of the speaker's char-

acter or of the general fallibility of mankind. We could never trust even the most reliable of witnesses as completely as we trust the author of the opening statement about Job.

We move immediately in Job to two scenes presented with no privileged information whatever: Satan's temptation of God and Job's first losses and lamentations. But we conclude the first section with another judgment which no real event could provide for any observer: "In all this Job sinned not, nor charged God foolishly." How do we know that Job sinned not? Who is to pronounce on such a question? Only God himself could know with certainty whether Job charged God foolishly. Yet the author pronounces judgment, and we accept his judgment without question.

It might at first appear that the author does not require us to rely on his unsupported word, since he gives us the testimonial of God himself, conversing with Satan, to confirm his view of Job's moral perfection. And after Job has been pestered by his three friends and has given his own opinion about his experience, God is brought on stage again to confirm the truth of Job's view. But clearly the reliability of God's statements ultimately depends on the author himself; it is he who names God and assures us that this voice is truly His.

This form of artificial authority has been present in most narrative until recent times. Though Aristotle praises Homer for speaking in his own voice less than other poets, even Homer writes scarcely a page without some kind of direct clarification of motives, of expectations, and of the relative importance of events. And though the gods themselves are often unreliable, Homer—the Homer we know—is not. What he tells us usually goes deeper and is more accurate than anything we are likely to learn about real people and events. In the opening lines of the *Iliad,* for example, we are told, under the half-pretense of an invocation, precisely what the tale is to be about: "the anger of Peleus' son Achilleus and its devastation."[1] We are told directly that we are to care more about the Greeks than the Trojans. We are told that they were "heroes" with "strong souls." We are told that it was the will of Zeus that they should be "the delicate feasting of dogs." And we learn that the particular conflict be-

[1] Trans. Richmond Lattimore (Chicago, 1951). All quotations are from this translation.

tween Agamemnon, "the lord of men," and "brilliant" Achilles was
set on by Apollo. We could never be sure of any of this information in real life, yet we are sure as we move through the *Iliad*
with Homer constantly at our elbow, controlling rigorously our
beliefs, our interests, and our sympathies. Though his commentary is generally brief and often disguised as simile, we learn
from it the precise quality of every heart; we know who dies
innocent and who guilty, who foolish and who wise. And we
know, whenever there is any reason for us to know, what the
characters are thinking: "the son of Tydeus pondered doubt-
fully/ . . . . Three times in his heart and spirit he pondered
turning . . ." (Book VIII, ll. 167–69).

In the *Odyssey* Homer works in the same explicit and systematic way to keep our judgments straight. Though E. V. Rieu
is no doubt correct in calling Homer an "impersonal" and "objective" author, in the sense that the life of the real Homer cannot be discovered in his work,[2] Homer "intrudes" deliberately and
obviously to insure that our judgment of the "heroic," "resource-
ful," "admirable," "wise" Odysseus will be sufficiently favorable.
"Yet all the gods were sorry for him, except Poseidon, who pursued the heroic Odysseus with relentless malice till the day when
he reached his own country."

Indeed, the major justification of the opening scene in the
palace of Zeus is not as mere exposition of the facts of Odysseus'
plight. What Homer requires of us is sympathetic involvement in
that plight, and Athene's opening reply to Zeus provides authoritative judgment on what is to follow. "It is for Odysseus that my
heart is wrung—the wise but unlucky Odysseus, who has been
parted so long from all his friends and is pining on a lonely island
far away in the middle of the seas." To her accusation of neglect,
Zeus replies, "How could I ever forget the admirable Odysseus?
He is not only the wisest man alive but has been the most generous in his offerings. . . . It is Poseidon . . . who is so implacable
towards him. . . ."

***

[2] The *Odyssey*, trans. E. V. Rieu (Penguin ed., 1959), p. 10. The quotations that follow are from Rieu's translation, Books I–IV. Different translations give different emphases to Homer's moral judgments, and some use
less forceful epithets than does Rieu. But no translator has been able to portray a neutral Homer.

When we come to Odysseus' enemies, the poet again does not hesitate either to speak in his own person or to give divine testimony. Penelope's suitors must look bad to us; Telemachus must be admired. Not only does Homer dwell on Athene's approval of Telemachus, he lays on his own direct judgments with bright colors. The "insolent," "swaggering," and "ruffianly" suitors are contrasted to the "wise" (though almost helplessly young) Telemachus and the "good" Mentor. "Telemachus now showed his good judgment." Mentor "showed his good will now by rising to admonish his compatriots." We seldom encounter the suitors without some explicit attack by the poet: "This was their boastful way, though it was they who little guessed how matters really stood." And whenever there might be some doubt about where a character stands, Homer sets us straight: " 'My Queen,' replied Medon, who was by no means a villain . . . ." Hundreds of pages later, when Medon is spared from Odysseus' slaughter, we can hardly be surprised.

The result of all this direct guidance, when it is joined with Athene's divine attestation that the gods "have no quarrel" with Telemachus and have settled that he "shall come home safe," is to leave us, as we enter upon Odysseus' first adventure in Book Five, perfectly clear about what we should hope for and what fear; we are unambiguously sympathetic toward the heroes and contemptuous of the suitors. It need hardly be said that another poet, working with the same episodes but treating them from the suitors' point of view, could easily have led us into the same adventures with radically different hopes and fears.

Direct and authoritative rhetoric of the kind we have seen in Job and in Homer's works has never completely disappeared from fiction. But as we all know, it is not what we are likely to find if we turn to a typical modern novel or short story.

Jim had a great trick that he used to play w'ile he was travelin'. For instance, he'd be ridin' on a train and they'd come to some little town like, well, like, we'll say, like Benton. Jim would look out of the train window and read the signs on the stores.

For instance, they'd be a sign, "Henry Smith, Dry Goods." Well, Jim would write down the name and the name of the town and when he got to wherever he was goin' he'd mail back a postal card to Henry Smith at Benton and not sign no name to it, but he'd write on the card, well, somethin' like "Ask your wife about that book agent that spent the afternoon last week," or "Ask your Missus who kept her from gettin' lonesome the last time you was in Carterville." And he'd sign the card, "A Friend."

Of course, he never knew what really come of none of these jokes, but he could picture what probably happened and that was enough. . . . Jim was a card.

Most readers of Lardner's "Haircut" (1926) have recognized that Lardner's opinion of Jim is radically different here from the speaker's. But no one in the story has said so. Lardner is not present to say so, not, at least, in the sense that Homer is present in his epics. Like many other modern authors, he has effaced himself, renounced the privilege of direct intervention, retreated to the wings and left his characters to work out their own fates upon the stage.

In sleep she knew she was in her bed, but not the bed she had lain down in a few hours since, and the room was not the same but it was a room she had known somewhere. Her heart was a stone lying upon her breast outside of her; her pulses lagged and paused, and she knew that something strange was going to happen, even as the early morning winds were cool through the lattice. . . .

Now I must get up and go while they are all quiet. Where are my things? Things have a will of their own in this place and hide where they like. . . . Now what horse shall I borrow for this journey I do not mean to take? . . . Come now, Graylie, she said, taking the bridle, we must outrun Death and the Devil. . . .

The relation between author and spokesman is more complex here. Katherine Anne Porter's Miranda ("Pale Horse, Pale Rider" [1936]) cannot be simply classified, like Lardner's barber, as morally and intellectually deficient; the ironies at work among character, author, and reader are considerably more difficult to describe. Yet the problem for the reader is essentially the same as in "Haircut." The story is presented without comment, leaving the reader without the guidance of explicit evaluation.

Since Flaubert, many authors and critics have been convinced that "objective" or "impersonal" or "dramatic" modes of narration are naturally superior to any mode that allows for direct appearances by the author or his reliable spokesman. Sometimes . . .

the complex issues involved in this shift have been reduced to a convenient distinction between "showing," which is artistic, and "telling," which is inartistic. "I shall not *tell* you anything," says a fine young novelist in defense of his art. "I shall allow you to eavesdrop on my people, and sometimes they will tell the truth and sometimes they will lie, and you must determine for yourself when they are doing which. You do this every day. Your butcher says, 'This is the best,' and you reply, 'That's you saying it.' Shall my people be less the captive of their desires than your butcher? I can *show* much, but show only. . . . You will no more expect the novelist to tell you precisely *how* something is said than you will expect him to stand by your chair and hold your book." [3]

But the changed attitudes toward the author's voice in fiction raise problems that go far deeper than this simplified version of point of view would suggest. Percy Lubbock taught us forty years ago to believe that "the art of fiction does not begin until the novelist thinks of his story as a matter to be *shown*, to be so exhibited that it will tell itself."[4] He may have been in some sense right—but to say so raises more questions than it answers.

Why is it that an episode "told" by Fielding can strike us as more fully realized than many of the scenes scrupulously "shown" by imitators of James or Hemingway? Why does some authorial commentary ruin the work in which it occurs, while the prolonged commentary of *Tristram Shandy* can still enthral us? What, after all, does an author do when he "intrudes" to "tell" us something about his story? Such questions force us to consider closely what happens when an author engages a reader fully with a work of fiction; they lead us to a view of fictional technique which necessarily goes far beyond the reductions that we have sometimes accepted under the concept of "point of view."

Two Stories from the "Decameron"

Our task will be simpler if we begin with some stories written long before anyone worried very much about cleaning out the

[3] Mark Harris, "Easy Does It Not," in *The Living Novel*, ed. Granville Hicks (New York, 1957), p. 117.
[4] *The Craft of Fiction* (London, 1921), p. 62.

rhetorical impurities from the house of fiction. The stories in Boccaccio's *Decameron,* for example, seem extremely simple—perhaps even simple-minded and inept—if we ask of them the questions which many modern stories invite us to ask. It is bad enough that the characters are what we call two-dimensional, with no revealed depths of any kind; what is much worse, the "point of view" of the narrator shifts among them with a total disregard for the kind of technical focus or consistency generally admired today. But if we read these stories in their own terms, we soon discover a splendid and complex skill underlying the simplicity of the effect.

The material of the ninth story of the fifth day is in itself conventional and shallow indeed. There was once a young lover, Federigo, who impoverished himself courting a chaste married woman, Monna Giovanna. Rejected, he withdrew to a life of poverty, with only a beloved falcon remaining of all his former possessions. The woman's husband died. Her son, who had grown fond of Federigo's falcon, became seriously ill and asked Monna to obtain the falcon for his comfort. She reluctantly went to Federigo to request the falcon. Federigo was overwhelmed with excitement by her visit, and he was determined, in spite of his poverty, to entertain her properly. But his cupboard was bare, so he killed the falcon and served it to her. They discovered their misunderstanding, and the mother returned empty-handed to her boy, who soon died. But the childless widow, impressed by Federigo's generous gesture in offering his falcon, chose him for her second husband.

Such a story, reduced in this way to a bare outline, could have been made into any number of fully realized plots with radically different effects. It could have been a farce, stressing Federigo's foolish extravagance, his ridiculous antics in trying to think of something to serve his beloved for breakfast, and the absurdity of the surprise ending. It could have been a meditative or a comic piece on the ironical twists of fate, emphasizing the transformation in Monna from proud resistance to quick surrender—something on the order of Christopher Fry's *A Phoenix Too Frequent* as derived from Petronius. It could have been a sardonic tale written from the point of view of the husband and son who, like the falcon, must be killed off, as it were, to make the survivors happy. And so on.

As it is, every stroke is in a direction different from these. The finished tale is designed to give the reader the greatest possible pleasure in the sympathetic comedy of Monna's and Federigo's deserved good fortune, to make the reader delight in this instance of the announced theme for all the tales told on the fifth day: "good fortune befalling lovers after divers direful or disastrous adventures."[5] Though one never views these characters or their "direful or disastrous adventures" in anything like a tragic light, and though, in fact, one laughs at the excesses of Federigo's passion and at his willingness to pursue it even to poverty, our laughter must always be sympathetic. Much as Federigo deserves his disasters, in the finished tale he also deserves the supreme good fortune of winning Monna.

To insure our pleasure in such an outcome—a pleasure which might have been mild indeed considering that there are nine other tales attempting something like the same effect—the two main characters must be established with great precision. First the heroine, Monna Giovanna, must be felt to be thoroughly worthy of Federigo's "extravagant" love. In a longer, different kind of story, this might have been done by showing her in virtuous action; one could take whatever space were required for episodes dramatizing her as worthy of Federigo's fantastic devotion. But here economy is at least as important as precision. And the economical method of imposing her virtues on the reader is for the narrator to *tell* us about them, supporting his telling with some judiciously chosen, and by modern standards very brief and unrealistic, episodes. These can be of two kinds, either in the form of what James was later to call "going behind" to reveal the true workings of the heroine's mind and heart or in the form of overt action. Thus, the narrator begins by describing her as the "fairest" and "most elegant," and as "no less virtuous than fair." In a simple story of this kind, her beauty and elegance require for validation no more than Federigo's dramatized passion. Our belief in her virtue, however—certainly in Boccaccio a more

[5] Trans. J. M. Rigg (Everyman ed., 1930). All quotations are from this edition.

unlikely gift than beauty and elegance—is supported both by
her sustained chastity in the face of his courtship and, far more
important, by the quality of what is revealed whenever we enter
her thoughts.

Whereupon the lady was silent a while, bethinking her what she
should do. She knew that Federigo had long loved her, and had never
had so much as a single kind look from her: wherefore she said to
herself:—How can I send or go to beg of him this falcon, which by
what I hear is the best that ever flew, and moreover is his sole comfort? And how could I be so unfeeling as to seek to deprive a gentleman of the one solace that is now left him? And so, albeit she very
well knew that she might have the falcon for the asking, she was
perplexed, and knew not what to say, and gave her son no answer. At
length, however, the love she bore the boy carried the day, and she
made up her mind, for his contentment . . . to go herself and fetch him
the falcon.

The interest in this passage lies of course in the moral choice
that it presents and in the effect upon our sentiments that is
implicit in that choice. Though the choice is in one respect a
relatively trivial one, it is far more important than most choices
faced by the characters who people Boccaccio's world. Dramatized at greater length, it could in fact have been made into the
central episode for the story—though the story that resulted
would be a far different one from what we now have. As it is
treated here, the choice is given precisely the degree of importance it should have in the whole. Because we experience Monna's
thoughts and feelings at first hand, we are forced to agree with
the narrator's assessment of her great worth. She is not simply
virtuous in conventional matters like chastity, but she is also
capable of moral delicacy in more fundamental matters: unlike
the majority of Boccaccio's women, she is above any casual manipulation of her lover for her own purposes. Even this delicacy,
admirable in itself, can be overridden by a more important value,
"the love she bore the boy." Yet all this is kept strictly serviceable
to our greater interest in Federigo and the falcon; there is never
any question of our becoming sidetracked into deep psychological
or sentimental involvement with her as a person.

Because the narrator has *told* us what to think of her, and then
shown her briefly in support of his claims, all the while keeping

our sympathy and admiration carefully subordinated to the comic effect of the whole, we can move to the most important episode with our expectations clear and—in their own kind—intense. We can move to Monna's relatively long and wonderfully delicate speech to Federigo requesting the falcon, with our hopes centered clearly on the "good fortune" of their ultimate union.

If all this skilful presentation of the admirable Monna is to succeed, we must see Federigo himself as an equally admirable, though not really heroic, figure. Too much moral stature will spoil the comedy; too little will destroy our desire for his success. It is not enough to show his virtues through his actions; his only admirable act is the gift of the falcon and that might be easily interpreted in itself as a further bit of foolish extravagance. Unless the story is to be lengthened unduly with episodes showing that he is worthy, in spite of his extravagance, the narrator must give us briefly and directly the necessary information about his true character. He is therefore described, unobtrusively but in terms that only an omniscient narrator could use with success, as "gallant," "full of courtesy," "patient," and most important of all, as "more in love than ever before"; the world of *his* desires is thus set off distinctly from the world of many of the other tales, where love is reduced for comic purposes to lust.

These completely straightforward statements of the narrator's opinions are supported by what we see of Federigo's own mind. His comic distress over not having anything to feed his beloved visitor, and his unflinching sacrifice of the bird, are rendered in intimate detail, with frequent—though by modern standards certainly shallow—inside views; his poverty "was brought home to him," he was "distressed beyond measure," he "inwardly" cursed "his evil fortune." "Sorely he longed that the lady might not leave his house altogether unhonoured, and yet to crave help of his own husbandman was more than his pride could brook." All this insures that the wonderful comedy of the breakfast will be the comedy of sympathetic laughter: we are throughout completely in favor of Federigo's suit. And our favor is heightened by the method of presenting the scene of discovery. "No sooner had Federigo apprehended what the lady wanted, than, *for grief that 'twas not in his power to serve her* . . . he fell a-weeping. . . ." At first Monna supposed that " 'twas only because he was loath to part with the brave falcon that he wept." *We* might have made the same mistake but for the author's help provided in the clause I have italicized.

Once we have become assured of his character in this way, Federigo's speeches, like Monna Giovanna's, become the equivalent of inside views, because we know that everything he says is a trustworthy reflection of his true state of mind. His long speech of explanation about the falcon serves, as a result, to confirm all we have learned of him; when he concludes, "I doubt I shall never know peace of mind more," we believe in his sincerity, though of course we know with complete certainty, and have known from the beginning, that the story is to end with "good fortune."

Having seen this much, we need little more. To make Monna the heiress as provided in the will, her son must die in a passage only one or two lines longer than the one or two lines earlier given to the death of the husband. Her "inward commendation" of Federigo's "magnanimity" leads her to the decision to marry him rather than a wealthy suitor: "I had rather have a man without wealth than wealth without a man." Federigo *is* a man, as we know by now. Though his portrait is conventional, "flat," "two-dimensional," it includes everything we need. We can thus accept without irony the narrator's concluding judgment that married to such a wife he lived happily to the end of his days. Fiammetta's auditors all "praised God that He had worthily rewarded Federigo."

If we share in the pleasure of seeing the comic but worthy hero worthily rewarded, the reason is thus not to be found in any inherent quality of the materials but rather in the skilful construction of a living plot out of materials that might have been used in many different ways. The deaths of the husband and son, which in the finished version are merely conveniences for Federigo's exaltation, would in any truly impartial account occupy considerably more space than Federigo's anxiety over not having anything to serve his mistress. Treated impartially, the boy's death would certainly be dramatized as fully as the mother's hesitation about troubling Federigo for his falcon. But the demands of this plot are for a technique that wins us to Federigo's side.

Quite obviously this technique cannot be judged by modern standards of consistency; the story could not have been written from a consistent point of view without stretching it to three times its present length and thereby losing its taut comic force. To tell it entirely through Federigo's eyes would require a much longer introductory section, and the comedy of the visit to fetch the falcon would be partially lost if we did not see more of the preparation for it than Federigo can possibly be aware of. Yet since it is primarily Federigo's story, to see it through Monna's eyes would require a great deal of manipulation and extension. Such conjectural emendations are in a way absurd, since they almost certainly would never have occurred to Boccaccio. But they help to make emphatic the great gap that separates Boccaccio's technique from the more obviously rigorous methods we have come to look for. In this story there is no important revelation of truth, no intensity of illusion, no ironic complexity, no prophetic vision, no rich portrayal of moral ambiguities. There is some incidental irony, it is true, but the greatness of the whole resides in unequivocal intensity not of illusion but of comic delight produced in extraordinarily brief compass.

Any temptation we might have to attribute its success to unconscious or accidental primitivism can be dispelled by looking at the radically different experience offered by other tales. Since his different effects are based on different moral codes, Boccaccio can never assume that his readers will hold precisely the correct attitudes as they approach any one story. He certainly does not assume that his readers will approve of the license of his most licentious tales. Even Dioneo, the most lewd of all the ten narrators, must spend a good deal of energy manipulating us into the camp of those who can laugh with a clear conscience at his bawdy and often cruel stories. In the potentially distressing tale of how the holy man, Rustico, debauches the young and innocent Alibech by teaching her how to put the devil in hell (third day, tenth tale), great care is taken with the character and ultimate fate of the simple-minded girl in order to lead us to laugh at conduct that in most worlds, including the world in which Boccaccio lived, would be considered cruel and sacrilegious rather than comic.

If Dioneo, the lusty young courtier, must use care with his rhetoric in a bawdy tale, Fiammetta, the lovely lady, must use even more when she comes to praise infidelity. On the seventh day the subject is "the tricks which, either for love or for their

deliverance from peril, ladies have heretofore played their husbands, and whether they were by the said husbands detected, or
no." In "The Falcon" Fiammetta worked to build admiration for
the virtue of Federigo and Monna Giovanna; she now (fifth tale)
employs a different rhetoric. Since her task is to insure our delight
in the punishment of a justifiably jealous husband, her commentary tells us directly what is borne out by our views of the husband's mind: he is "a poor creature, and of little sense" who deserves what he gets. More important, she prefaces the story with
a little oration, about one-seventh of the length of the whole story,
setting our values straight: "For which reason, to sum up, I say
that a wife is rather to be commended than censured, if she take
her revenge upon a husband that is jealous without cause."

In support of this general argument, the whole tale is manipu-
lated in such a way as to make the reader desire the comic punishment of the husband. Most of it is seen through the eyes of the
woman, with great stress on her comic suffering at the hands of
the great bullying fool. The climax is his full punishment, in the
form of a clever, lashing speech from his wife. Few readers can
feel that he has received anything but what he deserves when
Fiammetta concludes that the cuckold's wife has now earned her
"charter of indulgence."

These extremes by no means exhaust the variety of norms that
we are led to accept by the shifting rhetoric as we move through
the *Decameron*. The standards of judgment change so radically,
in fact, that it is difficult to discern any figure in Boccaccio's
carpet.[6] . . . What is important here is to recognize the radical
inadequacy of the telling-showing distinction in dealing with the

[6] Erich Auerbach, for example, complains that he can find no basic moral
attitude and no clear approach to reality lying back of all the tales. So long
as he considers what Boccaccio does "for the sake of the comic effect," he
has nothing but praise for his "critical sense" of the world, "firm yet elastic
in perspective, which, without abstract moralizing, allots phenomena their
specific, carefully nuanced moral value" (*Mimesis: The Representation of
Reality in Western Literature* [Berne, 1946], trans. Willard Trask [Anchor
Books ed., 1957], p. 193). It is only on the level of the most general qualities,
common to all the stories despite the differing needs of the moment, that
Auerbach encounters difficulties and complains of the "vagueness and uncertainty" of Boccaccio's "early humanism" (p. 202). Auerbach's account is
invaluable in showing how Boccaccio's style, in so far as it is common to all
of the tales, serves as a kind of rhetoric convincing the reader of the reality
of his world.

practice of this one author. Boccaccio's artistry lies not in adherence to any one supreme manner of narration but rather in his ability to order various forms of telling in the service of various forms of showing.

THE AUTHOR'S MANY VOICES

. . . [Most] of the more important arguments for authorial objectivity or impersonality . . . call for eliminating certain overt signs of the author's presence. As we might expect, however, one man's objectivity is another man's bête noire. If we are to have any degree of clarity as we make our way through attacks on the author's voice, we must have some preliminary notion of the variety of forms that voice can take, both in fiction and in attacks on fiction. What is it, in fact, that we might expunge if we attempted to drive the author from the house of fiction?

First, we must erase all direct addresses to the reader, all commentary in the author's own name. When the author of the *Decameron* speaks to us directly, in both the introduction and conclusion, whatever illusion we may have had that we are dealing immediately with Fiammetta and her friends is shattered. An astonishing number of authors and critics since Flaubert have agreed that such direct, unmediated commentary will not do. And even those authors who would allow it have often, like E. M. Forster, forbidden it except on certain limited subjects.[7]

But what, really, is "commentary"? If we agree to eliminate all personal intrusions of the kind used by Fielding, do we then agree to expunge less obtrusive comment? Is Flaubert violating his own principles of impersonality when he allows himself to tell us that in such and such a place one finds the worst Neufchatel cheeses of the entire district, or that Emma was "incapable of understanding what she didn't experience, or of recognizing anything that wasn't expressed in conventional terms"?[8]

Even if we eliminate all such explicit judgments, the author's presence will be obvious on every occasion when he moves into

[7] Forster would not allow the author to take "the reader into his confidence about his characters," since "intimacy is gained but at the expense of illusion and nobility." But he allows the author to take the reader into his confidence "about the universe" (*Aspects of the Novel* [London, 1927], pp. 111–12).

[8] *Madame Bovary*, trans. Francis Steegmuller (New York, 1957), p. 80.

or out of a character's mind—when he "shifts his point of view," as we have come to put it. Flaubert tells us that Emma's little attentions to Charles were "never, as he believed, for his sake . . . but for her own, out of exasperated vanity" (p. 69). It is clearly Flaubert who constructs this juxtaposition of Emma's motive with Charles' belief about the motive, and the same obtrusive "voice" is evident whenever a new mind is introduced. When Emma's father bids farewell to Emma and Charles, he remembers "his own wedding, his own earlier days. . . . He, too, had been very happy. . . . He felt dismal, like a stripped and empty house" (pp. 34–35). This momentary shift to Rouault is Flaubert's way of providing us with an evaluation of the marriage and a sense of what is to come. If we are troubled by all reminders of the author's presence, we shall be troubled here.

But if we are to object to this, why not go the next step and object to all inside views, not simply those that require a shift in point of view. In life such views are not to be had. The act of providing them in fiction is itself an obtrusion by the author.[9]

For that matter, we must object to the reliable statements of any dramatized character, not just the author in his own voice, because the act of narration as performed by even the most highly dramatized narrator is itself the author's presentation of a prolonged "inside view" of a character. When Fiammetta says "the love she bore the boy carried the day," she is giving us a reliable inside view of Monna, and she is also giving a view of her own evaluation of events. Both are reminders of the author's controlling hand.

But why stop here? The author is present in every speech given by any character who has had conferred upon him, in whatever

[9] Such obtrusions are especially obvious in narration that purports to be historical. And yet intelligent men were until quite recently able to read ostensibly historical accounts, like the Bible, packed with such illicit entries into private minds, with no distress whatever. For us it may seem strange that the writers of the Gospels should claim so much knowledge of what Christ is feeling and thinking. "Moved with pity, he stretched out his hand and touched him" (Mark 1:41). "And Jesus, perceiving in himself that power had gone forth from him . . ." (5:30). Who reported to the authors these internal events? Who told them what occurs in the Garden, when everyone but Jesus is asleep? Who reported to them that Christ prays to God to "let this cup pass"? Such questions, like the question of how Moses could have written an account of his own death and burial, may be indispensable in historical criticism, but they can easily be overdone in literary criticism.

manner, the badge of reliability. Once we know that God is God in Job, once we know that Monna speaks only truth in "The Falcon," the authors speak whenever God and Monna speak. Introducing the great Doctor Larivière, Flaubert says:

He belonged to that great surgical school created by Bichat—that generation, now vanished, of philosopher-practitioners, who cherished their art with fanatical love and applied it with enthusiasm and sagacity. Everyone in his hospital trembled when he was angry; and his students so revered him that the moment they set up for themselves they imitated him as much as they could. . . . Disdainful of decorations . . . hospitable, generous, a father to the poor, practicing Christian virtues although an unbeliever, he might have been thought of as a saint if he hadn't been feared as a devil because of the keenness of his mind [pp. 363–64].

This unambiguous bestowal of authority contributes greatly to the power of the next few pages, in which Larivière judges for us everything that we see. But helpful as he is, he must go—if the author's voice is a fault.

Even here we cannot stop, though many of the critics of the author's voice have stopped here. We can go on and on, purging the work of every recognizably personal touch, every distinctive literary allusion or colorful metaphor, every pattern of myth or symbol; they all implicitly evaluate. Any discerning reader can recognize that they are imposed by the author.[10]

Finally, we might even follow Jean-Paul Sartre and object, in the name of "durational realism," to all evidences of the author's meddling with the natural sequence, proportion, or duration of events. Earlier authors, Sartre says, tried to justify "the foolish business of storytelling by ceaselessly bringing to the reader's attention, explicitly or by allusion, the existence of an author." The existentialist novels, in contrast, will be "toboggans, forgotten, unnoticed," hurling the reader "into the midst of a universe where there are no witnesses." Novels should "exist in the manner of things, of plants, of events, and not at first like products of man."[11]

[10] Speaking of Joyce's *Ulysses*, Edmund Wilson once complained that as soon as "we are aware of Joyce himself systematically embroidering on his text," packing in puzzles, symbols, and puns, "the illusion of the dream is lost" ("James Joyce," *Axel's Castle* [New York, 1931], p. 235).

[11] "Situation of the Writer in 1947," *What Is Literature?* trans. Bernard Frechtman (London, 1950), p. 169.

If this is so, the author must never summarize, never curtail a conversation, never telescope the events of three days into a paragraph. "If I pack six months into a single page, the reader jumps out of the book" (p. 229).

Sartre is certainly right in claiming that all these things are signs of the author's manipulating presence. In *The Brothers Karamazov*, for example, the story of Father Zossima's conversion could logically be placed anywhere. The events of Zossima's story took place long before the novel begins; unless they are to be placed at the beginning, which is out of the question, there is no natural reason for giving them in one place rather than another. Wherever they are placed, they will call attention to the author's selecting presence, just as Homer is glaringly present to us whenever the *Odyssey* takes one of its many leaps back and forth over a nineteen-year period. It is not accident but Dostoevski's careful choice that gives us Zossima's story as the sequel to Ivan's dream of the Grand Inquisitor. It is intended as a judgment on the values implied by that dream, just as everything that happens to Ivan afterward is an explicit criticism of his own ideas. Since the sequence is obviously not dictated by anything other than the author's purposes, it betrays the author's voice, and according to Sartre, it presumably will not do.

But, as Sartre woefully admits, even with all these forms of the author's voice expunged, what we have left will reveal to us a shameful artificiality. Unless the author contents himself with simply retelling The Three Bears or the story of Oedipus in the precise form in which they exist in popular accounts—and even so there must be some choice of *which* popular form to tell—his very choice of what he tells will betray him to the reader. He chooses to tell the tale of Odysseus rather than that of Circe or Polyphemus. He chooses to tell the cheerful tale of Monna and Federigo rather than a pathetic account of Monna's husband and son. He chooses to tell the story of Emma Bovary rather than the potentially heroic tale of Dr. Larivière. The author's voice is as passionately revealed in the decision to write the *Odyssey*, "The Falcon," or *Madame Bovary* as it is in the most obtrusive direct comment of the kind employed by Fielding, Dickens, or George Eliot. Everything he *shows* will serve to *tell*; the line between showing and telling is always to some degree an arbitrary one.

In short, the author's judgment is always present, always evident to anyone who knows how to look for it. Whether its particular forms are harmful or serviceable is always a complex question, a question that cannot be settled by any easy reference to abstract rules. . . . [W]e must never forget that though the author can to some extent choose his disguises, he can never choose to disappear.

✦

Wayne C. Booth   Born in Utah in 1921, he graduated from The University of Chicago, where he is now Dean of the College. His widely acclaimed *The Rhetoric of Fiction*, of which "Telling and Showing" is the first chapter, is a significant contribution to modern criticism.

"Telling and Showing" (1961) Using the Socratic method, the author refutes a common argument by granting its tenets, then exploring them until they are seen to be unsound. The subject of this essay is important to any kind of writing, for the rhetoric of fiction as here defined also applies to non-fiction. Booth's style is lucid and direct, and he utilizes a variety of literary examples and allusions without pedantry or exhibitionism.

✦

1. *How did you display your own control the last time you told a funny story?* 2. *In what ways are Booth's examples especially appropriate to his argument?*

JOHN CIARDI

What Does It Take to Read a Poem?

What does it take to enjoy a poem?
  Let us begin with a really difficult piece of symbolism:

> Hickory, dickory, dock,
> The mouse ran up the clock.
> The clock struck one,
> The mouse ran down,
> Hickory, dickory, dock.

Not really complicated, you say? Consider these questions. What does it mean? Why a clock? Why a mouse? Isn't it fairly unusual for mice to run up clocks? What is the point of inventing this esoteric incident? And since the mouse ran up it and down again, the chances are it's a grandfather clock. What does that signify? And isn't it a fairly obsolete notion? Why did the clock strike one? (To rhyme with "down"? But is "down" a rhyme for "one," or is this another slovenly piece of modernism? Why didn't the poem make the clock strike three and the mouse turn to flee? It didn't, of course, but why?) What is the origin and significance of all these unexplained symbols? Or is this simply nonsense verse? (I find that hard to believe.) And even as nonsense, what is there in this particular combination of sounds and actions (symbolic actions?) that makes this jingle survive a long word-of-mouth transmission in the English voice-box? Why mightn't the poem as easily have read:

From *Dialogue with an Audience* by John Ciardi. Copyright 1949, 1963 by John Ciardi. Published by J. B. Lippincott Company.

Thickery, thackery, tea,
An owl flew into the tree.
The tree's down,
The owl's flown,
Thickery, thackery, tea.

I submit: (a) that my parody is a bad poem, that the original is a good one, and that a serious and learned series of lectures might be devoted to the reasons why each is so; (b) that none of the questions I have raised are meaningless and that in fact many critics have made a career of asking this sort of question of less perfect poems; and (c) that neither you nor I know what the poem "means." I further submit that such considerations have frightened many readers away from good poems.

But—and this is the point—the child in whose babble the poem is immediate and alive has no critical theories and no troubles. He is too busy enjoying the pleasure of poetry. The moral is obvious: do not ask the poem to be more rational than you are. The way to read a poem is with pleasure: with the child's pleasure in tasting the syllables on his tongue, with the marvel of the child's eye that can really see the mouse run up the clock, be panic-stricken, and run down again, with the child's hand-clapping, rhythmic joy. In short, to read a poem, come prepared for delight.

But if a child can do it why can't you?

That question deserves attention, but before considering it, I should like to say one thing of which I am fairly certain: everyone writes poetry sometime in his life. Bad poetry is what we all have in common. Such poetry generally occurs in three categories: as invective, as obscenity, and as love-yelps.

The obscenity I assume everyone to be capable of documenting. Here is an example of invective:

Billy Billy, dirty coat
Stinks like a nanny goat

And here is a fair example of the love-yelp:

Have you ever been in love?
I ask you: have you ever been in love?
Have you?

I have .... I know!

"Billy Billy," you will recognize as a kind of "Georgie-Porgie pud-din' and pie," but if you think it peculiar to your childhood or to grandfather's I urge you to look in the encyclopedia under Fescen-nine for an inkling of the antiquity of man's pleasure in jingling taunts at other men. "Billy Billy," as nearly as I know, was com-posed in our fourth-grade schoolyard by a former young poet now in the coal business and was used to taunt our local sloven, who has since washed up, cleaned up, grown up, and joined the police force. Almost inevitably it earned its young author a punch in the nose: a fair example of the way criticism operates in our society to kill the poetic impulse. The love-yelp, a reasonably deplorable specimen of its class, was submitted for the Tufts College literary magazine when I was an undergraduate assistant editor. Anyone who will take the trouble to be reasonably honest can almost cer-tainly summon from himself examples of at least one of these forms he has attempted at one time or another, and enjoyed attempting.

If, then, the impulse to bad poetry is so widespread (though I insist that "Billy Billy" is not at all bad), why is it so few people enjoy reading what passes as good poetry? Why is it, for example, that in a nation of 146,000,000 presumably literate people, the average sale for a book of poems is about five hundred copies? Is it that the pleasures and outlets one finds in composing are purely private—that only one's own creation, good or bad, is interesting? Considering the variety of egos that have banded together to pass as the human race, that seems one reasonably good guess, but there is obviously more to it.

First, it seems fairly obvious that the process of growing up in a nuts-and-bolts world inhibits the poetic impulse in most people. Somewhere along the line, they learn to say, "Let's face it; we must be practical." So the literalist on his rostrum demands the rational: "What *does* hickory-dickory-dock *mean*? It has to mean *some-thing*." It does indeed, but not anything you can paraphrase, not anything you can prove. To see what it does mean, you need only go read Mother Goose to a child: you will then be observing a natural audience busy with the process of receiving poetry as it was intended to be received.

Point one, then, is delight: if you mean to enjoy the poem as a poem, stop cross-examining it, stop trying to force it to "make sense." The poem *is* sense. Or if you must cross-examine, remember at least that the third degree is not the poem. Most poems do reveal themselves most richly after close examination, but the examination is, at best, only a preparation for reading the poem. It is never the reading itself.

More precisely put, an understanding of the rational surfaces of the poem (the prose part of the poem) may, in some cases, point a direction toward the poem. The poem is never experienced, however, until it is felt in the same complex of mind and nerve from which it arose—the subconscious. That experience sometimes happens immediately, and is sometimes helped along by our conscious (rational) perceptions. But to substitute rational analysis for the larger contact of the subconscious is to reject the poem. The kind of communication that happens in a poem is infinitely closer to that of music than to that of prose.

Second, poetry must never be read as an exercise in "reading-speed," that deplorable mental-mangle for increasing the rate of destruction of textbook English. The fastest reader is not the best reader any more than the best conductor of Beethoven is the man who gets the orchestra through the *Eroica* in the shortest elapsed time. Why not take a stop watch to the symphony, if speed is your measure? Obviously because music declares its own pace. But so does good poetry. By rhyme, by the word-values of the poem, by the sequence of syllables, and by all these taken together, good poetry contains its own notation. "We broke the brittle bright stubble like chaff" can no more be read at the same rate as "Bury the great duke with an Empire's lamentation" than *allegro vivace* can intelligently be played *adagio*.

Point two, then: leave your efficiency out of it and look for the notation within the poem. Every poem is in part an effort to reconstruct the poet's speaking voice. Listen for it. Listen to the poet on records and at public readings(but know the poems well before you do). You may discover more than you could have foreseen. In any case, when reading a book of poems you must be prepared to linger. That thin volume will take at least as much reading as a detective story.

Third (and of course related to our second consideration): read it aloud. Few poems will come whole at one hearing. Few piano pieces will. But once you have *learned* either, their pleasure is always ready to repeat itself. Even difficult poems are meant to go into the voice box. Put them there.

Fourth: there are still readers who must be specifically cautioned that twentieth-century poetry is not nineteenth-century poetry. That fact may seem rather obvious, but the point is not frivolously made. Your teachers and mine were products of nineteenth-century culture, and almost certainly the first poems you were given to read were nineteenth-century poems. And praise nineteenth-century literature as you will (and as all must), there yet remains the fact that it tended to take itself much too seriously. The mind of man seemed to suffer the illusion that it lived in a cathedral, and when man spoke he was not only too likely to pontificate, but he was pre-inclined to select from experience only the vast, the lofty, the divine-in-nature. The result was what Cleanth Brooks has called "the poetry of high-seriousness." Opposed to that tradition is the poetry of "wit," poetry in which the mind most definitely does not live in a cathedral but in the total world, open to the encounter of all sorts of diverse elements and prepared to take them as they come, fusing fleas and sunsets, love and Charley horses, beauty and trivia into what is conceived to be a more inclusive range of human experience. Judge the poet of "wit" by the standards of "high-seriousness" and he will likely appear crass and obnoxious; judge the poet of high-seriousness by the standards of wit and he will likely appear a rather pompous and myopic ass.

The point, then, is quite simple: judge the poet by his intent: if you tend to the illusion that you are on your way to church when you pick up a poem, stop off at the supermarket and watch man against his background of groceries for a while. The church is still next door, and I am quite sure that one of the things "modern" (whatever that is) poetry is trying to say is that the cities of our life contain both church spires and Wheaties, and that both of them, for better or worse, impinge upon man's consciousness, and are therefore the material of poetry.

A fifth consideration I can best present by asking a question: how do you, reader, distinguish between your responses to a very bad portrait of dear old Aunt Jane, and a very good one of Old Skinflint, the gentleman who holds your mortgage? The question is one that splits the reading audience straight down the middle. The tenacity with which the ladies of the poetry societies will hold on to Aunt Jane with a bluebird in her hair, and the persistency with which they reject all-that-is-not-bluebirds, reaches so far into the problem of a satisfactory approach to poetry (both reading and writing) that it has been necessary to evolve two terms: "poetry" for that which exists as an art form, "poesy" for that which exists as the sentimental bluebird in Aunt Jane's hair. Confusion is inevitable when these terms are not properly applied. The writers and readers of poesy always refer to their matter as poetry or true poetry, and defend it with as much violence as possible from "the ugly." Here is a piece of poesy—a sonnet of course:

THRENODY

Truth is a golden sunset far away
Above the misty hills. Its burning eye
Lights all the fading world. A bird flies by
Alive and singing on the dying day.
O mystic world, what shall the proud heart say
When beauty flies on beauty beautifully
While blue-gold hills look down to watch it die
Into the falling miracle of clay?

Say: "I have seen the wing of sunset lift
Into the golden vision of the hills
And truth come flooding through the cloud rift,
And known that souls survive their mortal ills."
Say: "Having seen such beauty in the air
I have seen truth and will no more despair."

"Threnody" is a fair example of what I have learned to call "prop-room poesy." It fills the stage as a poem might, but it fills it with pieces discarded from other poems and left to gather dust in the prop-room of tradition. It makes a stage of the stage, and brings the stage's own dust on as the play, rather than bringing on the life outside the theatre.

The result may look like a poem, but is really no more than a collection of poetic junk. For example: "golden sunsets far away" (question: have you ever seen a non-golden one nearby?), "misty hills," "burning eye," "fading world," "a bird flies by alive and

singing" (question: have you ever seen a non-live one fly by?),
"dying day," "the proud heart." . . .

I have tried many times to explain to the enthusiasts of this
school that any reasonably competent craftsman could concoct
such a poem in a matter of minutes, and with his tongue in his
cheek. I said exactly that from a public platform once and claimed
I could turn out such an illusion-of-the-sonnet in three minutes
flat. I was challenged and given a first line to start with, but I
failed: I discovered it is impossible, simply mechanically, to write
off fourteen lines in three minutes. It took four minutes and
eighteen seconds. The "sonnet" I have quoted above was the
poem produced in answer to that challenge, and by way of further
experimentation I sent it off to a magazine for "traditional" poetry
and had it accepted for publication. In a moment of cowardice I
withdrew the poem for fear someone I respected might see my
name attached to it. I was wrong, of course; no one whose poetic
opinion I could respect would have been reading that magazine.

The fact remains beyond all persuasion, however, that the de-
votees of poesy are violent in their charges against Modern Poetry
(their capitals) as ugly, coarse, immoral, and debased (their
adjectives). My good friend Geraldine Udell, business manager of
Poetry, A Magazine of Verse, the oldest magazine of good poetry
in America, once showed me thirty-four letters received in one
day's mail accusing the magazine of debasing the pure tradition
of English poetry, and enclosing pages of poesy from two magazines of "traditional poetry" as specimens of what should be
printed.

It is, you see, Aunt Jane and Old Skinflint with a vengeance.
Poesy (which is always anti-poetry) wants it pretty. It wants
comfortably worn-out props to which comfortable and vague
reactions are already conditioned. Everyone understands the bluebird in Aunt Jane's hair; the response to it is by now so stereo-
typed that it will do for a birthday card. Poetry, on the contrary,
insists on battering at life, and on making the poem capture the
thing seen and felt in its own unique complex. It does not repeat,
it creates. Therefore, some willingness to dismiss preconception
from the reader's mind is necessary if one is to partake of that vital
process. One is also required to get himself and his own loose-
afflatus out of the way of the poem.

The fifth point then is simple: poesy is not poetry.

A sixth and related consideration follows almost immediately: it concerns the preconception that demands moral affirmation of oneself from a poem, just as poesy demands a loose emotional affirmation of oneself. Consistently adhered to, this application of one's own morality as a test of the poem can lead to ridiculous ends. It would require, for example, the rejection of Milton by all who do not agree with his theology. It might reject beforehand all poems containing the word harlot, since harlots are immoral, and by that test we should have to reject such great lines as Blake's:

> The harlot's cry from street to street
> Shall weave Old England's winding sheet.

Or, shifted to political concern, it might require a new Communist manifesto against any poem in which the lover is rich in his love, since it is bourgeois, decadent, and just plain indecent to be rich.

Similarly, I have observed many present-day reviewers to reject a poem because it seems cheerful ("withdrawal from reality"), because it does not ("defeatist and negativist"), because it is immediately understandable ("facile and slight"), and because it requires rereading ("obscurantist"). These are cartoons, of course, but they are cartoons of a real trend. The simple fact is that none of us can hope to be wholly free of preconceptions of one sort or another. I must confess, for example, that I still find Milton's theology a bit silly, and that my feeling prevents me from experiencing *Paradise Lost* as richly as I might. Even Milton's language creates blocks for me that he could not have intended and for which I am solely responsible. For whatever reason, I cannot read of Satan mounted on his "bad eminence" without an impulse to smile. I don't know why I want to smile at such a phrase, but I am sure the reason is within me and that it has nothing to do with the poem. I am being blocked in this case by a pre-set subjective response. I must, therefore, recognize the obstruction and try to allow for it. Unless I can do so, I am not permitting the poet his right to his own kind of vision and existence.

Point six, then: the poem does not exist to conform moral, political, or religious prejudgments. The poem as a poem is in fact amoral. The poem, I say, not the poet. The poet may be the most moral of men, but when he writes poetry he is performing a ritual dance. He may even sermonize, but if the poem is to succeed as a poem, it must be a dancing sermon. What the poem says is always hickory-dickory-dock, that ineffable, wonderful, everlasting dance of syllables that moves the mouse and winds the clock over and over again, and sends the child to sleep among the swinging nebulae. Or perhaps it is hickory-dickory-God, but still what the poem says is what the child dreams: "Look, Universe, I'm dancing." There is no immorality more wretched than the habit of mind which *will* insist on moralizing that dance.

The last necessity for good reading that I shall discuss here is tradition. If you will grant me the existence of an unintellectualized basis for poetry upon which the responses of all readers may meet, we can probably agree that a fair example of such a response may be found in, say, Juliet on her balcony swooning into moonlight at the sound of Romeo's song rising from the shrubbery. Hers is certainly a non-intellectualized response. It is certainly a living response. And a world-wide one: Black Jade in her moony garden in Peiping will respond in an almost identical way to Pao-yii's serenade from beyond the garden wall.

But wait: let us switch singers. Now Pao-yii is in Veronà under Juliet's balcony, and Romeo is in Peiping outside Black Jade's garden. Both strike up a song. Why is it that both girls now hear not a swooning love-cry but something closer to the sound of sustained gargling? The answer is—Tradition.

For the fact is we are being educated when we know it least. We learn simply by the exposure of living, and what we learn most natively is the tradition in which we live. But the response acquired effortlessly within one tradition will not serve us in another, any more than speaking pure Tuscan will help us in Peiping.

In order to read poetry, then, one must read poetry. One may of course have read only bad poetry, and in that case he will read badly. The criterion Matthew Arnold set forth as "the touchstone method" may well be applied here. This critical theory states simply that all poetry is judged by great poetry. Poetry may be called great only when it has been acclaimed by so many generations of different poetical taste that its merit and universality are beyond dispute. The way to come to a poem, then, is with the memory of great singing in one's inner ear.

Greatness, however, can be a dangerous measure, for it immediately implies rendering a verdict. I for one cannot lose the belief that it is more important to experience the poem than to judge it. Certainly there is real pleasure to be had from poetry no one will ever think of as great or near-great. Certainly, too, every mental action implies a kind of judgment. Nevertheless, it seems to me more desirable in every way for the reader to conceive of himself as a participant in the action of the poem rather than as a trial judge pondering its claim to immortality.

Time, of course, will hand down that verdict, and in a way from which there is no appeal. It may then happen that the verdict will be against modern poets, and against the principles on which they write. But until that verdict has been achieved, it would be well to bear in mind that the reader is as liable to error as the poet, and that when the poem fails to communicate, the failure may as reasonably be charged against the one as against the other.

✓

JOHN CIARDI   Born in Boston in 1916, educated at Tufts and The University of Michigan, he is now professor of English at Rutgers and poetry editor of the *Saturday Review.* He is well known as a poet, critic, lecturer, and translator of Dante.

"*What Does It Take to Read a Poem?*" (1949) The style displays what Ciardi aptly calls "downrightness of tone." It is colloquial and vehement, and it is interspersed with strikingly appropriate quotations. The argument is largely commonsensical, though the questions it raises are subtle and complex.

✓

1. *Try answering Ciardi's questions about "Hickory, dickory, dock."*
2. *Is the seventh necessity for good reading—tradition—a contradiction to the six preceding requirements?*

LEO STEINBERG

The Eye Is a Part of the Mind

We begin with the interrogation of witnesses. Two men are called
to defend the reversal of aesthetic values in their time. The first is
Giorgio Vasari, the tireless biographer to whose *Lives of the
Painters* we owe half the facts and most of the figments current on the artists of the Renaissance. The other, Vasari's junior
by four centuries, is André Malraux, whose *Psychology of Art*[1]
forms a brilliant brief for the moot values of a neo-mystic, modern
taste in art.

Speaking of Masaccio, the great initiator of the naturalist trend
in Western art, Vasari states: "The things made before his time
may be termed paintings merely, and by comparison his (Masaccio's) creations are real."

And Malraux, hailing Manet as the initiator of the modern trend
in art, asks: "What then was painting becoming, now it no longer
imitated or transfigured?" And his answer: "Simply—painting."

A startling consonance this, the "painting merely" of Vasari
and the "simply painting" of Malraux. Strange also that the self-
same epithet should be scorn in one man's mouth and praise in
the other's, and yet for both bear the same connotation.

For what exactly did Vasari have in mind? That Masaccio's
work, and that which flowed from his influence to make the main-

Reprinted from *Partisan Review*, Vol. XX, No. 2 (March–April 1953), by
permission of the author and publisher. © 1953 by *Partisan Review*.

[1] Bollinger Series XXIV, 1949; later revised and published as *The Voices
of Silence*.

stream of the Renaissance, was a true representation of the external world; whereas the earlier Byzantine mosaics were pictorial patterns whose forms were not determined by reality. Being undetermined by nature, he called them "paintings merely"—just as he might have called scholastic metaphysics "thinking merely," since it too formed a speculative system adrift from verifiable experience. Vasari's point was that medieval pictures implied no referent outside themselves. Renaissance painting, on the contrary, was valid because in it every element corresponded with its prototype in nature.

And Malraux? What does *he* mean when he pits the "simply painting" of Manet against the styles of other ages? Why, precisely the same thing. Representational art for him is weighted with extraneous content and transcribed appeal, with reference to things and situations that exist outside the picture frame in general experience. Manet pries art loose from the world. "Modern art," says Malraux, "has liberated painting which is now triumphantly a law unto itself." No longer must a painting borrow its validity from natural analogues. Its meaning—if self-significance can be called meaning—lies wholly within itself. Wherever art is seen with modern eyes—seen, that is to say, as "a certain compelling balance in colors and lines"—there, says Malraux, "a magic casement opens on another world . . . a world incompatible with the world of reality." It was for this incompatibility that Vasari spurned medieval art; it is on this very account that Malraux exalts contemporary painting.

Thus juxtaposed our authors confess that what is here involved is not a difference in aesthetic judgment, nor even in the definition of art. We are dealing rather with two distinct valuations set upon reality, and the overt gap between the Renaissance and the modern aesthetician is evidence of a rift far more deeply grounded.

We will ask later whether either Malraux or Vasari was justified in seeing "merely painting" anywhere. For the moment we may say that Malraux speaks the mind of his generation when he declares that the representation of external nature has nothing to do with art. "Creating a work of art is so tremendous a business," says Clive Bell, "that it leaves no leisure for catching likenesses." As long ago as 1911, Laurence Binyon wrote with satisfaction:

"The theory that art is, above all things, imitative and representative, no longer holds the field with thinking minds." Albert C. Barnes reminds us that only painters "unable to master the means of plastic expression, seek to awaken emotion by portraying objects or situations which have an appeal in themselves. . . . This attraction, though it is all-important in determining popular preference, is plastically and aesthetically irrelevant." And, as Sheldon Cheney insists: "It can hardly be too often repeated that the modernist repudiates the Aristotelian principle 'Art is Imitation.'"

But this position presents a serious quandary, for the first glance at art through the ages shows unmistakably that most of it is dedicated precisely to the imitation of nature, to likeness-catching, to the portrayal of objects and situations—in short, to representation. Now there are three possible formulas by which this contradiction between evidence and creed may be resolved. The first asserts that representation has always been an adventitious element in art—a concession to state, populace or church. Modern art, then, differs from historic art not in essence but in degree of purity. This is the view put forth by Roger Fry and Barnes and their respective schools. The second choice is to concede that representation did function essentially in the arts of the past, and that modern art, by suppressing the outgoing reference, constitutes something radically different and new. This is the implication of such continental critics as Ortega y Gasset and Malraux, who endorse the meaning elements in the historic styles, yet claim for modern art exemption from associated values. It is also (aesthetics makes strange bedfellows!) the view of the bourgeois who repudiates all modern art as an unfunny and too long protracted hoax.

The third alternative is to suggest that modern art has not, after all, abandoned the imitation of nature, and that, in its most powerful expressions, representation is still an essential condition, not an expendable freight. It is this third view which this essay will seek to establish. It will try to show that representation is a central aesthetic function in all art; and that the formalist aesthetic, designed to champion the new abstract trend, was largely based on a misunderstanding and an underestimation of the art it set out to defend.

II

We have said that most historic art is vitally concerned with representation. And lest the word be thought to offer too much latitude, we will commit ourselves further to say that about half the great art generated by mankind is dedicated to the accurate transcription of the sensible world.[2] This is as true of the best paleolithic art as of Egyptian at its finest moments. It applies to the entire Hellenic effort down to third-century Rome.[3] It applies equally to the great Western wave that lies between Giotto and the Post-Impressionists. Nor is it any the less true of Chinese painting—so self-conscious that it operated for a thousand years within six explicit canons; of which the third called for "conformity with nature," or "the drawing of forms which answer to natural forms." All of these schools—and there are as many more —strove for the mastery of nature by convincing imitation.

Perhaps it will be said that artists closer to us in time would not have subscribed to this quest. Here is a sampling of their depositions: Manet declared (Malraux notwithstanding) that he painted what he saw. Van Gogh's avowed aim was to be "simply honest before nature." Cézanne exclaims: "Look at that cloud! I would like to be able to paint that!" And he says: "We must give the picture of what we see, forgetting everything that has appeared in the past." Even for Matisse "the problem is to maintain the intensity of the canvas whilst getting near to verisimilitude."

Such quotations, given a collector's leisure, could be amply multiplied. They are adequately summarized in Constable's dictum which defines the goal of painting as "the pure apprehension of natural fact."

Yet artists and critics, for half a century and more, have been denouncing the representation of nature as a fatal side-stepping of artistic purpose. And whoever has the least pretension to aes-

[2] It would be missing the point to include here only such art as looks convincingly lifelike to us. What matters is the artist's intent to push the truth of his representation to the limits of what is felt to be depictable. The changing pattern of these limits is the preoccupation of the history of art.

[3] "The story of Greek art is the story of a step-by-step discovery of the true nature of appearance by the liberation of vision from its conceptual bonds," wrote Roger Fry (*Last Lectures*, New York, 1939, p. 187).

thetic culture speaks with condescension of "that power which is nothing but technical capacity in the imitation of nature." [4] This famous slur, reverberating in the prejudice of almost every modern connoisseur, has become standard critical jargon. The picturing of overt nature is written off as mere factual reportage, worthy only of the amateur photographer, a mechanical skill, patently uncreative and therefore alien to the essence of art.

The objection to this view is not far to seek. To begin with, "technical capacity in imitation" implies what no one seriously believes: that nature confronts man with a fixed, invariant look. For what else does it mean to speak of "mere skill in copying the model" (the words are Malraux's), but that the model's appearance is an objective fact susceptible of mechanical reproduction? We know better than that. Appearances reach us through the eye, and the eye—whether we speak with the psychologist or the embryologist—is part of the brain and therefore inextricably involved in mysterious cerebral operations. Thus nature presents every generation (and every person who will use his eyes for more than nodding recognitions) with a unique and unrepeated facet of appearance. And the Ineluctible Modality of the Visible —young Dedalus' hypnotic phrase—is a myth that evaporates between any two works of representation. The encroaching archaism of old photographs is only the latest instance of an endless succession in which every new mode of nature-representation eventually resigns its claim to co-identity with natural appearance. And if appearances are thus unstable in the human eye, their representation in art is not a matter of mechanical reproduction but of progressive revelation.

We can therefore assert with confidence that "technical capacity in the imitation of nature" simply does not exist. What does exist is the skill of reproducing handy graphic symbols for natural appearances, of rendering familiar facts by set professional conventions. We have cited a canon from the beginning phase of Chinese painting; here is another from nearer its dead end:

There are ten ways, say the Chinese academicians, of depicting a mountain: by drawing wrinkles like the slashes of a large axe, or wrinkles like the hair on a cow's hide; by brushstrokes wrinkled

[4] The words are taken from Alois Riegl (died 1905).

like a heap of firewood, or like the veins of lotus leaves. The rest are to be wrinkled like the folds of a belt, or the twists of a rope; or like raindrops, or like convoluted clouds, etc.

With rigorous training the Ming painters could, and did, acquire a dazzling proficiency in drawing the right wrinkles so as to evoke some long-assimilated and familiar facts about natural panoramas. They had mastered the skill of applying certain academic tricks for the drawing of mountains—but this is most emphatically not the same as skill in drawing actual mountains. The mechanical, the uncreative element lies not therefore in imitating nature, but in academicism, which is the passionless employment of preformed devices. Representation in art is the fashioning of graphic symbols to act as analogues for certain areas of visual experience. There is every difference between this fashioning of symbols, this transmutation and reduction of experience to symbolic pattern, and the use of symbols ready-made. In works that seem to duplicate a visible aspect of nature we must therefore distinguish between the recitation of a known fact and the discovery thereof, between the dexterous use of tools and their invention.

This distinction must be upheld for all representational art. Seen in this light it becomes quite absurd to charge Victorian academicians with too fastidious an eye for natural forms. Their fault was not, as Roger Fry maintained, "the fervid pursuit of naturalistic appearances," but that they continued to see and represent the facts of nature in spent conventional terms. The so-called naturalism of certain nineteenth-century academicians was worthless because it was impelled by precept and by meritorious example, instead of by pure visual apprehension. These men never imitated nature; they copied earlier imitations and applied those formal principles which, they believed, had made their models so effective. That they sometimes painted from life is, of course, beside the point; for they still saw life in the aspect which their vision was conditioned to expect.[5] Thus the malady of Victorian art (and of some lingering official art today, notably in Soviet Russia) is not naturalism, nor literal representation, but the

[5] Even Sir Joshua Reynolds, in his first Discourse, laments that students "make a drawing rather of what they think the figure ought to be than of what it appears."

presumption to create living art out of impulses long dead and mummified; which ailment is not confined to realistic art. For academicism will blight non-objective figurations and abstractions as readily as illustrative, anecdotal pictures.

This is not to say that a convention invariably chokes artistic creativity. It does so only when too fully conned and understood, when the uphill drive of aspiration is relaxed and the professors of the brush can settle down to mass production. An artist searches for true vision, but having found it, leaves in his successors' hands the blueprint of a new academy. Almost anyone with a modicum of talent and sufficient application can appropriate another man's mode of representation. (Were this not so, the forger's craft would not exist.) But he cannot discover it. He can learn after one lesson in perspective how to give an illusion of depth to a design (an illusion, by the way, based largely on our habit of routine consent). But this lesson will not arm him with the passion of an early Florentine who first ventures through the picture plane and, like daydreaming Alice, finds a wonderland beyond. The same rules of perspective mean one thing at the Beaux Arts; in Mantegna's studio, in Uccello's workship, they meant quite another. Space, that had congealed into a solid crust during the Middle Ages, was here dented, pierced and vaporized. Bodies were inserted and, against resisting pressure, as on reluctant hinges, pivoted into depth. There is in Uccello's work a tensity which springs directly from his craving to know how bodies will behave in the *terra incognita* known as the third dimension. And the reports of his discoveries, such as the bold foreshortenings in *The Battle of San Romano,* are proclaimed in tense and urgent gestures. And what is true of perspective applies equally to anatomy. The gulf that separates a Pollaiuolo nude from one by Bouguereau is not all a matter of significant design. The one was born of nature's union with an avid sensibility; the other makes a parade of a habitual skill. One says, pointing to the array of anatomic facts—"Here lies the mystery"; the other says—"Here lies no mystery, I know it all."

The modern critic who belittles all representational concerns, because he sees them only as solved problems, underrates their power to inflame the artist's mind and to intensify his vision and his touch. He will fail in appreciation if he cannot relive the artist's will to formulate his found reality. Nor need he know how much of anatomic ignorance prevailed in Pollaiuolo's time to judge the measure of the artist's revelation. For Pollaiuolo's effort to articulate each muscular inflection is permanently sealed in the form. Like all works connected with discoveries of representation, his pictures lack the sweet ease of accomplishment. His images are ever aborning, swelling into space and taking life, like frozen fingers tingling as they warm. It is not facts they purvey; it is the thrill and wonder of cognition.

But is this sort of cognition relevant to aesthetic value? To be sure, it is. We are told that the artist's design seeks to impose enduring unity and order on the undifferentiated content of experience. To bring his organizing powers into fullest play, the painter must haul his perceptions out of their limbo and annex them to his plan. A Michelangelo, busying himself in anatomic studies, knows that the apparent turbulence of a man's muscles must become in his design as inevitably ordered as was the long, unswerving contour of Masaccio. A score of muscles newly differentiated, a new vocabulary of expressive gesture, a newly seen relation between motion and shape, these become part of that living diversity to which unification is the victorious response. They are the stuff of the aesthetic program. And in bringing novel visual experiences to his art, Michelangelo, so far from abandoning Masaccio's ground, is doing precisely what his forerunner had done. For he is still engaged in the "pure apprehension of natural fact." The Mannerist, on the other hand, he who displays Michelangelo's musculature over again, is not at all repeating Michelangelo, since what he arranges on the canvas lives already in the domesticated state. It had been won for art already.

In realistic art, then, it is the ever-novel influx of visual experience which incites the artist's synthesizing will, summons his energies and so contributes to the generation of aesthetic form. And this perhaps explains why periods of expanding iconography, of deepening observation and growing imitative skill so often coincide with supreme aesthetic achievement. When the limits of the depictable in nature suddenly recede before the searching gaze, when earlier works come to seem inadequately representative of truth, then the artist's power multiplies. Hence the beauty of those Fifth Dynasty reliefs in Egypt, when, almost suddenly, all life comes to be taken for the artist's province; or the unsurpassed grandeur of the Middle Kingdom heads, when the uniqueness of the human face is first perceived. Hence the upsurge of aesthetic force in Sixth and Fifth Century Greece, when new insights into human nature find embodiment; or in Quattrocento art when the untamed reality of space has to be disciplined and reduced to the coordinate system of the plane canvas or wall.

The Impressionists formed another group of passionate investigators into natural fact. Was it accident that these same men evolved powerful new formal conceptions? Malraux chooses to see no connection between the significance of their forms and their representational pursuits. "That the banks of the Seine might look more 'lifelike' in Sisley's than in Théodore Rousseau's work was beside the mark," he says. Beside the mark, possibly, for the modern doctrinaire, but obviously not so for Sisley.

And Cézanne? Nowadays every schoolboy knows that Cézanne was interested in picture construction. We incline to forget that he was just as concerned with the construction of Mont Sainte-Victoire and the vibration of sunlight; that he studied the subterranean geologic energies which had rolled up the landscape of Provence, and pondered those pervasive unities of nature in which forms are compacted despite their apparent edges. Today's fashionable cant ignores Cézanne's obsession with reality, "the spectacle that the Pater Omnipotens spreads before our eyes." When he warns his friend, Emile Bernard, to "beware of the literary spirit which so often causes painting to deviate from its true path—the concrete study of nature—to lose itself all too long in intangible speculations," he seems to be speaking not so much of the critics he knew, as of those more recent who profess to know him. The truth is that Cézanne's work embodies profound insights into nature. And the logic of his form is unthinkable without his ardent apprehension of natural fact.

By what hazard do these moments of whole-hearted nature-imitation synchronize so often with unforgettable art? In the formalistic system of ideas the recurrent coincidence of significant form with deepened observation remains unexplained. To avoid perversity we do better to grant that nature-imitation in art is neither mechanical skill nor irrelevant distraction. The most that can be said in its disfavor is that we of this century happen to have turned our interest elsewhere.

III

Where your treasure is, there (dropping the h) will your art be also. Every picture is to some degree a value judgment, since you cannot represent a thing without proclaiming it to be worthwhile.

Now the arts discussed in the foregoing section pertained to those schools whose purpose was, at least in part, to depict the open sights of nature. One and all they endorsed Constable's plea for the pure apprehension of natural fact.

But natural fact can be purely apprehended only where the human mind has first endowed it with the status of reality. Only then is the act of seeing backed by a passion, being focused on ultimate truth. From Masaccio to Cézanne men prized overt nature as the locus of reality, and to it they directed their capacities of apprehension. But if we invoke a civilization for whom nature was a pale and immaterial reflection of ideal types, we shall expect to find it careless of the outer shapes of things. Its art will strive to incarnate those forms which are the permanent exemplars behind the drift of sensuous appearances. This indeed is the course taken by Christian art after the fall of pagan Rome.

We can now modify Constable's dictum and propose that art seeks the pure apprehension of natural fact wherever natural fact, as registered by the senses, is regarded as meaningful reality. Where it is not so interpreted we shall find some form of antihumanist distortion, of hieratic stylization or abstraction. But—and this is crucial—such abstraction will continue to apprehend and to express reality. Though it rejects the intimations of mere sense perception, it does not thereby cease to be representational. Only the matter that now calls for representation is drawn from a new order of reality.

Let us list briefly some of the formal features governing Early Christian and Byzantine art. Comparing it to the preceding style of disenchanted Hellenism, we are struck by a rigid frontality in the disposition of figures, by a minimum of variation in gesture, and the replacement of individual likeness by canonic type. We note that movement is arrested, that the natural bulk of things is flattened and all forms are gathered in a single plane; distance is eliminated in favor of ideal space, purple or gold; color becomes pure, unmodulated, and the shadow—that negating spirit who haunts only the art of the West—vanishes in the diffusion of an unremitting light.

These devices sound, as indeed they look, other-worldly. Yet we can say without paradox that their employment proves how deeply involved was the art of Byzantium, and of the Western Dark and Middle Ages, in the effort at truthful representation. This is readily verified by reference to Neo-Platonist aesthetics.

The most valuable source here is Plotinus, whose thought, by way of Dionysius and Augustine, shaped the spirituality of the first Christian millennium. What, asks Plotinus, speaking of the plastic arts, are true distance and true size? And his answer is a philosophic premonition of the Byzantine manner.[6] If we see two men, the one close by, the other far away, the latter will appear ridiculously dwarfed, and the interval between the two will seem absurdly shrunken. A given distance, therefore, is so many measures of falsification. Since deep space is the occasion of delusion, true distance can exist only within the nearest facing plane; true size is the dimension of each form within that plane.

The argument may be extended to true color. If the red of a red object fades in distance, this effaced, degraded color is not "true." The truth must be an even red in the proximate plane. Furthermore, shadows are to be shunned for doing violence to truthful color, for their can be neither truth nor reality where there is not illumination. Thus to Plotinus the proper rendering of a red sphere would be a disk of pure, ungraduated hue. It is the chiaroscurist—a pander to the sense of sight—who mistakes the nature of reality and therefore sins against the light. "We dare not keep ourselves set toward the images of sense," Plotinus says.[7]

Do Byzantine images seem incorporeal? How else should they represent the truly real? "The body is brute," says Plotinus; "the true man is the other, going pure of body." And he proceeds to reprove them who on the evidence of thrust and resistance identify body with real being.

Do Early Christian figures seem monotonously like, immobile

[6] See A. Grabar on *"Plotin et l'Esthétique Médiévale"* in *Cahiers Archéologiques*, Vol. I, 1945.

[7] See, for this quotation and those following, *The Essence of Plotinus*, compiled by Grace H. Turnbull from the translation by Stephen MacKenna, Oxford, 1948.

and unchanging? We are forewarned by Plotinus that "bodies live in the species, and the individual in the whole class; from them they derive their life and maintainence, for life here is a thing of change, but in that prior realm it is unmoving."

Finally, do the eyes in medieval faces seem excessively prominent? The eye sees the sun, says Plotinus, because it is itself sunlike. Window of the soul, it bespeaks the presence in the body of that radiant emanation which sustains matter in being. Should not the artist therefore mark the eye's true nature rather than comparative size? Values having more reality than facts, it is they that determine the ethos and technique of medieval art.

Clearly, then, the formal conventions of this Christian art came into being in the interest of representational truth; not, to be sure, of direct visual facts, since such facts were metaphysically discredited, but of an ideal, extra-sensory reality.

Obedient to its mystic vision, Christian art proceeded to erect a system of representation by abstraction. Here a certain limited affinity with our own contemporary art suggests itself. There is indeed striking resemblance between the repudiation of naturalism in our time and in Plotinus' day. The latter had written that "the arts give no bare reproduction of the thing seen but go back to the ideas from which nature herself derives." Compare this with Paul Klee's: "The modern artist places more value on the powers that do the forming, than on the final forms (of nature) themselves." And even Roger Fry, who had no stomach for mystical speculation, says of Cézanne—who was all modern art to him— that he rendered "not appearances, but the causes of appearance in structure."

As the greatest apostle of the modern aesthetic faith, the case of Roger Fry is a rewarding study. And it is noteworthy that he was unaware of his own implications. He fervently believed that the prime business of art, in fact its sole legitimate concern, was "abstract unity of design." "Painting," he exclaimed, "has thrown representation to the winds; literature should do the same and follow suit!" Yet, gazing at an academic portrait, he passed this elegant quip (quoted in Virginia Woolf's *Roger Fry*): "I cannot," he said, "see the man for the likeness."

This went far deeper than Fry would have granted. He had meant to say that he could not see the essential man beneath the clutter of external traits. But he unwittingly confessed that he did want to see this inner man. While affirming that the valuable image did not manifest itself in mere visibility, he also admitted that the truth which lay concealed behind the model's mask, could and should be represented by some graphic symbol. It will be seen at once that Fry was speaking from a philosophic premise for which his formalistic theorizing left no room. He mistook for an aesthetic doctrine what was actually a shift in philosophic orientation. And he was not calling for the end of representation in art, but for the representation of a different content, to be tapped from a new order of reality.

Fry's sensitive recoil from Victorian academicism—or naturalism, to give it his preferred misnomer—was therefore based on two objections, neither of which he acknowledged. First, that it substituted standard commonplaces for pure vision, and second, that it continued to portray an aspect of nature which in the philosophic conscience of his age had lost reality and meaning. For the inversions of modern psychology and the iconoclasm of contemporary physics have once again, as in the Middle Ages, subverted our faith in the reality of palpable appearances. And it is right and proper for the modern artist who is worthy of his time that he should turn his back on the apparent, since he holds with Plotinus that "all perceptible things are but signs and symbols of the imperceptible." Thus the relevance of naturalistic representation to art depends on no aesthetic doctrines, but on prior metaphysical commitments. And the argument for and against representation, which has agitated critics for so long, has rarely been fought at its proper level.

IV

Has modern art, then, like Byzantium, broken with the sensible world? Is it true that art, having paid its debt to nature, is now finally at liberty? Let us consider first those modern works which still maintain natural forms at some degree of recognizability. To the formalist their distortions seem sufficiently justified as serving the higher needs of design. Yet in these works the illustrative element is there, and—no matter how abstracted—takes its point from its residual resemblance to familiar sights. "The deformation of natural forms" of which Klee speaks in his journals presupposes in us the expectation of natural forms undeformed. Meyer Schapiro, speaking of Picasso's *Girl before a Mirror,* points out that "Picasso and other moderns have discovered for art the internality of the body," that is, the inner image of the body as conjured up by fear and desire, pleasure and pain. But this inner image is communicable only as related contrast to the outer. Everyone knows how clumsy the human foot feels when pursuing a bird. The mammoth foot in Miro's *Man Throwing a Stone at a Bird* is thus an eloquent hyperbole, a piece of graphic gigantism. It makes its point not as largeness—a pure, abstract value—but as enlargement, which implies an external referent. The distance which the form has traveled in the way of distortion is apprehended by the beholder and becomes a vital element of the narrative structure. Familiar nature is not, after all, ignored. It survives as the distanced, but implicit, norm.

Exaggeration for expressive ends is found, of course, throughout the history of art. It is the common device of all caricatures. No matter how remotely they have ventured into fantasy, it is the stretch and span between norm and distortion that constitutes their wit. The same is true of expressionism and of much so-called abstract art. A term of reference still lies outside the picture frame in human recollection and experience, as it does for the most clinically realistic pictures.

To an eye still immersed in the visual habits of the nineteenth century, the abstract way often seems willful and offensive. To a mind indoctrinated with formalist theory, it often looks like— "simply painting," a manipulation of the medium itself. Both judgments, we believe, are failures of appreciation, since abstraction *from* nature is still a telling mode of representation, whose hyphen with common reality is stretched but never snapped, except in the most thinly decorative works.

There is another feature in contemporary abstract art which ties it to the world of sense and separates it from all anti-naturalistic styles of the past—its boundless freedom of selection from natural sights. The conceptualism of ancient Egypt or Byzantium had constrained itself to show every form from a preferred angle, convinced that one aspect alone could reveal its essential nature. Thus the Egyptian foot appears persistently in profile, as though the human foot in essence were a profile form, all other postures being accidentals. Domiciled in eternity, the Egyptian or Byzantine foot is not susceptible of change.

Modern abstraction brooks no such restraints. Six centuries of arduous research into the changing nature of appearance are not so easily dismissed. Accordingly, in modern art, a difficult, foreshortened front view of a foot is met head-on, and finds its abstract formulation as readily as the diagrammatic profile. The modern painter, if caught in the orbit of Picasso or Paul Klee, discovers a formative principle not in the foot as such, but in the foot in every possible predicament. He sees not one transcendent, universal formula for man, but a distinct abbreviation for man in every pose, mood, situation. Klee himself finds a symbolic cipher not for Woman, the Eternal Feminine, but for a certain middle-aged lady coming home loaded with packages.

It is quite true that Klee probes into the form-giving principle behind the thing, and strips it, like the mystic, of its superfluity; his representations rest upon his vision of a world whose surface forms conceal an occulted reality. In his own words, he seeks "a distant point at the source of creation, a kind of formula for man, earth, fire, water, air, and all the circling forces." Klee here seems to repeat a commonplace of mysticism. And yet his work, one of the most potent influences behind modern abstraction, is of devastating originality, utterly destructive of the mystic premise that there is one immutable reality available to detached contemplation. For Klee finds his occult reality incarnate in each fleeting, perjured gesture of this world. In his intuition the nature of man is not to be found in any timeless essence, soaring like Egyptian or Byzantine man above vicissitudes. Man, to Paul Klee, is what he does and where he is—a *Juggler in April,* an *Omphalocentric Lecturer,* an *Old Man Figuring,* a *Mocker Mocked.* Vainly you scan these works for any single pictographic type; in every sketch the symbol is freshly apprehended and invented anew. If this is mysticism it is certainly not of the medieval, contemplative kind. It is a restless, existential mysticism, peculiarly our own.

Or watch Picasso's *Three Musicians* in the Philadelphia version. Despite an apparently remote cubist formalism we can say with confidence that the three men in the picture are equipped with six hands. But saying this we have already said too much.

Having availed ourselves of the non-visual concept of *the human hand,* we have implied that Picasso here deals with a six-fold repetition of a single item. But he does nothing of the kind. He knows, or knew in 1921, that a man's hand may manifest itself as rake, pestle, mallet, pincer, vise or broom; as cantilever or as decorative fringe; that it is a nubile and unstable element, contracting easy marriages with other forms to build up into compound entities. In actual vision the hand is an infinity of variegated forms. Its common factor is not any ontological handshape, but a protean energy with only a positional and functional relation to the arm, and to the object handled. Thus, in the *Three Musicians,* a fist hugging a fiddle's neck is one sort of efficient force expressed by one decorative shape; four digits flat upon a keyboard are of another sort entirely. Picasso here banishes the *a priori* vision which must ever find conceptual permanence despite visible change. His manual formulae stand not for Being, but for function, operation. Adaptability and change are the sole measure of reality. And it is on behalf of such reality, as well as of design, that his sleights of hand are wrought. To describe the *Three Musicians* as a finely patterned abstraction of invented anatomies is an injustice to the matter of Picasso's revelation.

It follows that the modern abstractionist does not necessarily write off the "accidents" of visual appearance. He welcomes their occurrence, but pictures them as the negotiable shapes assumed by transient energy. And in this adaptability to every optic impulse modern art is more closely linked to its naturalistic ancestry than to the unworldly stylizations of the past. Its affinity with medieval art remains, after all, purely negative. Modern and medieval art agree that reality is not so much revealed as masked by surfaces. But, as at a carnival, the choice of a mask may betray the reveler's characteristic nature, so surfaces bespeak something as to the truth below. And the truths inferred by modern and by medieval artists lie at opposite poles of interpretation.

v

It remains to speak of so-called non-objective art. Here surely all connection with the outer world is cut. The forms that here emerge mean nothing, we are told, but private states of feeling;

and, for the rest, they are pure form, a music for the optic nerve. The following passage from Ortega y Gasset ("On Point of View in the Arts," *Partisan Review,* August 1949) may serve as an example of the common view: "Painting," Ortega writes, "completely reversed its function and, instead of putting us within what is outside, endeavored to pour out upon the canvas what is within: ideal invented objects. . . . The [artist's] eyes, instead of absorbing things, are converted into projectors of private flora and fauna. Before, the real world drained off into them; now they are reservoirs of irreality."

This seems to us an open question still. For we are forced to ask: by what faculty of mind or eye does the artist discover and distill the forms of his private irreality? Whence come the plastic symbols of his unconditioned subjectivity? Surely no amount of introspection will yield shapes to put on canvas. And if this is so, from what external quarter proceed those visual stimuli which the artist can identify as apt and corresponding to his inner state?

Obviously, any attempt to answer such a question rests on pure speculation. Yet it seems worth considering the testimony of those artists and critics who have pointed to the impact of science on contemporary art.

The impact operates on several levels and takes various forms. There is, first, a constant stream of suggestion issuing from the laboratories. Wittingly, or through unconscious exposure, the non-objective artist draws much of his imagery from the visual data of the scientist—from magnifications of minute natural textures, from telescopic vistas, submarine scenery and X-ray photographs. Not that he undertakes to render a particular bacterial culture or pattern of refracted light. The shapes of his choice are recruited in good faith for their suggestiveness as shapes, and for their obscure correspondence to his inner state. But it is significant how often the morphology he finds analogous to his own sentient being is that which has revealed itself to scientific vision. It is apparently in these gestating images, shapes antecedent to the visible, that many abstract painters recognize a more intimate manifestation of natural truth. On these uncharted realms of form they must impose aesthetic purpose; from them they wrest new decorative principles—such as the "biomorphic" motif. Nature they imitate no less than did Masaccio. But where the Renaissance had turned to nature's display windows, and to the finished forms of man and beast, the men of our time descend into nature's laboratories.

But the affinity with science probably goes further still. It has been suggested that the very conceptions of twentieth-century science are finding expression in modern abstract art. The scientist's sense of pervasive physical activity in space, his intuition of immaterial functions, his awareness of the constant mutability of forms, of their indefinable location, their mutual interpenetration, their renewal and decay—all these have found a visual echo in contemporary art; not because painters illustrate scientific concepts, but because an awareness of nature in its latest undisguise seems to be held in common by science and art.

The question is, of course, whether nature as the modern scientist conceives it can be represented at all, except in spectral mathematical equations. Philosophers of science concur in saying it cannot. Even such divergent thinkers as A. N. Whitehead and Bertrand Russell join hands when they declare that the abstractions of contemporary science have irrevocably passed beyond man's visual imagination. "Our understanding of nature has now reached a stage," says J. W. N. Sullivan, "when we cannot picture what we are talking about."

But this utterance of the philosophers contains an unwarranted assumption, to wit, that whereas man's capacity for intellectual abstraction is ever widening, his visual imagination is fixed and circumscribed. Here the philosophers are reckoning without the host, since our visualizing powers are determined for us not by them but by the men who paint. And this our visual imagination, thanks to those in whom it is creative, is also in perpetual growth, as unpredictable as the extension of thought.

Thus the art of the last half-century may well be schooling our eyes to live at ease with the new concepts forced upon our credulity by scientific reasoning. What we may be witnessing is the gradual condensation of abstract ideas into images that fall within the range of sensory imagination.[8] Modern painting in-

[8] In his *Art as Experience* John Dewey writes: "Nothing that man has ever reached by the highest flights of thought, or penetrated by any probing insight is inherently such that it may not become the heart and core of sense."

ures us to the aspect of a world housing not discrete forms but trajectories and vectors, lines of tension and strain. Form in the sense of solid substance melts away and resolves itself into dynamic process. Instead of bodies powered by muscle, or by gravity, we get energy propagating itself in the void. If, to the scientist, solidity and simple location are illusions born of the grossness of our senses, they are so also to the modern painter. His canvases are fields of force; his shapes the transient aggregates of energies that seem impatient to be on their way. In the imagery of modern art waves of matter have usurped the place of tangible, visible things.

The representation of the trajectory in art has its own history, like the representation of the visage of Christ. Emerging in certain Rembrandt drawings as a scribbled flourish in the wake of a volatile angel, it comes in the late work of Turner to invade painting itself. And in Brancusi's *Bird in Space* the path of motion at last claims the full sculptured dignity of mass. It is senseless to call such a work non-representational, for there is no ignoring here of nature. The trail of a projectile is, after all, as real as the object flung. And though it wants tangibility, it is as surely part of the natural world.

So much then for the dissolution of the solid in contemporary art; the substantial object has been activated into a continuing event. As for space, it is no longer a passive receptacle, wherein solid forms may disport themselves, as once they did in Renaissance or nineteenth-century art. In modern paintings—barring those which are nostalgic throwbacks to the past—space is an organic growth interacting with matter. There is a painting by Matta Echaurren, entitled *Grave Situation,* in which long tensile forms stretch through a space generated by their motion—a space which at the same time inflects the curvature of their path.

It takes some effort to concede the heroic creativity of such envisionings. Granted that they do not depict what we normally see. But to call them "simply painting," as though they had no referent outside themselves, is to miss both their meaning and their continuity with the art of the past. If our suggestion is valid, then even non-objective art continues to pursue art's social role of fixating thought in aesthetic form, pinning down the most ethereal conceptions of the age in vital designs, and rendering them accessible to the apparatus of sense.

✓

LEO STEINBERG Born in 1920, he received his Ph.D. from New York University. He is a well-known and wide-ranging art critic and art historian.

"The Eye Is a Part of the Mind" (1953) In a clear and vigorous style the author develops his much-disputed thesis by example, analysis, definition, and comparison. Undogmatic, he still manages to be convincing.

✓

1. Support or refute Steinberg's argument, using a modern painting with which you are familiar. 2. Is there such a thing as an artistic photograph?

Experimental Music

Formerly, whenever anyone said the music I presented was experimental, I objected. It seemed to me that composers knew what they were doing, and that the experiments that had been made had taken place prior to the finished works, just as sketches are made before paintings and rehearsals precede performances. But, giving the matter further thought, I realized that there is ordinarily an essential difference between making a piece of music and hearing one. A composer knows his work as a woodsman knows a path he has traced and retraced, while a listener is confronted by the same work as one is in the woods by a plant he has never seen before.

Now, on the other hand, times have changed; music has changed; and I no longer object to the word "experimental." I use it in fact to describe all the music that especially interests me and to which I am devoted, whether someone else wrote it or I myself did. What has happened is that I have become a listener and the music has become something to hear. Many people, of course, have given up saying "experimental" about this new music. Instead, they either move to a halfway point and say "controversial" or depart to a greater distance and question whether this "music" is music at all.

For in this new music nothing takes place but sounds: those that are notated and those that are not. Those that are not notated appear in the written music as silences, opening the doors of the music to the sounds that happen to be in the environment. This openness exists in the fields of modern sculpture and architecture. The glass houses of Mies van der Rohe reflect their environment, presenting to the eye images of clouds, trees, or grass, according to the situation. And while looking at the constructions in wire of the sculptor Richard Lippold, it is inevitable that one will see other things, and people too, if they happen to be there at the same time, through the network of wires. There is no such thing as an empty space or an empty time. There is always something to see, something to hear. In fact, try as we may to make a silence, we cannot. For certain engineering purposes, it is desirable to have as silent a situation as possible. Such a room is called an anechoic chamber, its six walls made of special material, a room without echoes. I entered one at Harvard University several years ago and heard two sounds, one high and one low. When I described them to the engineer in charge, he informed me that the high one was my nervous system in operation, the low one my blood in circulation. Until I die there will be sounds. And they will continue following my death. One need not fear about the future of music.

But this fearlessness only follows if, at the parting of the ways, where it is realized that sounds occur whether intended or not, one turns in the direction of those he does not intend. This turning is psychological and seems at first to be a giving up of everything that belongs to humanity—for a musician, the giving up of music. This psychological turning leads to the world of nature, where, gradually or suddenly, one sees that humanity and nature, not separate, are in this world together; that nothing was lost when everything was given away. In fact, everything is gained. In musical terms, any sounds may occur in any combination and in any continuity.

And it is a striking coincidence that just now the technical means to produce such a free-ranging music are available. When the Allies entered Germany towards the end of World War II, it was discovered that improvements had been made in recording sounds magnetically such that tape had become suitable for the high-fidelity recording of music. First in France with the work of Pierre Schaeffer, later here, in Germany, in Italy, in Japan, and perhaps, without my knowing it, in other places, magnetic tape was used not simply to record performances of music but to make a new music that was possible only because of it. Given a minimum of two tape recorders and a disk recorder, the following processes are possible: 1) a single recording of any sound may be made; 2) a rerecording may be made, in the course of which, by means of filters and circuits, any or all of the physical characteristics of a given recorded sound may be altered; 3) electronic mixing (combining on a third machine sounds issuing from two others) permits the presentation of any number of sounds in combination; 4) ordinary splicing permits the juxtaposition of any sounds, and when it includes unconventional cuts, it, like rerecording, brings about alterations of any or all of the original physical characteristics. The situation made available by these means is essentially a total sound-space, the limits of which are ear-determined only, the position of a particular sound in this space being the result of five determinants: frequency or pitch, amplitude or loudness, overtone structure or timbre, duration, and morphology (how the sound begins, goes on, and dies away). By the alteration of any one of these determinants, the position of the sound in sound-space changes. Any sound at any point in this total sound-space can move to become a sound at any other point. But advantage can be taken of these possibilities only if one is willing to change one's musical habits radically. That is, one may take advantage of the appearance of images without visible transition in distant places, which is a way of saying "television," if one is willing to stay at home instead of going to a theatre. Or one may fly if one is willing to give up walking.

Musical habits include scales, modes, theories of counterpoint and harmony, and the study of the timbres, singly and in combination of a limited number of sound-producing mechanisms. In mathematical terms these all concern discrete steps. They resemble walking—in the case of pitches, on steppingstones twelve in number. This cautious stepping is not characteristic of the possibilities of magnetic tape, which is revealing to us that musical action or existence can occur at any point or along any line or curve or what have you in total sound-space; that we are, in fact, technically equipped to transform our contemporary awareness of nature's manner of operation into art.

Again there is a parting of the ways. One has a choice. If he does not wish to give up his attempts to control sound, he may complicate his musical technique towards an approximation of the new possibilities and awareness. (I use the word "approximation" because a measuring mind can never finally measure nature.) Or, as before, one may give up the desire to control sound, clear his mind of music, and set about discovering means to let sounds be themselves rather than vehicles for man-made theories or expressions of human sentiments.

This project will seem fearsome to many, but on examination it gives no cause for alarm. Hearing sounds which are just sounds immediately sets the theorizing mind to theorizing, and the emotions of human beings are continually aroused by encounters with nature. Does not a mountain unintentionally evoke in us a sense of wonder? otters along a stream a sense of mirth? night in the woods a sense of fear? Do not rain falling and mists rising up suggest the love binding heaven and earth? Is not decaying flesh loathsome? Does not the death of someone we love bring sorrow? And is there a greater hero than the least plant that grows? What is more angry than the flash of lightning and the sound of thunder? These responses to nature are mine and will not necessarily correspond with another's. Emotion takes place in the person who has it. And sounds, when allowed to be themselves, do not require that those who hear them do so unfeelingly. The opposite is what is meant by response ability.

New music: new listening. Not an attempt to understand something that is being said, for, if something were being said, the sounds would be given the shapes of words. Just an attention to the activity of sounds.

Those involved with the composition of experimental music find ways and means to remove themselves from the activities of the sounds they make. Some employ chance operations, derived from sources as ancient as the Chinese *Book of Changes,* or as modern as the tables of random numbers used also by physicists in research. Or, analogous to the Rorschach tests of psychology, the interpretation of imperfections in the paper upon which one is writing may provide a music free from one's memory and imagination. Geometrical means employing spatial superimpositions at variance with the ultimate performance in time may be used. The total field of possibilities may be roughly divided and the actual sounds within these divisions may be indicated as to number but left to the performer or to the splicer to choose. In this latter case, the composer resembles the maker of a camera who allows someone else to take the picture.

Whether one uses tape or writes for conventional instruments, the present musical situation has changed from what it was before tape came into being. This also need not arouse alarm, for the coming into being of something new does not by that fact deprive what was of its proper place. Each thing has its own place, never takes the place of something else; and the more things there are, as is said, the merrier.

But several effects of tape on experimental music may be mentioned. Since so many inches of tape equal so many seconds of time, it has become more and more usual that notation is in space rather than in symbols of quarter, half, and sixteenth notes and so on. Thus where on a page a note appears will correspond to when in a time it is to occur. A stop watch is used to facilitate a performance; and a rhythm results which is a far cry from horse's hoofs and other regular beats.

Also it has been impossible with the playing of several separate tapes at once to achieve perfect synchronization. This fact has led some towards the manufacture of multiple-tracked tapes and machines with a corresponding number of heads; while others— those who have accepted the sounds they do not intend—now realize that the score, the requiring that many parts be played in a particular togetherness, is not an accurate representation of how things are. These now compose parts but not scores, and the parts may be combined in any unthought ways. This means that each performance of such a piece of music is unique, as interesting to a composer as to others listening. It is easy to see again the parallel with nature, for even with leaves of the same tree, no two are exactly alike. The parallel in art is the sculpture with moving parts, the mobile.

It goes without saying that dissonances and noises are welcome in this new music. But so is the dominant seventh chord if it happens to put in an appearance.

Rehearsals have shown that this new music, whether for tape or for instruments, is more clearly heard when the several loudspeakers or performers are separated in space rather than grouped closely together. For this music is not concerned with harmoniousness as generally understood, where the quality of harmony results from a blending of several elements. Here we are concerned with the coexistence of dissimilars, and the central points where fusion occurs are many: the ears of the listeners wherever they are. This disharmony, to paraphrase Bergson's statement about disorder, is simply a harmony to which many are unaccustomed.

Where do we go from here? Towards theatre. That art more than music resembles nature. We have eyes as well as ears, and it is our business while we are alive to use them.

And what is the purpose of writing music? One is, of course, not dealing with purposes but dealing with sounds. Or the answer must take the form of paradox: a purposeful purposelessness or a purposeless play. This play, however, is an affirmation of life—not an attempt to bring order out of chaos nor to suggest improvements in creation, but simply a way of waking up to the very life we're living, which is so excellent once one gets one's mind and one's desires out of its way and lets it act of its own accord.

❧

JOHN CAGE   Born in Los Angeles in 1912, he has composed a variety of music, and taught, lectured, and written in behalf of musical experimentation.

"Experimental Music" (1958) The style, though deliberately somewhat offbeat, is generally clear and direct; and the argument, though unconventional, is handled in a persuasive manner.

❧

1. *What is the author's definition of music?* 2. *Do you agree with it?* 3. *Are there any ways in which Cage's own prose is experimental?*

KATHERINE ANNE PORTER

The Future Is Now

Not so long ago I was reading in a magazine with an enormous circulation some instructions as to how to behave if and when we see that flash brighter than the sun which means that the atom bomb has arrived. I read of course with the intense interest of one who has everything to learn on this subject; but at the end, the advice dwindled to this: the only real safety seems to lie in simply being somewhere else at the time, the farther away the better; the next best, failing access to deep shelters, bombproof cellars and all, is to get under a stout table—that is, just what you might do if someone were throwing bricks through your window and you were too nervous to throw them back.

This comic anticlimax to what I had been taking as a serious educational piece surprised me into real laughter, hearty and carefree. It is such a relief to be told the truth, or even just the facts, so pleasant not to be coddled with unreasonable hopes. That very evening I was drawn away from my work table to my fifth-story window by one of those shrill terror-screaming sirens which our excitement-loving city government used then to affect for so many occasions: A fire? Police chasing a gangster? Somebody being got to the hospital in a hurry? Some distinguished public guest being transferred from one point to another? Strange aircraft coming over, maybe? Under the lights of the corner crossing of the great avenue, a huge closed vehicle whizzed past, screaming. I never knew what it was, had not in fact expected to know; no one I could possibly ask would know. Now that we have bells clamoring away instead for such events, we all have one doubt less, if perhaps one expectancy more. The single siren's voice means to tell us only one thing.

But at that doubtful moment, framed in a lighted window level with mine in the apartment house across the street, I saw a young man in a white T-shirt and white shorts at work polishing a long, beautiful dark table top. It was obviously his own table in his own flat, and he was enjoying his occupation. He was bent over in perfect concentration, rubbing, sandpapering, running the flat of his palm over the surface, standing back now and then to get the sheen of light on the fine wood. I am sure he had not even raised his head at the noise of the siren, much less had he come to the window. I stood there admiring his workmanlike devotion to a good job worth doing, and there flashed through me one of those pure fallacies of feeling which suddenly overleap reason: surely all that effort and energy so irreproachably employed were not going to be wasted on a table that was to be used merely for crawling under at some unspecified date. Then why take all those pains to make it beautiful? Any sort of old board would do.

I was so shocked at this treachery of the lurking Foul Fiend (despair *is* a foul fiend, and this was despair) I stood a moment longer, looking out and around, trying to collect my feelings, trying to think a little. Two windows away and a floor down in the house across the street, a young woman was lolling in a deep chair, reading and eating fruit from a little basket. On the sidewalk, a boy and a girl dressed alike in checkerboard cotton shirts and skin-tight blue denims, a costume which displayed acutely the structural differences of their shapes, strolled along with their arms around each other. I believe this custom of lovers walking enwreathed in public was imported by our soldiers of the First World War from France, from Paris indeed. "You didn't see that sort of thing here before," certain members of the older generation were heard to remark quite often, in a tone of voice. Well, one sees quite a lot of it now, and it is a very pretty, reassuring sight. Other citizens of all sizes and kinds and ages were crossing back and forth; lights flashed red and green, punctually. Motors zoomed by, and over the great city—but where am I going? I never read other peoples' descriptions of great cities, more particularly if it is a great city I know. It doesn't belong here anyway, except that I had again that quieting sense of the continuity of human experience on this earth, its perpetual aspirations, setbacks, failures and re-beginnings in eternal hope; and that, with some appreciable differences of dress, customs and means of conveyance, so people have lived and moved in the cities they have built for more millennia than we are yet able to account for, and will no doubt build and live for as many more.

Why did this console me? I cannot say; my mind is of the sort that can often be soothed with large generalities of that nature. The silence of the spaces between the stars does not affright me, as it did Pascal, because I am unable to imagine it except poetically; and my awe is not for the silence and space of the endless universe but for the inspired imagination of man, who can think and feel so, and turn a phrase like that to communicate it to us. Then too, I like the kind of honesty and directness of the young soldier who lately answered someone who asked him if he knew what he was fighting for. "I sure do," he said, "I am fighting to live." And as for the future, I was once reading the first writings of a young girl, an apprentice author, who was quite impatient to get on with the business and find her way into print. There is very little one can say of use in such matters, but I advised her against haste—she could so easily regret it. "Give yourself time," I said, "the future will take care of itself." This opinionated young person looked down her little nose at me and said, "The future is now." She may have heard the phrase somewhere and liked it, or she may just have naturally belonged to that school of metaphysics; I am sure she was too young to have investigated the thought deeply. But maybe she was right and the future does arrive every day and it is all we have, from one second to the next.

So I glanced again at the young man at work, a proper-looking candidate for the armed services, and realized the plain, homely fact: he was not preparing a possible shelter, something to cower under trembling; he was restoring a beautiful surface to put his books and papers on, to serve his plates from, to hold his cocktail tray and his lamp. He was full of the deep, right, instinctive, human belief that he and the table were going to be around together for a long time. Even if he is off to the army next week, it will be there when he gets back. At the very least, he is doing something he feels is worth doing now, and that is no small thing.

At once the difficulty, and the hope, of our special time in this world of Western Europe and America is that we have been brought up for many generations in the belief, however tacit, that all humanity was almost unanimously engaged in going forward, naturally to better things and to higher reaches. Since the eighteenth century at least when the Encyclopedists seized upon the Platonic theory that the highest pleasure of mankind was pursuit of the good, the true, and the beautiful, progress, in precisely the sense of perpetual, gradual amelioration of the hard human lot, has been taught popularly not just as theory of possibility but as an article of faith and the groundwork of a whole political doctrine. Mr. Toynbee has even simplified this view for us with picture diagrams of various sections of humanity, each in its own cycle rising to its own height, struggling beautifully on from craggy level to level, but always upward. Whole peoples are arrested at certain points, and perish there, but others go on. There is also the school of thought, Oriental and very ancient, which gives to life the spiral shape, and the spiral moves by nature upward. Even adherents of the circular or recurring-cycle school, also ancient and honorable, somehow do finally allow that the circle is a thread that spins itself out one layer above another, so that even though it is perpetually at every moment passing over a place it has been before, yet by its own width it will have risen just so much higher.

These are admirable attempts to get a little meaning and order into our view of our destiny, in that same spirit which moves the artist to labor with his little handful of chaos, bringing it to coherency within a frame; but on the visible evidence we must admit that in human nature the spirit of contradiction more than holds its own. Mankind has always built a little more than he has hitherto been able or willing to destroy; got more children than he has been able to kill; invented more laws and customs than he had any intention of observing; founded more religions than he was able to practice or even to believe in; made in general many more promises than he could keep; and has been known more than once to commit suicide through mere fear of death. Now in our time, in his pride to explore his universe to its unimaginable limits and to exceed his possible powers, he has at last produced an embarrassing series of engines too powerful for their containers and too tricky for their mechanicians; millions of labor-saving gadgets which can be rendered totally useless by the mere failure of the public power plants, and has reduced himself to such helplessness that a dozen or less of the enemy could disable a whole city by throwing a few switches. This paradoxical creature has committed all these extravagances and created all these dangers and sufferings in a quest—we are told—for peace and security.

How much of this are we to believe, when with the pride of Lucifer, the recklessness of Icarus, the boldness of Prometheus and the intellectual curiosity of Adam and Eve (yes, intellectual; the serpent promised them wisdom if . . .) man has obviously outreached himself, to the point where he cannot understand his own science or control his own inventions. Indeed he has become as the gods, who have over and over again suffered defeat and downfall at the hands of their creatures. Having devised the most exquisite and instantaneous means of communication to all corners of the earth, for years upon years friends were unable even to get a postcard message to each other across national frontiers. The newspapers assure us that from the kitchen tap there flows a chemical, cheap and available, to make a bomb more disturbing to the imagination even than the one we so appallingly have; yet no machine has been invented to purify that water so that it will not spoil even the best tea or coffee. Or at any rate, it is not in use. We are the proud possessors of rocket bombs that go higher and farther and faster than any ever before, and there is some talk of a rocket ship shortly to take off for the moon. (My plan is to stow away.) We may indeed reach the moon some day, and I dare predict that will happen before we have devised a decent system of city garbage disposal.

This lunatic atom bomb has succeeded in rousing the people of all nations to the highest point of unanimous moral dudgeon; great numbers of persons are frightened who never really had much cause to be frightened before. This world has always been a desperately dangerous place to live for the greater part of the earth's inhabitants; it was, however reluctantly, endured as the natural state of affairs. Yet the invention of every new weapon of war has always been greeted with horror and righteous indignation, especially by those who failed to invent it, or who were threatened with it first . . . bows and arrows, stone cannon balls, gunpowder, flintlocks, pistols, the dumdum bullet, the Maxim silencer, the machine gun, poison gas, armored tanks, and on and on to the grand climax—if it should prove to be—of the experiment on Hiroshima. Nagasaki was bombed too, remember? Or were we already growing accustomed to the idea? And as for Hiroshima, surely it could not have been the notion of sudden death of others that shocked us? How could it be, when in two great wars within one generation we have become familiar with millions of shocking deaths, by sudden violence of most cruel devices, and by agonies prolonged for years in prisons and hospitals and concentration camps. We take with apparent calmness the news of the deaths of millions by flood, famine, plague—no, all the frontiers of danger are down now, no one is safe, no one, and that, alas, really means all of us. It is our own deaths we fear, and so let's out with it and give up our fine debauch of moralistic frenzy over Hiroshima. I fail entirely to see why it is more criminal to kill a few thousand persons in one instant than it is to kill the same number slowly over a given stretch of time. If I have a choice, I'd as lief be killed by an atom bomb as by a hand grenade or a flame thrower. If dropping the atom bomb is an immoral act, then the making of it was too; and writing of the formula was a crime, since those who wrote it must have known what such a contrivance was good for. So, morally speaking, the bomb is only a magnified hand grenade, and the crime, if crime it is, is still murder. It was never anything else. Our protocriminal then was the man who first struck fire from flint, for from that moment we have been coming steadily to this day and this weapon and this use of it. What would you have advised instead? That the human race should have gone on sitting in caves gnawing raw meat and beating each other over the head with the bones?

And yet it may be that what we have is a world not on the verge of flying apart, but an uncreated one—still in shapeless frag-

394 KATHERINE ANNE PORTER

ments waiting to be put together properly. I imagine that when we want something better, we may have it: at perhaps no greater price than we have already paid for the worse.

✸

KATHERINE ANNE PORTER   Born in Texas in 1890, for many years she has been famous for her essays, short stories, and novels. Like E. M. Forster, she does not write much, but what she does publish is polished and meaningful.

"The Future Is Now" (1950) This essay grows out of a series of only casually connected experiences that, through rhetorical questions, enable the author to generalize with apparent objectivity. The mood, despite the subject, is easygoing; the tone, a bit irreverent. The diction is vivid, the syntax lively, the philosophy homespun. The style, simple on the surface, shifts with the state of mind of the author and with what she is observing.

✸

1. What devices and arguments does the author use to suggest that things really aren't so bad? 2. What are the major philosophical premises underlying her point of view?

Appendix

Editor's Note

The following three pieces are intended to provide a brief glimpse of the development of the essay in English. Francis Bacon is the earliest and probably the best known English essayist. "Of Studies" (1597, 1625) is a dissection of a single subject in moral and philosophical terms. The tone is didactic, the argument positive and succinct, the style highly polished. Indeed, the author makes skillful use of several rhetorical devices that Renaissance books on style recommended for eloquent writing: *anaphora*—consecutive statements beginning with the same word or words; *ellipsis*—omission of a word or words necessary for a complete construction; *isocolon*—successive clauses or phrases of the same length; *parison*—even balance between the parts of a sentence. Bacon also enjoys mixing learned and colloquial diction and using two words where one would serve the meaning—for example, "contradict and confute," "weigh and consider."

Jonathan Swift's "A Modest Proposal" (1729) reflects different times and tastes. A satire that operates on many levels, its political and social criticism is horrifyingly evident. But its moral satire, focused on the persona whom Swift creates to address the reader, is no less effective. That persona is ostensibly a modest and deferential fellow, yet somewhat of a snob who is pleased with his own patriotism and social conscience. He has a keenly theoretical mind and shows himself to be an able statistician and economist, as well as a shrewd businessman. At the same time, he also seems a man of broad and tolerant understanding—one who even has

Americans among his acquaintances. His smug personality, values, and assumptions are thus very much the subject—and the object—of Swift's satire.

Another satiric aspect of "A Modest Proposal" is literary. Swift's erudite persona models his essay on a Ciceronian oration, for what could be more convincing to his allegedly sophisticated audience. He begins with the *exordium*, to win their attention. Next comes the *narratio*, in which he sets up the problem by surveying existing conditions. This prepares for the *propositio*, in which he presents his thesis. In the *partitio* he divides his proposition into various supporting arguments, which he then amplifies in the *confirmatio*. Possible objections he first raises and then refutes in the *reprehensio*, finally bringing his piece to its irrefutable climax in the *peroratio*, where he sums up the essential achievement of his argument and proves his own disinterestedness. Though I have indicated these formal divisions in the text, they were not needed in Swift's day: such a formal organization was then clear to any educated man, for he had been trained in grammar school to write treatises according to the same format.

The nineteenth century witnessed a shift in taste from the classical and formal toward the personal and informal. Thoreau's *Walden* (1854) reflects this change. ("Where I Lived, and What I Lived For" is the second chapter of that book.) Swift used a first-person narrator in "A Modest Proposal," but that persona is obviously not to be confused with Swift himself; in *Walden* the relationship between author and persona is more subtle, more intimate. Though we are being personally addressed by Thoreau, we do not read far in "Where I Lived, and What I Lived For" before we discover that the "I" who speaks to us is a person of many faces. The man who first addresses us is a real-estate broker of sorts, a shrewd Yankee who can drive a hard bargain. Yet once we are attracted by that voice we find ourselves being charmed by no Yankee we have met before. This one changes into a poet whose bardic voice startles us by its gnomic assertions and who disturbs our religious sensibilities by his frankly pagan asides. Before the essay is over he has shifted his identity to that of a prophet, then to that of a philosopher. These changing aspects of the narrator are of course indicative of Thoreau's own complex personality, but they are also examples of how a careful writer can shift and control his voice for rhetorical ends. There is no set organizational format here as there was in "A Modest Proposal"; instead, the changes in the persona mark the progress of the argument.

Like Bacon and Swift, Thoreau is a master of the sentence. Though he and Bacon both strive for aphoristic effects, Thoreau relies less on parallel constructions, more on simple sentences which stand out because of their proverbial ring: "To be awake is to be alive." "Time is but the stream I go a-fishing in." He is also a master of metaphor, but where Bacon tends to use metaphor to decorate his argument, Thoreau generally employs it to convey his central message. These three essays, then, differ widely in style, intent, and impact; yet each is controlled, thought provoking, and effective.

Of Studies

Studies serve for delight, for ornament, and for ability. Their chief use for delight is in privateness and retiring; for ornament, is in discourse; and for ability, is in the judgment and disposition of business. For expert men can execute and perhaps judge of particulars, one by one; but the general counsels, and the plots and marshaling of affairs, come best from those that are learned. To spend too much time in studies is sloth; to use them too much for ornament is affectation; to make judgment wholly by their rules is the humor of a scholler. They perfect nature, and are perfected by experience; for natural abilities are like natural plants, that need proyning by study; and studies themselves do give forth directions too much at large, except they be bounded in by experience. Crafty men contemn studies, simple men admire them, and wise men use them; for they teach not their own use, but that is a wisdom without them, and above them, won by observation. Read not to contradict and confute, nor to believe and take for granted, nor to find talk and discourse, but to weigh and consider. Some books are to be tasted, others to be swallowed, and some few to be chewed and digested; that is, some books are to be read only in parts; others to be read, but not curiously; and some few to be read wholly, and with diligence and attention. Some books also may be read by deputy, and extracts made of them by others; but that would be only in the less important arguments, and the meaner sort of books; else distilled books are like common distilled waters, flashy things. Reading maketh a full man; conference a ready man; and writing an exact man. And therefore, if a man write little, he had need have a great memory; if he confer little, he had need have a present wit: and if he read little, he had need have much cunning, to seem to know that he doth not. Histories make men wise; poets witty; the mathematics subtile; natural philosophy deep; moral grave; logic and rhetoric able to contend. *Abeunt studia in mores.* Nay, there is no stond or impediment in the wit but may be wrought out by fit studies; like as diseases of the body may have appropriate exercises. Bowling is good for the stone and reins; shooting for the lungs and breast; gentle walking for the stomach; riding for the head; and the like. So if a man's wit be wand'ring, let him study the mathematics; for in demonstrations, if his wit be called away never so little, he must begin again. If his wit be not apt to distinguish or find difference, let him study the schoolmen; for they are *cymini sectores.* If he be not apt to beat over matters, and to call up one thing to prove and illustrate another, let him study the lawyers' cases. So every defect of the mind may have a special receit.

JONATHAN SWIFT

A Modest Proposal

For Preventing the Children of the Poor People in Ireland
from Being a Burden to Their Parents or Country,
and for Making them Beneficial to the Public

[Exordium] It is a melancholy object to those who walk
through this great town [Dublin] or travel in the country, when
they see the streets, the roads, and cabin doors crowded with beggars of the female sex, followed by three, four, or six children, all
in rags and importuning every passenger for an alms. These
mothers, instead of being able to work for their honest livelihood,
are forced to employ all their time in strolling to beg sustenance
for their helpless infants, who, as they grow up, either turn thieves
for want of work, or leave their dear native country to fight for
the Pretender in Spain, or sell themselves to the Barbadoes.

[Narratio] I think it is agreed by all parties that this prodigious number of children in the arms, or on the backs, or at the
heels of their mothers, and frequently of their fathers, is in the
present deplorable state of the kingdom a very great additional
grievance; and, therefore, whoever could find out a fair, cheap,
and easy method of making these children sound, useful members of the commonwealth, would deserve so well of the public as
to have his statue set up for a preserver of the nation.

But my intention is very far from being confined to provide
only for the children of professed beggars; it is of a much
greater extent, and shall take in the whole number of infants at a

certain age who are born of parents in effect as little able to support them as those who demand our charity in the streets.

As to my own part, having turned my thoughts for many years upon this important subject, and maturely weighed the several schemes of our projectors, I have always found them grossly mistaken in their computation. It is true, a child just dropped from its dam may be supported by her milk for a solar year with little other nourishment, at most not above the value of two shillings, which the mother may certainly get, or the value in scraps, by her lawful occupation of begging; and it is exactly at one year old that I propose to provide for them in such a manner as instead of being a charge upon their parents or the parish, or wanting food and raiment for the rest of their lives, they shall, on the contrary, contribute to the feeding and partly to the clothing of many thousands.

There is likewise another great advantage in my scheme, that it will prevent those voluntary abortions, and that horrid practice of women murdering their bastard children, alas! too frequent among us! sacrificing the poor innocent babies, I doubt, more to avoid the expense than the shame, which would move tears and pity in the most savage and inhuman breast.

The number of souls in this kingdom being usually reckoned one million and a half, of these, I calculate there may be about two hundred thousand couples whose wives are breeders; from which number I subtract thirty thousand couples, who are able to maintain their own children (although I apprehend there cannot be so many, under the present distress of the kingdom); but this being granted, there will remain one hundred and seventy thousand breeders. I again subtract fifty thousand for those women who miscarry, or whose children die by accident or disease within the year. There only remain an hundred and twenty thousand children of poor parents annually born. The question therefore is, how this number shall be reared and provided for? which, as I have already said, under the present situation of affairs, is utterly impossible by all the methods hitherto proposed. For we can neither employ them in handicraft or agriculture; we neither build houses (I mean in the country) nor cultivate land; they can very seldom pick up a livelihood by stealing till they arrive at six years old, except where they are of towardly parts, although I confess they learn the rudiments much earlier, during which time, they can, however, be properly looked upon only as probationers, as I have been informed by a principal gentleman in the country of Cavan, who protested to me that he never knew above one or two instances under the age of six, even in a part of the kingdom so renowned for the quickest proficiency in that art.

I am assured by our merchants that a boy or girl before twelve years old is no saleable commodity, and even when they come to this age they will not yield three pounds or three pounds and a half-crown at most on the exchange; which cannot turn to account either to the parents or the kingdom, the charge of nutriment and rags having been at least four times that value.

[Propositio] I shall now therefore humbly propose my own thoughts, which I hope will not be liable to the least objection.

I have been assured by a very knowing American of my acquaintance in London, that a young healthy child well nursed is at a year old a most delicious, nourishing, and wholesome food whether stewed, roasted, baked, or boiled; and I make no doubt that it will equally serve in a fricassee or a ragout.

I do therefore humbly offer it to public consideration that of the hundred and twenty thousand children already computed, twenty thousand may be reserved for breed, whereof only one-fourth part to be males, which is more than we allow to sheep, black cattle or swine; and my reason is that these children are seldom the fruits of marriage, a circumstance not much regarded by our savages; therefore one male will be sufficient to serve four females. That the remaining hundred thousand may, at a year old, be offered in sale to the persons of quality and fortune through the kingdom, always advising the mother to let them suck plentifully in the last month, so as to render them plump and fat for a good table. A child will make two dishes at an entertainment for friends, and when the family dines alone, the fore or hind quarter will make a reasonable dish, and seasoned with a little pepper or salt will be very good boiled on the fourth day, especially in winter.

[Partitio] I have reckoned upon a medium that a child just born will weigh twelve pounds, and in a solar year, if tolerably nursed, will increase to twenty-eight pounds.

I grant this food will be somewhat dear, and therefore very proper for landlords, who, as they have already devoured most of the parents, seem to have the best title to the children.

Infants' flesh will be in season throughout the year, but more plentiful in March, and a little before and after; for we are told by a grave author, an eminent French physician, that fish being a prolific diet, there are more children born in Roman Catholic countries about nine months after Lent than at any other season; therefore, reckoning a year after Lent, the markets will be more glutted than usual, because the number of popish infants is at least three to one in this kingdom, and therefore it will have one other collateral advantage, by lessening the number of papists among us.

I have already computed the charge of nursing a beggar's child (in which list I reckon all cottagers, laborers, and four-fifths of the farmers) to be about two shillings per annum, rags included; and I believe no gentleman would repine to give ten shillings for the carcass of a good fat child, which, as I have said, will make four dishes of excellent nutritive meat, when he has only some particular friend or his own family to dine with him. Thus the squire will learn to be a good landlord, and grow popular among his tenants; the mother will have eight shillings net profit, and be fit for work till she produces another child.

Those who are more thrifty (as I must confess the times require) may flay the carcass, the skin of which artificially dressed will make admirable gloves for ladies, and summer boots for fine gentlemen.

As to our city of Dublin, shambles may be appointed for this purpose in the most convenient parts of it, and butchers, we may be assured, will not be wanting, although I rather recommend buying the children alive, and dressing them hot from the knife as we do roasting pigs.

A very worthy person, a true lover of his country, and whose virtues I highly esteem, was lately pleased, in discoursing on this matter, to offer a refinement upon my scheme. He said that many gentlemen of this kingdom, having of late destroyed their deer, he conceived that the want of venison might be well supplied by the bodies of young lads and maidens, not exceeding fourteen years of age nor under twelve, so great a number of both sexes in every country being now ready to starve for want of work and service, and these to be disposed of by their parents, if alive, or otherwise by their nearest relations. But with due deference to so excellent a friend and so deserving a patriot, I cannot be altogether in his sentiments; for as to the males, my American acquaintance assured me from frequent experience that their flesh was generally tough and lean, like that of our school-boys, by continual exercise, and their taste disagreeable; and to fatten them would not answer the charge. Then as to the females, it would, I think, with humble submission, be a loss to the public, because they soon would become breeders themselves; and besides, it is not improbable that some scrupulous people might be apt to censure such a practice (although indeed very unjustly) as a little bordering upon cruelty, which, I confess, has always been with me the strongest objection against any project, however so well intended.

But in order to justify my friend, he confessed that this expedient was put into his head by the famous Psalmanazar, a native of the island Formosa, who came from thence to London above twenty years ago, and in conversation told my friend, that in his country when any young person happened to be put to death, the executioner sold the carcass to persons of quality as a prime dainty, and that in his time the body of a plump girl of fifteen, who was crucified for an attempt to poison the emperor, was sold to his imperial majesty's prime minister of state and other great mandarins of the court, in joints from the gibbet, at four hundred crowns. Neither indeed can I deny that if the same use were made of several plump young girls in this town, who, without one single groat to their fortunes, cannot stir abroad without a chair, and appear at the playhouse and assemblies in foreign fineries which they never will pay for, the kingdom would not be the worse.

Some persons of a desponding spirit are in great concern about that vast number of poor people, who are aged, diseased, or maimed, and I have been desired to employ my thoughts what course may be taken to ease the nation of so greivous an encumbrance. But I am not in the least pain upon that matter, because it is very well known that they are every day dying and rotting by cold, and famine, and filth, and vermin, as fast as can be reasonably expected. And as to the younger laborers, they are now in as hopeful a condition; they cannot get work, and consequently pine away for want of nourishment, to a degree that if at any time they are accidentally hired to common labor, they have not strength to perform it; and thus the country and themselves are happily delivered from the evils to come.

[Confirmatio] I have too long digressed, and therefore shall return to my subject. I think the advantages by the proposal which I have made are obvious, and many, as well as of the highest importance.

For first, as I have already observed, it would greatly lessen the number of papists, with whom we are yearly overrun, being the principal breeders of the nation as well as our most dangerous enemies; and who stay at home on purpose with a design to deliver the kingdom to the Pretender, hoping to take their advantage by the absence of so many good protestants, who have chosen rather to leave their country than stay at home and pay tithes against their conscience to an episcopal curate.

Secondly, The poorer tenants will have something valuable of their own, which by law may be made liable to distress, and help to pay their landlord's rent, their corn and cattle being already seized, and money a thing unknown.

Thirdly, Whereas the maintenance of an hundred thousand children, from two years old and upward, cannot be computed at less than ten shillings a-piece per annum, the nation's stock will be thereby increased fifty thousand pounds per annum, besides the profit of a new dish introduced to the tables of all gentlemen of fortune in the kingdom who have any refinement in taste. And the money will circulate among ourselves, the goods being entirely of our own growth and manufacture.

Fourthly, The constant breeders, besides the gain of eight shillings sterling per annum by the sale of their children, will be rid of the charge of maintaining them after the first year.

Fifthly, This food would likewise bring great custom to taverns, where the vintners will certainly be so prudent as to procure the best receipts for dressing it to perfection, and consequently have their houses frequented by all the fine gentlemen, who justly value themselves upon their knowledge in good eating; and a skillful cook, who understands how to oblige his guests, will contrive to make it as expensive as they please.

Sixthly, This would be a great inducement to marriage, which all wise nations have either encouraged by rewards or enforced by laws and penalties. It would increase the care and tenderness of mothers toward their children, when they were sure of a settlement for life to the poor babes, provided in some sort by the public, to their annual profit instead of expense. We should see an honest emulation among the married women, which of them could bring the fattest child to the market. Men would become as fond of their wives during the time of their pregnancy as they are now of their mares in foal, their cows in calf, or sows when they are ready to farrow; nor offer to beat or kick them (as is too frequent a practice) for fear of miscarriage.

Many other advantages might be enumerated. For instance, the addition of some thousand carcasses in our exportation of barreled beef, the propagation of swine's flesh, and improvement in the art of making good bacon, so much wanted among us by the great destruction of pigs, too frequent at our tables; which are in no way comparable in taste or magnificence to a well-grown, fat yearling child, which roasted whole will make a considerable figure at a lord mayor's feast, or any other public entertainment. But this and many others I omit, being studious of brevity.

Supposing that one thousand families in this city would be constant customers for infants' flesh, beside others who might have it at merry-meetings, particularly weddings and christenings, I compute that Dublin would take off annually about twenty thousand carcasses, and the rest of the kingdom (where probably they will be sold somewhat cheaper) the remaining eighty thousand.

[Reprehensio] I can think of no one objection that will possibly be raised against this proposal, unless it should be urged that the number of people will be thereby much lessened in the kingdom. This I freely own, and it was indeed one principal design in offering it to the world. I desire the reader will observe that I calculate my remedy for this one individual kingdom of Ireland, and for no other that ever was, is, or, I think, ever can be upon earth. Therefore let no man talk to me of other expedients: of taxing our absentees at five shillings a pound; of using neither clothes nor household furniture, except what is of our own growth and manufacture; of utterly rejecting the materials and instruments that promote foreign luxury; of curing the expensiveness of pride, vanity, idleness, and gaming in our women; of introducing a vein of parsimony, prudence, and temperance; of learning to love our country, in the want of which we differ even from Laplanders and the inhabitants of Topinamboo; of quitting our animosities and factions, nor act any longer like the Jews, who were murdering one another at the very moment their city was taken; of being a little cautious not to sell our country and consciences for nothing; of teaching landlords to have at least one degree of mercy toward their tenants; lastly, of putting a spirit of honesty, industry, and skill into our shopkeepers, who, if a resolution could now be taken to buy only our native goods, would immediately unite to cheat and exact upon us in the price, the measure, and the goodness, nor could ever yet be brought to make one fair proposal of just dealing, though often and earnestly invited to it.

Therefore, I repeat, let no man talk to me of these and the like expedients, till he has at least some glimpse of hope that there will be ever some hearty and sincere attempt to put them in practice.

[Peroratio] But as to myself, having been wearied out for many years with offering vain, idle, visionary thoughts, and at length utterly despairing of success, I fortunately fell upon this proposal, which, as it is wholly new, so it has something solid and real, of no expense and little trouble, full in our own power, and whereby we can incur no danger in disobliging England. For this kind of commodity will not bear exportation, the flesh being of too tender a consistence to admit a long continuance in salt, although perhaps I could name a country which would be glad to eat up our whole nation without it.

After all, I am not so violently bent upon my own opinion as to reject any offer proposed by wise men, which shall be found equally innocent, cheap, easy, and effectual. But before something of that kind shall be advanced in contradiction to my scheme, and offering a better, I desire the author or authors will be pleased maturely to consider two points. First, as things now stand, how they will be able to find food and raiment for an hundred thousand useless mouths and backs. And secondly, there being a round million creatures in human figure throughout this kingdom, whose whole subsistence put into a common stock would leave them in debt two millions of pounds sterling, adding those who are beggars by profession to the bulk of farmers, cottagers, and laborers, with their wives and children, who are beggars in effect; I desire those politicians, who dislike my overture, and may perhaps be so bold as to attempt an answer, that they will first ask the parents of these mortals, whether they would not at this day think it a great happiness to have been sold for food at a year old in the manner I prescribe, and thereby have avoided such a perpetual scene of misfortunes as they have since gone through by the oppression of landlords, the impossibility of paying rent without money or trade, the want of common sustenance, with neither house nor clothes to cover them from the inclemencies of the weather, and the most inevitable prospect of entailing the like or greater miseries upon their breed for ever.

I profess, in the sincerity of my heart, that I have not the least personal interest in endeavoring to promote this necessary work, having no other motive than the public good of my country, by advancing our trade, providing for infants, relieving the poor, and giving some pleasure to the rich. I have no children by which I can propose to get a single penny; the youngest being nine years old, and my wife past child-bearing.

HENRY DAVID THOREAU

Where I Lived, and What I Lived For

At a certain season of our life we are accustomed to consider every
spot as the possible site of a house. I have thus surveyed the
country on every side within a dozen miles of where I live. In
imagination I have bought all the farms in succession, for all were
to be bought, and I knew their price. I walked over each farmer's
premises, tasted his wild apples, discoursed on husbandry with
him, took his farm at his price, at any price, mortgaging it to him
in my mind; even put a higher price on it,—took everything but a
deed of it,—took his word for his deed, for I dearly love to talk,—
cultivated it, and him too to some extent, I trust, and withdrew
when I had enjoyed it long enough, leaving him to carry it on.
This experience entitled me to be regarded as a sort of real-estate
broker by my friends. Wherever I sat, there I might live, and the
landscape radiated from me accordingly. What is a house but a
sedes, a seat?—better if a country seat. I discovered many a site
for a house not likely to be soon improved, which some might
have thought too far from the village, but to my eyes the village
was too far from it. Well, there I might live, I said; and there I did
live, for an hour, a summer and a winter life; saw how I could let
the years run off, buffet the winter through, and see the spring
come in. The future inhabitants of this region, wherever they may
place their houses, may be sure that they have been anticipated.
An afternoon sufficed to lay out the land into orchard, wood-lot,
and pasture, and to decide what fine oaks or pines should be left
to stand before the door, and whence each blasted tree could be

seen to the best advantage; and then I let it lie, fallow perchance, for a man is rich in proportion to the number of things which he can afford to let alone.

My imagination carried me so far that I even had the refusal of several farms,—the refusal was all I wanted,—but I never got my fingers burned by actual possession. The nearest that I came to actual possession was when I bought the Hollowell place, and had begun to sort my seeds, and collected materials with which to make a wheelbarrow to carry it on or off with; but before the owner gave me a deed of it, his wife—every man has such a wife —changed her mind and wished to keep it, and he offered me ten dollars to release him. Now, to speak the truth, I had but ten cents in the world, and it surpassed my arithmetic to tell, if I was that man who had ten cents, or who had a farm, or ten dollars, or all together. However, I let him keep the ten dollars and the farm too, for I had carried it far enough; or rather, to be generous, I sold him the farm for just what I gave for it, and, as he was not a rich man, made him a present of ten dollars, and still had my ten cents, and seeds, and materials for a wheelbarrow left. I found thus that I had been a rich man without any damage to my poverty. But I retained the landscape, and I have since annually carried off what it yielded without a wheelbarrow. With respects to landscapes,—

> I am monarch of all I *survey,*
> My right there is none to dispute.

I have frequently seen a poet withdraw, having enjoyed the most valuable part of a farm, while the crusty farmer supposed that he had got a few wild apples only. Why, the owner does not know it for many years when a poet has put his farm in rhyme, the most admirable kind of invisible fence, has fairly impounded it, milked it, skimmed it, and got all the cream, and left the farmer only the skimmed milk.

The real attractions of the Hollowell farm, to me, were: its complete retirement, being about two miles from the village, half a mile from the nearest neighbor, and separated from the highway by a broad field; its bounding on the river, which the owner said protected it by its fogs from frosts in the spring, though that was nothing to me; the gray color and ruinous state of the house and barn, and the dilapidated fences, which put such an interval between me and the last occupant; the hollow and lichen-covered apple trees, gnawed by rabbits, showing what kind of neighbors I should have; but above all, the recollection I had of it from my earliest voyages up the river, when the house was concealed behind a dense grove of red maples, through which I heard the house-dog bark. I was in haste to buy it, before the proprietor finished getting out some rocks, cutting down the hollow apple trees, and grubbing up some young birches which had sprung up in the pasture, or in short, had made any more of his improvements. To enjoy these advantages I was ready to carry it on; like Atlas, to take the world on my shoulders,—I never heard what compensation he received for that,—and do all those things which had no other motive or excuse but that I might pay for it and be unmolested in my possession of it; for I knew all the while that it would yield the most abundant crop of the kind I wanted, if I could only afford to let it alone. But it turned out as I have said.

All that I could say, then, with respect to farming on a large scale—I have always cultivated a garden—was, that I had had my seeds ready. Many think that seeds improve with age. I have no doubt that time discriminates between the good and the bad; and when at last I shall plant, I shall be less likely to be disappointed. But I would say to my fellows, once for all, As long as possible live free and uncommitted. It makes but little difference whether you are committed to a farm or the county jail.

Old Cato, whose "De Re Rusticâ" is my "Cultivator," says,— and the only translation I have seen makes sheer nonsense of the passage,—"When you think of getting a farm turn it thus in your mind, not to buy greedily; nor spare your pains to look at it, and do not think it enough to go round it once. The oftener you go there the more it will please you, if it is good." I think I shall not buy greedily, but go round and round it as long as I live, and be buried in it first, that it may please me the more at last.

The present was my next experiment of this kind, which I purpose to describe more at length, for convenience putting the experience of two years into one. As I have said, I do not propose to write an ode to dejection, but to brag as lustily as chanticleer in the morning, standing on his roost, if only to wake my neighbors up.

When first I took up my abode in the woods, that is, began to spend my nights as well as days there, which, by accident, was on Independence Day, or the Fourth of July, 1845, my house was not finished for winter, but was merely a defence against the rain, without plastering or chimney, the walls being of rough, weather-stained boards, with wide chinks, which made it cool at night. The upright white hewn studs and freshly planed door and window casings gave it a clean and airy look, especially in the morning, when its timbers were saturated with dew, so that I fancied that by noon some sweet gum would exude from them. To my imagination it retained throughout the day more or less of this auroral character, reminding me of a certain house on a mountain which I had visited a year before. This was an airy and unplastered cabin, fit to entertain a travelling god, and where a goddess might trail her garments. The winds which passed over my dwelling were such as sweep over the ridges of mountains, bearing the broken strains, or celestial parts only, of terrestrial music. The morning wind forever blows, the poem of creation is uninterrupted; but few are the ears that hear it. Olympus is but the outside of the earth everywhere.

The only house I had been the owner of before, if I except a boat, was a tent, which I used occasionally when making excursions in the summer, and this is still rolled up in my garret; but the boat, after passing from hand to hand, has gone down the stream of time. With this more substantial shelter about me, I had made some progress toward settling in the world. This frame, so slightly clad, was a sort of crystallization around me, and reacted on the builder. It was suggestive somewhat as a picture in outlines. I did not need to go outdoors to take the air, for the atmosphere within had lost none of its freshness. It was not so much within-doors as behind a door where I sat, even in the rainiest weather. The Harivansa says, "An abode without birds is like a meat without seasoning." Such was not my abode, for I found myself suddenly neighbor to the birds; not by having imprisoned one, but having caged myself near them. I was not only nearer to some of those which commonly frequent the garden and the orchard, but to those wilder and more thrilling songsters of the forest which never, or rarely, serenade a villager,—the wood thrush, the veery, the scarlet tanager, the field sparrow, the whip-poor-will, and many others.

I was seated by the shore of a small pond, about a mile and a half south of the village of Concord and somewhat higher than it, in the midst of an extensive wood between that town and Lincoln, and about two miles south of that our only field known to fame, Concord Battle Ground; but I was so low in the woods that the opposite shore, half a mile off, like the rest, covered with wood, was my most distant horizon. For the first week, whenever I looked out on the pond it impressed me like a tarn high up on the side of a mountain, its bottom far above the surface of other lakes, and, as the sun arose, I saw it throwing off its nightly cloth-ing of mist, and here and there, by degrees, its soft ripples or its smooth reflecting surface was revealed, while the mists, like ghosts, were stealthily withdrawing in every direction into the woods, as at the breaking up of some nocturnal conventicle. The very dew seemed to hang upon the trees later into the day than usual, as on the sides of mountains.

This small lake was of most value as a neighbor in the intervals of a gentle rain-storm in August, when, both air and water being perfectly still, but the sky overcast, mid-afternoon had all the serenity of evening, and the wood thrush sang around, and was heard from shore to shore. A lake like this is never smoother than at such a time; and the clear portion of the air above it being shallow and darkened by clouds, the water, full of light and re-flections, becomes a lower heaven itself so much the more impor-tant. From a hill-top near by, where the wood had been recently cut off, there was a pleasing vista southward across the pond, through a wide indentation in the hills which form the shore there, where their opposite sides sloping toward each other sug-gested a stream flowing out in that direction through a wooded valley, but stream there was none. That way I looked between and over the near green hills to some distant and higher ones in the horizon, tinged with blue. Indeed, by standing on tiptoe I could catch a glimpse of some of the peaks of the still bluer and more distant mountain ranges in the northwest, those true-blue coins from heaven's own mint, and also of some portion of the village.

But in other directions, even from this point, I could not see over or beyond the woods which surrounded me. It is well to have some water in your neighborhood, to give buoyancy to and float the earth. One value even of the smallest well is, that when you look into it you see that earth is not continent but insular. This is as important as that it keeps butter cool. When I looked across the pond from this peak toward the Sudbury meadows, which in time of flood I distinguished elevated perhaps by a mirage in their seething valley, like a coin in a basin, all the earth beyond the pond appeared like a thin crust insulated and floated even by this small sheet of intervening water, and I was reminded that this on which I dwelt was but *dry land.*

Though the view from my door was still more contracted, I did not feel crowded or confined in the least. There was pasture enough for my imagination. The low shrub oak plateau to which the opposite shore arose stretched away toward the prairies of the West and the steppes of Tartary, affording ample room for all the roving families of men. "There are none happy in the world but beings who enjoy freely a vast horizon,"—said Damodara, when his herds required new and larger pastures.

Both place and time were changed, and I dwelt nearer to those parts of the universe and to those eras in history which had most attracted me. Where I lived was as far off as many a region viewed nightly by astronomers. We are wont to imagine rare and delectable places in some remote and more celestial corner of the system, behind the constellation of Cassiopeia's Chair, far from noise and disturbance. I discovered that my house actually had its site in such a withdrawn, but forever new and unprofaned, part of the universe. If it were worth the while to settle in those parts near to the Pleiades or the Hyades, to Aldebaran or Altair, then I was really there, or at an equal remoteness from the life which I had left behind, dwindled and twinkling with as fine a ray to my nearest neighbor, and to be seen only in moonless nights by him. Such was that part of creation where I had squatted;—

> There was a shepherd that did live,
>   And held his thoughts as high
> As were the mounts whereon his flocks
>   Did hourly feed him by.

What should we think of the shepherd's life if his flocks always wandered to higher pastures than his thoughts?

Every morning was a cheerful invitation to make my life of equal simplicity, and I may say innocence, with Nature herself. I have been as sincere a worshipper of Aurora as the Greeks. I got up early and bathed in the pond; that was a religious exercise, and one of the best things which I did. They say that characters were engraven on the bathing tub of King Tching-thang to this effect: "Renew thyself completely each day; do it again, and again, and forever again." I can understand that. Morning brings back the heroic ages. I was as much affected by the faint hum of a mosquito making its invisible and unimaginable tour through my apartment at earliest dawn, when I was sitting with door and windows open, as I could be by any trumpet that ever sang of fame. It was Homer's requiem; itself an Iliad and Odyssey in the air, singing its own wrath and wanderings. There was something cosmical about it; a standing advertisement, till forbidden, of the everlasting vigor and fertility of the world. The morning, which is the most memorable season of the day, is the awakening hour. Then there is least somnolence in us; and for an hour, at least, some part of us awakes which slumbers all the rest of the day and night. Little is to be expected of that day, if it can be called a day, to which we are not awakened by our Genius, but by the mechanical nudgings of some servitor, are not awakened by our own newly acquired force and aspirations from within, accompanied by the undulations of celestial music, instead of factory bells, and a fragrance filling the air—to a higher life than we fell asleep from; and thus the darkness bear its fruit, and prove itself to be good, no less than the light. That man who does not believe that each day contains an earlier, more sacred, and auroral hour than he has yet profaned, has despaired of life, and is pursuing a descending and darkening way. After a partial cessation of his sensuous life, the soul of man, or its organs rather, are reinvigorated each day, and his Genius tries again what noble life it can make. All memorable events, I should say, transpire in morning time and in a morning atmosphere. The Vedas say, "All intelligences awake with the morning." Poetry and art, and the fairest and most memorable of the actions of men, date from such an hour. All poets and heroes, like Memnon, are the children of Aurora, and emit their music at sunrise. To him whose elastic and vigorous thought keeps pace with the sun, the day is a perpetual morning. It matters not what the clocks say or the attitudes and labors of men. Morning is when I am awake and there is a dawn in me. Moral reform is the effort to throw off sleep. Why is it that men give so poor an account of their day if they have not been slumbering? They are not such poor calculators. If they had not been overcome with drowsiness, they would have performed something. The millions are awake enough for physical labor; but only one in a million is awake enough for effective intellectual exertion, only one in a hundred millions to a poetic or divine life. To be awake is to be alive. I have never yet met a man who was quite awake. How could I have looked him in the face?

We must learn to reawaken and keep ourselves awake, not by mechanical aids, but by an infinite expectation of the dawn, which does not forsake us in our soundest sleep. I know of no more encouraging fact than the unquestionable ability of man to elevate his life by a conscious endeavor. It is something to be able to paint a particular picture, or to carve a statue, and so to make a few objects beautiful; but it is far more glorious to carve and paint the very atmosphere and medium through which we look, which morally we can do. To affect the quality of the day, that is the highest of arts. Every man is tasked to make his life, even in its details, worthy of the contemplation of his most elevated and critical hour. If we refused, or rather used up, such paltry information as we get, the oracles would distinctly inform us how this might be done.

I went to the woods because I wished to live deliberately, to front only the essential facts of life, and see if I could not learn what it had to teach, and not, when I came to die, discover that I had not lived. I did not wish to live what was not life, living is so dear; nor did I wish to practise resignation, unless it was quite necessary. I wanted to live deep and suck out all the marrow of life, to live so sturdily and Spartan-like as to put to rout all that was not life, to cut a broad swath and shave close, to drive life into a corner, and reduce it to its lowest terms, and, if it proved to be mean, why then to get the whole and genuine meanness of it, and publish its meanness to the world; or if it were sublime, to know it by experience, and be able to give a true account of it in my next excursion. For most men, it appears to me, are in a strange uncertainty about it, whether it is of the devil or of God, and have *somewhat hastily* concluded that it is the chief end of man here to "glorify God and enjoy him forever."

Still we live meanly, like ants; though the fable tells us that we were long ago changed into men; like pygmies we fight with cranes; it is error upon error, and clout upon clout, and our best virtue has for its occasion a superfluous and evitable wretchedness. Our life is frittered away by detail. An honest man has hardly need to count more than his ten fingers, or in extreme cases he may add his ten toes, and lump the rest. Simplicity, simplicity, simplicity! I say, let your affairs be as two or three, and not a hundred or a thousand; instead of a million count half a dozen, and keep your accounts on your thumb-nail. In the midst of this chopping sea of civilized life, such are the clouds and storms and quicksands and thousand-and-one items to be allowed for, that a man has to live, if he would not founder and go to the bottom and not make his port at all, by dead reckoning, and he must be a great calculator indeed who succeeds. Simplify, simplify. Instead of three meals a day, if it be necessary eat but one; instead of a hundred dishes, five; and reduce other things in proportion. Our life is like a German Confederacy, made up of petty states, with its boundary forever fluctuating, so that even a German cannot tell you how it is bounded at any moment. The nation itself, with all its so-called internal improvements, which, by the way are all external and superficial, is just an unwieldy and overgrown establishment, cluttered with furniture and tripped up by its own traps, ruined by luxury and heedless expense, by want of calculation and a worthy aim, as the million households in the land; and the only cure for it, as for them, is in a rigid economy, a stern and more than Spartan simplicity of life and elevation of purpose. It lives too fast. Men think that it is essential that the *Nation* have commerce, and export ice, and talk through a telegraph, and ride thirty miles an hour, without a doubt, whether *they* do or not; but whether we should live like baboons or like men, is a little uncertain. If we do not get out sleepers, and forge rails, and devote days and nights to the work, but go to tinkering upon our *lives* to improve *them,* who will build railroads? And if railroads are not built, how shall we get to heaven in season? But if we stay at home and mind our business, who will want railroads? We do not ride on the railroad; it rides upon us. Did you ever think what those sleepers are that underlie the railroad? Each one is a man, an Irishman, or a Yankee man. The rails are laid on them, and they are covered with sand, and the cars run smoothly over them. They are sound sleepers, I assure you. And every few years a new lot is laid down and run over; so that, if some have the pleasure of riding on a rail, others have the misfortune to be ridden upon. And when they run over a man that is walking in his sleep, a supernumerary sleeper in the wrong position, and wake him up, they suddenly stop the cars, and make a hue and cry about it, as if this were an exception. I am glad to know that it takes a gang of men for every five miles to keep the sleepers down and level in their beds as it is, for this is a sign that they may sometime get up again.

Why should we live with such hurry and waste of life? We are determined to be starved before we are hungry. Men say that a stitch in time saves nine, and so they take a thousand stitches to-day to save nine to-morrow. As for *work*, we haven't any of any consequence. We have the Saint Vitus' dance, and cannot possibly keep our heads still. If I should only give a few pulls at the parish bell-rope, as for a fire, that is, without setting the bell, there is hardly a man on his farm in the outskirts of Concord, not-withstanding that press of engagements which was his excuse so many times this morning, nor a boy, nor a woman, I might almost say, but would forsake all and follow that sound, not mainly to save property from the flames, but, if we will confess the truth, much more to see it burn, since burn it must, and we, be it known, did not set it on fire,—or to see it put out, and have a hand in it, if that is done as handsomely; yes, even if it were the parish church itself. Hardly a man takes a half-hour's nap after dinner, but when he wakes he holds up his head and asks, "What's the news?" as if the rest of mankind had stood his sentinels. Some give directions to be waked every half-hour, doubtless for no other purpose; and then, to pay for it, they tell what they have dreamed. After a night's sleep the news is as indispensable as the breakfast. "Pray tell me anything new that has happened to a man any-where on this globe,"—and he reads it over his coffee and rolls, that a man has had his eyes gouged out this morning on the Wachito River; never dreaming the while that he lives in the dark unfathomed mammoth cave of this world, and has but the rudiment of an eye himself.

For my part, I could easily do without the post-office. I think that there are very few important communications made through it. To speak critically, I never received more than one or two letters in my life—I wrote this some years ago—that were worth the postage. The penny-post is, commonly, an institution through which you seriously offer a man that penny for his thoughts which is so often safely offered in jest. And I am sure that I never read any memorable news in a newspaper. If we read of one man robbed, or murdered, or killed by accident, or one house burned, or one vessel wrecked, or one steamboat blown up, or one cow run over on the Western Railroad, or one mad dog killed, or one lot of grasshoppers in the winter,—we never read of another. One is enough. If you are acquainted with the principle, what do you care for a myriad instances and applications? To a philosopher all news, as it is called, is gossip, and they who edit and read it are old women over their tea. Yet not a few are greedy after this gossip. There was such a rush, as I hear, the other day at one of the offices to learn the foreign news by the last arrival, that several large squares of plate glass belonging to the establishment were broken by the pressure,—news which I seriously think a ready wit might write a twelvemonth, or twelve years, beforehand with sufficient accuracy. As for Spain, for instance, if you know how to throw in Don Carlos and the Infanta, and Don Pedro and Seville and Granada, from time to time in the right proportions,—they may have changed the names a little since I saw the papers,— and serve up a bull-fight when other entertainments fail, it will be true to the letter, and give us as good an idea of the exact state or ruin of things in Spain as the most succinct and lucid reports under this head in the newspapers: and as for England, almost the last significant scrap of news from that quarter was the revolution of 1649; and if you have learned the history of her crops for an average year, you never need attend to that thing again, unless your speculations are of a merely pecuniary character. If one may judge who rarely looks into the newspapers, nothing new does ever happen in foreign parts, a French revolution not excepted.

What news! how much more important to know what that is which was never old! "Kieou-he-yu (great dignitary of the state of Wei) sent a man to Khoung-tseu to know his news. Khoung-tseu caused the messenger to be seated near him, and questioned him in these terms: What is your master doing? The messenger answered with respect: My master desires to diminish the number of his faults, but he cannot come to the end of them. The messenger being gone, the philosopher remarked: What a worthy messenger! What a worthy messenger!" The preacher, instead of vexing the ears of drowsy farmers on their day of rest at the end of the week,—for Sunday is the fit conclusion of an ill-spent week, and not the fresh and brave beginning of a new one,—with this one other draggle-tail of a sermon, should shout with thundering voice, "Pause! Avast! Why so seeming fast, but deadly slow?"

Shams and delusions are esteemed for soundest truths, while reality is fabulous. If men would steadily observe realities only, and not allow themselves to be deluded, life, to compare it with such things as we know, would be like a fairy tale and the Arabian Nights' Entertainments. If we respected only what is inevitable and has a right to be, music and poetry would resound along the streets. When we are unhurried and wise, we perceive that only great and worthy things have any permanent and absolute existence, that petty fears and petty pleasures are but the shadow of the reality. This is always exhilarating and sublime. By closing the eyes and slumbering, and consenting to be deceived by shows, men establish and confirm their daily life of routine and habit everywhere, which still is built on purely illusory foundations. Children, who play life, discern its true law and relations more clearly than men, who fail to live it worthily, but who think that they are wiser by experience, that is, by failure. I have read in a Hindoo book, that "there was a king's son, who, being expelled in infancy from his native city, was brought up by a forester, and, growing up to maturity in that state, imagined himself to belong to the barbarous race with which he lived. One of his father's ministers having discovered him, revealed to him what he was, and the misconception of his character was removed, and he knew himself to be a prince. So soul," continues the Hindoo philosopher, "from the circumstances in which it is placed, mistakes its own character, until the truth is revealed to it by some holy teacher, and then it knows itself to be *Brahme*." I perceive that we inhabitants of New England live this mean life that we do because our vision does not penetrate the surface of things. We think that that *is* which *appears* to be. If a man should walk through this town and see only the reality, where, think you, would the "Mill-dam" go to? If he should give us an account of the realities he beheld there, we should not recognize the place in his description. Look at a meeting-house, or a court-house, or a jail, or a shop, or a dwelling-house, and say what that thing really is before a true gaze, and they would all go to pieces in your account of them. Men esteem truth remote, in the outskirts of the system, behind the farthest star, before Adam and after the last man. In eternity there is indeed something true and sublime. But all these times and places and occasions are now and here. God himself culminates in the present moment, and will never be more divine in the lapse of all the ages. And we are enabled to apprehend at all what is sublime and noble only by the perpetual instilling and drenching of the reality that surrounds us. The universe constantly and obediently answers to our conceptions; whether we travel fast or slow, the track is laid for us. Let us spend our lives in conceiving then. The poet or the artist never yet had so fair and noble a design but some of his posterity at least could accomplish it.

Let us spend one day as deliberately as Nature, and not be thrown off the track by every nutshell and mosquito's wing that falls on the rails. Let us rise early and fast, or break fast, gently and without perturbation; let company come and let company go, let the bells ring and the children cry,—determined to make a day of it. Why should we knock under and go with the stream? Let us not be upset and overwhelmed in that terrible rapid and whirlpool called a dinner, situated in the meridian shallows. Weather this danger and you are safe, for the rest of the way is down hill. With unrelaxed nerves, with morning vigor, sail by it, looking another way, tied to the mast like Ulysses. If the engine whistles, let it whistle till it is hoarse for its pains. If the bell rings, why should we run? We will consider what kind of music they are like. Let us settle ourselves, and work and wedge our feet downward through the mud and slush of opinion, and prejudice, and tradition, and delusion, and appearance, that alluvion which covers the globe, through Paris and London, through New York and Boston and Concord, through Church and State, through poetry and philosophy and religion, till we come to a hard bottom and rocks in place, which we can call *reality*, and say, This is, and no mistake; and then begin, having a *point d'appui*, below freshet and frost and fire, a place where you might found a wall or a state, or set a lamp-post safely, or perhaps a gauge, not a Nilometer, but a Realometer, that future ages might know how deep a freshet of shams and appearances had gathered from time to time. If you stand right fronting and face to face to a fact, you will see the sun glimmer on both its surfaces, as if it were a cimeter, and feel its sweet edge dividing you through the heart and marrow, and so you will happily conclude your mortal career. Be it life or death, we crave only reality. If we are really dying, let us hear the rattle in our throats and feel cold in the extremities; if we are alive, let us go about our business.

Time is but the stream I go a-fishing in. I drink at it; but while I drink I see the sandy bottom and detect how shallow it is. Its thin current slides away, but eternity remains. I would drink deeper; fish in the sky, whose bottom is pebbly with stars. I cannot count one. I know not the first letter of the alphabet. I have always been regretting that I was not as wise as the day I was born. The intellect is a cleaver; it discerns and rifts its way into the secret of things. I do not wish to be any more busy with my hands than is necessary. My head is hands and feet. I feel all my best faculties concentrated in it. My instinct tells me that my head is an organ for burrowing, as some creatures use their snout and fore paws, and with it I would mine and burrow my way through these hills. I think that the richest vein is somewhere hereabouts; so by the divining-rod and thin rising vapors I judge; and here I will begin to mine.